COMPENDIUM OF BAR CORKSCREWS

by Wayne Meadows

Copy editing by Sal Robinson

Production by Hunter Communications Group Inc.

"Art and the Bar Corkscrew" cover photograph by Derek Lepper.

Clockwise from the upper right: an art nouveau ALEXANDERWERK with a bottle neck rest; a baroque-embellished BEAUMONT; an art nouveau ALEXANDERWERK with a bottle lip rest; a grape and leaf decoration on a FORTSCHRITT; an arts and crafts PIX; a William Morris inspired MODERN; an art deco CHAMPION; a William Morris inspired TRIUMPH; an art nouveau HENVI; an art deco CHAMPION; a William Morris inspired UNIQUE; a rococo 5th AVENUE (centre).

Published by
Kitsilano Cellars
Vancouver, British Columbia

Printed in Canada
ISBN 0-9689294-0-0

Compendium of Bar Corkscrews

This book is dedicated to my wife Sal, who has put up with my bar corkscrew obsession for the last nine years and to Fred MacAdam. Without Fred's knowledge and vast collection of bar corkscrews and Sal's assistance and encouragement, this book could not have been produced.

"I am sensible the reader has no occasion to know all this, but I feel a kind of necessity for relating it."

Jean-Jacques Rousseau, Les confessions

Table of contents

Acknowledgments

It is not possible to gather this much information without the assistance of a great many corkscrew collectors and dealers. I have worked away at this book for many years, and in the beginning I did not realize how long it would take and that I should keep careful records of the contributors. I apologize if I have missed any contributors.

For photographs or illustrations in the IDENTIFICATION SECTION, I would like to thank Elide Albert (W01.1.1), Jack Bandy (B08.1.2, F04.1.1, H05.2.1, K99.1.1, L04.3.1, P06.2.1, P07.1.3, S10.1.3, S10.1.5, S19.2.1, U3.1.1, U99.1.1), Buster Berntson (L06.1.1, S23.1.1), Gérard Bidault (A14.1.1, P03.1.1), Dennis Bosa (E04.1.1), Don Bull (P01.1.1, R01.1.1, V02.1.1), Ed Bystran (A13.4.1), Herb Danziger (S19.3.1), Heinz ten Doornkaat (A13.3.1), Bert Giulian (N01.1.1, V03.1.1), Mannfred Heckmann (B09.1.1, B09.2.1, H08.1.1, I04.1.1, Q01.1.1), Tom Kijek (F04.2.1), Fred Kincaid (B08.3.1), Paul Luchsinger (Y02.2.1), Ron McLean (C04.1.2, D04.3.1, L04.1.1, M99.3.2, S08.1.1), Alfonso Martinez (A12.1.1, A13.1.1, A13.3.2, J99.1.1, S14.1.1), Paolo Montecchi (I99.1.1, I99.1.2, I9.2.1, I99.3.1, I99.3.2, M08.1.1, Z99.1.1), John Morris (S10.2.6), Fred O'Leary (O01.1.1), Joe Paradi (S05.1.1), Klaus Pumpenmeier (S07.1.1), Bob Roger (V06.1.1), Christopher Sykes (E06.1.1), Barry Taylor (G99.4.1), Fletcher Wallace (L05.1.1, L05.2.1), Joe Young (R07.2.1).

Advertising and parts lists are particularly hard to find. Without the assistance of Frank Ellis and his many, many hours at the Public Records Office in London, this would be a much slimmer book. I would also like to thank Reinhold Berndt, Don Bull, Heinz ten Doornkaat, Ron McLean, Guy Olive, Ferd Peters and Klaus Pumpenmeier for their contributions.

I have extracted illustrations and information from a number of books, newsletters, catalogues and patents. I would like to thank the following contributors: a 1901 Walker catalogue (all of the Walker advertising and parts lists) courtesy of Jack Bandy; *Scandinavian Corkscrews* by Buster Berntson & Per Ekman; the *Quarterly Worme* of the Canadian Corkscrew Collectors Club; corkscrew sales catalogues from Christie's London; *Fabriques les Françaises de Tire-bouchons 1820-1970* by Gérard Bidault; *Five Hundred and Seven Mechanical Movements* by Henry Brown; *The Ultimate Corkscrew Book* by Don Bull; catalogues from Aaron Corenman; *Korkenzieher* by Mannfred Heckmann; an 1897 and 1913 Arcade catalogue (all of the Arcade advertising and parts lists) courtesy of Fred MacAdam; *Corkscrews (1000 patented ways to open a bottle)* by Fred O'Leary; *Tire-Bouchons Français Brevets 1828 - 1974* by Guy Olive; *German Corkscrew Patents and German Corkscrew Registrations* by Ferd Peters; *Mechanical Corkscrews* by Ferd Peters; a 1910 Gaskell catalogue(all of the Gaskell advertising and parts lists) courtesy of J. J. Stratton of Gaskell & Chambers; catalogues from Christopher Sykes; *Tavern Treasures* by Charles Tresise; *British Corkscrew Patents from 1795* by Fletcher Wallis; *Cavatappi d'Epoca* catalogue of Vineide, 1989.

Thank you to Maurice Dancer, Frank Ellis, Sally Lloyd, Stan Mullery, Fred O'Leary and Ferd Peters for their assistance in finding patent and registration documentation.

I am indebted to Jack Bandy, Ron McLean and Joe Paradi for their many helpful thoughts and comments on content, to Ferd Peters for his extensive help with German content, in particular information relating to Gerhard Frings, and to Dennis Cox for his general assistance.

Wayne Meadows
September 1st, 2001

Foreword

Bar corkscrews, mounted corkscrews, automatic corkscrews - whatever you choose to call them - have long been an enigma in the corkscrew-collecting world. While a few collectors with a bent for the mechanical have found these ingenious pieces of machinery interesting, even fascinating, even they have often shunned them. The reasons some have given for overlooking these corkscrews centered around their shear bulk, awkwardness and difficulty of display. Then there were many who might have overlooked these perceived shortcomings, but suffered from a common misconception that aside from the massive, but exquisite, English brass *Eclipse*, there were really only three bar corkscrews anyway - the *Champion*, the *Yankee* and the *Quick and Easy* - so what was there to collect? And, finally, there were those collectors who, having little affinity, interest or curiosity for the mechanical, were quite intimidated by the mysteries concealed within those imposing brass or cast iron carcasses. So, with these real or imagined handicaps, is it any wonder bar corkscrews have lingered in the backwaters of corkscrew collecting for so long?

Quite a reputation to overcome! But, even though some of the resistance to collecting these corkscrews seems to have been on the decline in recent years, any lingering misconceptions in collectors' minds are destined to be finally dispelled with this *Compendium of Bar Corkscrews*. In this work, Wayne Meadows has succeeded in stripping away the myths, misunderstandings and mysteries about bar corkscrews. Although Wayne has amassed a personal collection of over 200, as well as sheaves of old advertisements, catalogues, parts lists, patents and any other related materials, this was just the beginning. Mere collecting is one thing. What Wayne has done with this material is to open the door for us and turn on the light to the world of these mechanical marvels. From examining their evolution, to studying their unique nomenclature, to explaining and illustrating the major mechanisms, to organizing, coding, and cataloguing hundreds of markings identifying the patentees, makers and other sources, this compendium is a warehouse of bar corkscrew knowledge much needed, and all too long in coming.

Fortunately, Wayne has had the curiosity, knowledge and persistence to "get under the hood" of these ingenious pieces of machinery to see what makes them tick. And, he has presented the result of his years of work in a way that makes it understandable, even to those of us who find difficulty in dealing with the inner workings of a screwdriver. Wayne has inspected, dissected, dismantled, dislodged, disassembled, examined, poked and probed every bar corkscrew he owns or could lay his hands on, and has recorded, catalogued and studied every marking and nuance his eyes, magnifying glass, flash light and magnet could detect. Bringing all of this together has taken years of work, and was no small challenge. The corkscrew-collecting world will long be in Wayne's debt for his having created this definitive work on these long overlooked corkscrews.

So bar corkscrews, mounted corkscrews, automatic corkscrews - whatever you choose to call them - this *Compendium of Bar Corkscrews* will transform these ugly ducklings of the corkscrew-collecting world into their rightful place as knights in shining armour.

Jack D. Bandy

Compendium of Bar Corkscrews

Introduction

Nine years ago, I purchased my first bar corkscrew collection from Dennis Bosa. On arriving home with my six pieces I immediately started to disassemble them to see what was inside. Shortly after that I started to look for published information about them; much to my surprise, there was almost nothing available. It seemed to me that there was a simple solution to this problem. When I first began thinking about producing a book about bar corkscrews, I estimated that probably about 50 different kinds had been manufactured, and that I should be able to compile an illustrated reference in a couple of years. As I worked away on my simple book, many things happened. First, Ron McLean told me about a collector in Freeport, Illinois, who had "a lot" of bar corkscrews.

I decided to visit Fred MacAdam and when I turned into his driveway I was impressed to see ARCADE on his license plates; of course at that time I did not realize that Freeport had been the world capital of bar corkscrews. It was dinnertime so we went out to a restaurant and talked bar corkscrews. I told Fred all about my ideas for the book, noticing that I sure was making him happy, as almost every time I opened my mouth he would smile. Later that evening Fred asked if I wanted to see a few of his corkscrews. Upon going upstairs to his bar corkscrew room, I was stunned to see a room filled with hundreds of bar corkscrews, most of which I had never heard of. I was particularly impressed with discovering that Arcade had actually made a corkscrew marked ARCADE, and that Fred owned five different versions of something I did not know existed. With great excitement I spent the next two days discussing, fondling and photographing dozens and dozens of corkscrews.

On the last day I drove back to Chicago, stopping in to see Joe Young on the way. Still reeling from my MacAdam experience, I was not prepared for even more bar corkscrews that I had not seen at Fred's. More photographs, more talk. The next day found me in Tulsa, Oklahoma, where I stopped in to see Larry Gralla. Larry showed me a bar corkscrew he had just acquired and wanted to know what I knew about it. There in his hand was an ARCADE, and better than that, a version that Fred did not have. Lacking the patience of a good negotiator, I immediately popped the question. With the words that every collector hates to hear, Larry responded, "It is not for sale or trade." On hearing these words I reflected back on a story that Fred had told me.

It seems that a friend of Fred's had phoned him to brag about a bar corkscrew that he had just found. Fred, being a quick thinker, told his friend that by a great coincidence he had planned to drive over to Centerville the next day, and as his friend's house was close to the highway Fred would be traveling, he would pop in on his way and take a look at it. His friend said, "Okay Fred, but remember 'it is not for sale or trade.'" The next day Fred placed a dozen bar corkscrews in his trunk and drove over to his friend's home. They sat under a tree in the back yard for a while talking. After a while Fred said, "I must remember to take a look at that corkscrew you found." It was produced shortly after that. Upon seeing it, Fred mentally determined that he had to have it, while pointing out its defects to his friend. After some more general conversation Fred made a trip to his trunk, selected two reasonable bar corkscrews and laid them on the table without saying a word. No comment from his friend. After another period of discussion, Fred again went to the trunk, and selecting a pretty nice one, put another corkscrew on the table. Still no comments passed about a trade. Later, Fred made another trip to the trunk; this time he selected a really nice one. He lay the fourth one down on the table. His friend studied the four corkscrews for a while then, still with no comment, pushed his bar corkscrew across to Fred.

So, Fred said, "When someone says it is not for sale or trade, they just leave out the word 'reasonable'".

I left Larry's plus one ARCADE and minus one ECLIPSE.

This started off as a simple little book when I had six bar corkscrews, but over the past nine years it has taken on a life of its own, becoming a history of the manufacturers and the inventors. Distribution and manufacturing methods became a passion; patents were explored in ever-growing detail; later it became mandatory to analyze and compare the mechanisms. Then came the internet, and the number of collectors I came into contact with blossomed such that it is now a very rare day that I do not receive a number of e-mails, telephone calls or letters about something to do with bar corkscrews. I now own a few over 200 different versions and I still discover well over a dozen "new" corkscrews every year. Fearing that *the book* was going to become a life long project, I decided to publish this summary of the information that I have.

In this case, procrastination proved somewhat virtuous as the long gestation brought continued additions until the number of different versions and variants of mounted corkscrews in this volume is over 350. While this summary is not exhaustive, it will provide the references to identify a large percentage of the bar corkscrews you own or find, facilitate easier communications among all of us collectors and, most importantly, allow fellow collectors to know if they are in possession of "unknown" information. I hope that this book will result in the turning up of all of those corkscrews, patents, advertising and parts lists that I have yet to see. I apologize in advance for the very likely possibility that I have made a number of errors.

In this book, I deal only with corkscrews that are mounted on a wall or counter top and have the worm permanently attached to the extraction mechanism. There were many possible names for this class of corkscrew. Some patents use "lever operated", but they do not all have levers. Collectors commonly call them barscrews, but many were not designed for or used in bars. The one thing they all have in common is that they are mounted. I used this term for years, but in the end I did an unusual thing and went with the crowd, bowing to common usage, so "bar corkscrews" it is. I have also tried to limit this book to corkscrews that probably exist, in that an example has been found or at least advertised.

Many organizational formats can be used for a volume such as this. Mine is admittedly arbitrary but, after very many false starts, I settled on organizing the book around the advertised names. The rationale was that most pieces either had a name marked on the corkscrew or were advertised under a name.

There are many bar corkscrews not listed in this book. I have copies of the patents for about 75 of these. So, adding these to the many versions and variants yet to be found I would estimate that there are more than 100 models, versions and variants of bar corkscrews waiting for discovery, if only they have survived the decades.

There is a great reluctance on the part of most collectors to disassemble and clean up their bar corkscrews, so that even external marks are often obscured by dirt and rust. I think that it is a great shame to let these rare examples of late 19th century mechanical ingenuity return to the earth as iron oxide, when even small preservation steps could extend their life almost indefinitely.

Inevitably the question of value of a bar corkscrew arises. The value of a collectible item is based on three things: popularity, condition and scarcity. As all bar corkscrews are rare, I believe that they are still a great bargain, even though they have increased in price dramatically over the past few years. I know of no other collecting area where one can sometimes find a rare, 100+ year old, patent dated collectible for a few hundred dollars. When an item is bought and sold repeatedly, some measure of its market price can be ascertained. However, many of these corkscrews are so rare that they have never been auctioned; they change hands privately so a "market" price is never established. I have obtained very rare bar corkscrews for less than a hundred dollars while I was unable to purchase others with a five-figure offer. Some relatively common (in mounted corkscrew terms) items such as the British ECLIPSE are very popular with corkscrew collectors, often fetching prices far higher than do less showy but far more rare corkscrews. Any "mint" corkscrew will usually be valued at many times the price of a similar piece with normal wear and tear. I see no reason why a marked only-existing example of a patented bar corkscrew mechanism should be valued any differently than the equivalent of any other type of corkscrew.

If this publication serves as a base of information that can be built on by helixophiles, authors and researchers in the future, I will feel very well rewarded.

I learned a huge amount and enjoyed putting it together.

Wayne Meadows
September 1st, 2001

Section I
MECHANISMS

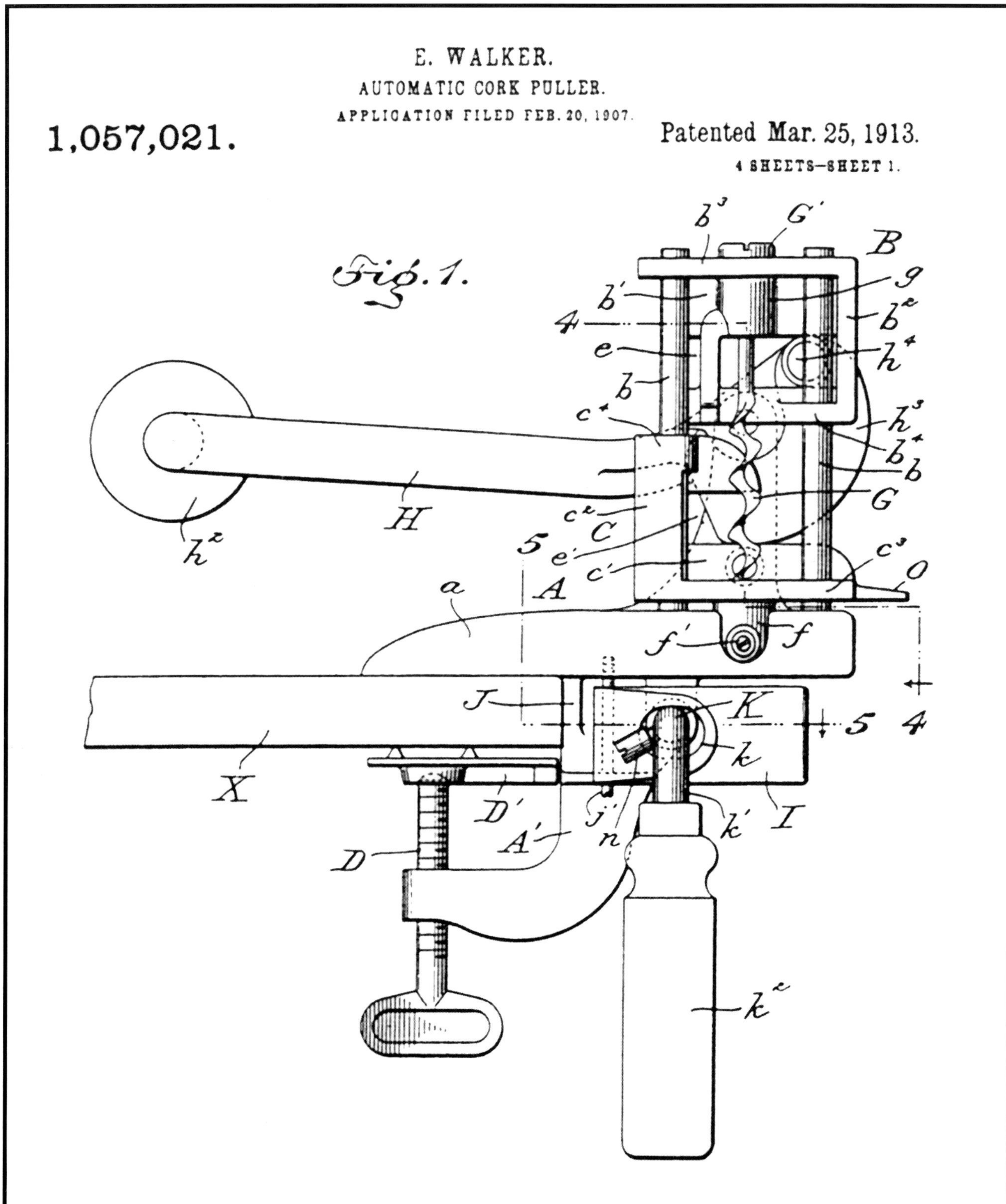

This section shows and explains both the operation of the various mechanisms found in bar corkscrews and the details of what was claimed in each patent. In some cases the patent was not for a new type of internal mechanism, but rather some additional feature or attachment that made the corkscrew easier to use. A large number of corkscrews were manufactured, with and without patents, utilizing hand cranks, levers, multiple combinations of gear trains, counter-rotating stems, stem-nuts and worm-nut mechanisms. In general this section includes only the corkscrew mechanisms that are known to exist, or believed to exist, as they have been advertised for sale. Except in one or two cases, this section does not include bar corkscrews that were granted a patent, but for which no examples or advertising have been found.

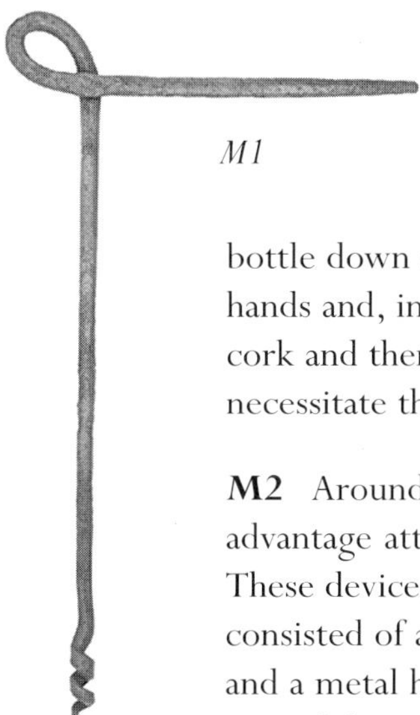

M1

M1 In the beginning, corkscrews were very simple. They consisted of a handle attached to a stem, which was attached to a worm. With these simple corkscrews one could pull a cork from a bottle, but neither easily or quickly.

The hard part about using a simple "T" type corkscrew was (and is) holding the bottle down and pulling the cork out. Grasping a large bottle and pulling the cork required large hands and, in many cases, considerable strength. The slow part was turning the worm into the cork and then turning the cork off of the worm. Eventually, bottled beer (with corks) would necessitate the invention of a faster, simpler method of removing corks.

M2 Around the middle of the 18th century, a frame with a mechanical advantage attacked the hold-bottle-down-and-pull-cork-out problem. These devices could not in themselves be classified as corkscrews; they consisted of a frame incorporating a bracket that held the bottle down and a metal hook that pulled almost any "T" handled corkscrew up. One turned the corkscrew into the cork, held the bottle and protruding corkscrew in the frame, and then pulled the lever that hooked the "T" handled corkscrew and extracted the cork. The mechanical advantage incorporated into these frames consisted of various types of rack and pinion, gear or lever mechanisms. This greatly improved on the effort required to pull a cork from a bottle of wine, but, as there was no requirement at this time, did not address the problem of speed.

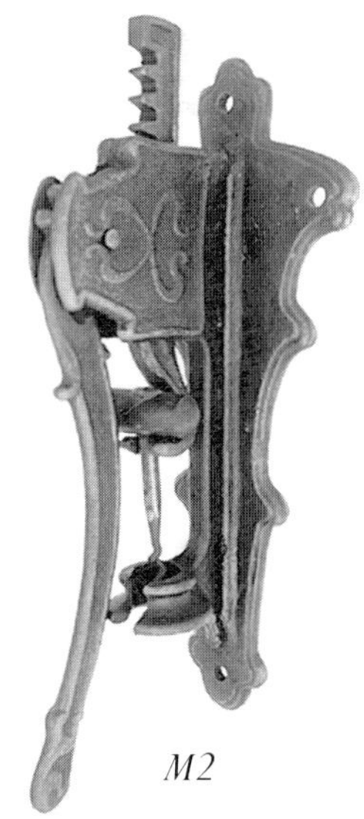

M2

Mounted corkscrew mechanisms

The first, simplest, form of mounted corkscrew, introduced in the late 1800's, saw the corkscrew and mechanical advantage combined in one device. These corkscrews are commonly known as "coffee grinders" or "crank and pump" in the collector community. In most cases the worm was attached to a stem with a crank on it. This stem was inserted through a frame that included a lever to assist in the extraction process. In most examples one cranked the worm into the cork and pressed or pulled a lever to extract the cork. With this system, the operator then held the cork steady and reversed the direction of the crank to remove the cork from the worm. While this provided a much more compact and economical mechanical advantage than the corkscrew frame, the crank-operated worm only marginally improved on the speed. Various mechanical devices were added to speed up the turn-out-of-the-cork problem. One of these centered around fixing a blade to the frame, such that stacking up corks on the stem caused the uppermost to split, letting the pieces fall where they might. Probably no speed was gained due to the very considerable turning force required, not to mention the mess produced by the broken cork bits. Many attempts to incorporate other types of mechanical advantages into this style of corkscrew were patented. These included devices utilizing mechanisms such as rack and pinion, various lever configurations and screw threads. Many of these were copies of mechanisms found in the smaller portable corkscrews of this era, with some type of mounting bracket added to the frame. Ultimately, this style of corkscrew was confined to the home consumer market.

Note: The patent drawings in this section have been heavily edited, with all of the original lines, arrows, numbers and letters deleted to more clearly show the underlying mechanism. The many pages of words found in a patent document have in most cases been reduced to a sentence or two, or what is considered to be the essence of the mechanism patented. Quotes from the patent are in italics. To view the original drawings and words one should obtain a complete copy of the patent. The American patent system dates a patent from the date it was granted, not from the date of filing the application as in the British system. The American system can be quite misleading as to the chronological order of inventions, as some patents spend many years in the "pending" file. To keep the comments in chronological order, the USA "Application filed" date has been used, not the "issued" date that is normally used.

The mechanisms and related patents

M3 This American application was filed in 1884 by William Redlich, #303,400. In this application Redlich claimed a mounted version of the wide rack "London Rack", with a lever operated pinion. In the patent Redlich claimed many innovations, including the crank (C) on the worm shaft and a padded collar (D) in the throat to prevent bottle breakage (in this case a wooden collar). In the left diagram he claimed the rack (A) and pinion (B) mechanism and the clamp mount (E) with thumbscrew. In the right diagram he claimed an alternate design utilizing a shaft with a collar (F) and lever mechanism (G) to extract the cork, and the top-mounting frame (H). Corkscrews containing this mechanism were sold under the SULLIVAN name.

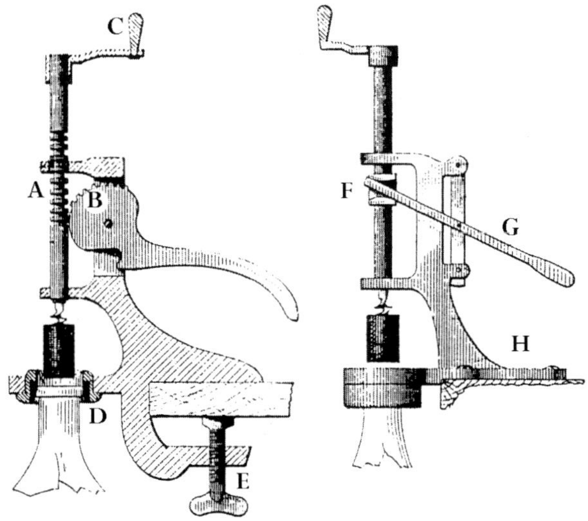

M3

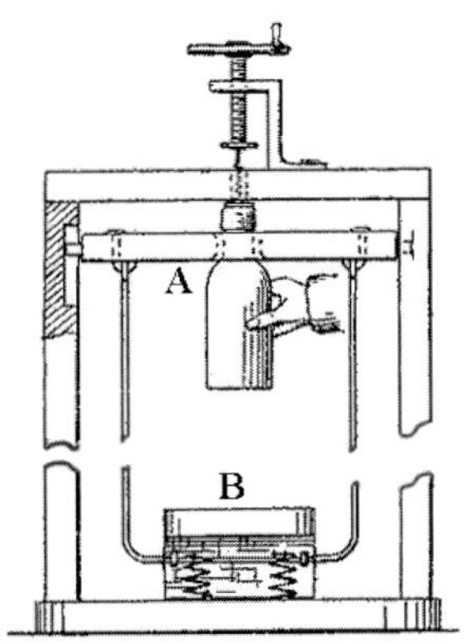

M4

M4 In this American application filed in 1885 by John Bloeser, #337,921, Bloeser claimed a corkscrew mounted on a frame containing a foot operated yoke (A). In the only production model known, the hinged wooden foot plate (B) that operated the yoke had been changed to a much longer, cast iron, levered foot pedal to actuate the yoke; presumably the original design required a fairly heavy person to operate it. The cast iron pedal version could be operated with very little foot pressure. To operate this corkscrew the bottle was inserted under the worm through a tapered hole carved into the wooden yoke; the crank-operated worm entered the cork through a small hole in a metal plate on top of the frame. The foot lever pulled the yoke down and the bottle off of the cork. Unwinding the crank released the cork, as the cork could not pass up through the hole in the plate. No name for corkscrews containing this mechanism has been found.

M5 This American application was filed in October 1885, and assigned to the F. F. Adams Company, by John A. Hurley, #348,743. In this application Hurley claimed a lever operated mounted corkscrew where the stem and crank (A) rode in a hollow plunger (B) mechanism. The corkscrew stem was free to turn or move up and down in the plunger. The plunger, which was the same size as a cork, was free to slide up and down in the barrel (C) of the corkscrew. The plunger had a round stud (D) fixed in its side, which protruded through a slot cut into the barrel. A short straight slot cut out of the operating lever engaged the stud. Pulling on the operating lever raised the plunger, thus the worm and cork.

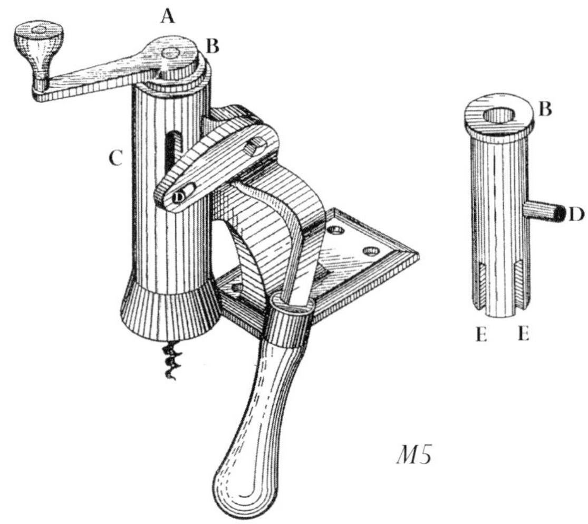

M5

The original patent envisioned pins through the barrel of the corkscrew to prevent the cork from turning when the crank was unwound, and slots (E) cut into the plunger to clear the pins. One version of this corkscrew, manufactured very close to the patent document, did not have the pins or the slots; instead a wire breaker was fixed to the front of the barrel with two screws and a groove was cut into the front of the plunger, such that the plunger cleared the protruding screws. The two screws protruded through the barrel into the path of the cork, holding the cork from turning when the worm was unwound. A sharp rap on the top of the crank drove the cork down, out of the barrel. This version also had very limited leverage; moving the lever 45° lifted the worm 1 5/8" (40 mm). No name for corkscrews containing this version of the mechanism has been found.

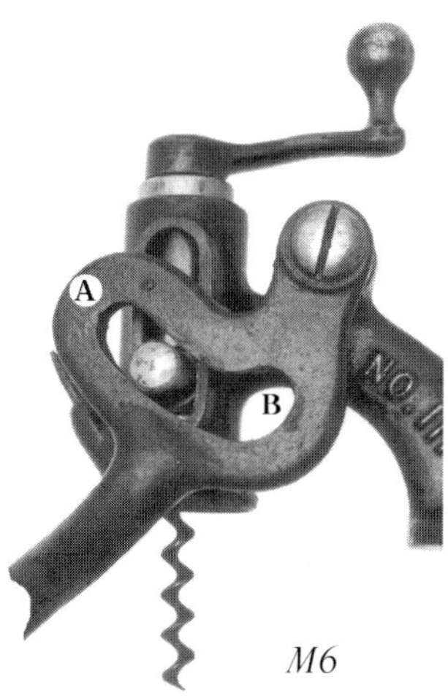

M6

M6 In a corkscrew that we know as the ENTERPRISE, this same Hurley mechanism was used, however the operating lever (A) was expanded such that it could swing through 90° and a long curved slot (B) could be cut into it. This modification increased the leverage by more than four times during the initial phase of pulling a cork. Due to the shape of the slot, the first 45° of lever movement lifted the plunger and worm only 3/8" (9mm); the remaining 45° of movement resulted in the final 1¼" (31mm) of lift. It seems doubtful that a patent could be granted for a different shaped slot in the arm. The ENTERPRISE was offered for sale for many years, with the advertising featuring a little girl using it to open a bottle of wine. If the ENTERPRISE had infringed on Hurley's patent one would assume that he would not have allowed it to be offered for sale. If the slot shape were patentable, the patent would have been granted and found. Hurley does not appear to have prevented the sale of the ENTERPRISE and no patent for it has been found, thus this would appear to be an improved version of Hurley's original patent. Corkscrews containing this mechanism were sold under the ENTERPRISE and AJAX name.

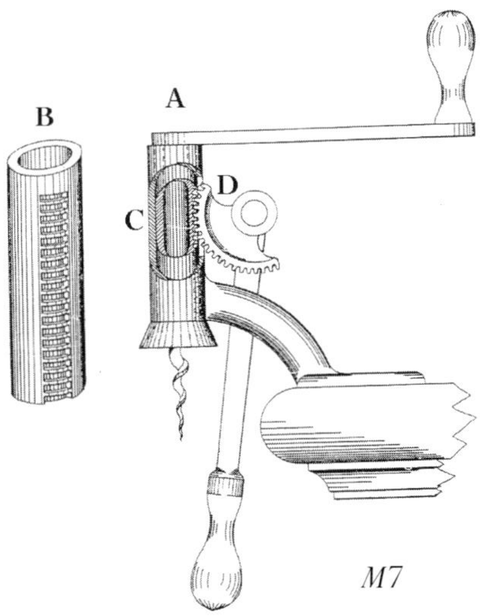

M7

M7 & M8 This American application was filed in June 1886, and assigned to the F. F. Adams Company, by John A. Hurley, #350,308. In this application Hurley claimed a rack and pinion mounted corkscrew containing a hollow, narrow rack plunger mechanism. The corkscrew stem and crank (A) was free to turn or move up and down in the plunger (B). The plunger, which was the same size as a cork, was free to slide up and down in the barrel (C) of the corkscrew. Raising the operating arm caused the pinion (D) to lift the plunger, thus the worm and cork, into the barrel. In the production versions, a wire breaker was fixed to the front of the barrel with two screws and a groove was cut into the front of the plunger, such that the plunger cleared the protruding screws, as in Hurley's patent #348,743. Around 1901 E. Walker manufactured a different version of this corkscrew with the operating arm and pinion cast as a single unit. The pinion mounting bracket (E) cast as part of the barrel was moved to the right side of the corkscrew. Corkscrews containing this mechanism were sold under the ADAMS, SAMSON and SAMPSON names.

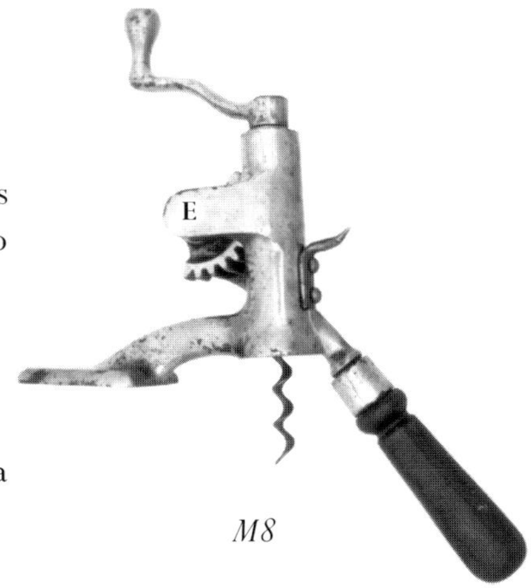

M8

M9 This American application was filed in July 1886 by Daniel Hurley, #372,266. Hurley claimed a cross over crank handled lever (A) pivoted on a rotating collar (B) around the barrel of the corkscrew. The patent included two "V" shaped ribs cast inside the barrel; these were to prevent the cork from turning when it was being stripped. Hurley noted that he was aware of the 1878 Tucker, 1883 White and the 1862 Russel patents. A later version of this corkscrew was produced with a slightly lighter frame and a wire or string-breaking hook on the tip of the operating lever. Corkscrews containing this mechanism were sold under the LEVER name.

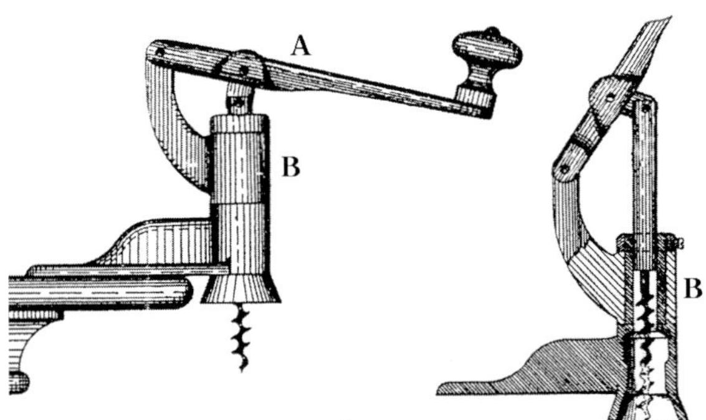

M9

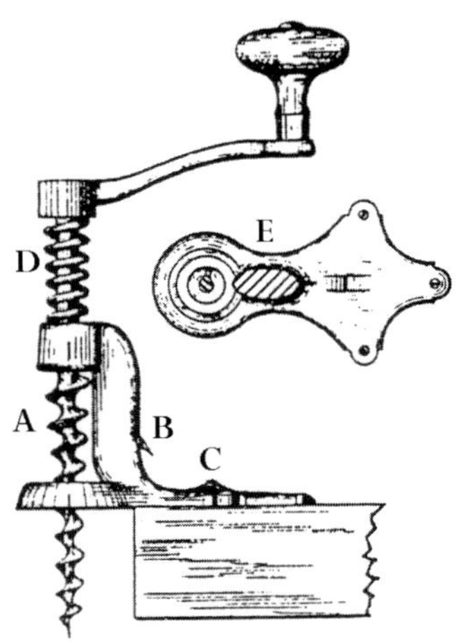

M10

M10 This American application was filed in 1886 by Newton Linsley & Arthur B. Curtis, #388,888. Linsley and Curtis claimed the wire cutter (B) the neck rest formed by the curve between (B) and (C). They described, but did not claim, the tapered worm (A) that was designed to split the cork, the spring assisted cork pulling stem and the blade (E) that was designed to prevent the cork from turning. No name for corkscrews containing this mechanism has been found.

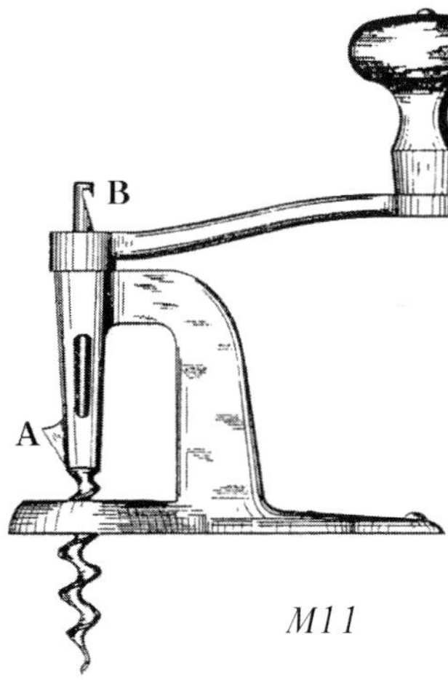

M11

M11 This American application was filed in 1887 by Charles & Edgar H. Morgan, #390,183. The Morgan brothers claimed a crank operated corkscrew with a cork splitting blade (A) cast into the front of the frame. The patent claim is for a blade that cuts from the inside of the cork. The concept behind this corkscrew was that the cork would be forced up the frame, be split apart by the blade, and fall off the corkscrew. The patent specifications mention the wire or string breaker (B), but Morgan does not claim it. No name for corkscrews containing this mechanism has been found.

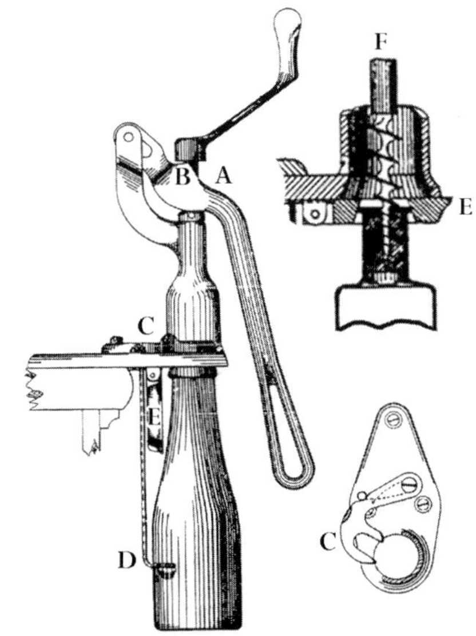

M12

M12 This American application was filed in 1887 by Edwin Walker, #377,790. Walker claimed a slotted-lever operated corkscrew. The worm stem with its crank arm was inserted through the slot (A) in the arm; the cam shaped bearing surfaces (B) on the top of the slot varied the required lifting force or leverage during the initial phase of pulling a cork. The patent also included a spring-loaded cork-stripping arm (C). In the specifications Walker envisioned a bracket or guide (D) to help center the bottle. Walker also envisioned a hinged plate (E) that contained a smaller throat; this plate could be swung up into place when a cork was to be pulled from a very small bottle. Combined with the throat size reducer was a worm manufactured with two different diameters (F), very small at the end and the normal size for the rest of its length. In this patent Walker claimed only the slotted lever and the cork stripper. No name for corkscrews containing this mechanism has been found.

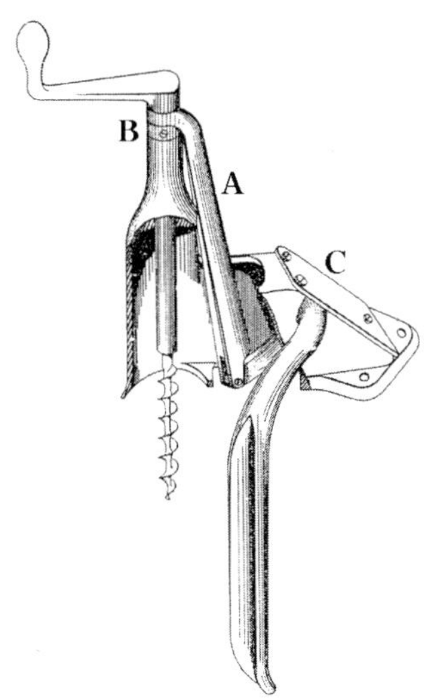

M13

M13 This American application was filed in 1889 by Edwin Walker, #452,625. Walker claimed a crank operated corkscrew, with the stem directly linked to the operating lever with a link or push bar (A). In his patent Walker noted the previous Hurley patents and made the comment that Hurley's mechanisms utilized a sleeve (plunger), rather than being directly connected to the corkscrew stem as his was. (Note that Walker did not mention the Redlich patent #303,400.) The collar (B) holding the stem with a setscrew was later replaced with a threaded stem that screwed into the crank handle. Walker noted the potential to use the case cover plate (C) as a nameplate, but did not claim it in the patent. Corkscrews containing this mechanism were sold under the ERIE and THE WALKER name.

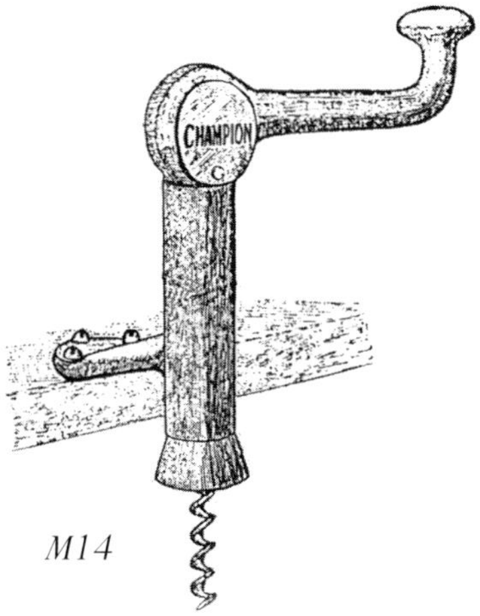

M14

M14 & M15 This American corkscrew was advertised for sale in 1893. This is a mounted version of the 1862 Russel patent with a crank operated worm, an amazingly simple corkscrew consisting of only three components: the barrel and mount, a single cast crank and disk, and the plunger and worm pinned to the edge of the disk. As shown in the position in the illustration, one cranked the worm into the cork, then as shown in the photograph, lifted the crank up and over to extract the cork. Corkscrews containing this mechanism were sold under the CHAMPION name.

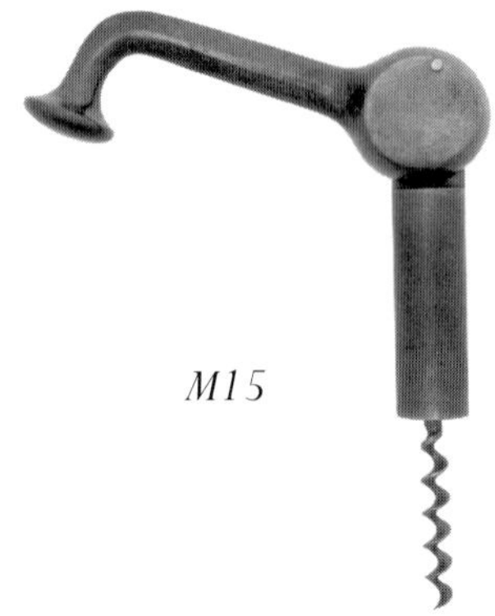

M15

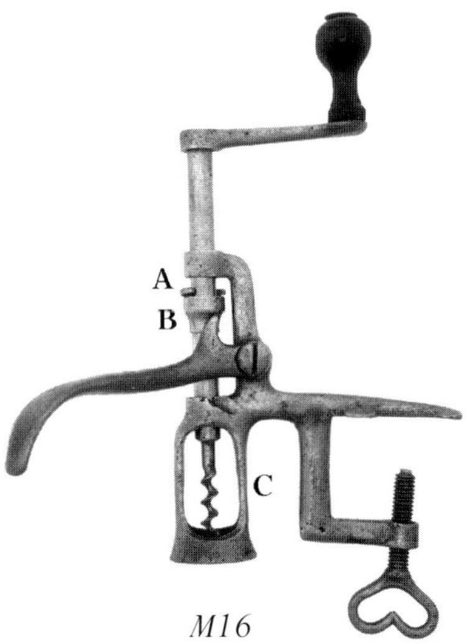

M16

M16 This is a British corkscrew, presumably produced in the 1870 – 1890 time frame. No patent or registration has been found for this crank and lever operated corkscrew. There were three holes in the stem; inserting a cotter pin (A) in any one of the holes allowed the worm to be set to penetrate a given cork to three different depths. (When most bottle containers were stopped by a cork, one did not want the worm to completely penetrate the cork as this would allow air to enter a stopped bottle.) The tapered collar (B) had an internal spring that kept the collar from sliding down the stem, away from the pin. As the lever was pulled forward and up, the projection on the operating lever caught the tapered collar, lifting the cork up, depending on the depth setting; at some point the lever and its projection slid off the collar and the lever was free to continue to swing through 360°. There was a slot (C) cut out of the back of the throat. It seems reasonable that this slot at one time contained a mechanism to prevent the cork from turning while it was being stripped. Presumably, this missing mechanism would have been actuated when the lever was pointing approximately straight down. This interesting little mounted corkscrew does not have enough pulling power to open wine or beer bottles; possibly it was designed to be used in a pharmacy. No name for corkscrews containing this mechanism has been found.

M17 This American application was filed in 1893 by Harry J. Williams, #531,670. Williams claimed a mounted version of the 1802 Thomason patent with a crank operated worm. There are three known versions of this mechanism. Two of the versions attack the same problem: how to insure that turning the crank caused the inner screw to descend rather than the outer screw to ascend (to operate properly, the outer screw must remain down against the cork until the inner screw is fully extended). Without some method of clamping the outer screw, any wear, lack of lubrication or thread damage would cause the outer screw to rise rather than the inner screw to descend.

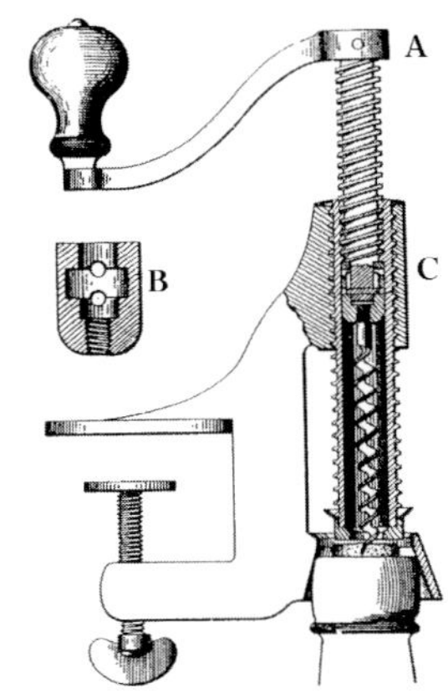

M17

Version #1 is very similar to the patent, with a nut holding the crank on rather than a pin (A) and no clutch (B) as shown in the patent drawing. This version has no hole or clip in the front (C) of the frame. It is unlikely that any clutch existed that solved the problem and it seems questionable whether Williams himself was aware of any such clutch existing. To quote from his patent: "*it is obvious that any of the well known forms of clutches which will answer the purpose may be employed between the cork screw and its supporting screw and at one or both ends of the elevating screw to lock it against rotation until the inner or supporting screw reaches the limit of its independent movement, or for that matter, in some instances the clutch may be entirely omitted.*" Turning the crank on an example of the version #1 INFANTA caused the outer screw to ascend unless it was held down by hand.

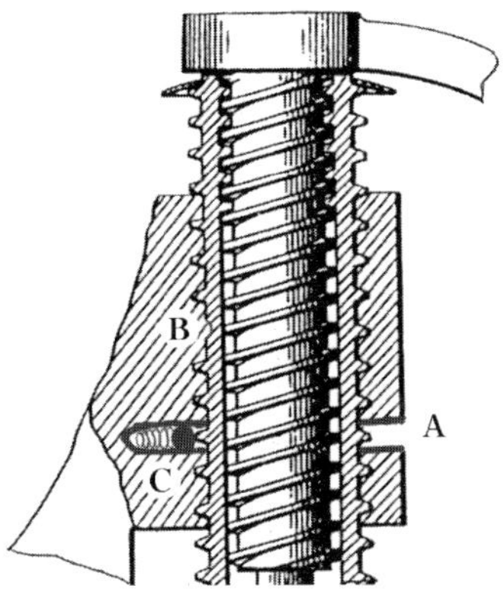

M18

M18 The version #2 INFANTA is identical to version #1, except that a hole (A) was drilled in the front of the frame. As the threaded shafts moved up and down, one could hear a "click" and feel positive pull just as the outer screw reached the lower end of its travel. A shallow hole (B) was drilled into one thread of the outer shaft. The hole in the front of the frame was the result of drilling through the front to reach the back of the frame. If one could disassemble the piece, one would find a spring and a single ball bearing (C) inset into the back of the frame. Thus, when the outer screw reached its lower limit, the spring-loaded ball pressed into the shallow hole drilled into the thread, applying a modest amount of resistance to the upward movement of the outer screw.

M19 The version #3 INFANTA, and the most common, had a spring clip (A) set into a channel cut into the front of the frame. The clip held the outer screw down by engaging a slot cut into the upper washer (B), thus hard-clamping the outer screw when it reached its lower limit. This version also had a one-piece cap (C) and handle on the stem. The lip of the cap (D) pushed the spring clip out of the slot when the inner screw reached its lower limit. This last version of the INFANTA is not as elegant a solution as the one devised for version #2, but it is extremely effective and presumably was the only version put into mass production. Corkscrews containing this mechanism were sold under the INFANTA No 8 name.

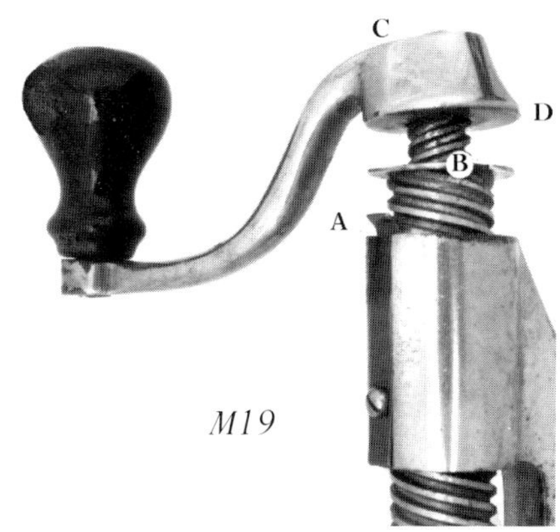

M19

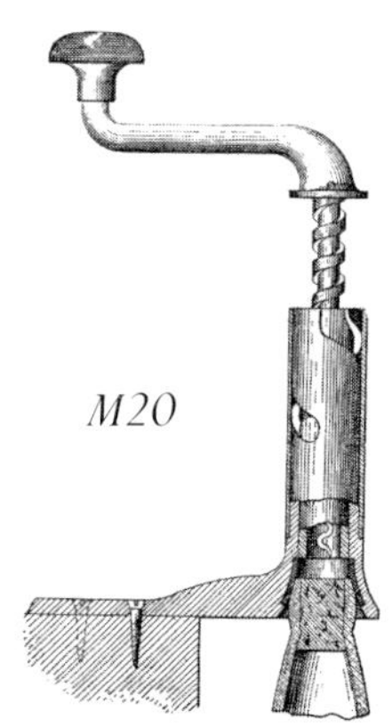

M20

M20 & M21 This is an American manufactured corkscrew. Henry Cliff patented it in 1894 in England, France and Germany, but no American patent has been discovered. This is a crank operated corkscrew with a mechanism somewhat similar to the German L. Kummer patent. The barrel of the corkscrew had a left handed spiral slot (A) cut into it; the plunger had a roller bearing (B) that rode in this slot and a babbitt guide-nut fixed in the lower end of the plunger. As shown in the photograph the crank and plunger had mating snail faces (C). Turning the crank clockwise caused the worm to pass through the guide-nut and into the cork; at this point the snail faces engaged and the plunger rode up the spiral slot, pulling the cork. Turning the crank counter clockwise caused the plunger to ride down the spiral slot; when it reached the bottom the cork was stripped from the worm as the worm was retracted through the guide-nut. Cliff described two methods of driving this mechanism, one with a threaded stem as shown in the patent drawing and the other with a guide-nut in the plunger as produced and described. Corkscrews containing this mechanism were sold under the SIMPLEX name.

There are many more American patents for mounted corkscrew mechanisms not shown in this section, but to date no advertising or examples of the patents have been found. Other than the one British example shown, no examples of this type of corkscrew have been found in any other country, indicating that they were almost exclusively an American phenomenon.

M21

The automatic corkscrew

With the advent of the mass production of beer in corked bottles and the proliferation of large hotel bars, the speed at which one could open hundreds of bottles in an evening became important. Required was a low cost, faster mechanical system to insert the worm and eject the cork; a way was found to combine the two handles into one operating lever, pulling and ejecting the cork in a forward and rearward stroke of the handle. The many ways of doing this were the subject of the bulk of the mounted corkscrew patents aimed at the commercial market in the late 1800's and early 1900's.

At first glance, automatic corkscrew mechanisms appear to be extremely complex, but only the most impractical designs were so. When one stops and thinks about it, there are very few operations required. First a worm is turned into the cork, and then the worm is pulled away from the bottle, removing the cork. In its simplest form, that's it. In an automatic corkscrew, one final operation is performed in that the worm is turned in the opposite direction, unscrewing or stripping the cork from the worm.

To make a corkscrew automatic, one must devise a method of turning the worm in both directions, while preventing it from turning during the cork extraction phase of the operation.

There are only three ways to cause the worm to turn in an automatic corkscrew. Two of these involve fastening a stem to the worm and causing the stem to turn. This can be accomplished either by attaching a gear to the stem or threading the stem and pushing it through a nut.

M22

M22 In the gear mechanisms, a gear (A) is attached to the stem (B) that is in turn attached to, or formed into, the worm (C). The usual method of turning the gear is to mesh it with a larger gear on a shaft, which is connected to a crank handle. The operator, to remove the cork, turns the crank handle. This mechanism was usually made from cast iron.

M23 In the stem-nut mechanism a stem carrier (A) holds a threaded stem (C) which is free to revolve in its bearing. The worm (E) is screwed into the end of the threaded stem. The stem-nut (D) causes the stem to turn when the stem is pushed or pulled through it. In this example a bolt passes through the operating lever and through the hole (B) in the worm carrier; pushing or pulling the operating lever causes the worm to turn clockwise or counter clockwise. Other than the worm, this mechanism was usually made from brass, cast and then machined.

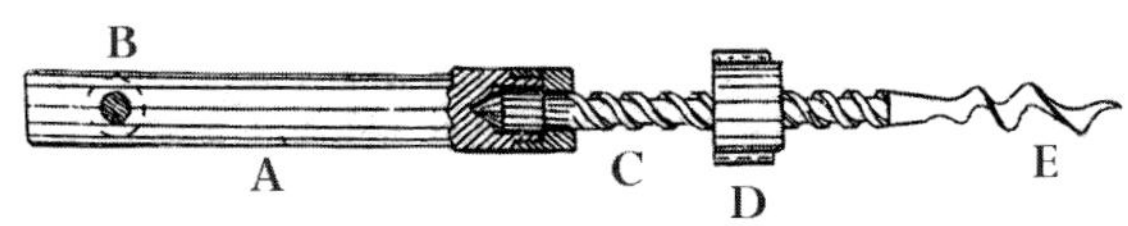

M23

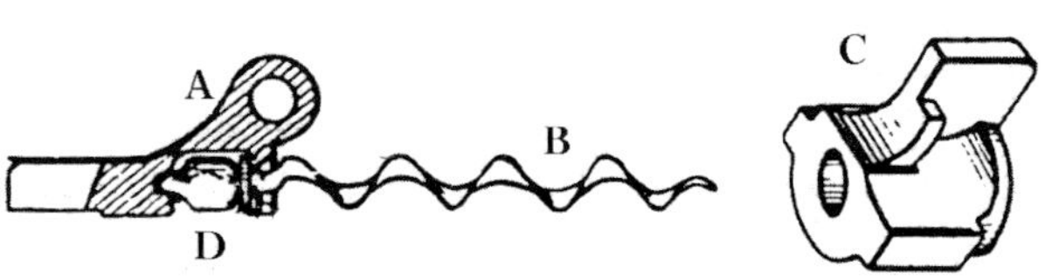

M24

M24 The third way to turn a worm is the worm-nut mechanism. As the worm (B) is already a form of screw, one can push or pull the worm through a worm-nut (C), causing it to rotate clockwise or counter clockwise. In the worm-nut mechanism a worm carrier (A) holds the worm which is free to revolve in its bearing (D). Other than the worm, this mechanism was usually made entirely from cast iron, with a lead or babbitt lining in the nut; little or no machining was required.

The following illustrations show one complete cycle of an automatic corkscrew: entering, pulling, and ejecting a cork.

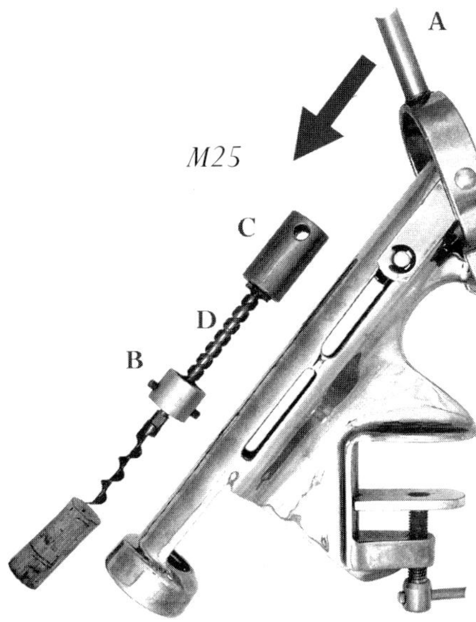

M25

M25 The operating lever (A) is half way through its forward stroke. The stem-nut (B) has been pushed down to the lower limit of its slot. The stem carrier (C) is in position to start pushing the stem (D) through the stem-nut. The cork is in the bottle.

M26 The operating lever has reached the end of its forward stroke, having pushed the stem carrier down to the lower limit of its slot. During this action the stem was pushed through the nut, turning the worm into the cork. The stem-nut remains at its lower limit. The cork is in the bottle.

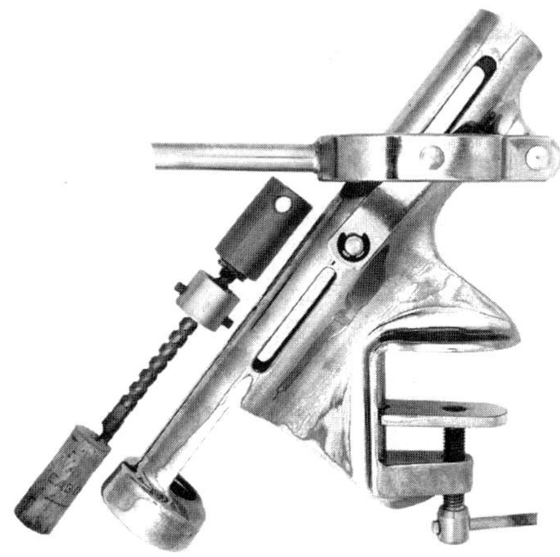

M26

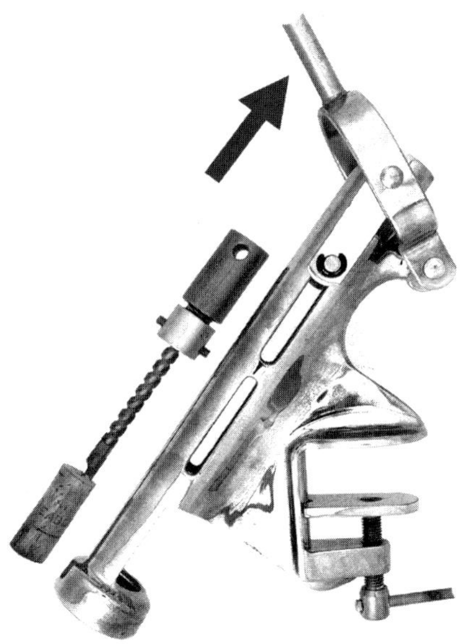

M27

M27 The operating lever is half way through its rearward stroke, pulling the stem carrier half way up its slot, causing the stem to pull the worm and cork with it. The stem-nut has been pulled to the upper limit of its slot. The cork has been pulled from the bottle.

M28 The operating lever has reached the end of its rearward stroke, pulling the stem carrier up to the upper limit of its slot. During this action the stem has been pu lled through the nut, turning the worm out of the cork. The stem-nut remains at its upper limit. The cork falls out through the barrel of the corkscrew.

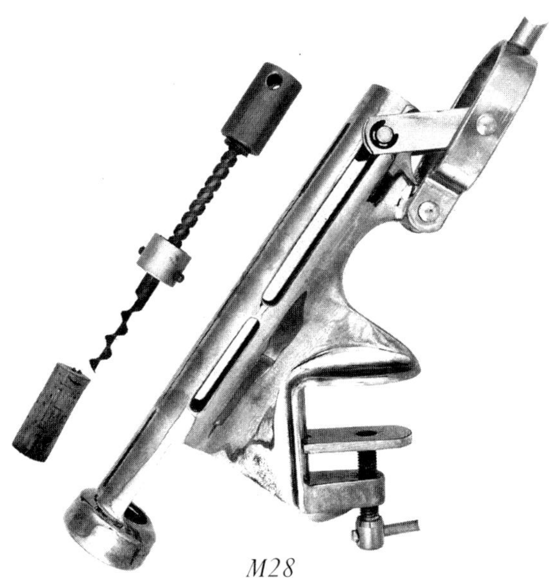

M28

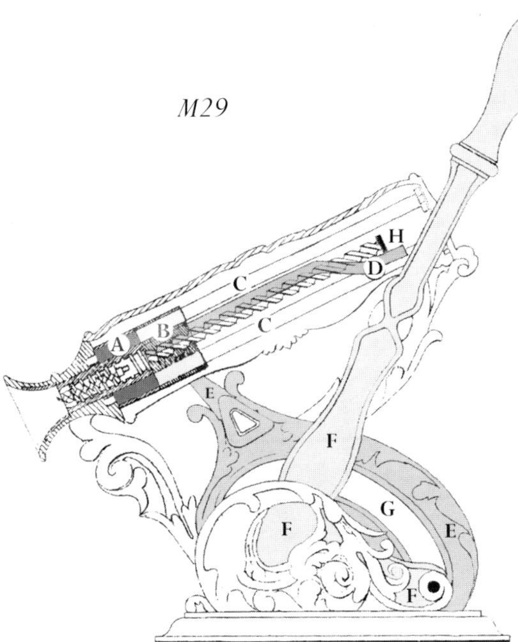

M29

M29 One of the very early automatic corkscrews was patented by P. F. Lindstrom of Stockholm, Sweden, in 1870. In this corkscrew the operating lever (F) had a roller (black) installed at the end of its "L" shaped arm. The roller operated in slot (G) of the reeling lever (E). The bottom end of the reeling lever was pivoted at the rear of the base and the top end of the reeling lever contained a fork, which engaged stem-nut (B). The stem-nut and guide-nut (A) both traveled on the guide rods (C). The guide-nut was a partially stationary nut moving only sufficiently to withdraw the cork. Locking bar (D) prevented the guide-nut from moving until it was lifted up when the stem-nut contacted the incline at its upper end. Pulling forward on the operating lever caused the reeling lever to push the stem-nut up the threaded stem, causing the threaded stem and worm to turn clockwise. After the stem-nut lifted the locking bar off of the guide-nut it reached the stop (H) on the end of the threaded stem. The operating lever, continuing in its forward direction now, caused the stem-nut to pull the threaded stem, guide-nut and worm backwards, removing the cork.

The rest of the "known to exist" automatic corkscrews fall into one of four different categories of mechanism types: Walker's corkscrew carrier mechanism, a very few gear driven mechanisms from three different countries, the British stem-nut mechanism and the American worm-nut mechanism.

The corkscrew carrier mechanism

M30, 31, 32 The corkscrew carrier mechanism was an American invention by Edwin Walker. Walker's first corkscrew carrier mechanism consisted of two tubes. Tube (A) consisted of a worm carrier with a fixed worm-nut (C), a transverse guide (D) and a screw acting as a lug (E). Tube (B) consisted of a worm carrier with a transverse guide (F) attached to it. Tube (B) was free to slide up and down inside tube (A). The roller pin (G) on the semi-disk moved both the nut and worm up and down relative to each other as the roller pin acted alternately on the two transverse guides. The cam surface (H) on the edge of the semi-disk operated on the lug (E) locking the worm-nut in place while the cork was stripped.

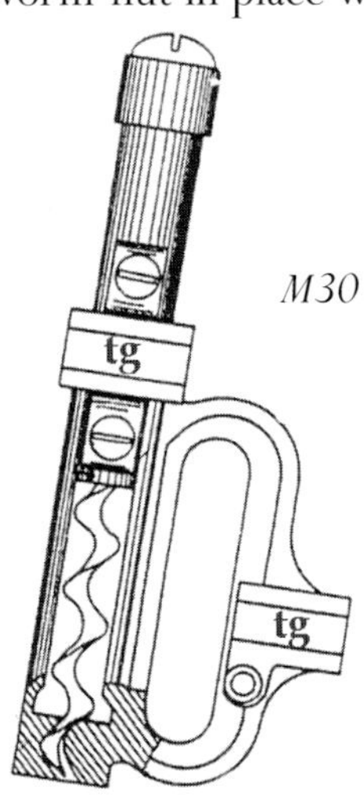

M30

M31

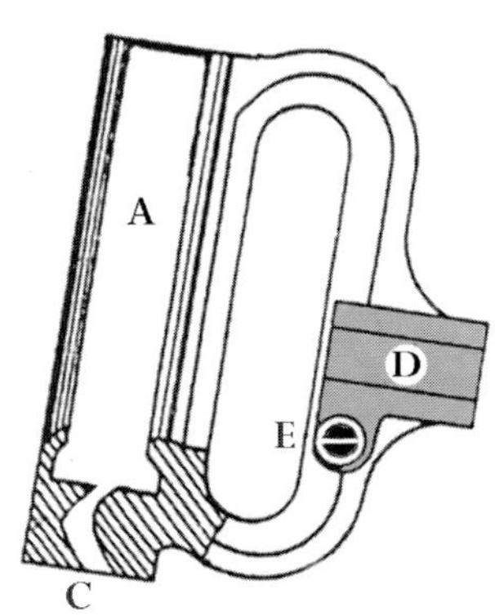

M32

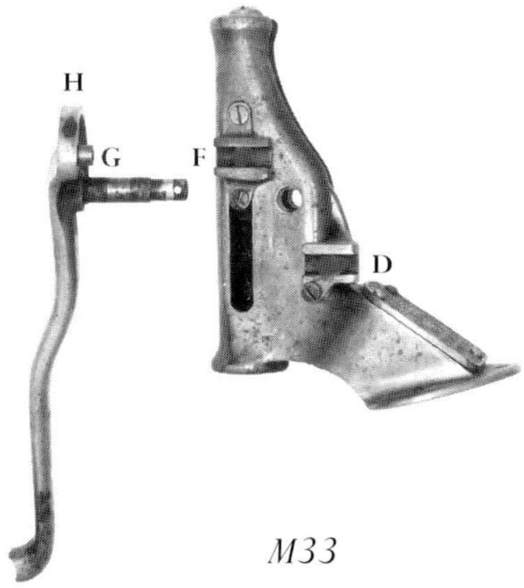

M33

M33 This American application was filed in 1893 by Edwin Walker, #515,412. In this application Walker claimed a corkscrew carrier. This first, almost vertical, design used only one pin (G) in the operating arm to control both tubes in the carrier and was soon replaced with a new and improved mechanism. (The operating arm required a rather long 270° of movement to complete a cycle and a very small amount of wear in the worm-nut allowed the transverse guides (F) and (D) to slip out of position, such that the roller pin would catch on the edge of the guide, jamming the mechanism.) The large size and complexity of this mechanism would allow Walker very little flexibility in reducing the cost, shape or size of his corkscrews in the future. Corkscrews containing this mechanism were sold under the QUICK & EASY name in the USA and the UNIQUE name in England.

M34 This American application was filed in 1895 by Edwin Walker, #543,224. Walker claimed some improvements and new features to his earlier design. These improvements included a much more inclined frame; Walker also claimed the bottleneck rest (J), cast as part of the frame in this patent. A second roller pin (G) was added to the semi-disk as the new inclined frame prevented the operating arm from traveling backwards the full 270°. The second roller pin reduced the required travel to 180°. The cam surface (H) on the edge of the semi-disk now operated on a cast lug (E) which replaced the screw lug. Walker showed the cap lifter and wire breaker (K) in the patent drawings, but did not claim them. Corkscrews containing this mechanism are marked "1895 Design" inside the semi-disk and were sold under the QUICK & EASY name in the USA.

M34
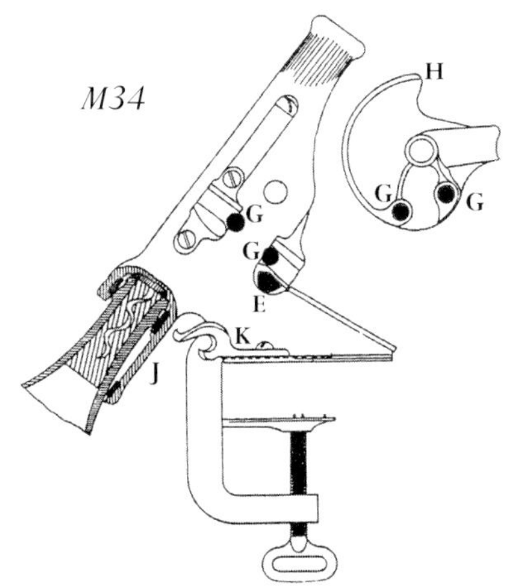

M35
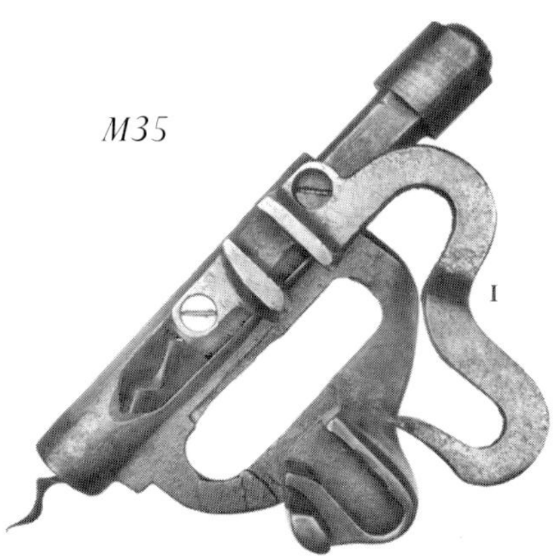

M35 & M36 In this American application filed in 1896 by Edwin Walker, #557,734, Walker claimed an additional improvement to his earlier designs by adding a yoke (I) to his corkscrew carrier. The yoke was designed to guide the lower roller pin into the transverse guide and lock the two carriers together during the cork extraction phase of the cycle. This prevented the roller pin from jamming on the edge of the guide and the worm from jamming in the worm-nut even when there was considerable wear in the worm-nut. This claim also included a bottle clasp mechanism (L). The offset operating arm (M) is found on the models named QUICK & EASY, and other than on the 1898 UNIQUE, a straight arm is found on all other corkscrews marked with a UNIQUE name. Walker spent a few years perfecting the space relationship between the two roller pins and the central shaft on the operating arm. These changes are denoted by the "design" year cast into the inside of the semi-disk on the operating arm. These include this 1896 Design, the 1897 Design and the final 1898 Design. (From the number of each design type found, it seems probable that this mechanism was not very successful before 1898.) Corkscrews containing this mechanism were sold under the QUICK & EASY name in the USA and 1898 UNIQUE, NEW UNIQUE and THE UNIQUE names in England.

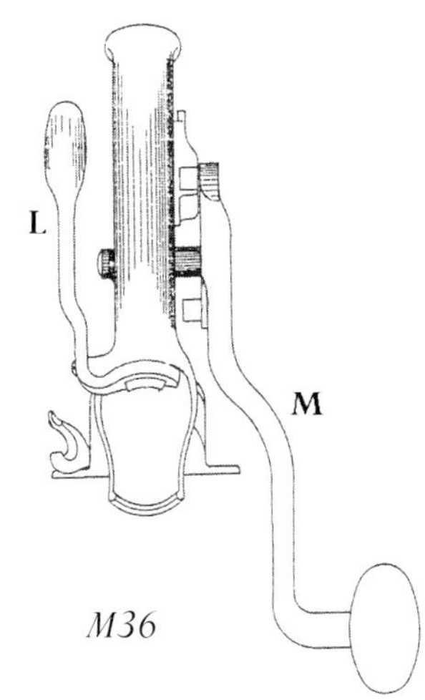

M36

M37 & M38 This American application was filed in 1907 by Edwin Walker, #1,057,021. Walker claimed a corkscrew utilizing a vertically operating version of his corkscrew carrier patent. In this application the nut carrier (A) and the worm carrier (B) slid up and down vertically on two guideposts (C). The operating arm contained the equivalent lugs and cam surface to those found in his earlier patents. This corkscrew also utilized his bottle clasp patent applied for two months later. (This corkscrew is so complex and thus expensive to manufacture that it is doubtful that it could have become a commercial success.)

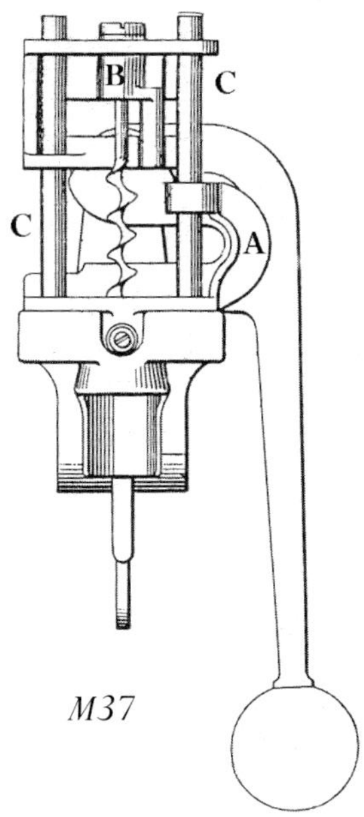

M37

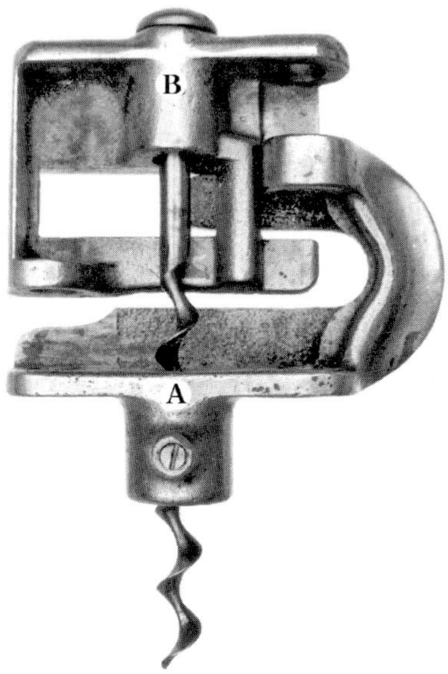

M38

Other Walker mechanisms, as found in the BULL DOG and the LITTLE QUICKER, are not corkscrew carrier mechanisms. In both of these Walker used the worm carrier similar to his QUICK & EASY; however, in both cases, the worm-nut was free to slide in guides and was not in a carrier. As the worm-nuts in these mechanisms were captured and released, the mechanisms may have infringed on Arcade's patents. If this were true, it would possibly explain why there are so few of these bar corkscrews found and why one of the LITTLE QUICKER patents was granted in Canada but no equivalent patent is found in the USA.

The gear mechanisms

While a number of gear driven mechanisms were patented over the years, the ECLIPSE was the only one that was manufactured over an extended period of time. Very few examples of any other types of gear driven corkscrews have been discovered.

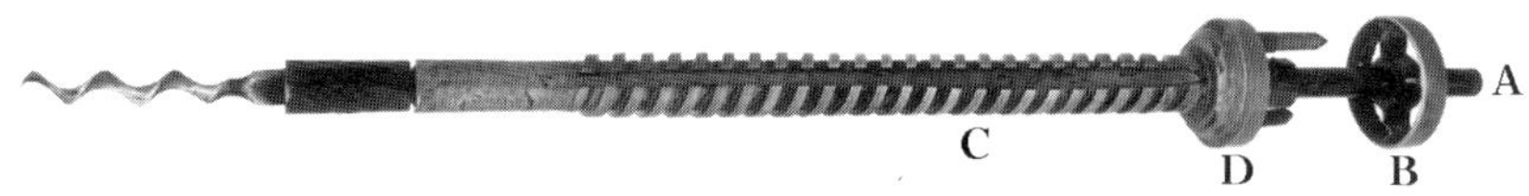

M39

M39 This English patent was filed in 1885 by Frederick Thomas Marwood, #3,871. In this patent Marwood claimed a gear and clutch driven mechanism. This corkscrew was not manufactured exactly as described in the patent. The stem (A) of the left-handed worm had a slot or keyway cut lengthwise into it, which engaged the upper half of the clutch (B). The upper half of the clutch consisted of a disk in the shape of a four-spoke wagon wheel, sliding loosely on the keyed stem; stops cast into the barrel of the corkscrew limited the distance this disk could slide up and down on the stem. The stem and worm revolved inside of a threaded shaft (C). The threaded shaft had two keyways cut lengthwise into it, which engaged the beveled gear turning the shaft through a nut. Fixed to the top of the threaded shaft was the lower half of the clutch (D), consisting of a disk with two projecting pins and a spring-loaded ratchet and pawl. The ratchet and pawl allowed the worm stem to slip during the cork extraction portion of the cycle. These two disks engaged and locked the stem to the threaded shaft causing the worm to turn when the threaded shaft's two projecting pins slid through the holes in the upper half of the clutch. To remove a cork, one turned the crank arm, which caused the main gear to turn the beveled gear and thus the threaded shaft. The ratchet and pawl in the clutch locked the worm spindle to the threaded shaft and the worm entered the cork. On reversing the crank arm, the threaded shaft turned in the opposite direction; however, the ratchet and pawl allowed the spindle to stop rotating and the cork was pulled from the bottle. As the threaded shaft approached the end of the barrel, the two pins in the lower clutch engaged the holes in the upper clutch plate, such that the spindle was again locked to the threaded shaft and the worm turned out of the cork. Corkscrews containing this mechanism were sold under the ECLIPSE trade name.

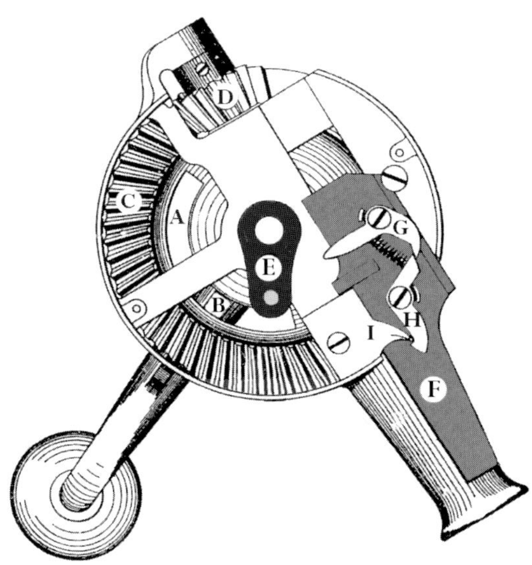

M40

M40 This American application was filed in 1883 by Edwin Walker, #515,411. Walker claimed a gear driven mechanism, as follows. The left side of the case had a semi-circular slot (A) cut out of it; a stud (B) on the crank arm protruded through this slot. Inside the case was a disk (C) cut with gear teeth around part of its circumference; this main gear also had a semi-circular slot (A) cut into it. The stud on the crank arm caused the main gear to turn when it was in contact with either end of the slot cut out of the gear. The main gear meshed with a small beveled gear (D), which was attached to a hollow tubular shaft. The tubular shaft had a keyway cut nearly its entire length. Inside the tubular shaft, free to slide longitudinally, was installed the worm stem with its spline. A small crank (E) containing a stud (light gray) was mounted on this side of the crank arm shaft. A sliding plate (F) had two spring-loaded latches (G) and (H) mounted on it. Working together, they locked the plate to the frame (I). Unseen, the plate also had a guide-nut mounted on the other side of the plate. (This guide-nut acted as a guide to center the worm, to provide reciprocal motion to the worm when the stem was turned and to strip the cork.) To operate, the sliding plate would initially be locked to the frame and the crank arm was turned counter clockwise, causing the beveled gear to turn the tubular shaft and thus the worm through the guide-nut into the cork. At this point the stud on the small crank contacted the top of, and then slipped past, the upper latch (G), which in turn lifted the lower latch (H) off the catch (I) unlocking the sliding plate from the frame. The crank arm was then turned clockwise; as the stud on the small crank (E) was now under the arm of the upper latch (G), the stud lifted the latch and the sliding plate up its guide rail, pulling the cork without turning the worm. At this point the lug on the crank arm contacted the end of the slot in the main gear causing it to rotate, and the cork was stripped. (The screw holding latch (G) to the sliding plate would have been required to be very sturdy to handle all of the force required to extract a cork.) Corkscrews containing this mechanism were sold under the WALKER AUTOMATIC name.

M41

M41 & M42 This Swedish gear driven mechanism was patented in 1883, in Germany by N. P. Krichau of Denmark, DRP #39,103; no Swedish patent has been found. This corkscrew was designed to partially pull corks made in a wide variety of lengths. The slotted pin (A) in the top of the frame controlled how far the cork was pulled out of the bottle before the cork was stripped from the worm. This distance was adjustable in eleven 1/8th inch steps. On the back of the corkscrew, three holes (B) were drilled in an arc at the end of the operating lever. A spring-loaded pin (I) allowed the operator to select one of three settings; these settings determined the depth that the worm would penetrate into the cork before it was pulled. Combining these two adjustments, the operator had a total of 33 different combinations to select from! The worm was attached to a stem (E), which had a keyway cut lengthwise into it. The keyed stem was free to ride up or down inside the small beveled gear (F). Pushing the operating lever in one direction turned the main gear (G), which turned the beveled gear, causing the spindle, thus worm, to turn in a guide-nut. (This guide-nut acted as a guide to center the worm, to provide reciprocal motion to the worm when the stem was turned and to strip the cork.) When the worm reached the pre-set depth, the operating lever contacted a roller pin (C) on the frame. The roller pin, acting as the fulcrum point, allowed the operating lever to lift the head of the corkscrew mechanism by sliding it up guide rails, pulling the cork. Just before the operating lever was about to lift the head, a stud on the operating lever released the spring-loaded catch (D) that was locking the head to the frame. On the cork-stripping portion of the cycle, this spring-loaded catch prevented the head from rising, and the cork was stripped. No name for corkscrews containing this mechanism has been found.

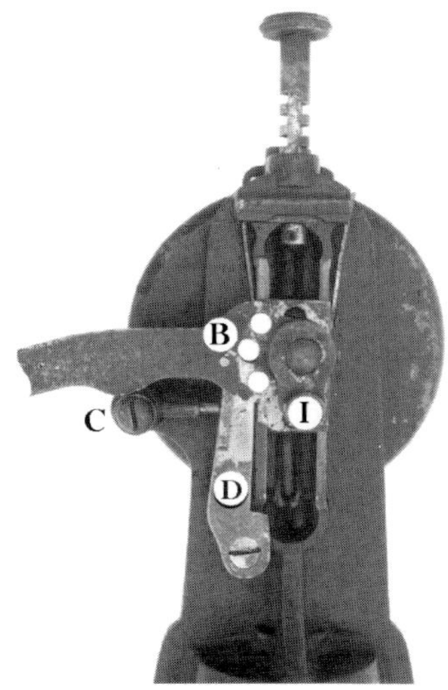

M42

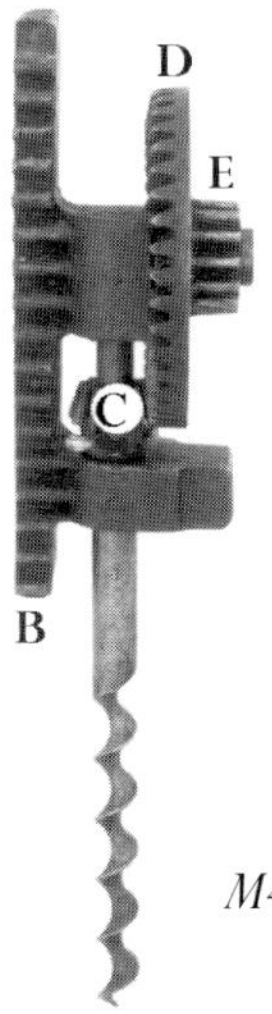

M43

M43 & M44 This is a French gear driven mechanism, for which the patent has yet to be found. This mechanism consisted of two racks and pinions. The pinion (A) on the operating lever drove the lifting rack (B), which housed three gears. These gears consisted of a beveled gear (C) pinned to the worm shaft and a disk with one side cut into a large diameter gear (D) and the other side of the disk having a small diameter gear (E). The second rack (F) was the driving rack, causing the gears to turn when the pinion on the operating lever raised and lowered the lifting rack. The driving rack consisted of a sliding plate (F) with rack teeth cut into its edge; this rack was allowed to freely travel up and down, the length of a cork, on guide pins inserted into the back plate of the corkscrew. To operate this mechanism the operating lever was pulled, causing the gear housing and the driving rack to slide down its guides. On reaching the lower limit of travel the driving rack caused the small gear to turn, which caused the large gear to turn the beveled gear on the worm, turning the worm into the cork. On reversing the direction of the operating lever the gear housing and driving rack slid up the guides, pulling the cork. On reaching the upper limit of its travel, the driving rack caused the small gear to turn in the opposite direction, resulting in the cork being stripped. Another version of this corkscrew utilized a second back plate for the driving rack. Corkscrews containing this mechanism were sold under the L'AUTOMATIQUE name.

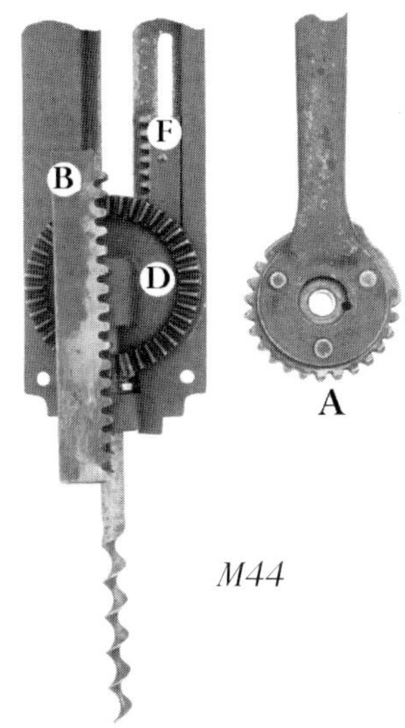

M44

There were a number of other patents received for bar corkscrews with gear driven mechanisms; unfortunately none of them have been found.

Stem-nut mechanisms and related patents

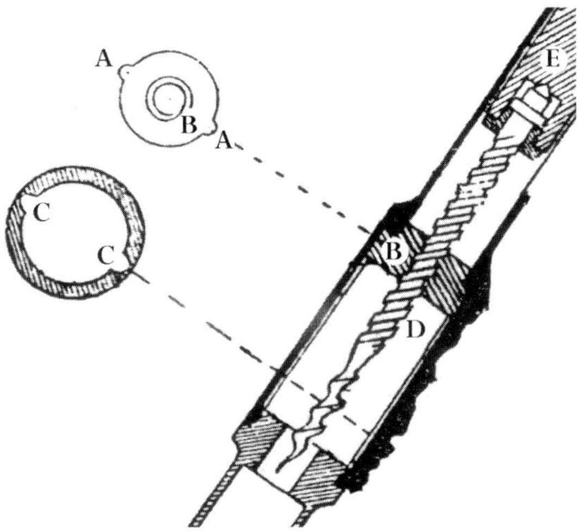

M45

M45 The stem-nut mechanism was a British invention. In this mechanism the tabs (A) on the side of the stem-nut (B) slide up and down in two guides or channels (C) cut into the inside of the barrel of the corkscrew, as shown in this cross section from a patent drawing. The length of these slots controls the distance that the stem-nut can travel up or down the barrel. Pushing down on the stem carrier (E) causes the stem-nut to slide down the barrel. When the stem-nut reaches the bottom end of the guide, the threaded stem is forced to turn clockwise, screwing the worm into the cork. Pulling up on the stem carrier causes the stem-nut to slide up the barrel. When the nut reaches the top end of the guide, the threaded stem is forced to turn counterclockwise, stripping the worm from the cork. Until the introduction of the worm-nut mechanism in the early 1890s, the stem-nut mechanism, manufactured in England, was the dominant automatic corkscrew mechanism. It is still the system of choice in many modern corkscrews. The two negative features of this original mechanism were that it was expensive to manufacture and large; they used up a lot of counter top space. (On the other hand, if one wanted a big shiny decoration on the bar, why not something as dramatic as a MERRITT?)

M46 These stem-nut mechanisms are shown with both the worm and the stem carrier attached. The one on the left is from an ACME; the stem carrier is also the rack which mates with the pinion turned by the operating lever. The other stem carriers are out of various English corkscrews: the A1, MERRITT, XXX, RAPID and SWIFT. The last five all have a hole drilled through the rear of the stem carrier. A bolt passed through this hole connecting the carrier to the operating lever or the lever's connecting links, thus converting the forward and rearward motion of the operating lever into a turning worm as the stem passed through the nut.

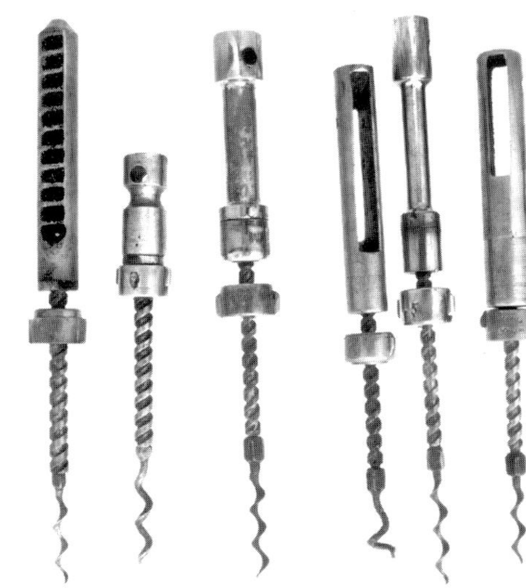

M46

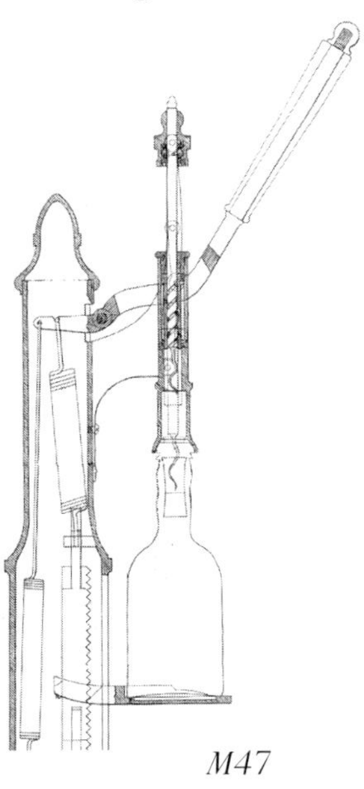

M47

M47 This English application was filed in 1865 by Henry John Sanders, #2,844. In this application Sanders claimed the first stem-nut mechanism with automatic cork ejection. *"As the lever and spindle continue to descend, the nut, when it has ceased to descend, causes the spindle and screw to revolve."* Pushing or pulling the threaded stem through the nut caused the attached worm to turn in or out of the cork, and, during the cork extraction phase, the nut slid up with the stem, keeping the worm from turning out of the cork. He also patented a bottle stand that moved up into place as the lever was pulled down. How the stem-nut was to be restrained from turning is not mentioned in the patent claim. Corkscrews containing these mechanisms were sold under the CRYSTAL PALACE name.

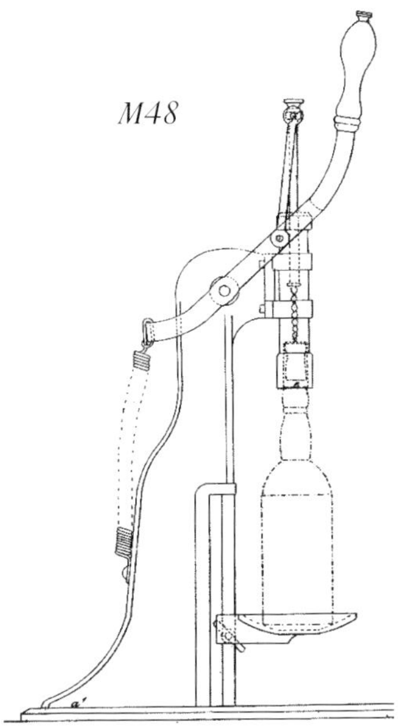

M48

M48 This English application was filed in 1878 by Martin Kosminski, #2,434. Kosminski claimed a mechanism very similar to Sanders' 1865 patent. In this case the spring assisting the cork extraction was moved outside the case. Possibly this patent was granted due to Kosminski being specific about the guides cut into the barrel. An excerpt from his patent states: *"The stem of the 'screw', or instrument for entering the cork is formed with a thread thereon, which passes through a nut capable of movement endwise without rotation in suitable guides."* He also claimed an adjustable base to support bottles of varying heights. No name for corkscrews containing this mechanism has been found.

M49 This English application was filed in 1885 by John Henry Smiles, #5,878. In this application Smiles claimed a complicated double linked (A) and (B), guide-nut (C) and stem-nut (D) mechanism with a flywheel finial (F) on the tube. While this is not a true stem-nut mechanism or known to exist, it is interesting to note that he received this patent, which also claimed the idea of securing the frame to a counter with a center bolted base (E).

M49

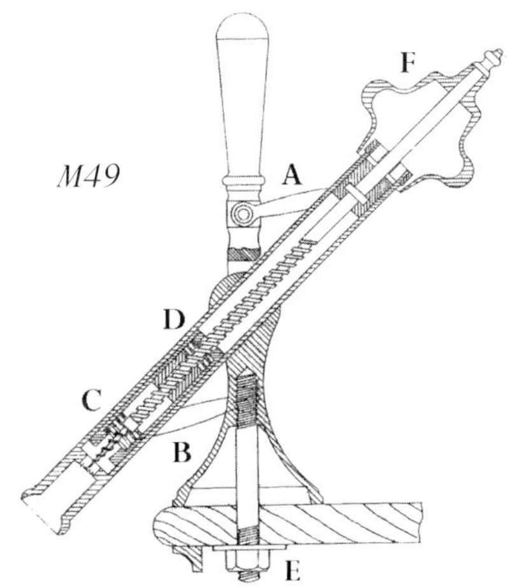

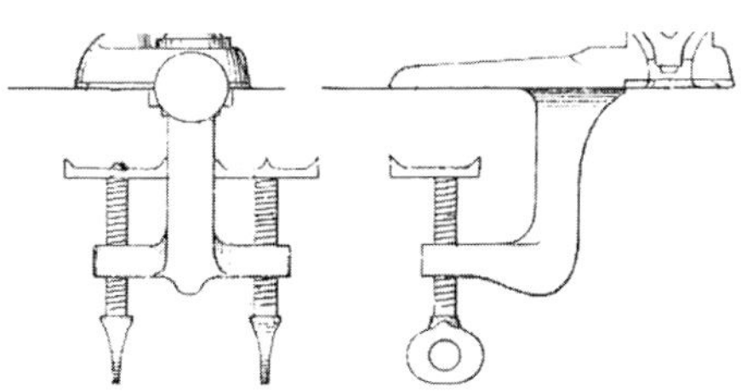

M50

M50 This English application was filed in 1886 by Walter Vaughan, #10,459. In this application Vaughan claimed the double clamp arrangement found on early versions of his ACME patent.

M51 & M52 In this English application filed in 1887 by Walter Vaughan, #11,104, Vaughan claimed a rack (A) and pinion (B) driven stem carrier and a bottle holder bracket as part of the frame. Corkscrews containing this mechanism were sold under the ACME and EXHIBITION name.

M51

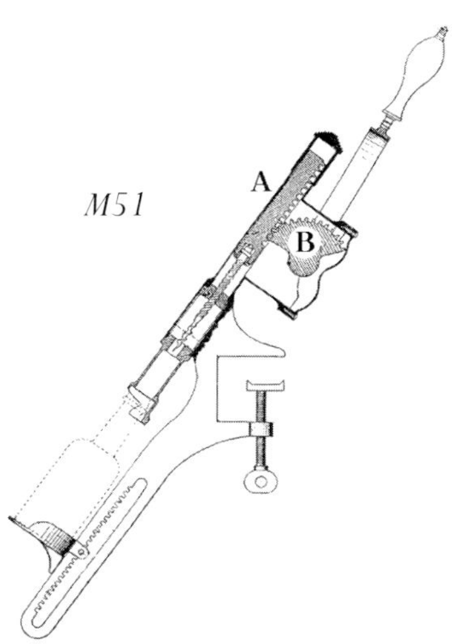

M52

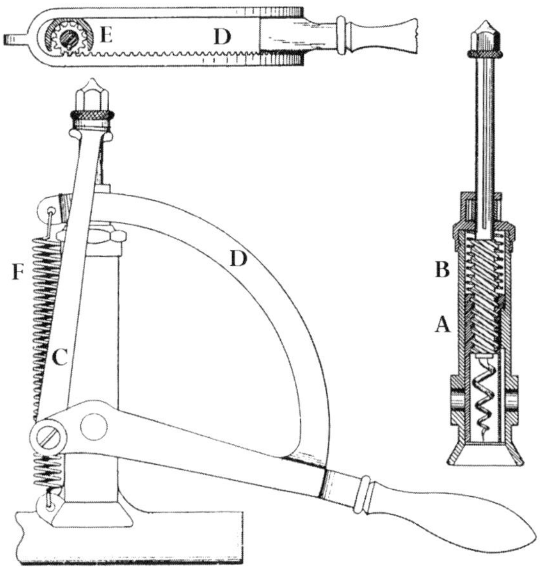

M53

M53 This American application was filed January 05, 1888 by Raymond Beardsley Gilchrist, #384,839. Gilchrist claimed the following stem-nut mechanism. Stem-nut (A) was free to travel up and down the length of a cork. A spring (B) was designed to hold the stem-nut down while the worm was entering the cork. The stem was turned by the pinion gear (E), which was rotated by the teeth on the rack (D). The lifting arm (C) was pivoted to the operating lever and pushed the stem up, pulling the cork; this operation was assisted by spring (F). No name for corkscrews containing this mechanism has been found.

M54 This American application was filed on May 19, 1888 by Raymond Beardsley Gilchrist, #392,116. The stem-nut spring in Gilchrist's previous patent probably did not work very well and this design corrected the problem. Gilchrist claimed the following captured stem-nut mechanism. The stem-nut (A) was captured at the bottom of its travel by a stud (B) passing through the front of the frame. The stud was attached to a flat leaf spring (C) mounted on the front of the barrel. When it was pulled all the way back, the operating lever pressed down on a swinging lever (D) pivoted to the frame. This action caused the other end of the lever (E) to lift up the stem-nut and cork. Immediately before the lever started to lift up, cams on the operating lever fork pushed the flat spring away from the frame, releasing the nut. Capturing a nut effectively reduced the distance it travelled by half, reducing the length of the barrel and reducing the size and cost of the corkscrew. Gilchrist further reduced the length of the barrel by allowing the stem to protrude through the cap on the barrel. Gilchrist and Arcade went on to make great use of the principle of catching and releasing a nut in their worm-nut designs. No name for corkscrews containing this mechanism, other than "Gilchrist Mfg. Co.", has been found.

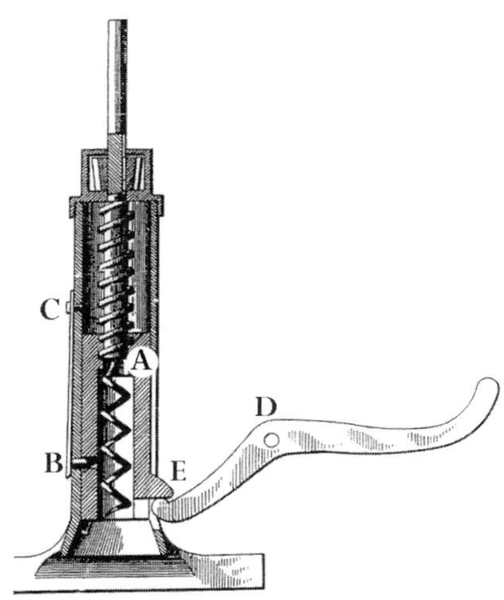

M54

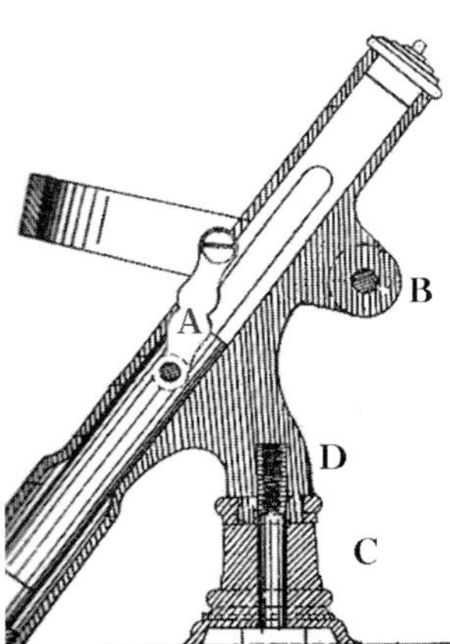

M55

M55 This English application was filed in 1888 by Cornelius Chambers, #4,564. In this application Chambers claimed an operating lever pivoted on the back of the barrel (B) with side links (A) between the operating lever and the stem carrier. He also claimed a circular base and pillar or pedestal (C), bolted to a projecting frame (D) on the barrel of the corkscrew. Corkscrews containing these mechanisms were sold under the MERRITT name.

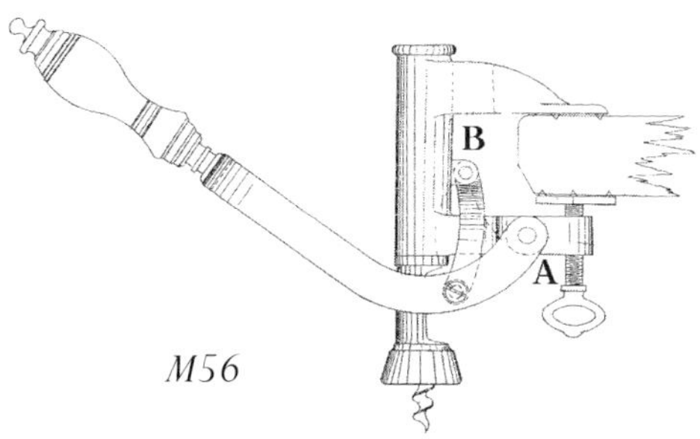

M56

M56 & M57 In this English application filed in 1888 by Cornelius Chambers, #6,230, Chambers claimed an operating lever pivoted from the clamp frame (A), and a single link between the lever and the back of the stem carrier (B). The most important claim in this patent was for the single ball bearing (C) inserted between the end of the stem (D) and the socket (E) in the stem carrier. The ball bearing was very important as it reduced wear and friction; it has been found in all stem-nut mechanisms examined by the author. With this simple invention Chambers probably locked up the market for all new and replacement stem-nut mechanisms sold in England.

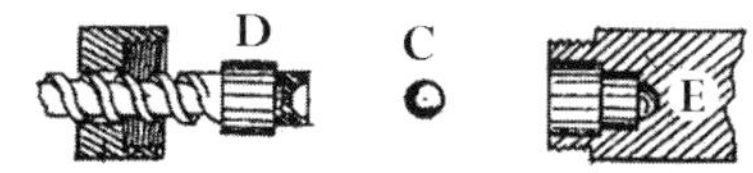

M57

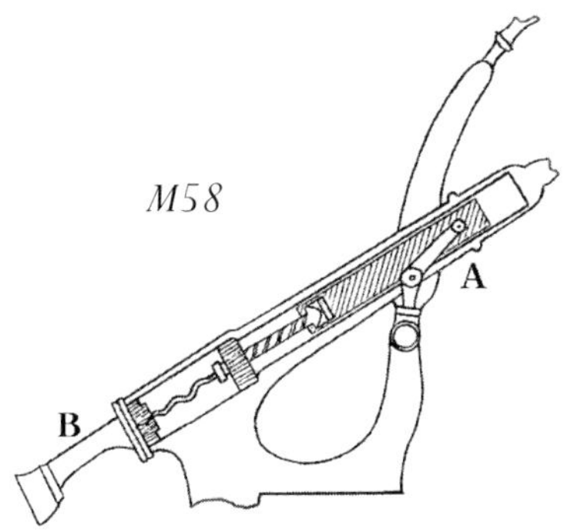

M58

M58 This English application was filed in 1889 by John and Thomas Joseph Haslam, #1,640. In this application the Haslams claimed a linkage between the operating lever and the bottom of the stem carrier (A). This patent also claimed the idea of cutting a hole in the top of the throat (B) to see if the bottle was aligned with the worm. See Appendix 4 for more details on the hole patterns found in various screw-in throats. This mechanism is found in a corkscrew marked XXX. (Yes, it is marked with three large X's.)

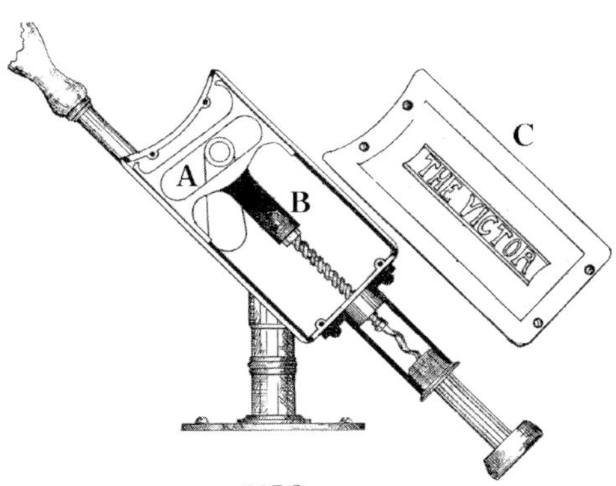

M59

M59 & M60 This English application was filed in 1890 by Samuel George Mason, #2,725. Mason claimed a slotted yoke driven mechanism (A) attached to the stem carrier (B) and advertising space (C) on the side of the corkscrew where "THE VICTOR" is printed, also projecting guide ribs rather than guide channels for the stem-nut. This resulted in a stem-nut with channels (D) cut into the nut, rather than the barrel as shown in this cross section of the stem-nut, from the patent drawings. Corkscrews containing this mechanism were sold under the VICTOR name.

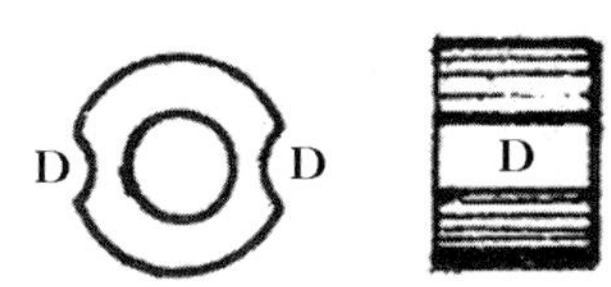

M60

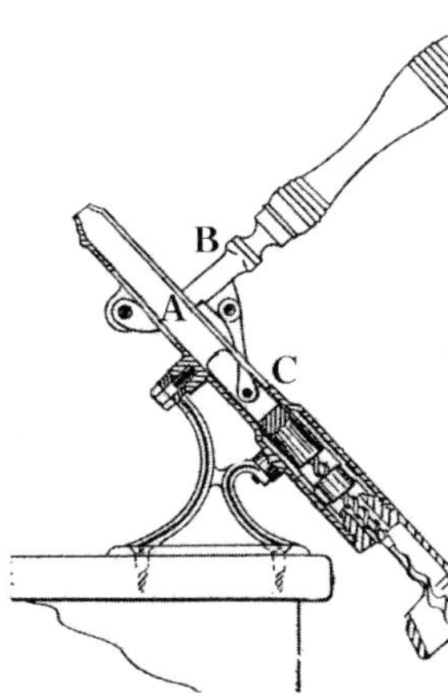

M61

M61 This English application was filed in 1891 by Cornelius Chambers, #4,225. Chambers claimed a slot (A) cut through the barrel of the corkscrew, such that the operating lever (B) passed through the corkscrew. This claim included a single link to the top of the stem carrier (C). (This was also the first bar corkscrew to receive a registered design, #168,629 March 23, 1891 in England.)

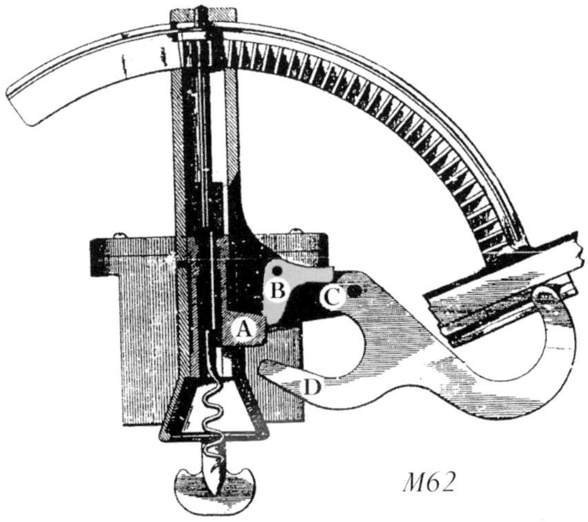

M62

M62 This American application was filed in 1891 by Raymond Beardsley Gilchrist, #478,545. The stem-nut catch stud on Gilchrist's previous patent was probably rather weak and this design corrected the problem. Gilchrist replaced the stud and leaf spring in this patent. Stem-nut (A) was captured by a swinging catch (B). Just prior to the extension (D) on the operating lever lifting up the stem-nut, a second extension (C) pushed the swinging catch off of the stem-nut. In this patent Gilchrist explains that this corkscrew is very quiet, and strong. He also discusses a separate mounting attachment for wall mounting or clamp mounting; these were not claimed in the application. Corkscrews containing this mechanism were sold under the COLUMBIA name.

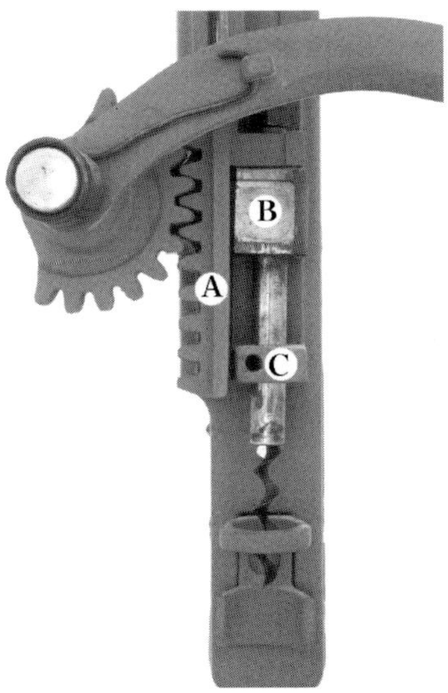

M63

M63 & M64 This French stem-nut mechanism has been offered for sale since at least 1898. In this stem-nut mechanism, the rack (A) driven stem carrier (E) pushed the stem-nut (B) down to the lower stop (C); this stop also acted as a guide for the tube (D) enclosing the worm. When the nut reached the lower stop, the threaded stem was pushed through the stem-nut, turning the worm. During the extraction cycle the rack pulled the threaded stem up, pulling the worm and cork out of the bottle. When the nut reached the upper stop the threaded stem was pulled through the nut, turning the worm up inside the tube and out of the cork. Corkscrews containing this mechanism were sold under the BL name.

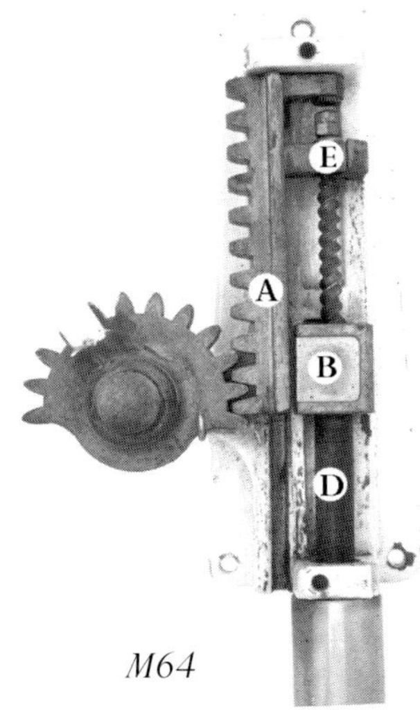

M64

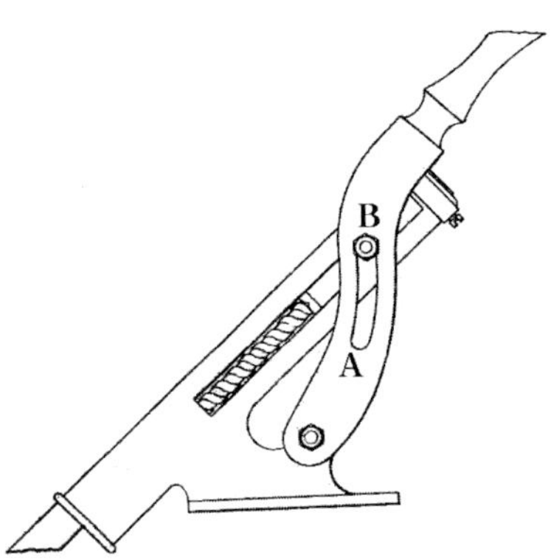

M65

M65 This English application was filed in 1902 by Samuel George Mason, #23,675. In this application Mason claimed a curved slot (A) cut into both sides of the operating lever yoke, such that a bolt (B) could pass through these slots and the hole in the end of the stem carrier. This eliminated the need for a link or links. Corkscrews containing this mechanism were sold under the A1 and A739 name.

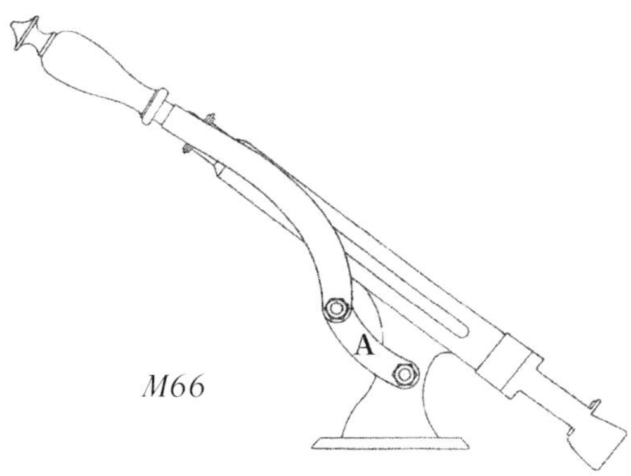

M66

M66, M67, M68 This English application was filed in 1903 by William George Deacle, #24,183. This patent was for a corkscrew containing not one, but three, stem-nuts, mounted on a very convoluted stem. The operating lever pivoted on a single link (A) from the frame was very distinctive, but research to date has not shown that it was ever patented. Deacle had described the lever and linkage shown only briefly in the forward to his claim, but he had not claimed it. Some literature describes the RAPID as a Deacle patent, but the mechanisms found in the RAPIDs are standard stem-nut mechanisms, not Deacle's mechanism as patented. The earliest known instance of this lever and link system was shown in a RAPID POWERFUL illustration in a circa 1895 advertisement pre-dating Deacle's patent by at least eight years.

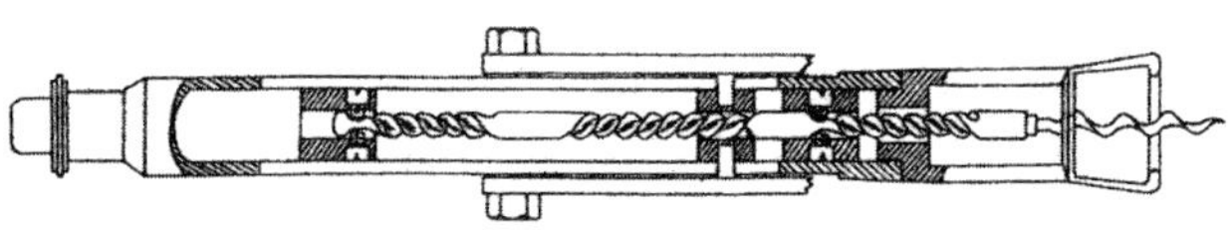

M68

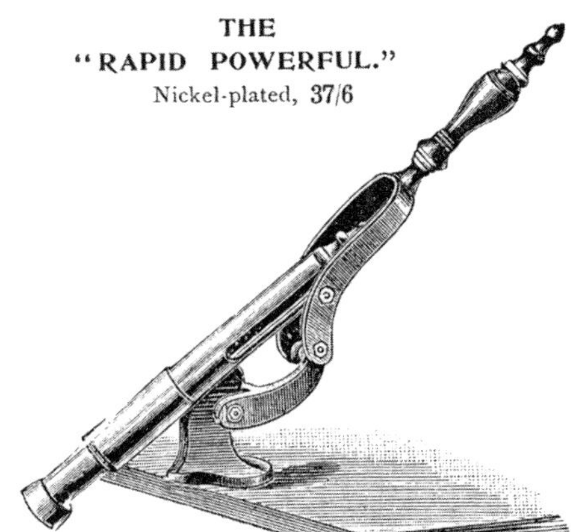

M67

M69 This English application was filed in 1903 by Cornelius Chambers, #18,006. Chambers claimed a guide rod (A) threaded on one end, screwed into the stem-nut (B) and passing through a slot (C) in the stem carrier. The rod hitting the cap on the end of the tube frame provided the means of limiting the distance the nut traveled. This patent greatly reduced the cost of manufacturing a corkscrew containing a stem-nut mechanism. His invention eliminated the need for guide channels to be cut into the inside of the brass casting, which in turn eliminated the need for the extra wall thickness on the lower third of the barrel of the frame. This invention also eliminated the need for an expensive, removable, threaded throat, which had previously been required to allow the insertion of the stem-nut mechanism. Corkscrews containing this mechanism were sold under the DON name.

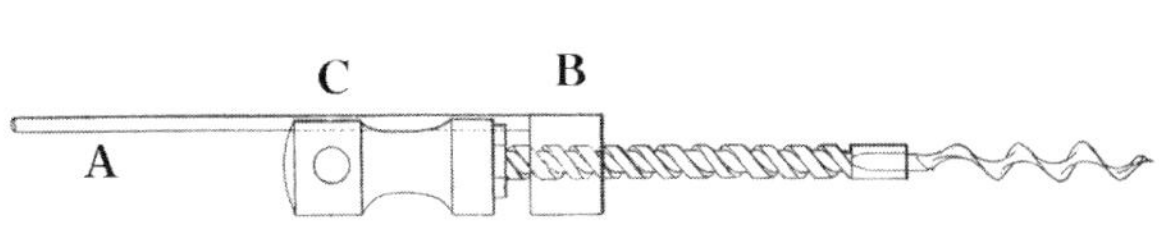

M69

M70

M70 At some later date, Chambers changed the single guide rod to two rods, one on each side. (Perhaps the single rod configuration proved to be too weak to hold the nut over years of use.) No patent was granted for this configuration. Corkscrews containing this mechanism were sold under the NEW DON name.

M71

M71 This Italian application was filed in 1959 by Leonardo Zerbinato and Ennio Masin, #604,312. In this mechanism, two sets of slots were cut out of both sides of the barrel. The upper set, as in the English mechanism, was for the operating lever's link bolt to pass through the hole (A) in the stem carrier. The lower set of slots allowed a screw (B) to be turned into each side of the stem-nut such that the protruding screws prevented the nut from turning and determined the stem-nut's travel limits. No name has been found for corkscrews containing this mechanism.

Worm-nut mechanisms and related patents

M72 The third way to turn a worm is the worm-nut mechanism. The worm-nut mechanism was an American invention. As the worm is already a form of screw, one can push or pull the worm through a worm-nut, causing it to rotate. In this mechanism, a worm carrier (B) is usually connected to some form of lever (C). Raising and lowering the lever causes the attached worm to be pushed or pulled through the worm-nut (A) causing the worm to turn into or out of the cork. The worm carrier usually has a lug or connecting point that is linked to the operating lever. The method varied with the patent. The worm-nut also usually has some lug or catch (D) that locks the worm-nut to the worm carrier during the extraction portion of the cycle and down to the frame during the cork stripping cycle. The lug or catch could be in many forms and was the subject of many different patents. This mechanism was both low cost and very compact. By the early 1900s, the worm-nut mechanism manufactured in the USA had become the dominant automatic corkscrew mechanism. This basic mechanism was utilized in probably more than eighty percent of the bar cork-screws sold around the world. These included the most popular models such as the English SAFETY, the American CHAMPION and YANKEE NO7 and the German PHR and HEKTOR corkscrews. It is still found in some modern cork-screws. The negative feature of this mechanism was that the babbitt worm-nut wore out quickly. It was, however, very cheap to produce.

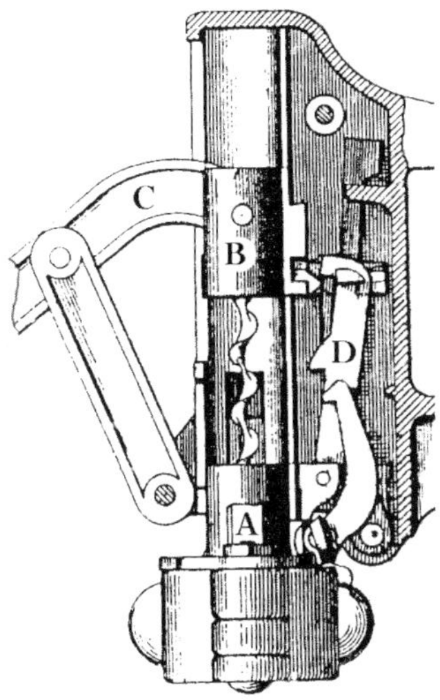

M72

M73 This was an American application filed in 1886 by William Nobel Barrett, #385,834. In this application Barrett claimed the first worm-nut mechanism. An excerpt from his patent states: "*As the plunger is forced down by the lever, the spiral screw enters the cork, is turned by its passage through the nut, and when the lever is raised the cork is drawn up against the nut and with it until the screw reaches the upper end of the slot, after which the plunger is revolved by passing up through the nut so as to carry the screw out of the cork.*" Obviously at this point Barrett did not appreciate the significance of his ideas; the actual patent claim is incredibly short, exactly one sentence long. As seen in the patent diagram, Barrett patented a sliding worm-nut (A). The worm-nut had a screw (B) inserted into it through a slot cut in the bottom of the throat; this screw kept the worm-nut from turning but allowed the required forward and rearward travel. Pushing the worm carrier (C) and the worm through the nut caused the worm to turn into the cork as the lever was pulled forward. During the cork extraction phase, the nut slid up the slot with the worm, keeping the worm from turning out of the cork until after the cork had been extracted from the bottle. When the screw in the worm-nut reached the upper end of the slot, the worm was pulled through the nut, causing it to turn out of the cork, ejecting it.

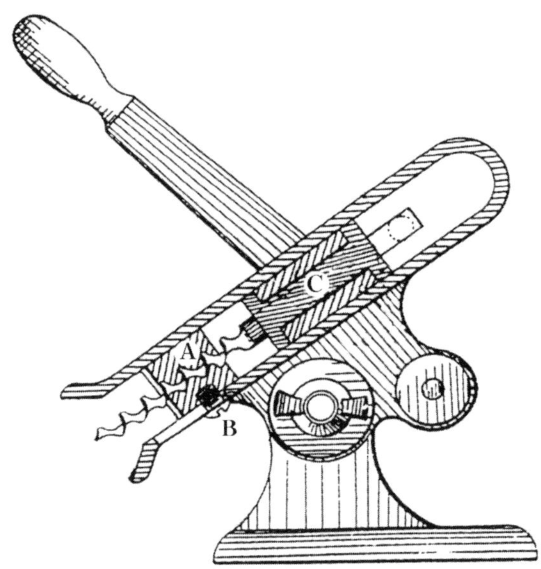

M73

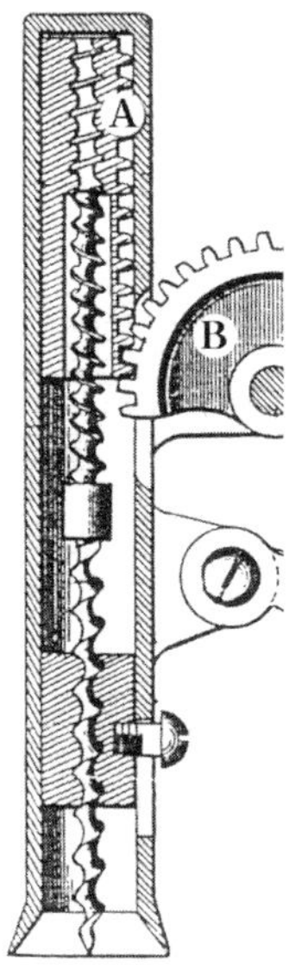

M74

M74 This American application was filed in 1887 by William Nobel Barrett, #388,945. Barrett claimed an improvement to his previous patent adding a complex mechanism involving a long rack (A) and pinion (B) driven stem-nut to his original worm-nut patent. This resulted in a two-nut system, adding all of the original stem-nut size and expense to what should have been his low cost worm-nut invention. (Unfortunately, Barrett lost his way and his chance at fame and fortune by taking his invention down this path. Adding a second slot and another screw in the worm-nut might have made his original invention a viable mechanism.)

M75 This American application was filed in 1890 by Harry J. Williams, #450,957. In this application Williams claimed a rack (A) and pinion (B) worm carrier combined with a spiral guide or worm-nut (C) fixed in the barrel and an operating lever with a cam or projection that pushed the bottle off the cork via a slotted sliding sleeve (D). In the patent claim, the sleeve was said to have a wire or cord severing edge. As seen in the diagram, Williams' patent was for a fixed worm-nut; thus without moving the nut, Williams achieved automatic cork stripping by pushing the bottle off of the cork. Corkscrews containing this mechanism were sold under the RAPID name.

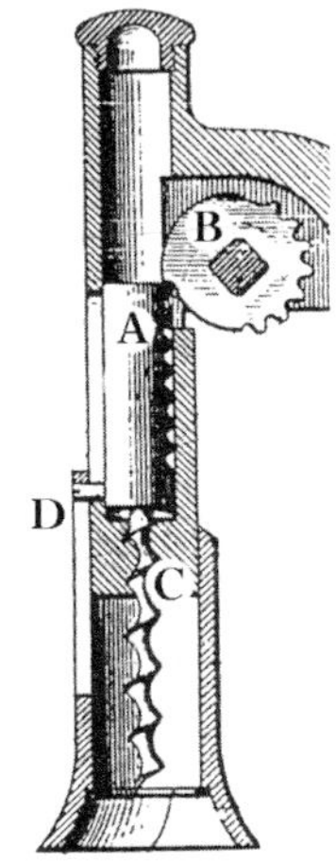

M75

M76 This American application was filed in 1893 by Michael Redlinger, #589,574. Redlinger claimed a reciprocating (moving up and down under control of the mechanism) worm-nut. During one cork extraction cycle the semi-disk (B) on the operating arm alternately extended and retracted the worm via the link rod (C) to the worm carrier (D). During a portion of each oscillation of the arm, the guide rod attached to the worm-nut (A) prevented vertical movement of the nut. The backside of the semi-disk on the operating lever had a raised section or cam surface (F) around part of its circumference. This cam prevented the guide rod and worm-nut from rising. The worm-nut was cast with two flanges that rode up and down in two grooves cast into the frame, like the guide channels in a stem-nut mechanism. The concept of controlling the worm-nut's movement relative to the worm carrier movement and the guide slots was a key invention. This invention allowed Arcade to become the dominant bar corkscrew supplier to the world and was the basis for all of their subsequent worm-nut patents. A few of the corkscrews containing this mechanism were sold under the ARCADE name in the USA, but shortly after its invention the design was seemingly acquired by S. Mason and, or, P. Gaskell in England. Both companies produced this mechanism and in early 1900 Mason threatened legal action against Gaskell & Chambers for patent infringement; he alternatively suggested a possible merger. Corkscrews containing this mechanism were sold in England under the SAFETY, THE SAFETY, ORIGINAL SAFETY, SUNOID, STANPAT and SIMPLE names. This mechanism was also sold under the ALEXANDERWERK and STEINER name in Europe.

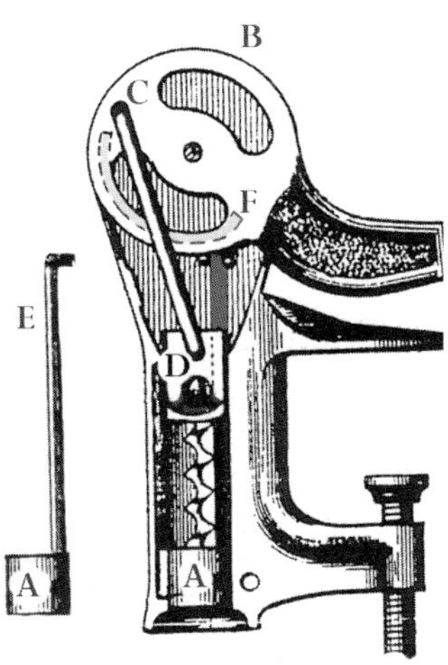

M76

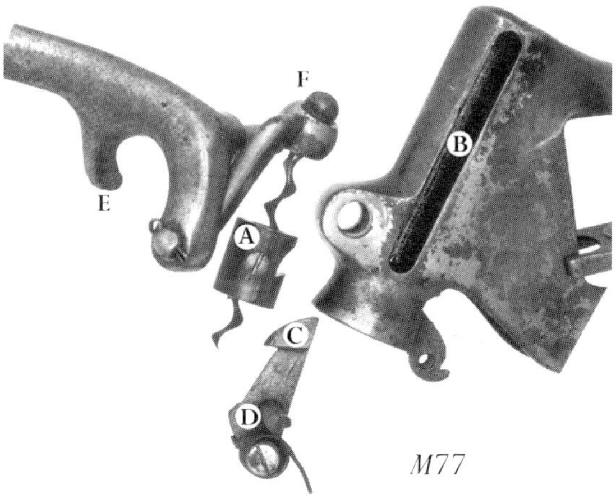

M77

M77 This was an American mechanism first offered for sale in the USA circa 1893 by Raymond Beardsley Gilchrist. This very small corkscrew was not patented in the USA, but a later version with a different bottle clasp was patented in 1896 and 1897 in England and Germany. In this mechanism the worm-nut (A) had a screw in the side of it, which slid up and down in the slot (B). A spring-loaded catch (C) was mounted in the throat; this catch alternately clasped the lip of a beer bottle (D) or locked the nut down. The operating lever had a rod attached to the worm carrier (F) that was free to slide up and down in the slot (B). A lug (E) on the operating arm triggered the latch, releasing the worm-nut and engaging the bottle clasp during the cork extraction portion of the cycle. Corkscrews containing this mechanism were sold under the MIDGET name.

M78 This American application was filed in 1894 by Charles Morgan, #532,575. In this application Morgan claimed a captured worm-nut and the first bottle clasp. A lug (A) on the front of the spring loaded bottle clasp lever caught and held the worm-nut (B) down. On pulling the bottle clasp lever forward the nut was released as the bottle clasp jaws gripped the bottle. In a two-cycle operation, the first cycle, with the bottle clasped, removed the cork; the second cycle, with the bottle clasp lever released, stripped the cork. This is also the first patent drawing showing a dual mount, with both a screw-on top mount or with a custom clamp inserted through the base; this idea was not claimed in the patent. This is the first version of the DAISY with a plain case and a flat top; a slightly later version incorporated a round top frame and some scroll design work on the side of the case. Corkscrews containing this mechanism were sold under the DAISY and THE DAISY names.

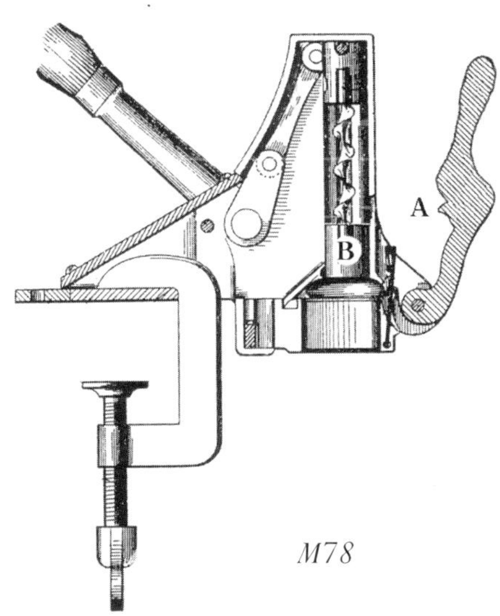

M78

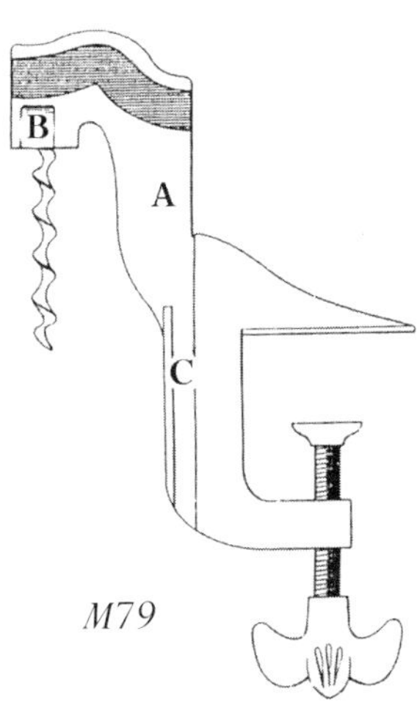

M79

M79 This American application was filed in 1895 by Michael & Matthias Redlinger Jr., #546,747. In it the Redlingers claimed a frame (A) with a rotatably mounted worm (B). Over this frame, a bottle carriage and mechanism to control the worm-nut slid up and down on the guide rail (C) as the operating arm was oscillated. This carriage included a very strong, spring loaded, automatic bottle clasp. The idea was that the carriage clasped the bottle and pulled the bottle (cork) up into the worm. On reversing the operating arm, the bottle was pulled off the cork and the cork was pulled off the worm. In 1899, H. H. Beaumont from Milwaukee patented this design in England. Corkscrews containing this mechanism were sold under the BEAUMONT name.

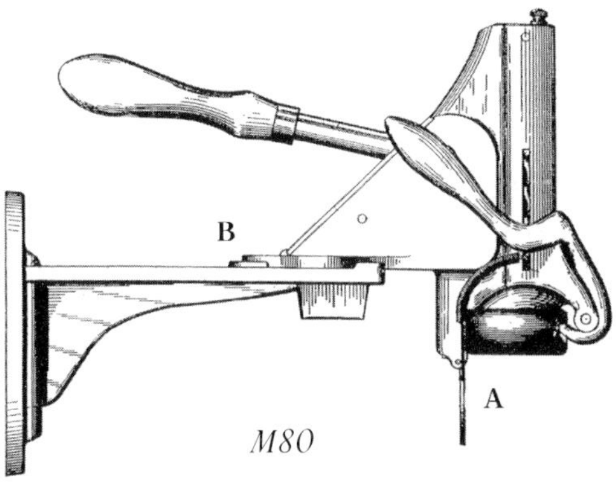

M80

M80 This American application was filed in 1895 by Charles Morgan, #549,607. In this application Morgan claimed new features for the DAISY, a plate or flapper (A) that flipped up and covered the throat when a cork was on the worm. The idea was to prevent the operator from trying to open another bottle when the cork from the previous bottle was still on the worm. This patent claim also included a wall mount bracket (B) that facilitated the quick mounting and releasing of the machine. This mechanism is shown only because some Arcade patent dates marked on their corkscrews incorrectly refer to this patent.

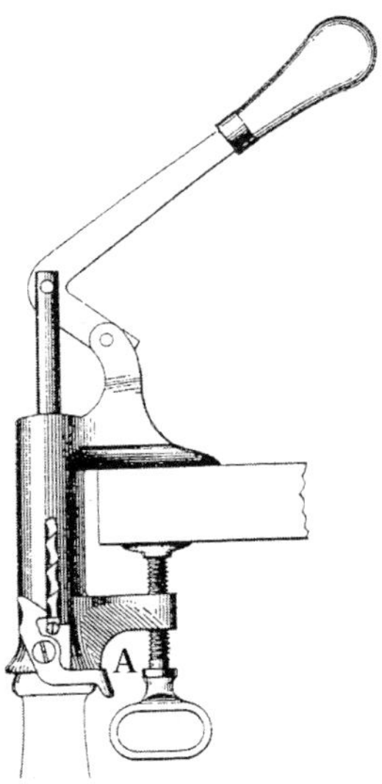

M80

M80 & M81 In this American application filed in 1895 by Lyman McMaster, #562,645, he claimed a worm-nut that was captured by a spring-loaded catch and lever mechanism (A), mounted on the throat. Pressing the bottle lip into the throat pressed on the lever, releasing the nut. When the cork was pulled and the bottle removed, the second forward stroke of the lever would push the nut into the catch and thus strip the cork on the rearward stroke. A wall mount version of this design extends the lever downward, such that grasping the neck of the bottle pulls the lever. (Presumably this modification was to alleviate the problem that, in a private home, the user would have wanted to open bottles with a wide variety of neck diameters. The original design relied on a consistent size of bottleneck, such as a beer bottle.) In 1899 Manning, Bowman & Co. received patent #9,409 in England for this same mechanism, incorporated in an inclined frame (B) version.

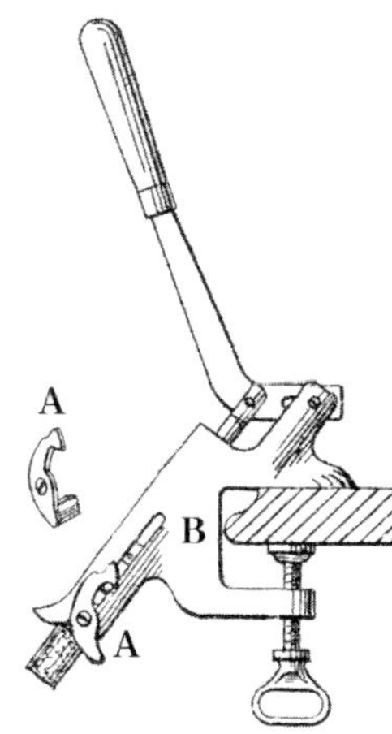

M81

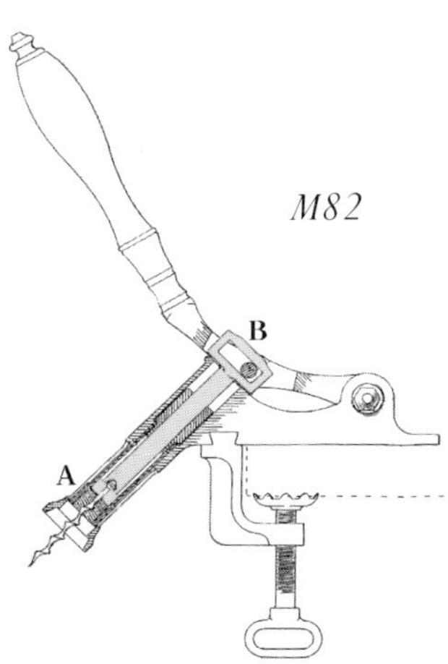

M82

M82 This English application was filed in 1896 by Walter Vaughan, #9,519. In this application Vaughn claimed a worm nut fixed in a sliding tube (A); fitted within the tube was a worm carrier consisting of a plunger terminating in a cross slide (B). As the cork was extracted, the sliding tube slid up the barrel of the corkscrew until it reached the stop in the tube; at that point the cork had been extracted. Continued rearward motion of the operating lever pulled the worm through the worm-nut, stripping the cork. On the forward stroke the plunger slid down the barrel until it reached the stop in the tube; at that point the plunger pushed the worm through the worm-nut, into the cork. Corkscrews containing this mechanism were sold under the LUXURY name.

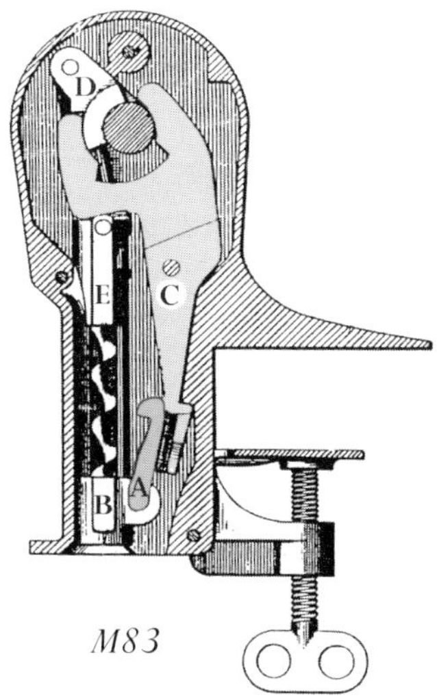

M83

M83 This American application was filed in 1898 by Charles Morgan, #620,949. In this application Morgan claimed a lifting hook (A) pivoted to the worm-nut (B) and a rocker arm (C) actuated by an internal stud (D) on the shaft of the operating arm, which also was linked to the worm carrier (E). The rocker arm alternately locked the worm-nut hook to the case or to the worm carrier. Corkscrews containing this mechanism were sold under the CHAMPION name and a shorter adaptation of this mechanism was found in corkscrews sold under the FAVORITE name.

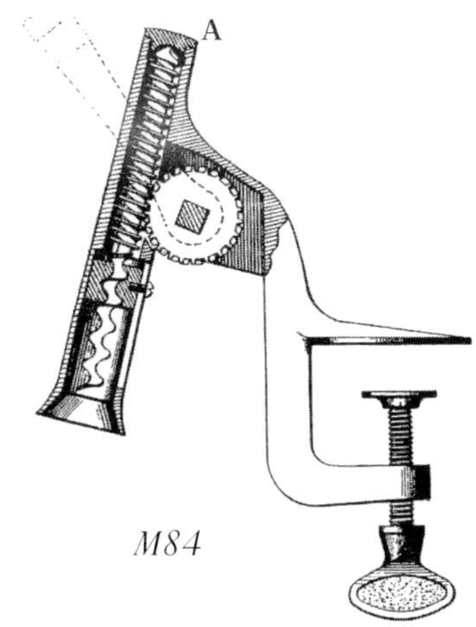

M84

M84 This American application was filed in 1898 by Harry J. Williams, #619,648. Williams claimed the cone shaped bearing (A) in the cap of the tube case. This bearing mated with the shape cut into the end of the rack driven stem carrier. This mechanism is identical to the second Barrett patent, except for the addition of the bearing surface, which appears to have no useful function. No advertised name has been found for corkscrews containing this mechanism.

M85 & M86 This American application was filed in 1899 by Edwin Walker, #649,498, claiming this mechanism. The worm was mounted in a worm carrier which also had a worm-nut release mechanism attached to it. The free-swinging plate (A) attached to the side of the throat rose up over the stud (B) on the worm-nut, as it descended. When the worm-nut reached its lowest point the plate fell down, capturing the nut. The carrier had a spring loaded "bird's head" lever (C) attached to the side of it. Screwing the worm into a cork caused the spring on the worm carrier to compress, moving the sliding pin (D), which changed the angle of the "beak". On the forward stroke, with a cork on the worm, the beak slid under the swinging plate, lifting it up and releasing the nut. Walker manufactured at least three different versions of this corkscrew, all utilizing different mechanisms to release the worm-nut. Corkscrews containing all three mechanisms were sold under the LITTLE QUICKER name.

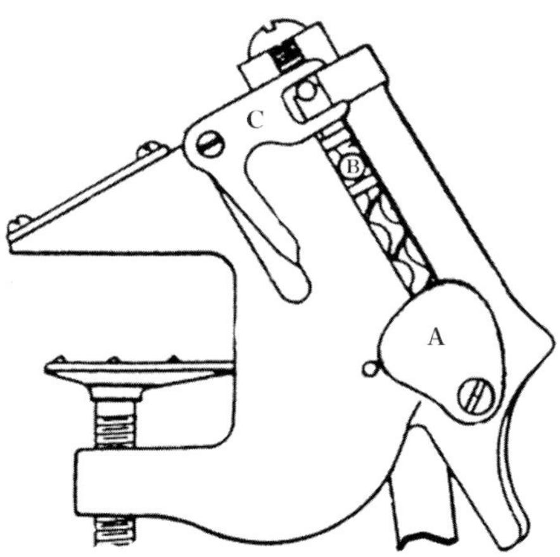

M85

M86

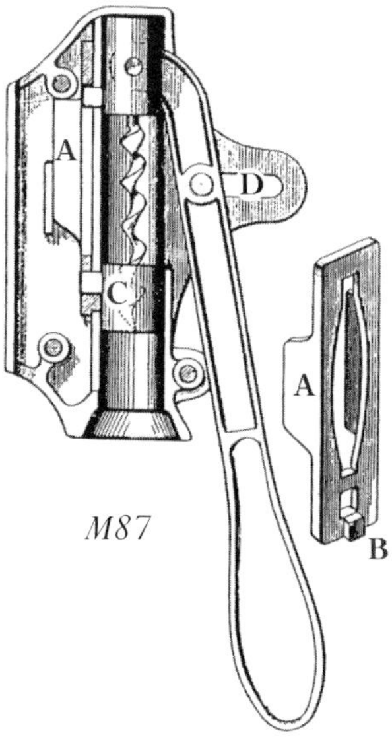

M87

M87 This was an American application filed in 1900 by Albert Baumgarten, #675,051. In this application Baumgarten claimed a sliding plate (A) with studs (B) that controlled the reciprocal movement of the worm-nut (C). Also, a bearing slot (D) for the operating lever to both pivot and slide in (eliminating a link and reducing cost). Corkscrews containing this mechanism were sold under the FAMLEE name as a wall mount with no bottle clasp mechanism, and the PULLMEE name when the bottle clasp mechanism, patented in 1907, was included.

M88 In this American application filed in 1900 by John J. Schermack, # 683,004, Schermack claimed the only known, patented example of a rack (A) and pinion (B) driven worm carrier (C). This mechanism included a spring-loaded latch to catch and release the worm-nut (D). Corkscrews containing this mechanism were sold under the TRIUMPH name.

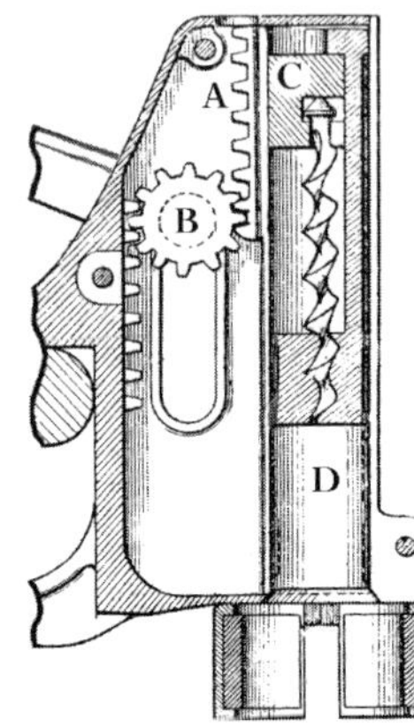

M88

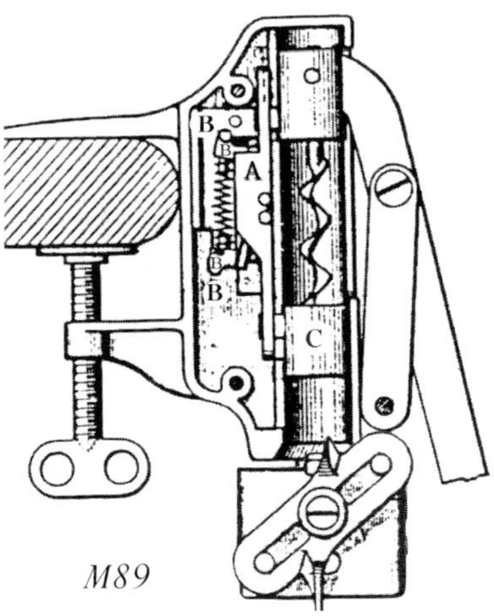

M89

M89 This American application was filed in 1900 by Albert Baumgarten, # 675,032. Baumgarten claimed a sliding plate (A) containing spring-loaded cams (B). These cams controlled the locking and releasing of the worm-nut (C). A lever, marked “short” “long” on the outside of the case, was used to control the point at which the upper cam was triggered. This allowed for the partial pulling of a cork. Also, this patent included Baumgarten’s first bottle clasp mechanism. Corkscrews containing this mechanism were sold under the SHOMEE name when the bottle clasp mechanism was included, and the PULLMEE name, as a wall mount version, without the bottle clasp mechanism.

M90 This American application was filed in 1900 by John Rogginger, #676,205. Rogginger claimed a rod (A) with projections that engaged slots in the worm-nut (C) and worm carrier (B). Guides cast into the frame caused the rod to turn, such that the worm-nut was locked to, or disengaged from, the worm carrier. Also claimed in this application was a locking lever (D) attached to the bottle clasp lever. The locking lever was designed such that the bottle clasp could be locked in the clamped position, allowing the operator to remove his hands from the bottle before pulling the cork. Corkscrews containing this mechanism were sold under the LITTLE GIANT name.

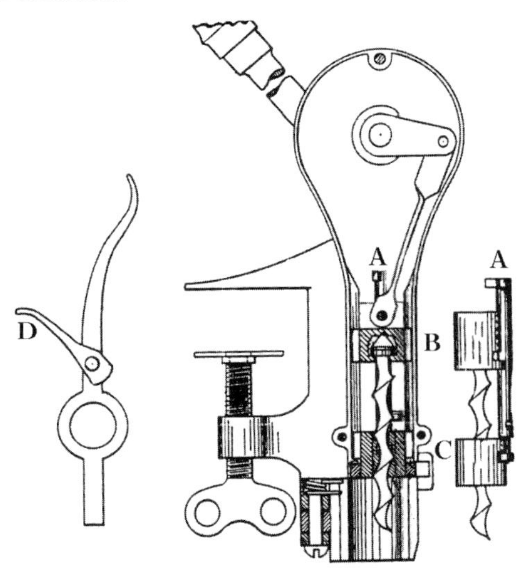

M90

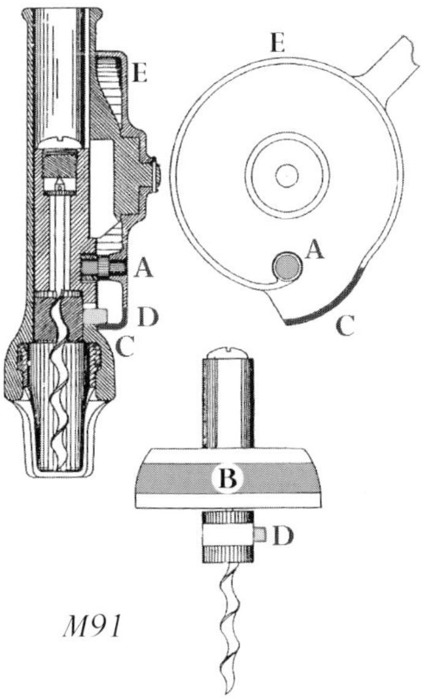

M91

M91 In this American application filed in 1900 by Edwin Walker, #676,013, Walker claimed this mechanism that consisted of a worm carrier, which incorporated a long transverse guide (B) and a worm-nut with a stud (D). The operating arm terminated in a hollow metal case (E), which contained a roller pin (A) and a flange around most of its circumference; a portion of this flange contained a cam shaped surface (C). This corkscrew was operated by the roller pin engaging the transverse guide, causing a pushing or pulling of the worm carrier when the operating arm moved forward or rearward. The surface of the flange pushed, pulled or held steady the worm-nut stud (D) depending on whether the inner or outer surface of the flange was contacting the stud. Corkscrews containing this mechanism were sold under the BULL DOG name.

M92 This American application was filed in 1901 by Albert Baumgarten, #696,399. Baumgarten claimed the addition of new features to his SHOMEE patent. These included a projection (A) to the front of the operating lever and a tray (B) to catch the spent cork. The concept was that as the worm was pulled out of the cork, the projection on the handle would kick the cork into the tray. Corkscrews containing this mechanism were sold under the EXTRACTEE name.

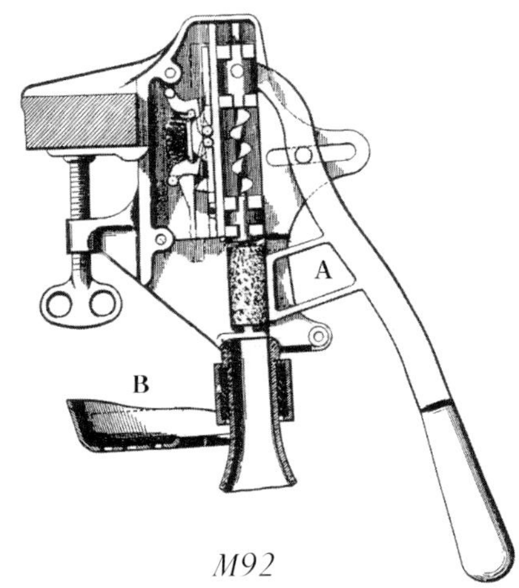

M92

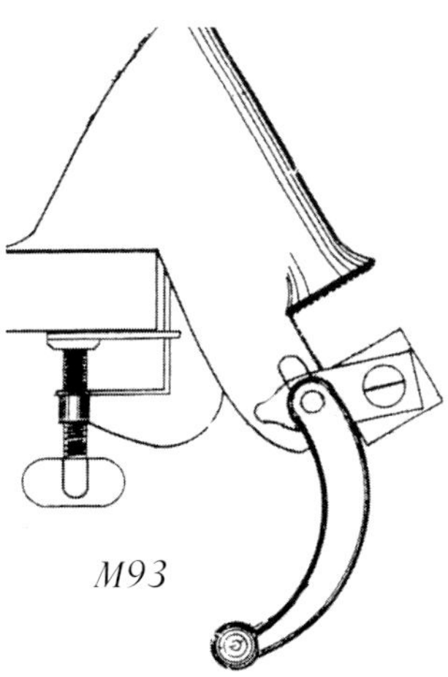

M93

M93 In this American application filed in 1901 by Edwin Walker, #713,540, Walker claimed a bottle clasp mechanism. (Bottle clasps were a key feature required to ensure bar corkscrew sales. There are many references to the danger of a bottle breaking in the bartender's hand. This would have been due to the inconsistent thickness of the glass in beer bottles made in this era.) This very convoluted and expensive-to-manufacture bottle clasp is found on some corkscrews sold under the QUICK & EASY name.

M94 This American application was filed in 1901 by Henry Tscherning, #728,517. In this application Tscherning claimed a bottle clasp, which included a lever that lifted a spring-loaded catch (A) off the worm-nut (B) and a gravity-catch (C) on the worm carrier (D) that caught and pulled the worm-nut up. This gravity-catch rode up over the lower catch on the forward stroke of the lever, releasing its grip on the worm-nut. This allowed the nut to be captured and held down by the spring-loaded catch. On the next stroke the bottle clasp lever lifted the lower catch up allowing the gravity-catch to slip under it, capturing the nut. Corkscrews containing this mechanism were sold under the PHOENIX 40, PHOENIX 60 and PHOENIX 100 name.

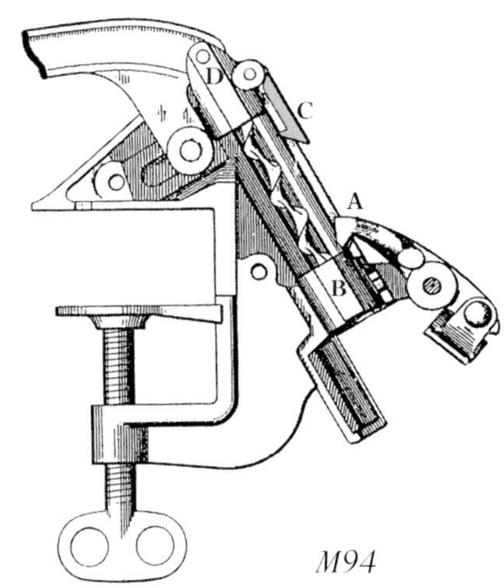

M94

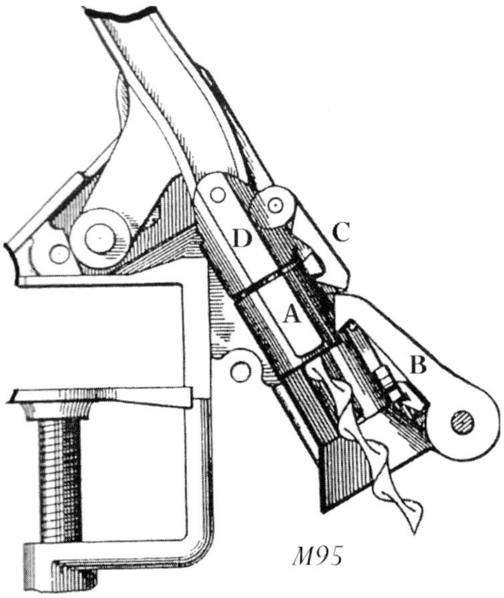

M95

M95 This American application was filed in 1901 by Charles Morgan, # 728,806. Morgan claimed a worm-nut (A) captured by a lower spring-loaded catch (B) on the frame and a gravity catch (C) on the worm carrier (D). On alternate oscillations of the operating lever these catches slid under and over each other, alternately catching and releasing the worm-nut at each end of its travel. This was accomplished by the lower catch sitting at two slightly different angles, depending on whether it was in a slightly raised position grasping the nut, or down slightly resting on the frame. Corkscrews containing this mechanism were sold under the PHOENIX 20, PHOENIX 30 and PHOENIX 50 name. Also, Arcade manufactured this design as a private label to Williamsons, who sold it under the NEW ERA name in both an inclined version and a vertical version with bottle clasps.

M96 This American application was filed in 1901 by Raymond Beardsley Gilchrist, #857,992. In this application Gilchrist claimed a mechanism that did not rely on springs or gravity to lock the worm-nut and included an exposed worm carrier (A) and worm-nut (B) riding on an exposed rail or guide. In this mechanism the operating lever had a flange (C) close to its pivot point that pushed the catch (D) off of the front worm-nut lug (E), releasing the nut. The worm-nut had two lugs on its side. The front lug (E) was a wing shaped cam that could pull the catch (D) down with its lower edge or alternately lock into the catch with its upper edge. While it was rising or descending, the double beveled cam lug (F) on the rear of the worm-nut pushed the catch over far enough for the worm-nut lugs to act on it when there was a cork on the worm. This resulted in the catch being able to be reset as soon as the cork started to lift from the bottle. This very short distance required only that the lower edge of the winged cam had cleared the lower edge of the notch in the catch. Gilchrist designed this corkscrew as a wall mount, to be both very economical to manufacture and home user friendly, as it could automatically pull even the shortest cork, without piercing the cork all the way through. He noted in his patent that it could also be made as a clamp mount. Judging from the patent drawings, Gilchrist's original concept was that this very low cost corkscrew was to be made almost entirely from stamped sheet metal. Corkscrews containing this mechanism were sold under the The YANKEE No1 and YANKEE No2 name. (A much fancier version with a "vine & leaf" decoration was sold under the MODERN name; in that version the rear cam on the nut was moved to the back of the catch.)

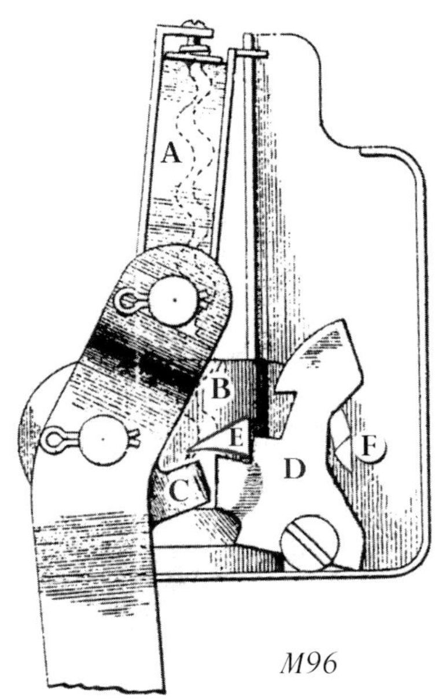

M96

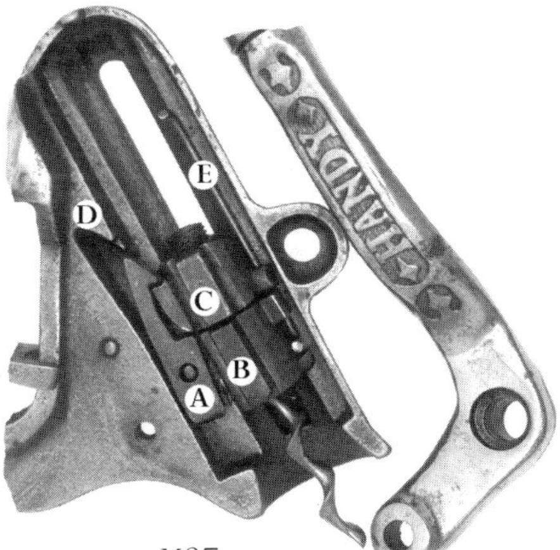

M97

M97 & M98 This American application was filed in 1902 by Henry Tscherning, #728,519. Tscherning claimed a mechanism that used a spring-loaded catch (A) to lock the worm-nut (B) to the worm carrier (C). When the cork was extracted, the top edge of the spring-loaded catch was released from the worm-nut when it contacted the catch release (D). Continued upward movement of the worm carrier stripped the cork. In the original patent the worm-nut's travel distance was limited by a lug on the worm-nut sliding up and down in the channel (F). In the HANDY implementation of this mechanism, this same function was performed by a wire rod (E). Corkscrews containing the original patent mechanism were sold under the STANDARD name. Corkscrews containing a much more compact version of this mechanism were sold under the HANDY name.

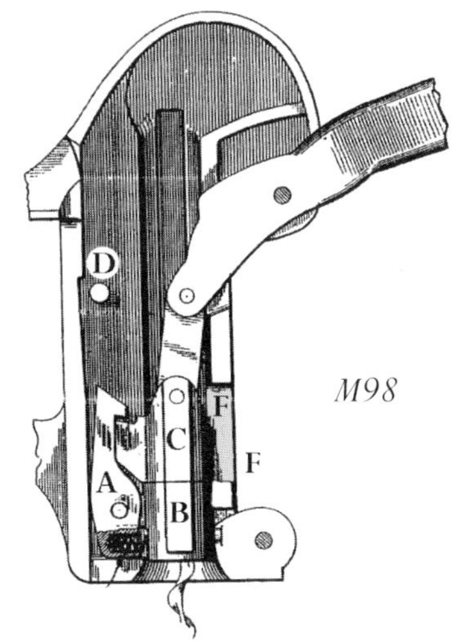

M98

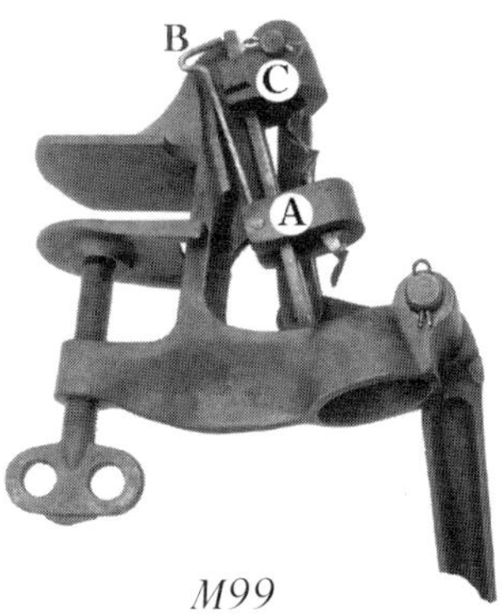

M99

M99 This was an American corkscrew advertised for sale in France around 1902. This mechanism contains an upside down "L" shaped rod (B) embedded in the worm-nut (A). The arm of the "L" clips into the worm carrier (C) at the top of the stroke, after the cork has been ejected. On the down stroke, the nut descends until it hits the cork; at that point the worm carrier slips off the clip and is then pushed through the nut. This mechanism allows the corkscrew to extract and strip the cork in a single cycle. The name is a play on English words, as it was manufactured by Arcade in the USA. Corkscrews containing this mechanism were sold under the CLIPPER name.

M100 & M101 In this American application filed in 1904 by Raymond Beardsley Gilchrist, #1,058,361, Gilchrist claimed a latching link (A) pivoted to an arm (B) on the operating lever and to the worm carrier (C). The hook (E) on the bottom of the latching link engaged a catch lug (F) on the worm-nut (D), lifting it up. A rocker arm mounted on the same side of the case as the operating arm swung down to hold the nut in place during the cork stripping action. (The mechanism has been described as manufactured; this patent illustration shows a different method of preventing the nut from rising up.) The original mechanism, as shown in the photograph, with the rocker arm mounted on the other half of the split case, and the latching link facing the other way is found in the YANKEE NO6, HERO NO5 and all of the German HEKTOR style corkscrews. Corkscrews containing this patented mechanism, in the Arcade FAVORITE case, were sold under the YANKEE NO7 name.

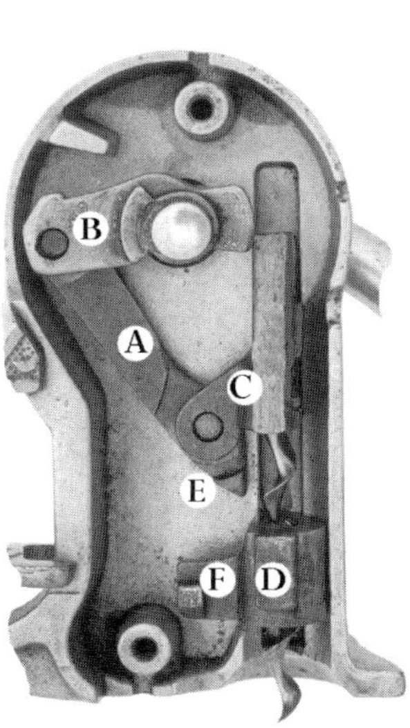

M101

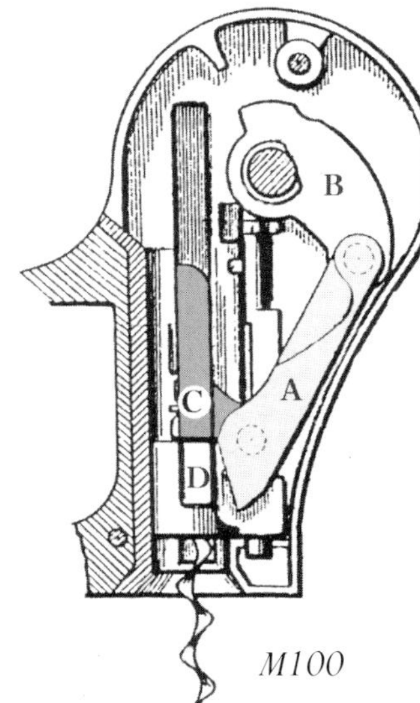

M100

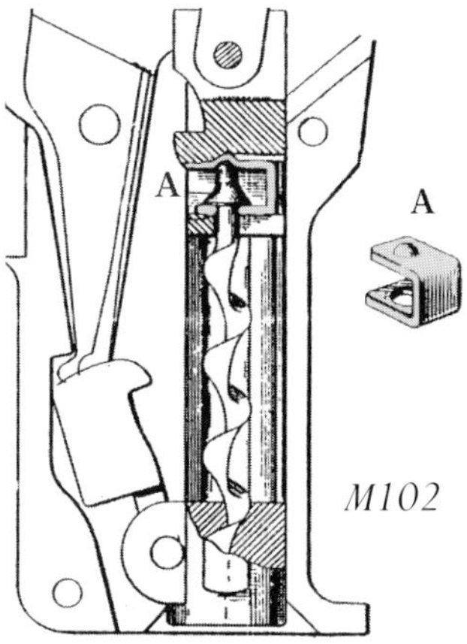

M102

M102 This American application was filed in 1905 by Harry Bittner, #845,608. In this application Bittner claimed a clip (A) to hold the worm in the worm carrier. (Bittner was the patent attorney used by Arcade.) This clip has not been found in any CHAMPION mechanism inspected.

M103 This American application was filed in 1905 by Raymond Beardsley Gilchrist, #823,678. In this application Gilchrist claimed a bottle grip: "*A bottle holder in which the jaws have pivots relatively eccentric with respect to each other and are connected to each other by a pin extending through both of the jaws to connect them for simultaneous and equidistant shift*." In other words, self-centering bottle clasp handles as found on the YANKEE NO6 and YANKEE NO7. The "U" pin (A) was initially held in place by two cotter pins, one in each leg of the "U" pin; at some later date the direction of the holes drilled into the legs of the "U" pin was changed by 90° so that a single long cotter pin could extend through both legs of the "U" pin.

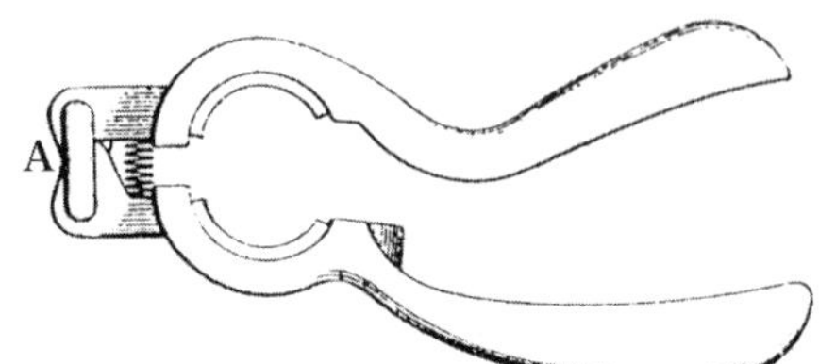

M103

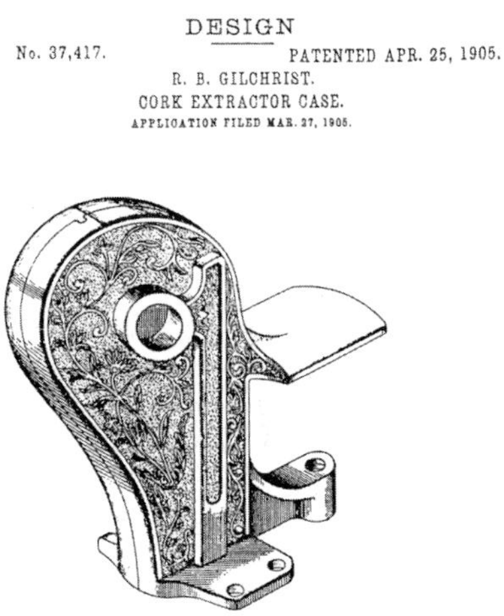

M104

M104 This American application was filed in 1905 by Raymond Beardsley Gilchrist, DES #37,417. In this application Gilchrist claimed "*The ornamental design for a cork-extractor case, as shown*". In other words he was not claiming the shape of the YANKEE NO7 case, only the decorative design on any corkscrew case.

M105 In this American application filed in 1905 by Albert Baumgarten, #853,151, Baumgarten claimed a bottle grip. "*In a bottle-holder the combination of a supporting frame, a pair of jaws having open seats formed therein, pivot-studs integrally formed with the supporting-frame, and a spring between the jaws, pressing said jaws into position to be retained by said pivots*." The bottle clasp handles were not attached to the frame (A), but held in place, on their pivots (B), by the pressure of a spring (C). This style of bottle clasp is found on the clamp-mounted version of the SHOMEE. (Because the bottle clasp mechanism was not physically attached to the frame, SHOMEEs are found with their bottle clasps missing.)

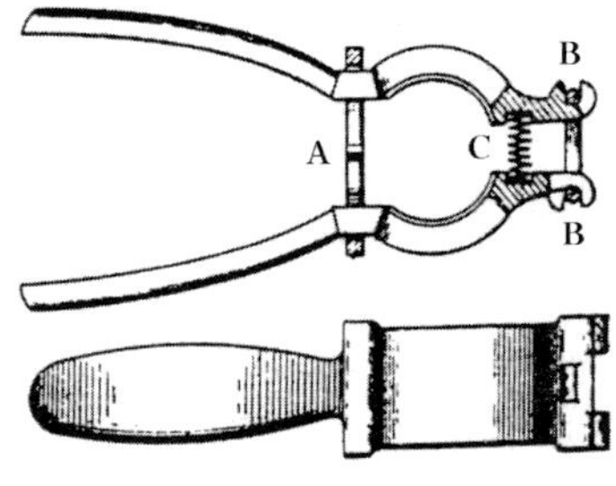

M105

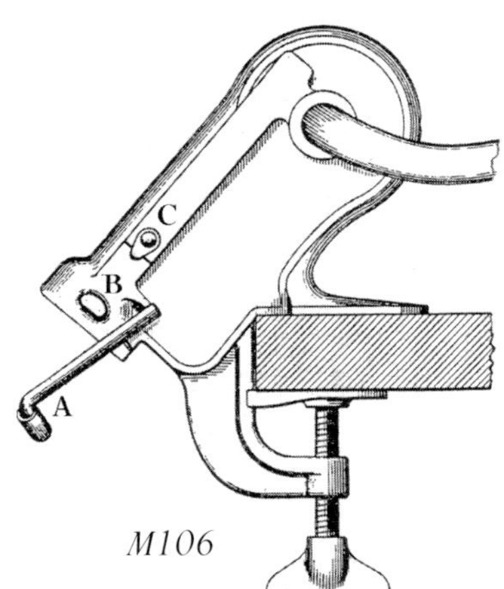

M106

M106 This American application was filed in 1906 by Raymond Beardsley Gilchrist, #1,058,362. In this application Gilchrist claimed a wire neck rest (A) that slid in and out to best match and center all different types and shapes of bottlenecks. Gilchrist showed but did not claim the thumb rest (B) or the wire or string breaker (C). Corkscrews containing this mechanism were sold under the HERO NO5 name and are found on many German corkscrews including the CYKLOP and HEKTOR types.

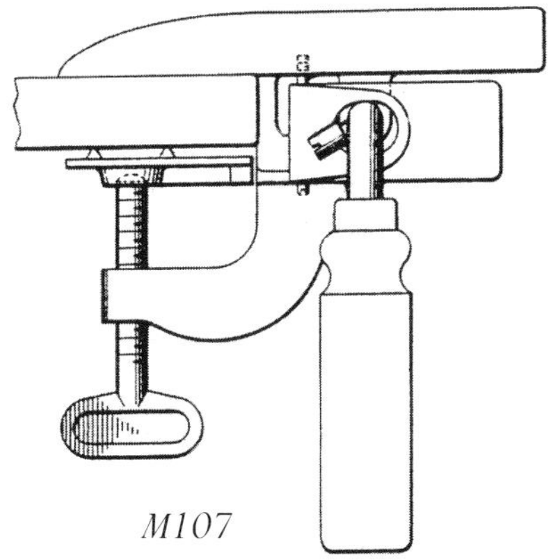

M107

M107 This American application was filed in 1907 by Edwin Walker, #964,588. Walker claimed a bottle clasp mechanism utilizing cam projection surfaces on the jaws, such that they opened and closed when a shaft with projections was turned forward and backward. (This bottle clasp design is found on very few Walker bar corkscrews.)

M108 & M109 In 1904 Raymond Beardsley Gilchrist patented his YANKEE NO 6 and YANKEE NO7 mechanism in Germany. Around that time he introduced his HERO NO5 into the German market. In the HERO NO5 the rocker arm (A) pivoted on a small "L" shaped rod (B) held in place by a force-fitting lug cast into the case. Gilchrist later produced a private label HERO NO5 named the BISON No5, for distribution by Helmut Gebel of Berlin. A short time later, the BISON No6 was introduced. In the BISON No6 the lug was tapped for screw threads and the wire rod was replaced with a screw and washer (C). All later versions of the HEKTORs and PHRs included this rocker arm improvement.

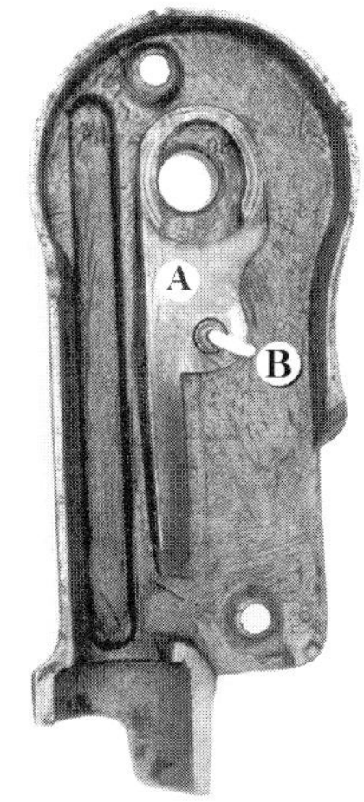

M108

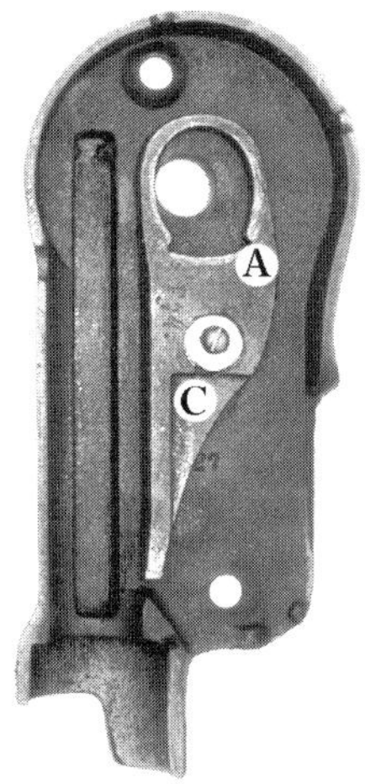

M109

M110 This English application was filed in 1911 by Cornelius Chambers, #23,06. In this application Chambers claimed a longer wearing worm-nut. One of the major problems with the worm-nut was the very rapid wearing of the babbitt in the nut. Chambers' invention greatly reduced this, by casting the iron nut (A) with ridges inside it. The steel worm would be lubricated by the babbitt, but would also ride on a tiny bit of cast iron that both guided the worm and kept it from wearing completely through the softer material. These nuts marked "patent BB nut" (presumably the BB stood for babbitt) are found in most SAFETY and SIMPLE corkscrews. So, again Chambers locked up the market, in this case for both the new and replacement worm-nuts!

M110

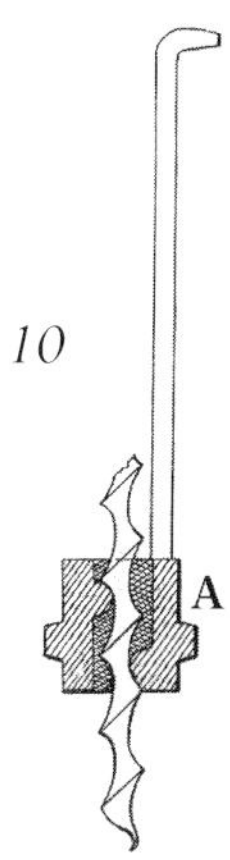

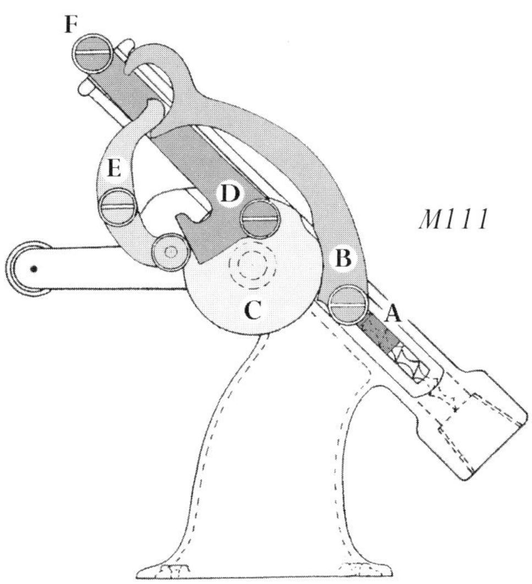

M111

M111 This Swedish application was filed in 1916 by Edvin Sönnergren, #43,176. Not inspected, but in this patent Sönnergren appears to have utilized cam surfaces for all aspects of controlling the worm-nut rather than the usual springs or catches. In this mechanism the wheel (C) is turned by the operating arm. Attached to the wheel is arm (D), which connects to the worm carrier at (F). Turning the operating arm caused the worm to be pushed or pulled through the worm-nut (A). During the cork extraction and stripping cycle the hook on the arm (D) engaged the top or bottom of the roller on the end of the arm (E) causing it to engage arm (B), which is connected to the worm-nut. Arm (B) controlled the worm-nut, pulling it up with the worm during cork extraction and holding it steady during the cork-stripping portion of the cycle.

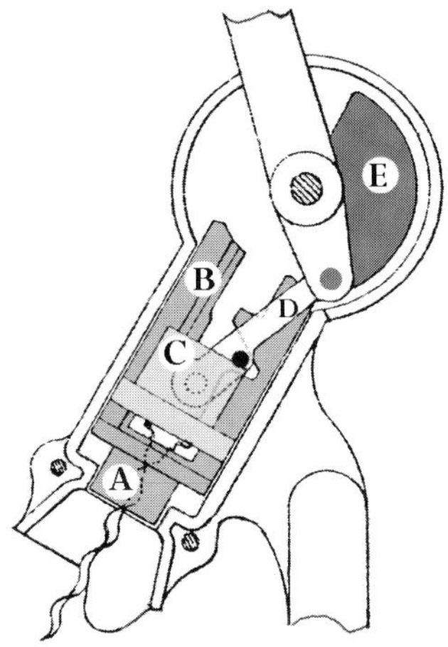

M112

M112 This was a French application filed in 1921 by Eugénie Sitbon, SGDG #537,989. In this mechanism Sitbon utilized a sliding worm-nut carrier (B) with the worm-nut at (A). The operating arm was attached to an internal semi-disk (E) and a connecting link (D) pivoted to the worm carrier (C), which was free to slide in the guides cast into the worm-nut carrier. The stud (black) on the connecting link locked the worm-nut carrier and the worm carrier together and pulled them up during the cork extraction portion of the cycle. On the rearward stroke of the operating arm, the semi-disk locked the worm-nut carrier down while the worm carrier was pulled up, stripping the cork.

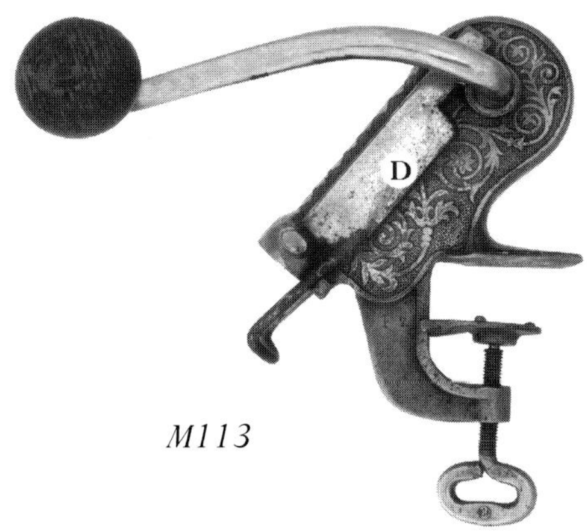

M113

M114

M113 & M114 & M115 This was probably a German application filed in 1925 by Gerhard Frings, DRGM #930,900. In the HERO NO5 the latching link (A) connecting the operating arm to the worm-nut was free to move at an angle, thus pulling the nut sideways as well as vertically. This sideways force would have caused the worm-nut to bind on the worm and wear quickly. This German improvement involved adding a round stud (B) to the back of the latching link and casting a channel in the case, such that the link and worm-nut were guided in a vertical path only, as they traveled up and down. To allow for the channel, the left side case (C) required some additional width (D) to accommodate the channel cast into the case. Looking at the left hand view of this style of corkscrew one can immediately see whether or not this latching link improvement had been incorporated in the corkscrew. Complete German patent and design documentation is extremely sketchy or non-existent, however it is almost certain that this improvement was registered by G. Frings. Corkscrews containing this mechanism were sold under the HEKTOR, HEKTOR 1, HEKTOR 2, HEKTOR 3, PHR, RIMO and HELIOS names.

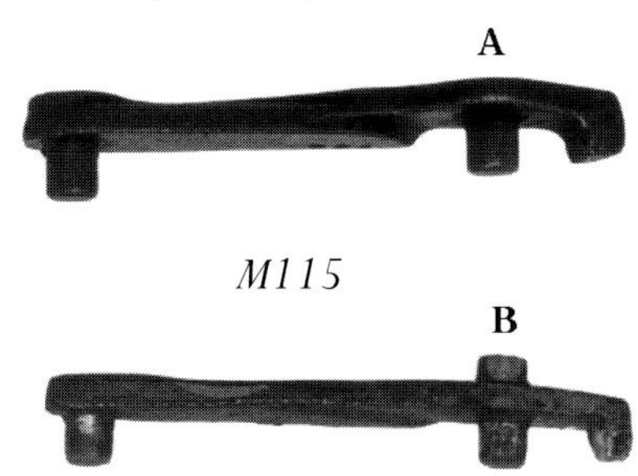

M115

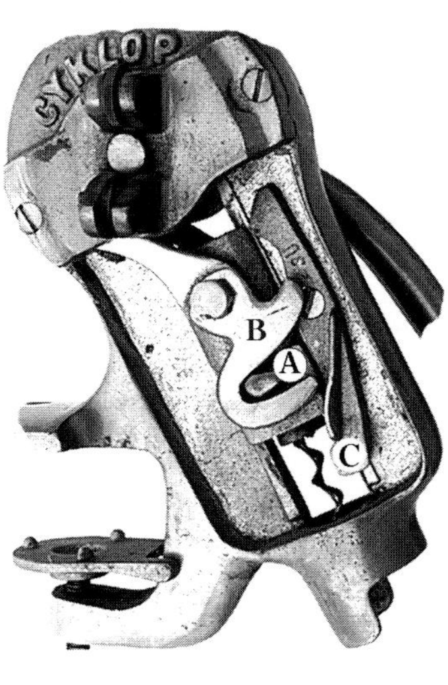

M116

M116 This was a German application probably filed in 1925 by Gerhard Frings, DRGM #926,839. In this DRGM design, one can see the heavy-duty mechanism, as it was completely open. It contained a worm-nut (A) with a pair of latching links (B). The two links had hooks on the ends, which hooked the studs on the worm-nut and pulled the nut up during cork removal. A narrow rocker arm (C) swung out to hold the nut down. The link part of the mechanism was somewhat like a dual YANKEE NO7 mechanism. Corkscrews containing this mechanism were sold under the CYKLOP name.

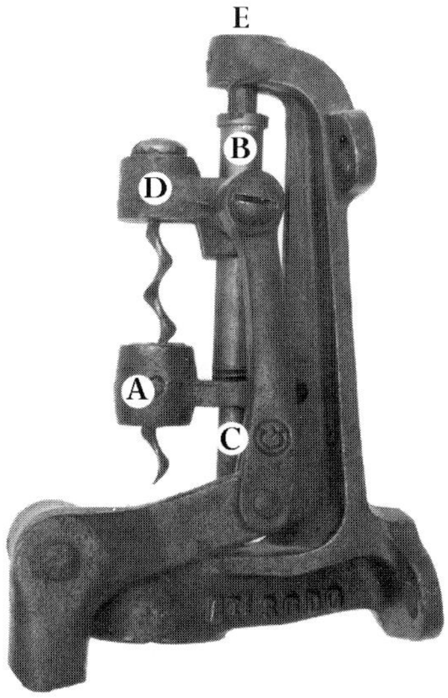

M117

M117 This was a French application filed in 1932 by Paul Wintenberger, SGDG #771,129. Forty-six years after the first American worm-nut patent by W. Barrett the worm-nut mechanism had come full circle. In this application Wintenberger did away with all of the levers, catches and springs on which many members of the Arcade group worked so hard. In Barrett's original application the worm-nut slid inside a tube and a screw limited its travel. In this application, a short threaded section of the steel rod (C) was screwed into the frame and extended to the top of the frame (E). The worm-nut (A) had a short threaded section of the brass tube (B) screwed into it and it slid up and down on this tube, which also limited its travel. The worm carrier (D) slid on the same tube (B). The link from the operating arm was attached to the worm carrier. Pulling the operating arm up caused the worm to rotate through the worm-nut into the cork. Pushing the operating arm down pulled the cork; at that point the brass tube had reached its upper limit and prevented the worm-nut from rising higher. Continuing to push the operating arm down raised the worm carrier, stripping the cork. A later version extended the frame at (E) allowing space for a coil spring to be added between the worm-nut and the worm carrier, assisting in the pulling of the cork. Corkscrews containing this mechanism were sold under the PRESTO name.

M118 This is a DRGM German corkscrew probably circa 1930 - 1940, but no registration has been found. This design utilized a slotted yoke (A) driven mechanism that contained the worm carrier (B). The disk (C) contained the crank pin (D) and on the other side had a cam surface along part of its circumference (like the cam surface in the ARCADE). This cam surface acted on a spring-loaded lever to hold or release the worm-nut. The VICTOR utilized a very similar slotted yoke mechanism, but in a stem-nut configuration. Corkscrews containing this mechanism were sold under the FORTSCHRITT name.

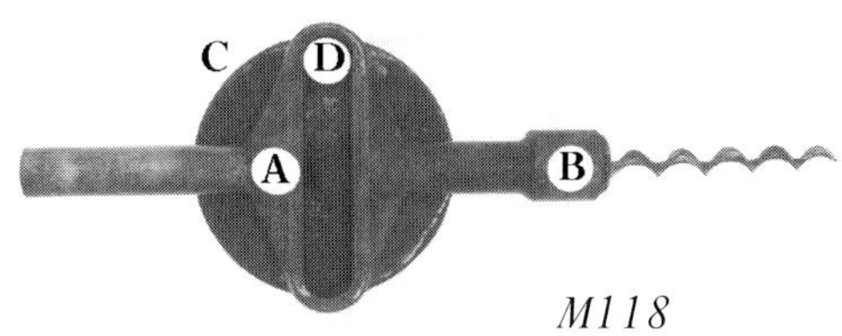

M118

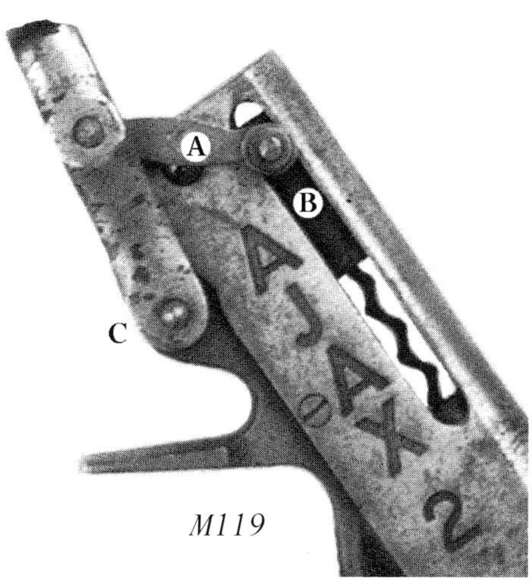

M119

M119 This is a German corkscrew, offered for sale in the 1940s and registered by G. Frings, but the DRGM registration has not been found. It was not inspected, but from the photograph it appears to have used a pair of side links (A) connected between the operating lever and the worm carrier (B). The side links and pivot point (C) on the back of the case are very similar to the lever system used in the MERRITT, but in this application they drove a worm-nut mechanism. Corkscrews containing this mechanism were sold under the AJAX 2 name.

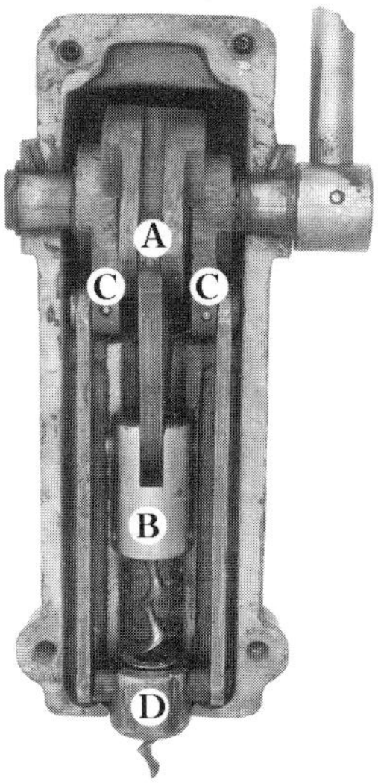

M120

M120 & M121 This is a German corkscrew probably circa 1950 - 1960, but no registration has been found. While this corkscrew may have been unreasonably ugly on the outside, the internal mechanism was a work of art. This was a crank driven worm-nut design with the center lobe (A) driving the worm carrier (B) and the two side lobes (C) driving the worm-nut (D). The side lobes were free to turn during the cork extraction portion of the cycle, but were forced to turn by flanges (E) around a portion of the main lobe during the cork stripping operation. (The side view of the mechanism is shown in a position that reveals the most components; it could never be in this position when it was installed in its case.) Corkscrews containing this mechanism were sold under the VAMPIR name.

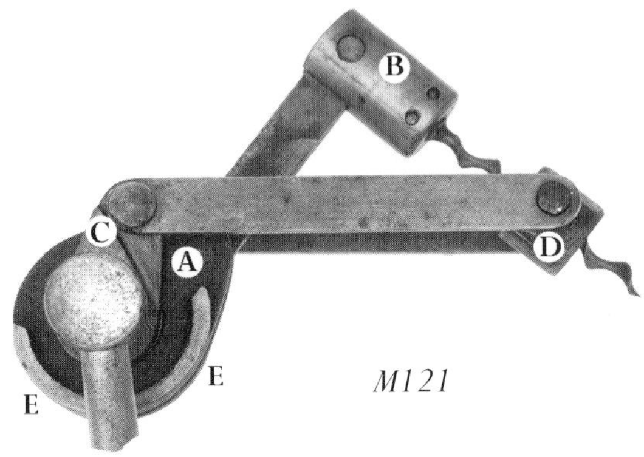

M121

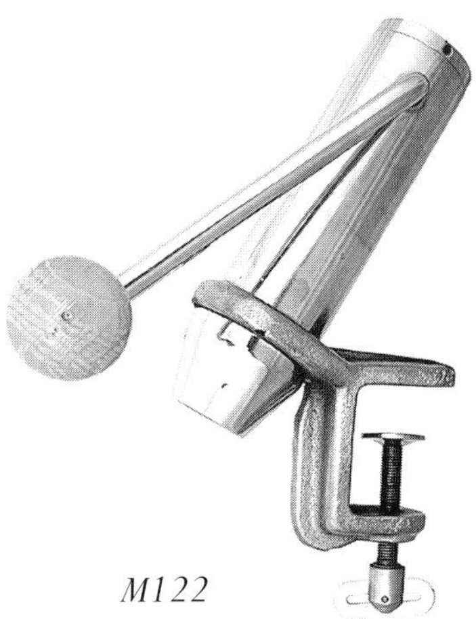

M122

M122 This is an East German corkscrew probably circa 1960 - 1990s, but no registration has been found. This corkscrew used a cam driven lever to hold the nut in place. Wonderfully machined, it is doubtful that this worm-nut mechanism was engineered with any consideration for the cost of production. All of the internal components were contained in, and slid in, some very hard, almost glass-like foam material. Corkscrews containing this mechanism were sold under the DREKO name.

Over a 100-year time span, starting in 1865, an incredible amount of inventive energy has gone into developing a "better" bar corkscrew. Considering that there are very few basic mechanisms options, it is amazing that so many different methods of converting the movement of a lever or crank into a turning worm with automatic cork ejection have been developed.

The bar corkscrew mechanism families

A few of the basic bar corkscrew mechanisms were extremely popular; these few produced a large number of offspring with different model and marketing names. There are some slight differences in some of the mechanisms; these include the DON offspring, where they all utilized Chambers DON patent, but a number of different operating lever and linkage configurations were used. It is interesting that the DON name is the only one where the father's name was used in some of its offspring's names, such as DONAR, DION and CEDON. The YANKEE No1 and No2 offspring were the MODERN and its offspring, which used a different location for one of the cams. The YANKEE NO6 offspring included the YANKEE NO7, which utilized a mirror image of the YANKEE NO6 mechanism and the Hero NO5 line with its inclined case. The German offspring of the HERO NO5, such as the HEKTORs, included an improvement presumably patented by G. Frings.

Derivative mechanism	Also marked as, or advertised as
A1	A739, OK
ACME	BRODERNE HERRMANN, EXHIBITION, PATENT ACME, THE ACME
ALFREDO P	ALFREDO M, SISTEMA
ARCADE	ALEXANDERWERK, EMPIRE, ORIGINAL SAFETY, THE SAFETY, SAFETY, SIMPLE, STANPAT, STEINER, SUNOID
BL	BORDEAUX, JPf
CHAMPION	BACCHUS, ESTATE, LE GRAPE, MILANO, MONTEREY, PIX, PUNTIGAM BRAUEREI, VINTNER, VITIPUM
DAISY	THE DAISY
DON	BISON-DONAR, BOJ, CEDON, DION, FALEAU, PERFECT, SLAM, THE DON, THE KING, THE RITZ, TITAN, ZEUS
ECLIPSE	THE ECLIPSE, THE ORIGINAL ECLIPSE, THE PATENT ECLIPSE
ENTERPRISE	AJAX
IMPROVED	JUMBO
MERRITT	DON (not the normal version), SUN
MIDGET	THE CROWN
PHOENIX 20	PHOENIX 40
PHOENIX 30	NEW ERA, PHOENIX 50, PHOENIX 60, PHOENIX 100
QUICK & EASY	ALEXANDERWERK, BISON-HEBE, BISON-UNIQUE, ESKILSTUNA, JUPP, L'ÉLÉGANT, HENVI, 1898 UNIQUE, NEW UNIQUE, THE EXPRESS, THE UNIQUE
RAPID (US)	SCHNELL, MOSCA
RAPID (UK)	INVICTA, RAPID POWERFUL, SHAMROCK, SWIFT, THE JUBILEE, THE RAPID CORK DRAWER
SAMSON	ADAMS, SAMPSON
WALKER, THE	ERIE
YANKEE No1 & No 2	BLITZ, NEW CENTURY, NEW ENGLAND, THE MODERN, THE KING, THE REX, US MODERN, VICTOR JR
YANKEE NO 6	BISON NO 5, BISON NO 6, HERO NO 5, HEKTOR, HEKTOR 1, HEKTOR 2, HEKTOR 3, HELIOS, HGB 7, JHE, PHR, QUICK, RIMO, ROTHCHILD NO 7, YANKEE NO 7

Cliff's SIMPLEX

A Swedish version of the ACME

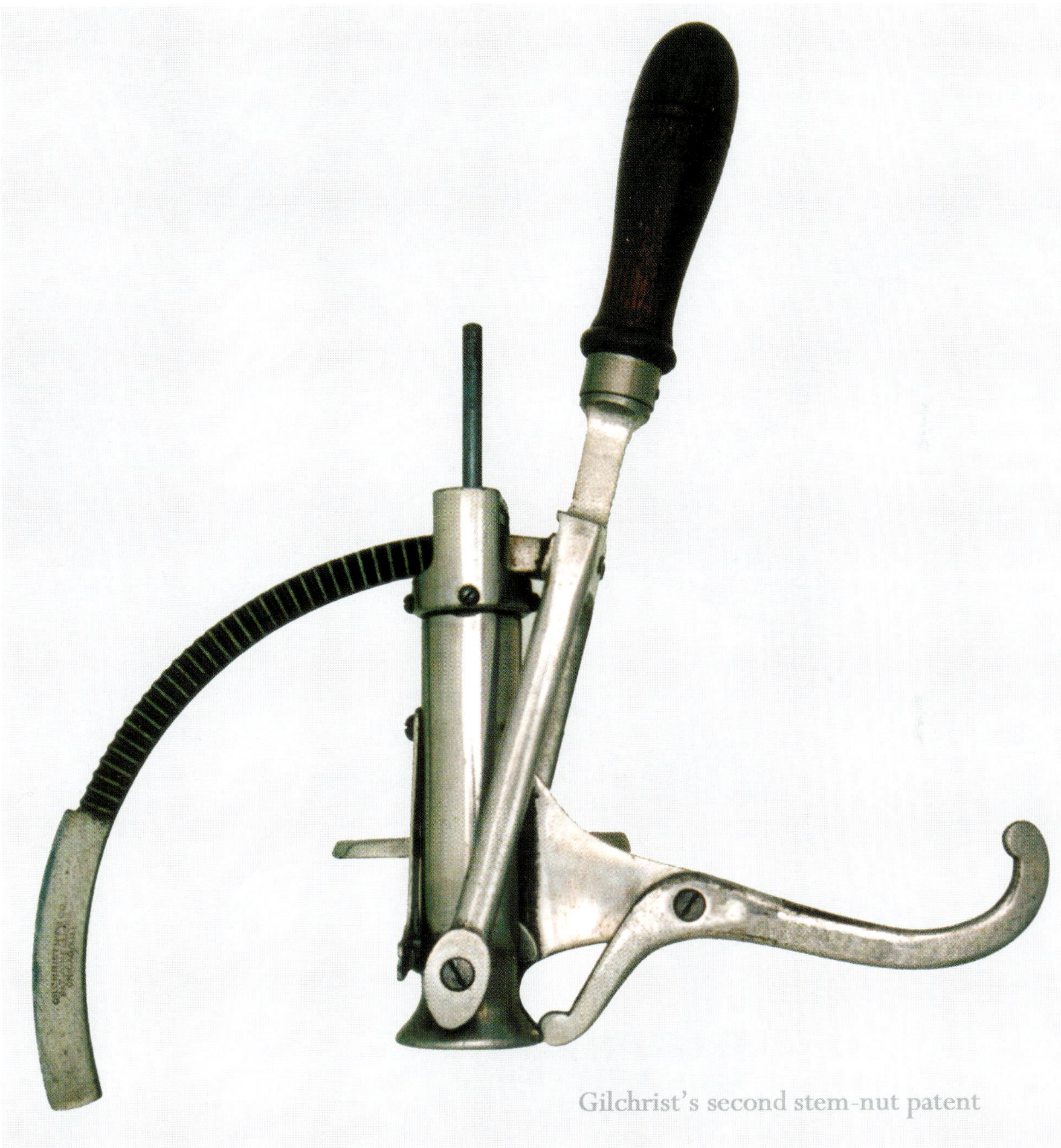

Gilchrist's second stem-nut patent

Haslam's 1889 patent

A French gear driven corkscrew

A cider opener from Gijon, Spain

A copper plated version of the US RAPID

ERIE
SPECIALTY CO.
1901
ERIE, PA.
U.S.A.

Walker's 1900 LITTLE QUICKER patent

Walker's 1913 patent

ARCADE
MANUFACTURING
COMPANY

M. Redlinger's 1897 patent

An Arcade bronze version of the ARCADE with bottle grips

Mason's version of the ARCADE

Alexanderwerk's version of the ARCADE

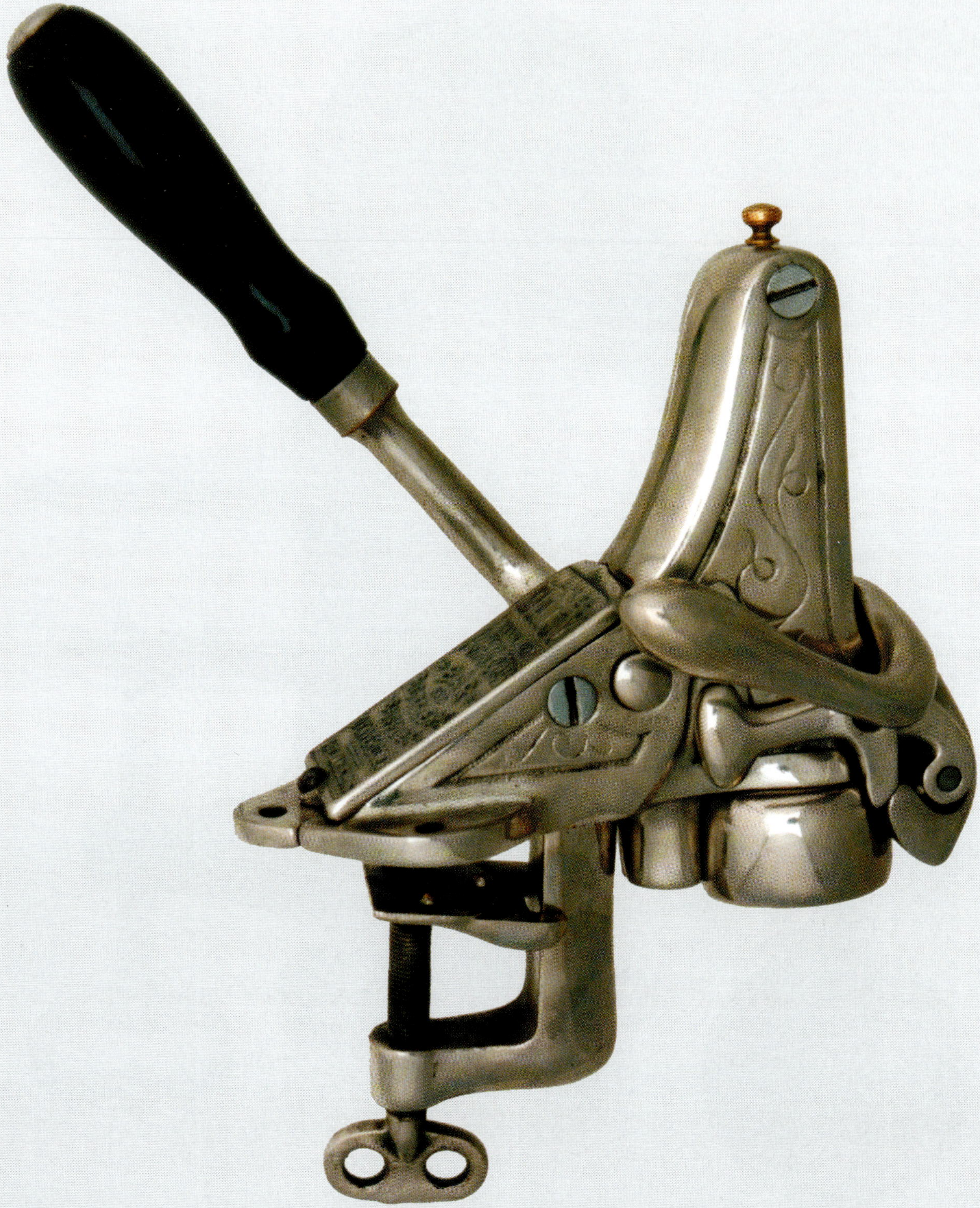

Morgan's 1895 DAISY patent

Section II
IDENTIFICATION

10 GOLD MEDALS — GASKELLS — HIGHEST AWARDS

PATENT

"SAFETY" CORK DRAWER.

With Bottle-holding Attachment.

PLAIN PATTERN (Improved)

BRASS

HIGHLY RECOMMENDED.

BRASS,
Prevents
breakages.

BRASS,
Strong and
Reliable.

No. **5011**—CLAMP PATTERN.

POLISHED BRASS	**25/-**
NICKEL-PLATED ON BRASS	**27/6**

No. **5012**—STAND PATTERN.

POLISHED BRASS	**27/6**
NICKEL-PLATED ON BRASS	**30/-**

The "SAFETY," made in BRASS, is strongly recommended; prevents annoyance of Breakages; is strong and durable.

IMPORTANT NOTICE.—The Patentees give notice that proceedings have been taken, and injunctions obtained against INFRINGERS of the "SAFETY" CORK DRAWER, and any persons pirating that Machine render themselves liable to be proceeded against.

How the Identification Section is arranged

The identification section was designed to assist corkscrew collectors in identifying bar corkscrews they own or are interested in. It consists of two groups of corkscrews. The first group includes all corkscrews marked with a NAME or for which an advertised NAME has been found. The second group includes the corkscrews which are unmarked and for which no NAME has been found to date.

It is interesting to note in this section that there is a bar corkscrew name for every letter in the alphabet.

Possibly the most interesting aspect of the IDENTIFICATION section is the discovery that there is so much misinformation marked on the corkscrews. For years collectors have been saying, "It is marked 'PAT SEPT 31 1899', but it sure does not look like the patent drawing." There are two reasons for this: the first is that the patent was usually for some device in the internal mechanism (in most cases the patentee was very specific about not claiming the shape of the case); second, and most startling, is that the patent dates as marked on the corkscrews were very seldom correct.

The following information is presented on each corkscrew.

NAME

These are the NAMES marked on the corkscrew or found in advertising. In some cases, the first corkscrew produced by a company simply carried the manufacturer's name or the patentee's name. In some instances the only marked NAME was a private label; in general, these have been used if the marked or advertised NAME does not appear on the corkscrew. In the case of a removable advertising plate, these have been included if they were deemed to assist in identifying a particular corkscrew.

The NAME is followed by "marked", "unmarked" or "not inspected", denoting whether or not the corkscrew has the name marked on it, or that it was not inspected, so the marks are unknown.

For those corkscrews at the back of this section where no marked or advertised NAME has been found "no name found" was used, preceded by the most important knowledge available. These include the inventor's name, the manufacturer, the country it was manufactured or sold in, or, failing any of the above, unknown.

The NAME used for a corkscrew would normally have been created for the following reasons: a new case and mechanism; a new internal mechanism in a previously used case; production of the same model by another manufacturer; protection of a new distribution channel.

The NAME is usually found cast into the corkscrew frame or the clamp frame on the corkscrews containing stem-nut mechanisms. On the corkscrews containing worm-nut mechanisms the NAME is usually cast into the side of the case or the operating lever. On wall mounts the NAME is usually cast into the front of the case.

TRADEMARK

The abbreviation for the TRADEMARK is shown. Trademarks were popular in Europe but almost never used on North American bar corkscrews. Close inspection is often required for trademarks to be found or read. On brass components this is due both to their delicate lines and to the practice of collectors and dealers of grinding or polishing off the nickel-plating, removing the trademark with the plating. This latter practice may account for some "unmarked" British brass corkscrews. On sand-cast iron components they often show only as a blob due to their very small size. Trademarks, if they can be found, are almost anywhere on the corkscrew. Other than the ones located on the front of the barrel just above the oil hole, they tend to be hidden away on the under side of the clamp plate, on the thumb piece or on the operating lever pivot point when it is located at the back of the barrel. A list of TRADEMARKS and their abbreviations is found in Appendix 3.

OTHER MARKS

These include marks on the corkscrew other than the NAME (if marked) and the TRADEMARK. Many mounted corkscrews are very well marked internally, but have no external marks. The internal marks have been noted only when there are no external markings or where the information could be useful in future research.

As indicated by "not inspected", there are corkscrews that the author has not examined, so the markings cannot be confirmed.

Many corkscrews had various numbers besides patent or registered design numbers on them. For general information the various types of numbers are as follows:

Serial numbers

A five or six digit serial number could be found *hand stamped* on the side of many of the British brass corkscrews. Manufacturers tend to build a date code into the serial number, but no date code has been deciphered to date.

Part number

On many cast iron pieces, a one or two digit number could be found *cast into* most or all of the internal components. Each component had a different number; these were the manufacturer's part numbers as found in their parts list.

Unit number

On many of the British brass pieces a one or two digit number could be found *hand stamped* into most or all of the components. This was the unit number, implying that each component was hand fitted to make up a complete unit. It is strange that these numbers are often in the 5 - 15 range and very rarely exceed 25, implying that very few were produced.

NOTICE

These notes point out details that might not be obvious in the illustration. Alternate I.D.#s for different finish variants are also listed here. Finish variant corkscrews listed here are not shown in the illustrations.

I.D. #

The I.D.# consists of a letter and three numbers for the named corkscrew. The letter indicates the first letter of the corkscrew's NAME. The first number consists of two digits and is assigned to all corkscrews with the same NAME and internal mechanisms, while the second number distinguishes frame differences in corkscrews bearing the same NAME. Finally, the third number denotes minor variations in the same basic corkscrew. This section attempts to list all of the known NAMES, versions and variations, including finish differences. While some of these differences may not appear very significant, it is possible that this information could be a useful research tool in the future.

An I.D.# example is C04.2.2, which identifies a corkscrew as the fourth type of mounted corkscrew listed having a NAME starting with "C", in this case CHAMPION. It is the second CHAMPION shown, but with notable differences from all the other "C04" corkscrews, such as the type of mounting, added attachments, pre-patent or post-patent examples or the material that it is made from. There are also two minor variations of this corkscrew, and this is the second one. This numbering system was designed to allow for the addition of all unfound NAMES, versions and variations in the future, without disrupting the overall numbering system.

Unmarked corkscrews for which a NAME has yet to be found are grouped at the back of this section in the no-name group with "99" as the first number. An I. D. # example is B99.1.1 used to identify a Bloeser patented corkscrew which is unmarked and for which no advertised NAME has been found.

INVENTOR & DATE

This is the name of the original inventor (without regard to whether the registration or patent may have expired before any specific version of this corkscrew was placed in production) and the date, for the country that it is believed to have been sold or manufactured in. The date shown here will often be different than the marked dates, due to the vagaries of manufacturers. Most Arcade corkscrews are marked with patent dates from previous patents and are almost never marked with the correct patent date.

> It would appear that a correctly marked patent date was of very little concern to the manufacturers. When the corkscrew was first put into production the foundry workers seem to have used whatever date plate was handy. Later, when the patent was granted, the manufacturer seldom bothered to change the dates on the casting model. In some cases, as is common in any information transfer, they just made a mistake. Sometimes these incorrect dates are later corrected, but not often.

REGISTRATION

The number is preceded by the patent or registration type. The following abbreviations have been used where it was felt that there could be some confusion as to which country the patent applied to: **England** – LP (utility), REG (design); **French** – SGDG (utility); **German** – DRP (utility), DRGM (design); **US, Canada and all other countries** – P (utility), DES (design). When the marks indicated that a patent had been applied for, the application filed date is used.

CIRCA

This is the period of time over which a corkscrew was manufactured. It would have varied widely from not at all, in the case of a single prototype, to many years of production on the popular models. An approximate date range has been given, based on patent application dates, dated catalogues, dated advertising and physical attributes of the corkscrew. Reliably dated advertising and catalogues are very difficult to find, so many circa dates are only a best estimate, as denoted by "?". The date when production ended is especially difficult to pin down. In many cases you will note that the circa date starts many years before the patent date. This is due to many patents being issued years after the application was made. It is assumed that production started at about the same time as the application was filed.

FREQUENCY

In this book, "frequency" must of necessity mean *how many the author has seen or heard about in the last nine years*. Information about specific corkscrews in other people's collections decreases rapidly as the distance increases. This is a very difficult area to be definitive about, so the categories are quite broad. A few dozen mounted corkscrews drift out of attics and cellars into the hands of collectors every year, so will almost certainly turn into over time. Almost any mounted corkscrew in mint condition is extremely hard to find; the categories assume "normal" condition. (Normal is considered to mean "showing normal wear and tear on a 100 year old item". It would still be operational, and not have missing or broken components.)

Frequency is indicated by the following symbols.

Almost unknown to the author: none or one.
The author is aware of very, very few, less than a half-dozen.
The author is aware of a few, maybe up to a dozen or so.
The author is aware of, maybe, a couple of dozen.
Quite a few; a collector might be able to find one in a year of searching.
"?" There is not enough data available to be meaningful.
(Blank) Still in production.

It should be reiterated that this is how many corkscrews the author thinks he remembers having seen or heard about. Many of the corkscrews look as if they should be far more common, but in nine years only one or no examples of these corkscrews have been heard of. It is difficult to be definitive about many versions and variants as the owner will not have been aware of the slight differences that are pointed out in IDENTIFICATION; sometimes these are all combined giving each version the same frequency rating. Over time, with the information published here, more accurate information will evolve. By the standards of almost any other collectible item, all mounted corkscrews are hard to find.

MANUFACTURER

The manufacturer or the suspected (denoted by "?") manufacturer is listed. Identifying the manufacturer or foundry is hazardous, due to many factors, including patents that were manufactured by more than one manufacturer, in more than one country. Also, as they do today, manufacturers went out of business, changed their name, merged and distributed "private label" products that they did not manufacture. Because bar corkscrews would have represented a minute portion of a foundry's production capacity, they have left almost no tracks in the sands of time. Many of the answers about which company or foundry manufactured which corkscrew will remain speculative forever. Firmer answers require more catalogues, company records and advertising.

Appendix 3 lists the distributors and manufacturers found and cited in this book.

MATERIAL

This indicates the metal used in the construction of the corkscrew.

FINISH

This is what the original finish is believed to have been, or was advertised as being (the photographs do not always show this). In many cases the original finish has long since oxidized away, been removed, painted over or re-plated. Some proprietary finishes were used, such as "Masonoid Silver", a silver colored plating used by Mason, or "Tuscan Bronze", a copper/lacquer finish used by Arcade (also advertised as "Arcadian Bronze"). Corkscrews with these finishes intact are extremely hard to find.

COMMENTS

These include additional information about the corkscrew that might be of interest.

The Illustrations

The illustrations are photographs taken by the author or by fellow collectors, printed advertising and, unfortunately in some cases, third or fourth generation copies of the above. Some of the older, poorer illustrations have been "fixed", and this process may have inadvertently left out or added important details. In some illustrations, advertising or patent drawings have been used in place of a photograph, if the photograph were very poor or the advertising were more interesting. In some cases the information provided is from an existing corkscrew, despite the illustration being from an advertisement; this is noted in the COMMENTS. Some of the advertising copy has been retyped and re-formatted where the original was almost unreadable, or where the copy was scattered around the page. When it was not possible to acquire an illustration, or only a verbal description was available, a computer-generated bas-relief illustration of the corkscrew was used. In many photographs, a penny is included for scale; the penny is 19 mm or ¾".

General Identification Guidelines

If the reader has searched through this book and not found his corkscrew, here are a few guidelines.

The number one identification tool is matching up the thumbscrew shape (see Appendix 5) with a known manufacturer's thumbscrew. This usually provides a very good idea of who manufactured the unknown corkscrew.

Other more general indicators are as follows:

- If the frame is vertical, it is probably an American manufactured or designed corkscrew.
- If the frame is inclined, it was probably designed for the European market, or manufactured in Europe. (The QUICK & EASY is an exception.)
- If it is made from brass, it was probably manufactured in England.
- If the operating arm has a crank handle, it was probably designed for the European market, or manufactured in Europe. (The QUICK & EASY is an exception.)
- If the operating arm has a crank handle attached by a bolt, it was probably manufactured for the European market or in Germany.
- If it has a wire neck rest it was probably designed for, or manufactured in, Germany.
- If it is a wall mount corkscrew, it was probably designed for, or manufactured in, France. (The YANKEE No 1 is an exception.)
- If it looks like a QUICK & EASY, but without the bottleneck rest, it was probably designed for the European market, or manufactured in Europe.
- If it has a bottle grip, it was probably manufactured or designed in America.
- If it has very delicate decorations on a cast iron case, it was probably manufactured by Arcade.
- If it has a removable throat, it was probably manufactured or designed in England.
- If it has a worm-nut mechanism, it was probably manufactured in American or Germany.
- If it has a stem-nut mechanism, it was probably manufactured in England.

Screw threads

At various times, the British, Americans and Europeans all used different types of screw threads. In many cases it is possible to use a thread gauge or a known nut or screw to ascertain whether a corkscrew was made in Europe, America or Britain. While this will not tell you who the manufacturer was, it may, at least, rule out a couple of continents.

NAME:	**A1** (not inspected)
TRADEMARK:	not inspected
OTHER MARKS:	not inspected
NOTICE:	thumb piece, open throat
I.D. #:	**A01.1.1**
INVENTOR & DATE:	S. Mason Oct 30, 1902
REGISTRATION #:	LP 23,675
CIRCA:	1902 - 1910
FREQUENCY:	
MANUFACTURER:	Samuel Mason Ltd.
MATERIAL:	brass
FINISH:	not inspected
COMMENTS:	As seen in this advertisement, the open throat and large thumb piece would indicate a very early version. A1 is found marked on the tube cap.

NAME:	**A1** (marked)
TRADEMARK:	none
OTHER MARKS:	none
NOTICE:	thumb piece, one hole throat, A1 tube cap out of scale
I.D. #:	**A01.1.2**
INVENTOR & DATE:	S. Mason Oct 30, 1902
REGISTRATION #:	LP 23,675
CIRCA:	1902 - 1910
FREQUENCY:	
MANUFACTURER:	Samuel Mason Ltd.
MATERIAL:	brass
FINISH:	nickel
COMMENTS:	This thumb piece and clamp plate are found on known Mason corkscrews.

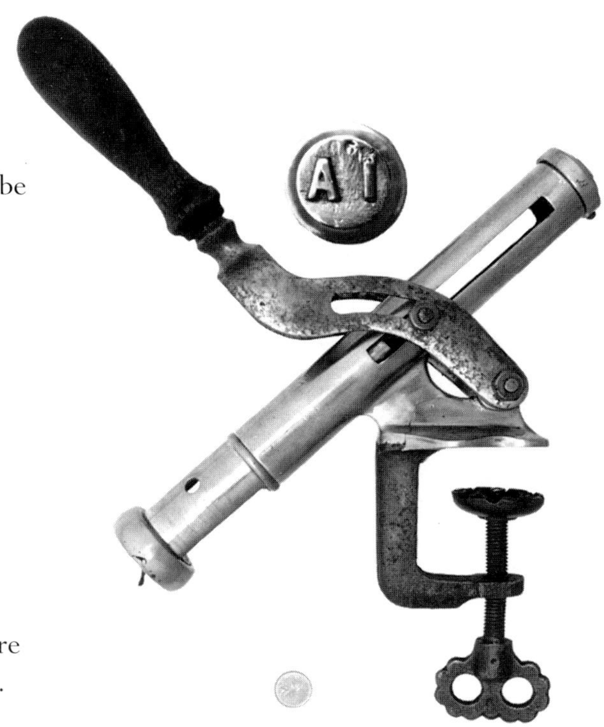

NAME:	**A1** (marked)
TRADEMARK:	hand & star
OTHER MARKS:	none
NOTICE:	Gaskell thumb piece, open throat, wire worm, A1 tube cap out of scale
I.D. #:	**A01.1.3**
INVENTOR & DATE:	S. Mason Oct 30, 1902
REGISTRATION #:	LP 23,675
CIRCA:	1910? - 1920?
FREQUENCY:	
MANUFACTURER:	Gaskell
MATERIAL:	brass
FINISH:	nickel
COMMENTS:	Gaskell & Chambers stopped using the hand & star trademark shortly after the optic trademark was registered.

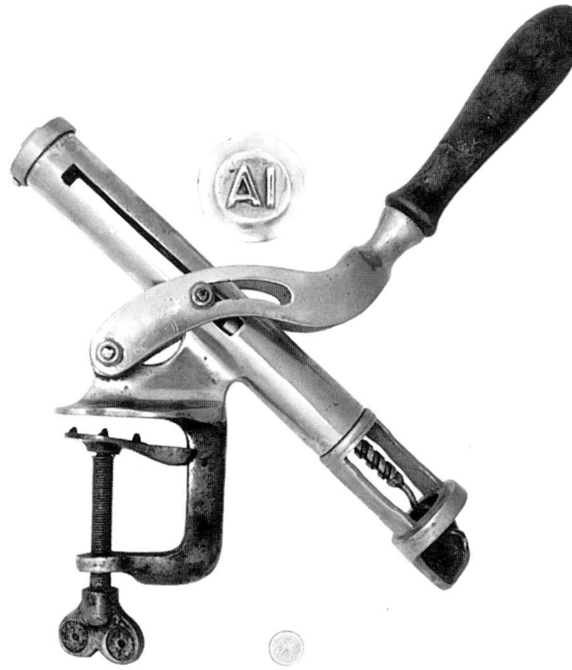

NAME:	**A739** (marked)
TRADEMARK:	none
OTHER MARKS:	PATENT
NOTICE:	three point clamp plate, thumb piece, A739 tube cap out of scale
I.D. #:	**A02.1.1**
INVENTOR & DATE:	S. Mason Oct 30, 1902
REGISTRATION #:	LP 23,675
CIRCA:	1902 - 1910
FREQUENCY:	
MANUFACTURER:	Samuel Mason Ltd.
MATERIAL:	brass
FINISH:	nickel
COMMENTS:	The three point clamp plate is found on the very early ACME; no A739 advertising has been found to date.

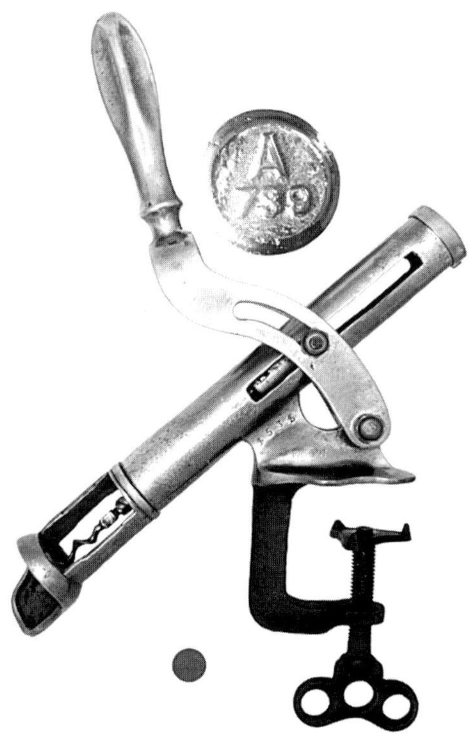

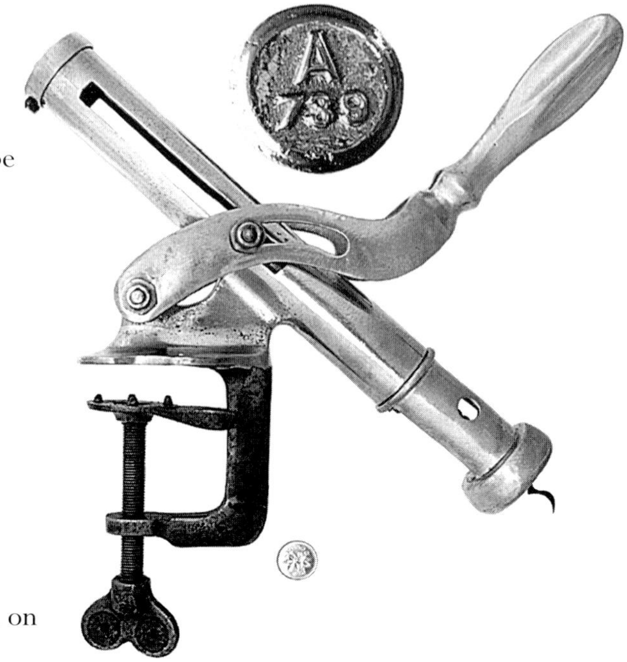

NAME:	**A739** (marked)
TRADEMARK:	hand & star
OTHER MARKS:	none
NOTICE:	throat, Gaskell thumb piece, A739 tube cap out of scale
I.D. #:	**A02.1.2**
INVENTOR & DATE:	S. Mason Oct 30, 1902
REGISTRATION #:	LP 23,675
CIRCA:	1910? - 1920?
FREQUENCY:	
MANUFACTURER:	Gaskell
MATERIAL:	brass
FINISH:	nickel
COMMENTS:	The cast brass operating lever is found on all A739s; possibly the A739 was a private label for someone.

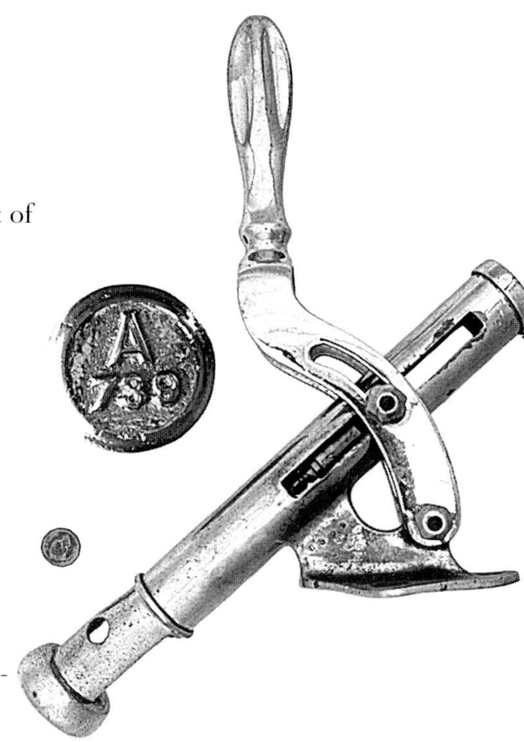

NAME:	**A739** (marked)
TRADEMARK:	hand & star
OTHER MARKS:	none
NOTICE:	top mount, throat, A739 tube cap out of scale
I.D. #:	**A02.2.1**
INVENTOR & DATE:	S. Mason Oct 30, 1902
REGISTRATION #:	LP 23,675
CIRCA:	1910? - 1920?
FREQUENCY:	
MANUFACTURER:	Gaskell
MATERIAL:	brass
FINISH:	nickel
COMMENTS:	Gaskell would have been the manufacturer.

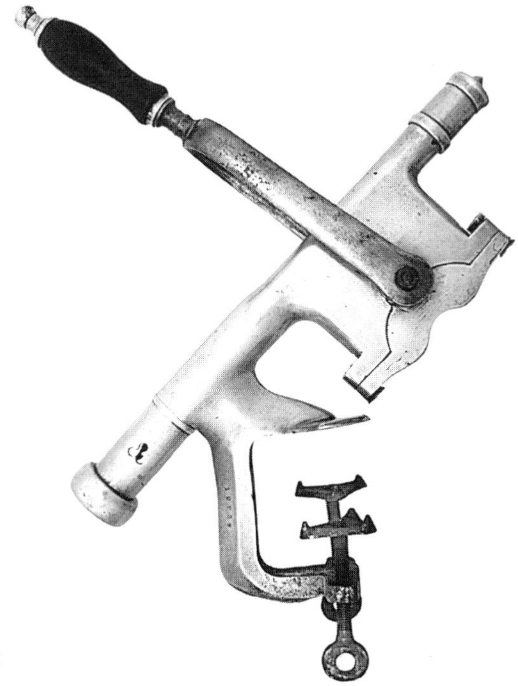

NAME:	**ACME, THE PATENT** (Marked)
TRADEMARK:	none
OTHER MARKS:	none
NOTICE:	double clamp
I.D. #:	**A03.1.1**
INVENTOR & DATE:	W. Vaughan Aug 15, 1887
REGISTRATION #:	LP 11,104
CIRCA:	1887? - 1895?
FREQUENCY:	
MANUFACTURER:	Samuel Mason Ltd.
MATERIAL:	brass
FINISH:	nickel
COMMENTS:	The brass double clamp frame would not have been very sturdy and is usually found only on prototypes; there does not appear to be any iron inside the brass.

No. P 4653—"Acme" Cork Drawer, With Cramp or Plate to screw to Counter.

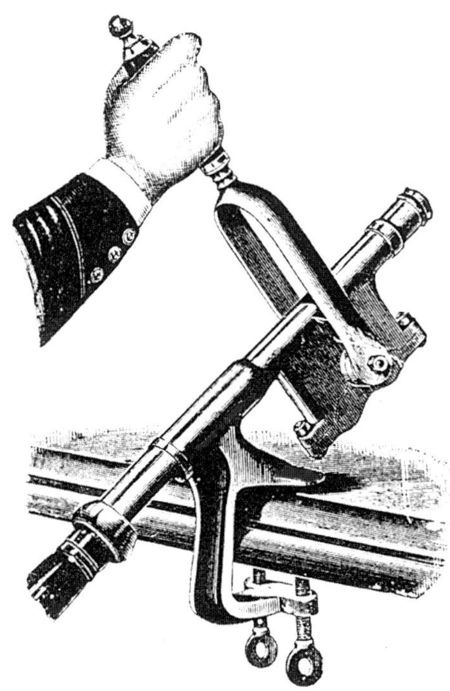

Brass, ...	...	58/6 each.
Nickel-plated,...	...	60/ ,,
Masonoid Silver,	...	68/3 ,,

NAME:	**ACME, THE PATENT** (not inspected)
TRADEMARK:	not inspected
OTHER MARKS:	not inspected
NOTICE:	masonoid finish, brass finish variant *A03.1.2*
I.D. #:	**A03.1.3**
INVENTOR & DATE:	W. Vaughan Aug 15, 1887
REGISTRATION #:	LP 11,104
CIRCA:	1887? - 1895?
FREQUENCY:	
MANUFACTURER:	Samuel Mason Ltd.
MATERIAL:	brass
FINISH:	Masonoid silver
COMMENTS:	This advertisement dates to 1898.

NAME: **ACME, THE PATENT** (marked)
TRADEMARK: not inspected
OTHER MARKS: not inspected
NOTICE: top mount, brass finish variant *A03.2.2*, Masonoid silver finish variant *A03.2.3*
I.D. #: **A03.2.1**
INVENTOR & DATE: W. Vaughan Aug 15, 1887
REGISTRATION #: LP 11,104
CIRCA: 1895? - 1900?
FREQUENCY:
MANUFACTURER: Samuel Mason Ltd.
MATERIAL: brass
FINISH: nickel
COMMENTS: This is the "Plate to screw to Counter" version described in the **A03.1.3** advertisement. Mason also used this pedestal top mount on the ECLIPSE and the VICTOR.

NAME: **ACME, THE PATENT** (marked)
TRADEMARK: none
OTHER MARKS: none
NOTICE: double clamp style frame, lower section replaced
I.D. #: **A03.3.1**
INVENTOR & DATE: W. Vaughan Aug 15, 1887
REGISTRATION #: LP 11,104
CIRCA: 1895? - 1900?
FREQUENCY:
MANUFACTURER: Samuel Mason Ltd.
MATERIAL: brass
FINISH: brass
COMMENTS: This appears to be a prototype during the transition from the double clamp to the single clamp; on the original double clamp frame the frame clamp plate was very thin, like this one is.

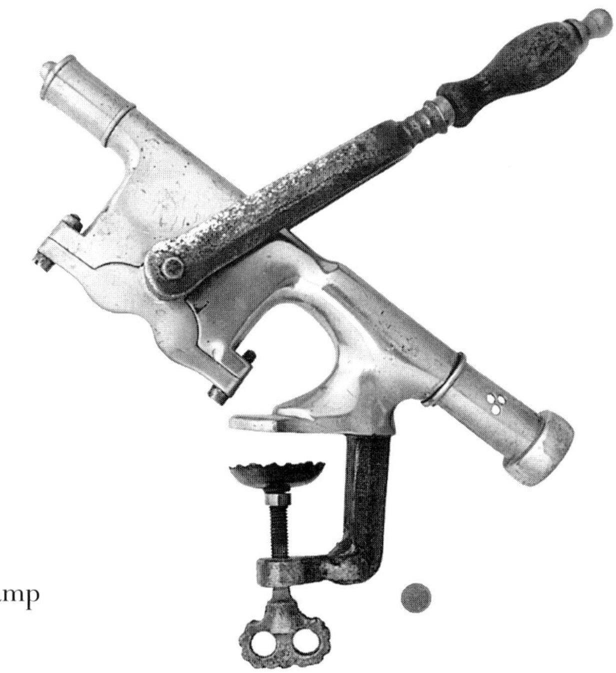

NAME:	**ACME** (marked)
TRADEMARK:	none
OTHER MARKS:	S. MASON on thumb piece
NOTICE:	lower section of the clamp frame broken off and welded back on
I.D. #:	**A04.1.1**
INVENTOR & DATE:	W. Vaughan Aug 15, 1887
REGISTRATION #:	LP 11,104
CIRCA:	1895? - 1910?
FREQUENCY:	
MANUFACTURER:	Samuel Mason Ltd.
MATERIAL:	brass
FINISH:	nickel
COMMENTS:	ACME is cast into the cast iron clamp frame.

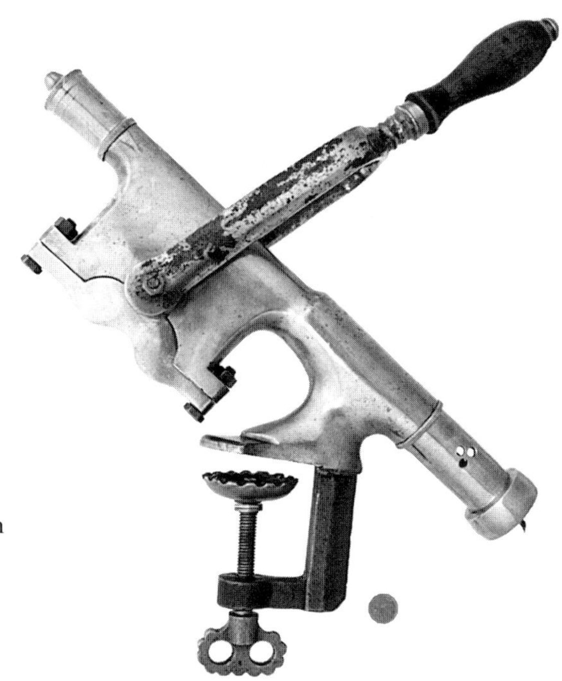

NAME:	**ACME** (unmarked)
TRADEMARK:	none
OTHER MARKS:	S. MASON on thumb piece
NOTICE:	brass thumb screw and clamp plate
I.D. #:	**A04.1.2**
INVENTOR & DATE:	W. Vaughan Aug 15, 1887
REGISTRATION #:	LP 11,104
CIRCA:	1895? - 1910?
FREQUENCY:	
MANUFACTURER:	Samuel Mason Ltd.
MATERIAL:	brass
FINISH:	nickel
COMMENTS:	Because of the brass clamp mechanism and no marked name, this is likely a prototype or very early version.

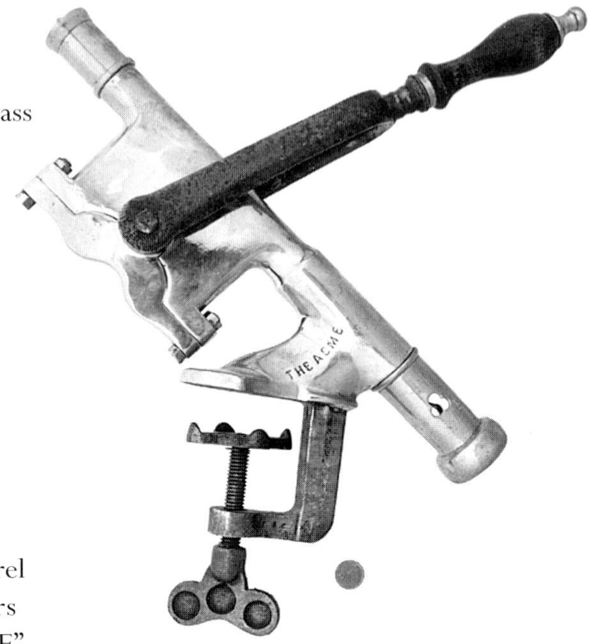

NAME:	**ACME, THE** (marked)
TRADEMARK:	hand & star
OTHER MARKS:	G&C
NOTICE:	Gaskell clamp plate, thumb piece, brass finish variant *A05.1.2*
I.D. #:	**A05.1.1**
INVENTOR & DATE:	W. Vaughan Aug 15, 1887
REGISTRATION #:	LP 11,104
CIRCA:	1910?-1920?
FREQUENCY:	
MANUFACTURER:	Gaskell
MATERIAL:	brass
FINISH:	nickel
COMMENTS:	THE ACME is cast into both the barrel frame and the clamp frame. It appears that Gaskell & Chambers added "THE" when they began manufacturing corkscrews previously manufactured by Mason.

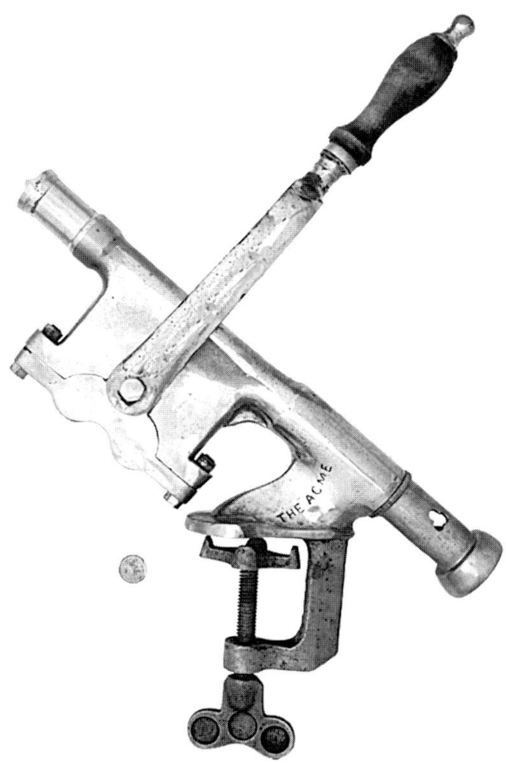

NAME:	**ACME, THE** (marked)
TRADEMARK:	optic
OTHER MARKS:	G&C
NOTICE:	heavier frame components, brass finish variant *A05.1.4*
I.D. #:	**A05.1.3**
INVENTOR & DATE:	W. Vaughan Aug 15, 1887
REGISTRATION #:	LP 11,104
CIRCA:	1920?-1930?
FREQUENCY:	
MANUFACTURER:	Gaskell & Chambers Ltd.
MATERIAL:	brass
FINISH:	nickel
COMMENTS:	This is a later version of THE ACME.

NAME:	**ACME, THE** (not inspected)
TRADEMARK:	not inspected
OTHER MARKS:	not inspected
NOTICE:	thumb piece, heavier frame, brass finish variant *A05.1.6*
I.D. #:	**A05.1.5**
INVENTOR & DATE:	W. Vaughan Aug 15, 1887
REGISTRATION #:	LP 11,104
CIRCA:	1910?-1930?
FREQUENCY:	
MANUFACTURER:	Gaskell & Chambers Ltd.
MATERIAL:	brass
FINISH:	nickel
COMMENTS:	This is a 1926 Gaskell & Chambers advertisement for what is probably the final version manufactured.

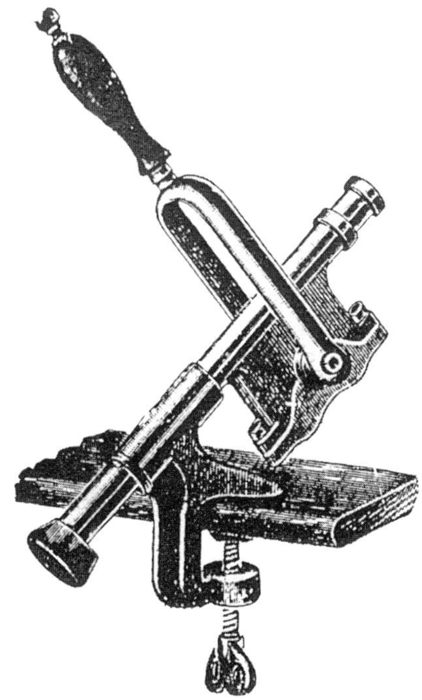

NAME:	**ADAMS** (not inspected)
TRADEMARK:	not inspected
OTHER MARKS:	not inspected
NOTICE:	
I.D. #:	**A06.1.1**
INVENTOR & DATE:	J. Hurley Oct 5,1886
REGISTRATION #:	P 350,308
CIRCA:	1886? - 1896?
FREQUENCY:	see SAMSON
MANUFACTURER:	F. F. Adams Co.
MATERIAL:	cast iron
FINISH:	nickel
COMMENTS:	ADAMS was a name for the SAMSON as found in an 1896 advertisement. In this case the manufacturer's name was used.

PATENT BAR COUNTER CORK PULLERS.

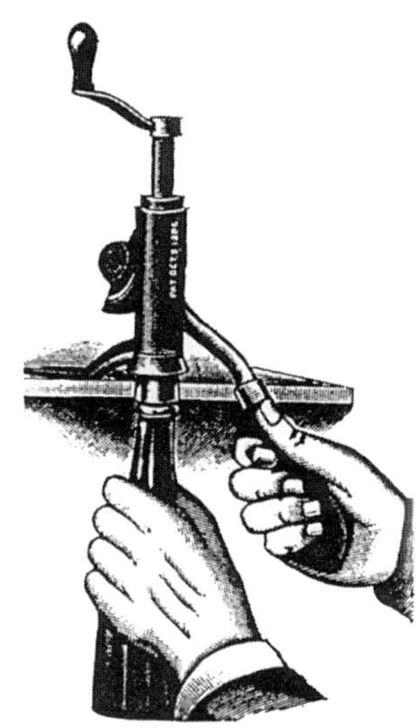

14819 Adams, plated, as per cut, each.............. 2.50

NAME: **AJAX** (not inspected)

TRADEMARK: not inspected

OTHER MARKS: not inspected

NOTICE: top mount shown but clamp mount advertised

I.D. #: **A07.1.1**

INVENTOR & DATE: presumably J. Hurley Sep 7,1886

REGISTRATION #: P 348,743

CIRCA: 1895? - 1900 ?

FREQUENCY:

MANUFACTURER: Enterprise Manufacturing Co.

MATERIAL: cast iron

FINISH: nickel

COMMENTS: The British name for the ENTERPRISE, presumably it was manufactured in the USA. Nickel plated versions are unknown.

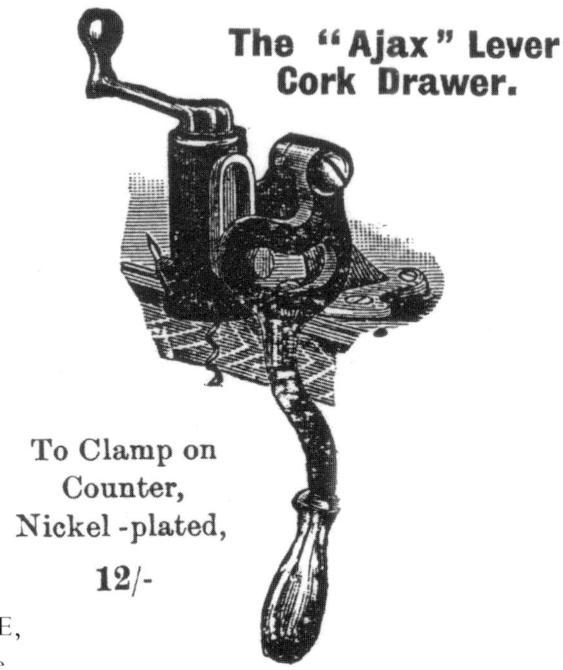

NAME: **AJAX** (not inspected)

TRADEMARK: not inspected

OTHER MARKS: not inspected

NOTICE: Gilchrist style thumb piece, wire neck rest

I.D. #: **A08.1.1**

INVENTOR & DATE: no German patent or registration found

REGISTRATION #:

CIRCA: 1910? - 1930?

FREQUENCY:

MANUFACTURER: FRINGS & CO. o. H. G.

MATERIAL: cast iron

FINISH: not inspected

COMMENTS: As found in a 1930 advertisement, this looks very much like an inclined version of Baumgarten's May 28th 1901 patent; see also the INVINCIBLE.

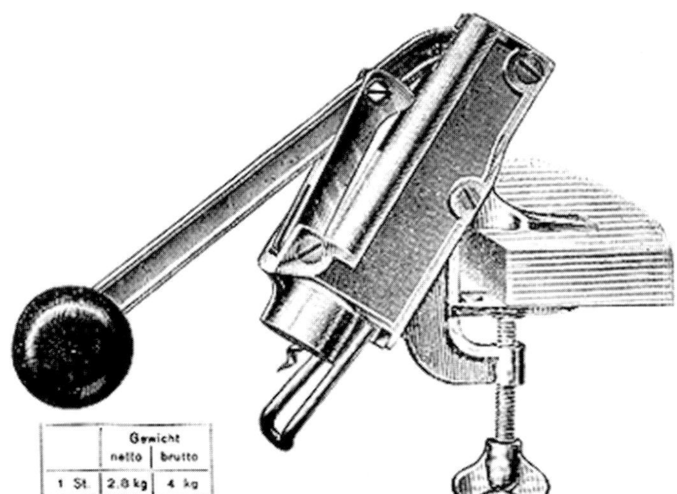

	Gewicht	
	netto	brutto
1 St.	2.8 kg	4 kg
6 St.	17 kg	22 kg

Entkorkmaschine Ajax

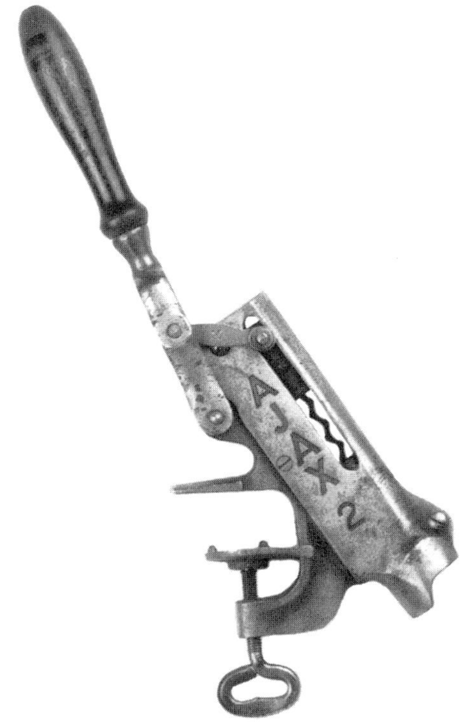

NAME:	**AJAX 2** (marked)
TRADEMARK:	not inspected
OTHER MARKS:	DRGM
NOTICE:	side links
I.D. #:	**A09.1.1**
INVENTOR & DATE:	Frings, no German registration found
REGISTRATION #:	
CIRCA:	1900? - 1920?
FREQUENCY:	
MANUFACTURER:	FRINGS & CO. o. H. G.
MATERIAL:	cast iron
FINISH:	nickel
COMMENTS:	This was a worm-nut version of the MERRITT lever and link arrangement.

NAME:	**ALEXANDERWERK** (marked)
TRADEMARK:	none
OTHER MARKS:	DR PATENT
NOTICE:	
I.D. #:	**A10.1.1**
INVENTOR & DATE:	A. Pick Aug 01,1895
REGISTRATION #:	DRP 85195
CIRCA:	1893 - 1900?
FREQUENCY:	
MANUFACTURER:	Arcade Manufacturing Co. ?
MATERIAL:	cast iron
FINISH:	green paint
COMMENTS:	USA screw threads would indicate a private label by Arcade for Alexanderwerk.

NAME:	**ALEXANDERWERK** (marked)
TRADEMARK:	none
OTHER MARKS:	D.R. PATENT
NOTICE:	based on Arcade's ARCADE mechanism
I.D. #:	**A10.1.2**
INVENTOR & DATE:	A. Pick Aug 01,1895
REGISTRATION #:	DRP 85195
CIRCA:	1893 - 1900?
FREQUENCY:	
MANUFACTURER:	Arcade Manufacturing Co. ?
MATERIAL:	cast iron
FINISH:	nickel
COMMENTS:	USA screw threads would indicate a private label by Arcade for Alexanderwerk; includes internal modifications to increase reliability.

NAME:	**ALEXANDERWERK** (marked)
TRADEMARK:	none
OTHER MARKS:	hand stamped **10** on all components
NOTICE:	
I.D. #:	**A11.1.1**
INVENTOR & DATE:	E. Walker Aug 04, 1896
REGISTRATION #:	DRP 90732
CIRCA:	1896 - ?
FREQUENCY:	
MANUFACTURER:	Erie Specialty Co. ?
MATERIAL:	cast iron
FINISH:	nickel
COMMENTS:	USA screw threads would indicate a private label by Walker for Alexanderwerk.

NAME:	**ALEXANDERWERK** (marked)
TRADEMARK:	none
OTHER MARKS:	hand stamped **23** on all components
NOTICE:	no bottle lip
I.D. #:	**A11.2.1**
INVENTOR & DATE:	E. Walker Aug 04, 1896
REGISTRATION #:	DRP 90732
CIRCA:	1896 - ?
FREQUENCY:	
MANUFACTURER:	Erie Specialty Co. ?
MATERIAL:	cast iron
FINISH:	nickel
COMMENTS:	USA screw threads would indicate a private label by Walker for Alexanderwerk.

NAME:	**ALFREDO M.** (marked)
TRADEMARK:	bottle, AYM
OTHER MARKS:	
NOTICE:	
I.D. #:	**A12.1.1**
INVENTOR & DATE:	no Spanish patent or registration found
REGISTRATION #:	
CIRCA:	1940?
FREQUENCY:	
MANUFACTURER:	Perez-Quintanilla
MATERIAL:	brass, cast iron and wood
FINISH:	brass
COMMENTS:	All of the ALFREDO corkscrews were sold mounted on large wooden wall mounting plates which included a bottle stand.

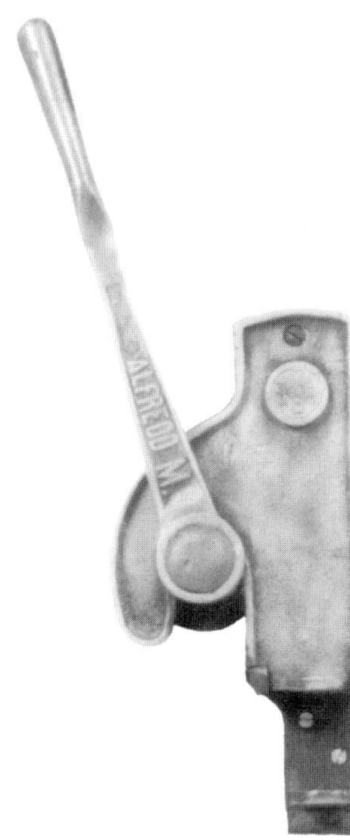

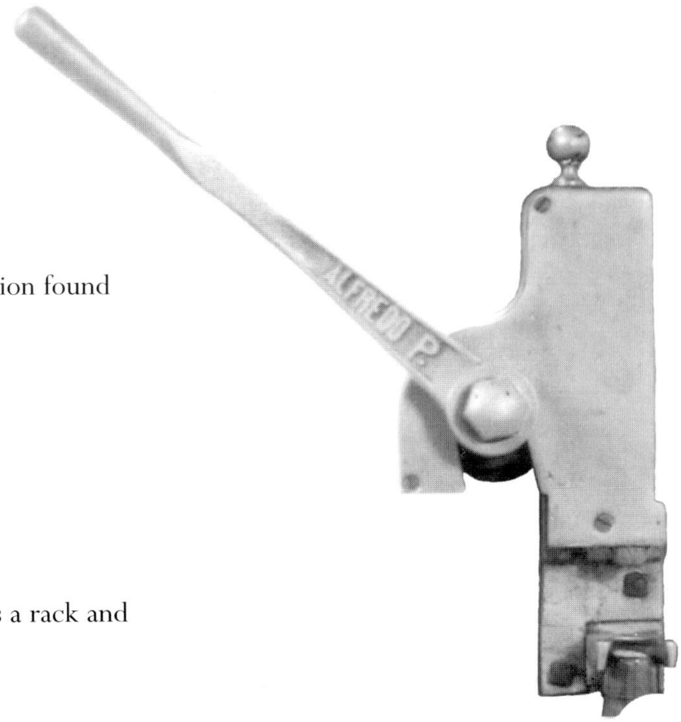

NAME: **ALFREDO P.** (marked)
TRADEMARK: not inspected
OTHER MARKS: not inspected
NOTICE: adjusting knob on the top
I.D. #: **A13.1.1**
INVENTOR & DATE: no Spanish patent or registration found
REGISTRATION #:
CIRCA: 1930?
FREQUENCY:
MANUFACTURER: Perez-Quintanilla
MATERIAL: brass, cast iron and wood
FINISH: brass
COMMENTS: The ALFREDO mechanism is a rack and pinion driven worm-nut.

NAME: **ALFREDO P.** (marked)
TRADEMARK: bottle, A
OTHER MARKS: GIJON, all components hand stamped 573
NOTICE:
I.D. #: **A13.2.1**
INVENTOR & DATE: no Spanish patent or registration found
REGISTRATION #:
CIRCA: 1960?
FREQUENCY:
MANUFACTURER: Perez-Quintanilla
MATERIAL: brass, cast iron and wood
FINISH: brass
COMMENTS: In Spain these are known as cider corkscrews.

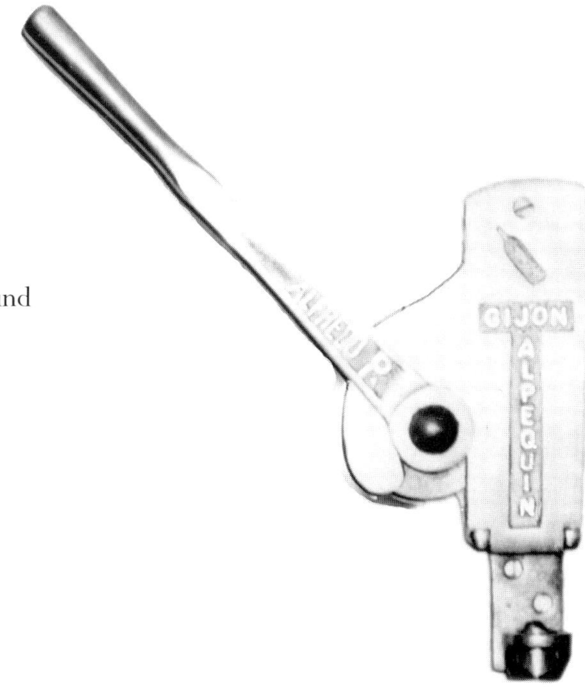

NAME:	**ALFREDO P.** (marked)
TRADEMARK:	not inspected
OTHER MARKS:	GIJON, ALPEQUIN
NOTICE:	
I.D. #:	**A13.3.1**
INVENTOR & DATE:	no Spanish patent or registration found
REGISTRATION #:	
CIRCA:	?
FREQUENCY:	
MANUFACTURER:	Perez-Quintanilla
MATERIAL:	brass, cast iron and wood
FINISH:	brass
COMMENTS:	These are massive, very well built corkscrews.

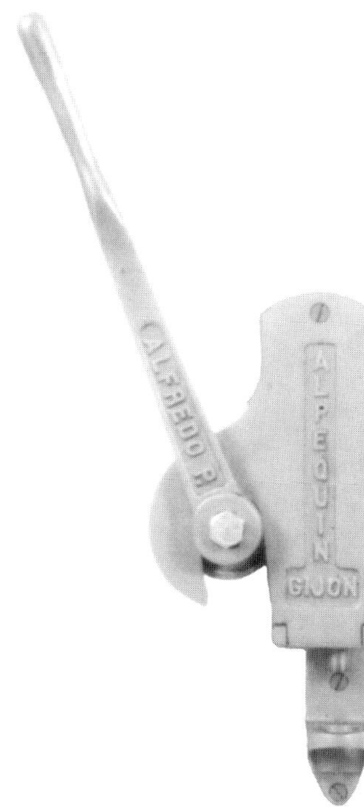

NAME:	**ALFREDO P.** (marked)
TRADEMARK:	not inspected
OTHER MARKS:	GIJON, ALPEQUIN
NOTICE:	
I.D. #:	**A13.3.2**
INVENTOR & DATE:	no Spanish patent or registration found
REGISTRATION #:	
CIRCA:	1980?
FREQUENCY:	
MANUFACTURER:	Perez-Quintanilla
MATERIAL:	brass, cast iron and wood
FINISH:	brass
COMMENTS:	–

NAME:	**ALFREDO P.** (unmarked)
TRADEMARK:	none
OTHER MARKS:	none
NOTICE:	clamp mount
I.D. #:	**A13.4.1**
INVENTOR & DATE:	no Spanish patent or registration found
REGISTRATION #:	
CIRCA:	1999
FREQUENCY:	
MANUFACTURER:	Perez-Quintanilla ?
MATERIAL:	brass, cast iron and wood
FINISH:	brass
COMMENTS:	Advertised and sold in Mexico, it was presumably made in Spain.

NAME:	**ALP** (marked)
TRADEMARK:	none
OTHER MARKS:	none
NOTICE:	
I.D. #:	**A14.1.1**
INVENTOR & DATE:	possibly J. Funt Dec 12, 1903
REGISTRATION #:	SGDG 335,730
CIRCA:	1920 - 1950?
FREQUENCY:	
MANUFACTURER:	Markt & Co.?
MATERIAL:	cast iron
FINISH:	black paint
COMMENTS:	The patent document shows an exact copy of the YANKEE No 2, not this version with the spring assist. This corkscrew may have been manufactured for Markt & Co. by a third party.

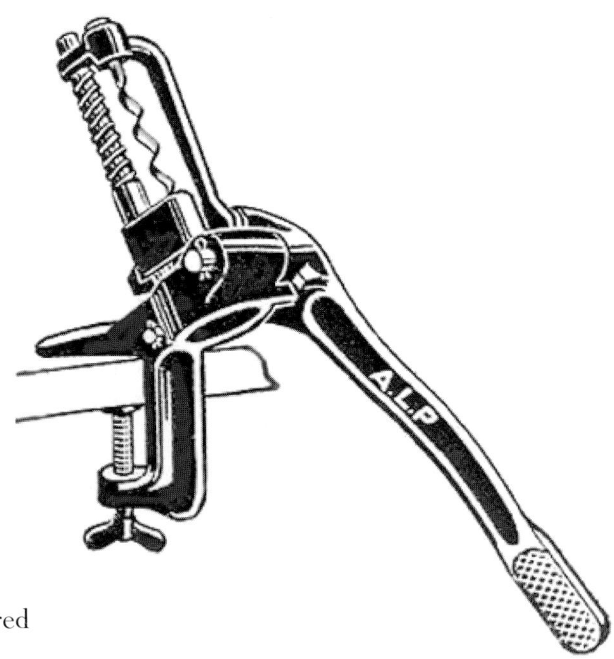

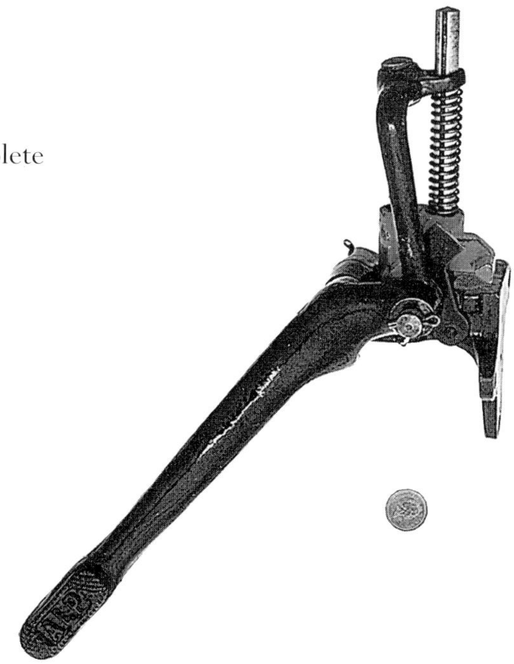

NAME:	**ALP** (marked)
TRADEMARK:	none
OTHER MARKS:	ICI, GRA??? FR
NOTICE:	part of the decal is missing, incomplete markings
I.D. #:	**A14.2.1**
INVENTOR & DATE:	possibly J. Funt Dec 12, 1903
REGISTRATION #:	SGDG 335,730
CIRCA:	1920 - 1950?
FREQUENCY:	
MANUFACTURER:	Markt & Co.?
MATERIAL:	cast iron
FINISH:	black and red paint
COMMENTS:	This is a French version of the YANKEE No 1. This corkscrew may have been manufactured for Markt & Co. by a third party.

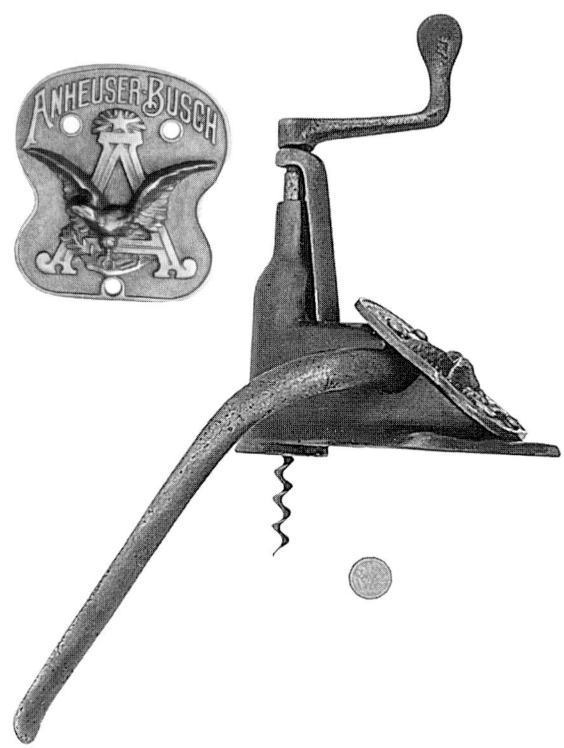

NAME:	**ANHEUSER BUSCH** (marked)
TRADEMARK:	none
OTHER MARKS:	none
NOTICE:	advertising plate out of scale
I.D. #:	**A15.1.1**
INVENTOR & DATE:	E. Walker May 19, 1891
REGISTRATION #:	P 452,625
CIRCA:	1890 -1908?
FREQUENCY:	
MANUFACTURER:	Erie Specialty Mfg. Co.
MATERIAL:	cast iron
FINISH:	nickel
COMMENTS:	This is a private label version of THE WALKER.

NAME:	**ARCADE, THE** (marked)
TRADEMARK:	none
OTHER MARKS:	PAT. AP'D, FOR
NOTICE:	early thumb piece, later found on the SAFETY, without the hole
I.D. #:	**A16.1.1**
INVENTOR & DATE:	M. Redlinger, application filed Dec 23, 1893
REGISTRATION #:	P 589,574
CIRCA:	1893 - 1897
FREQUENCY:	
MANUFACTURER:	Arcade Manufacturing Co.
MATERIAL:	cast iron
FINISH:	nickel
COMMENTS:	This is the first version with a "spade" shaped frame clamp and pinned handle; the 1896 patent was for the frame design.

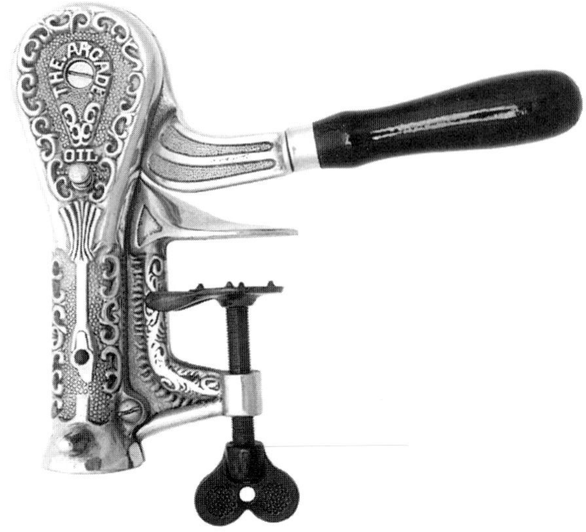

NAME:	**ARCADE, THE** (marked)
TRADEMARK:	none
OTHER MARKS:	PAT. AP'D, FOR
NOTICE:	thumb piece, nickel finish variant *A16.1.2*
I.D. #:	**A16.1.3**
INVENTOR & DATE:	M. Redlinger, application filed Dec 23, 1893
REGISTRATION #:	P 589,574
CIRCA:	1893 - 1897
FREQUENCY:	
MANUFACTURER:	Arcade Manufacturing Co.
MATERIAL:	cast iron
FINISH:	tuscan bronze
COMMENTS:	This slightly later version, still with spade shaped clamp bracket, has a bolted handle and the final thumb piece design. This version of the ARCADE became the SIMPLE in England.

NAME: **ARCADE, THE** (marked)
TRADEMARK: none
OTHER MARKS: PAT. AP'D, FOR
NOTICE: top mount, tuscan bronze finish variant *A16.2.2*
I.D. #: **A16.2.1**
INVENTOR & DATE: M. Redlinger, application filed Dec 23, 1893
REGISTRATION #: P 589,574
CIRCA: 1893 - 1897
FREQUENCY:
MANUFACTURER: Arcade Manufacturing Co.
MATERIAL: cast iron
FINISH: nickel
COMMENTS: This Arcade advertisement dates to 1897.

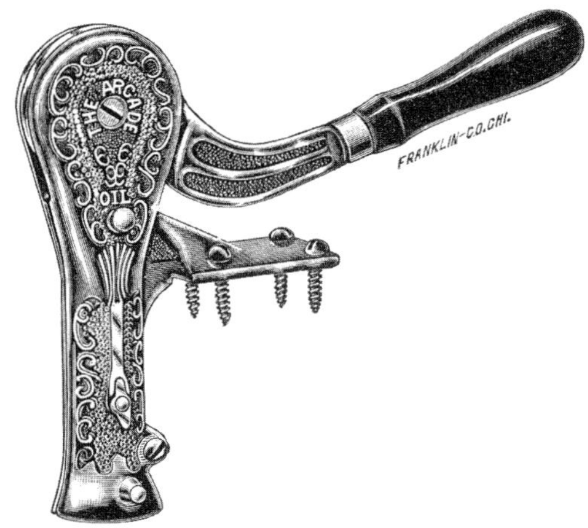

Each puller packed in a substantial wooden box. One dozen in a case.
No. 2, Nickel Plated..................$3 00
No. 4, Tuscan Bronze.................. 2 50

NAME: **ARCADE, THE** (marked)
TRADEMARK: none
OTHER MARKS: PAT. AP'D, FOR
NOTICE: thumb piece, bottle clasp handles, pinned handle
I.D. #: **A16.3.1**
INVENTOR & DATE: M. Redlinger, application filed Dec 23, 1893
REGISTRATION #: P 589,574
CIRCA: 1893 - 1897
FREQUENCY:
MANUFACTURER: Arcade Manufacturing Co.
MATERIAL: cast iron
FINISH: nickel
COMMENTS: The earliest bottle clasp version with square clamp bracket, pinned handle, bottle clasp handle and the original thumb piece; this version became the SAFETY in England.

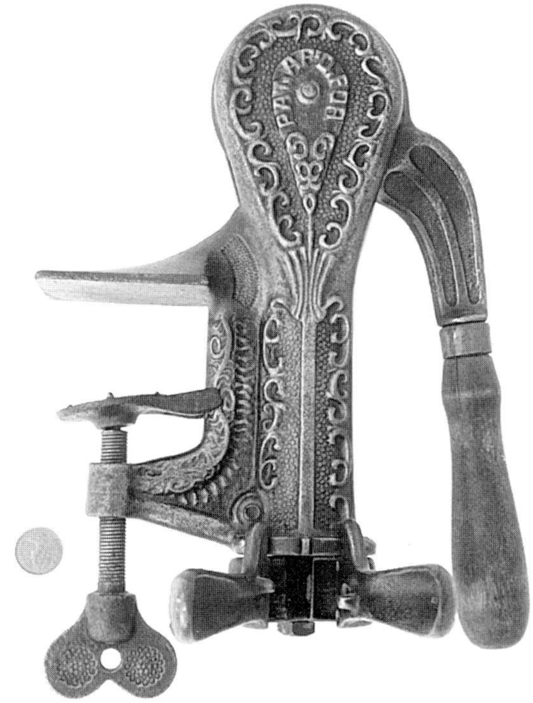

NAME:	**ARCADE, THE** (marked)
TRADEMARK:	none
OTHER MARKS:	PAT. AP'D, FOR
NOTICE:	thumb piece, bottle clasp handles, pinned handle
I.D. #:	**A16.3.2**
INVENTOR & DATE:	M. Redlinger, application filed Dec 23, 1893
REGISTRATION #:	P 589,574
CIRCA:	1893 - 1897
FREQUENCY:	
MANUFACTURER:	Arcade Manufacturing Co.
MATERIAL:	cast iron
FINISH:	tuscan bronze
COMMENTS:	This slightly later version has the final Arcade thumb piece design.

NAME:	**AUTOMATIQUE, L'** (marked)
TRADEMARK:	anchor
OTHER MARKS:	BRE-TE, S.G.D.G.
NOTICE:	
I.D. #:	**A17.1.1**
INVENTOR & DATE:	no French patent found
REGISTRATION #:	SGDG
CIRCA:	1930? -1935?
FREQUENCY:	
MANUFACTURER:	Camion Frères
MATERIAL:	cast iron
FINISH:	white paint with gold letters
COMMENTS:	This entirely gear driven mechanism has no stem or worm nut; part of the mechanism is in the base of the wall mount. It is assumed to be the earlier version.

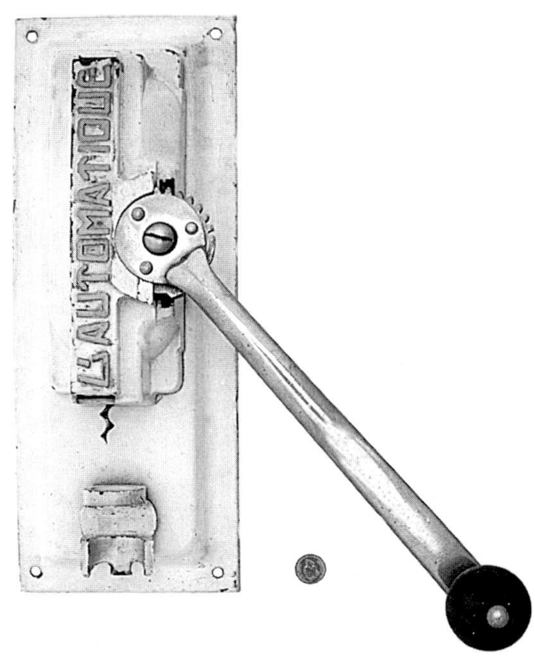

NAME:	**AUTOMATIQUE, L'** (marked)
TRADEMARK:	anchor
OTHER MARKS:	BRE-TE, S.G.D.G.
NOTICE:	cast iron bottle lip rest missing
I.D. #:	**A17.2.1**
INVENTOR & DATE:	no French patent found
REGISTRATION #:	SGDG
CIRCA:	1930? -1935?
FREQUENCY:	[corkscrew icon ×1]
MANUFACTURER:	Camion Frères
MATERIAL:	cast iron
FINISH:	blue paint
COMMENTS:	This is assumed to be a later version, as the complete mechanism is in the single housing.

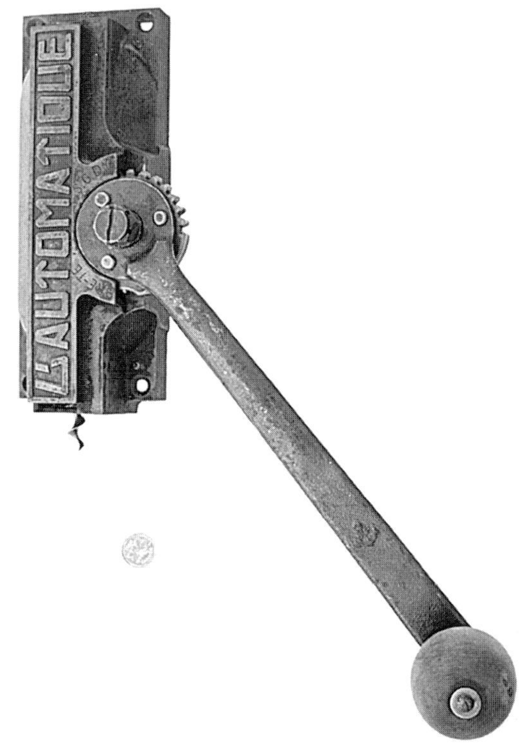

NAME:	**BACCHUS** (marked)
TRADEMARK:	none
OTHER MARKS:	PAT PEND, GC
NOTICE:	material, handle
I.D. #:	**B01.1.1**
INVENTOR & DATE:	
REGISTRATION #:	
CIRCA:	1940 - 1960?
FREQUENCY:	[corkscrew icon ×2]
MANUFACTURER:	unknown
MATERIAL:	bronze
FINISH:	high lighted bronze
COMMENTS:	This is a very well made bronze version of the CHAMPION.

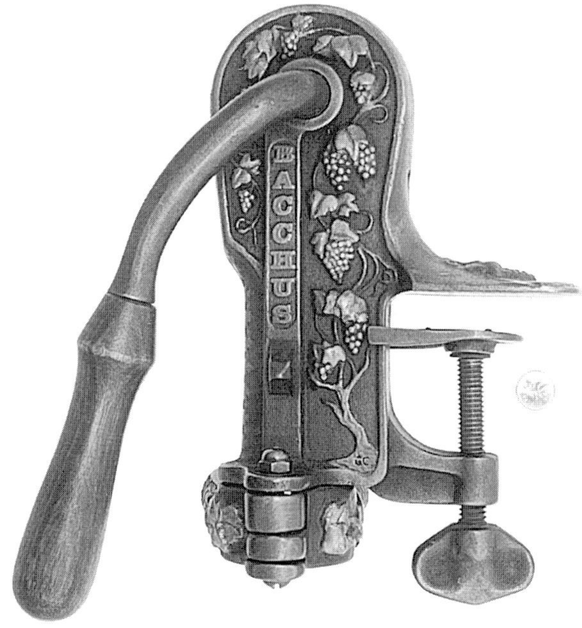

NAME:	**BACCHUS** (marked)
TRADEMARK:	none
OTHER MARKS:	PAT PEND, GC
NOTICE:	material, handle
I.D. #:	**B01.1.2**
INVENTOR & DATE:	
REGISTRATION #:	
CIRCA:	1940 - 1960?
FREQUENCY:	
MANUFACTURER:	unknown
MATERIAL:	brass
FINISH:	brass
COMMENTS:	This is a less elegant and assumed later version of the BACCHUS.

NAME:	**BALLANTINE'S ALES & BEERS** (marked)
TRADEMARK:	none
OTHER MARKS:	none
NOTICE:	
I.D. #:	**B02.1.1**
INVENTOR & DATE:	R. Gilchrist Jun 25, 1907
REGISTRATION #:	P 857,992
CIRCA:	1901? - ?
FREQUENCY:	
MANUFACTURER:	Arcade Manufacturing Co.
MATERIAL:	cast iron
FINISH:	nickel
COMMENTS:	This is a private label YANKEE No 1.

NAME: **BARRETT** (marked)

TRADEMARK: none

OTHER MARKS: V. & T. CO. MEADVILLE PA, PAT. JULY 10, 1888

NOTICE: unmarked version *B99.1.2*

I.D. #: **B12.1.1**

INVENTOR & DATE: Barrett Sep 04, 1888

REGISTRATION #: P 388,945

CIRCA: 1888?

FREQUENCY:

MANUFACTURER: V. & T. Co

MATERIAL: cast iron

FINISH: none visible

COMMENTS: This marked patent date is for Barrett's first worm-nut patent, so possibly he manufactured this corkscrew during the patent pending period.

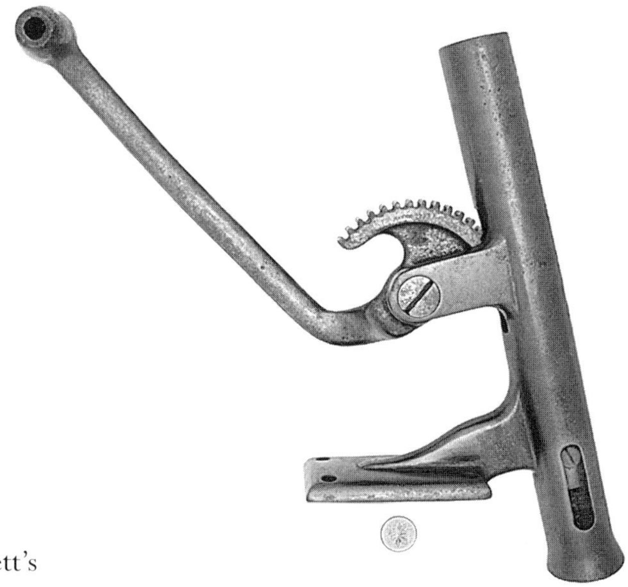

NAME: **BEAUMONT** (unmarked)

TRADEMARK: none

OTHER MARKS: none

NOTICE: thumb piece, a great art nouveau case design

I.D. #: **B03.1.1**

INVENTOR & DATE: M. Redlinger Sep 24, 1894

REGISTRATION #: P 546,747

CIRCA: 1895 - 1899?

FREQUENCY:

MANUFACTURER: Arcade Manufacturing Co.

MATERIAL: cast iron

FINISH: nickel

COMMENTS: This 1899 advertising shows the version with the thumb piece as shown in the patent; this bottle clasp was a dangerous tool, which could explain their rarity.

No. 101–"Beaumont," nickel plated, with bottle clasp attachment, stands about 5 in. above counter, screw clamp, - - - each $4.50

Press the bottle against back of puller's mouth, which closes and holds it firmly; pull the lever which draws cork, and remove bottle by pulling it towards you. To recork, place bottle in same position and reverse movement of lever.

ONE IN A BOX.

NAME: **BEAUMONT** (unmarked)

TRADEMARK: none

OTHER MARKS: none

NOTICE: thumb piece, close to the final Arcade thumb piece design

I.D. #: **B03.1.2**

INVENTOR & DATE: M. Redlinger Sep 24, 1895

REGISTRATION #: P 546,747

CIRCA: 1895 - 1899?

FREQUENCY:

MANUFACTURER: Arcade Manufacturing Co.

MATERIAL: cast iron

FINISH: nickel

COMMENTS: The BEAUMONT has a very strong automatic bottle clasp, capable of compressing your thumb into the shape of the bottle neck.

NAME: **BISON-DONAR** (not inspected)

TRADEMARK: not inspected

OTHER MARKS: not inspected

NOTICE: clamp mount, top mount version *B04.2.1*

I.D. #: **B04.1.1**

INVENTOR & DATE: no German patent or registration found

REGISTRATION #:

CIRCA: 1932 - 1940?

FREQUENCY: unknown

MANUFACTURER: Helmut Gebel

MATERIAL: cast iron

FINISH: nickel

COMMENTS: This 1936 advertisement, shows a "hand & star" trademark on the frame; presumably Helmut Gebel saved a little time and money by using the British artwork. No BISON-DONAR marked with that name has been found, leading to the belief that they were never marked.

NAME:	**BISON-HEBE** (not inspected)
TRADEMARK:	not inspected
OTHER MARKS:	not inspected
NOTICE:	silver bronze finish variant *B05.1.2*
I.D. #:	**B05.1.1**
INVENTOR & DATE:	E. Walker Aug 04,1896
REGISTRATION #:	DRP 90732
CIRCA:	1896 - 1940
FREQUENCY:	
MANUFACTURER:	Helmut Gebel or Erie Specialty Co.?
MATERIAL:	cast iron
FINISH:	nickel
COMMENTS:	This 1936 advertising shows a dual mount.

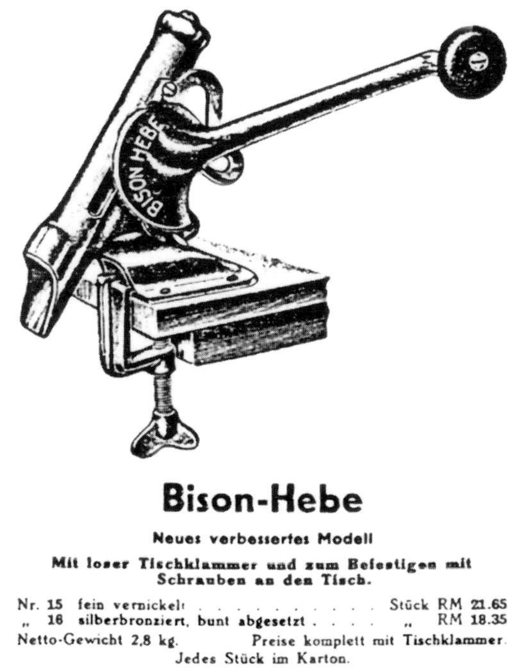

NAME:	**BISON No 5** (marked)
TRADEMARK:	none
OTHER MARKS:	BISON
NOTICE:	nickel plated finish variant *B12.1.1.*
I.D. #:	**B12.1.2**
INVENTOR & DATE:	R. Gilchrist Jun 14, 1904
REGISTRATION #:	DRP 162,930
CIRCA:	1908? - 1913?
FREQUENCY:	
MANUFACTURER:	Arcade Manufacturing Co.
MATERIAL:	cast iron
FINISH:	dark red paint
COMMENTS:	USA screw threads would indicate a private label HERO NO5 for Helmut Gebel; there are no improvements from the HERO NO5 mechanism.

NAME: **BISON No 6** (marked)
TRADEMARK: none
OTHER MARKS: BISON
NOTICE: nickel plated finish variant *B06.1.1*.
I.D. #: **B06.1.2**
INVENTOR & DATE: R. Gilchrist Jun 14, 1904
REGISTRATION #: DRP 162,930
CIRCA: 1908? - 1913?
FREQUENCY:
MANUFACTURER: Arcade Manufacturing Co.
MATERIAL: cast iron
FINISH: black paint with gold letters
COMMENTS: USA screw threads would indicate a private label HERO NO5 for Helmut Gebel. The rocker arm screw improvement has been implemented; see *MECHANISMS* for additional information.

NAME: **BISON-UNIQUE** (marked)
TRADEMARK: none
OTHER MARKS: HGB on all internal components
NOTICE:
I.D. #: **B07.1.1**
INVENTOR & DATE: E. Walker Aug 04,1896
REGISTRATION #: DRP 90732
CIRCA: 1913 - 1940?
FREQUENCY:
MANUFACTURER: Helmut Gebel
MATERIAL: cast iron
FINISH: nickel
COMMENTS: HGB manufactured this version of the QUICK & EASY.

NAME: **BISON-UNIQUE** (marked)
TRADEMARK: none
OTHER MARKS: HGB on all internal components
NOTICE:
I.D. #: **B07.1.2**
INVENTOR & DATE: E. Walker Aug 04,1896
REGISTRATION #: DRP 90732
CIRCA: 1913 - 1940?
FREQUENCY:
MANUFACTURER: Helmut Gebel
MATERIAL: cast iron
FINISH: silver bronze
COMMENTS: This corkscrew has a nickel finish, but silver bronze was available.

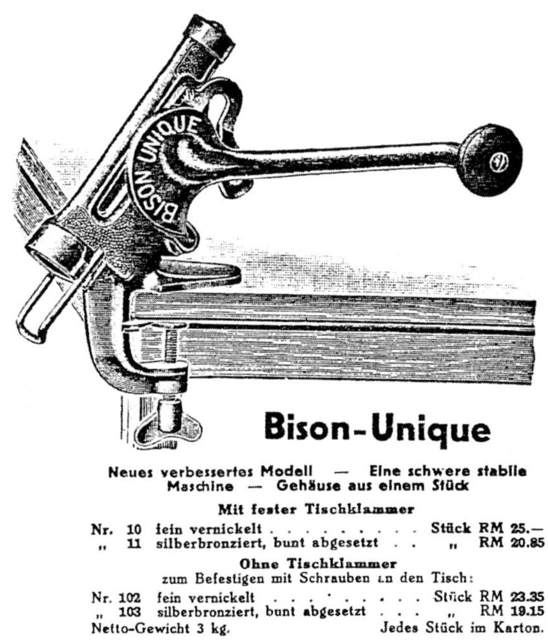

NAME: **BISON-UNIQUE** (marked)
TRADEMARK: none
OTHER MARKS: not inspected
NOTICE: silver bronze finish variant *B07.2.2*
I.D. #: **B07.2.1**
INVENTOR & DATE: E. Walker Aug 04,1896
REGISTRATION #: DRP 90732
CIRCA: 1913 - 1940?
FREQUENCY:
MANUFACTURER: Helmut Gebel
MATERIAL: cast iron
FINISH: nickel
COMMENTS: A dual mount version of the BISON-HEBE was manufactured by HGB. This 1936 advertisement does not show this version, but lists it in the advertising copy.

NAME:	**BL** (marked)
TRADEMARK:	BL
OTHER MARKS:	none
NOTICE:	handle, spring fixing
I.D. #:	**B08.1.1**
INVENTOR & DATE:	no French patent found
REGISTRATION #:	
CIRCA:	1890 - 1925?
FREQUENCY:	
MANUFACTURER:	Barraud & Lerenard
MATERIAL:	cast iron
FINISH:	not inspected
COMMENTS:	As found in this 1925 advertising, this early version had a bolt mounted crank handle and the spring end held to the operating lever by a screw.

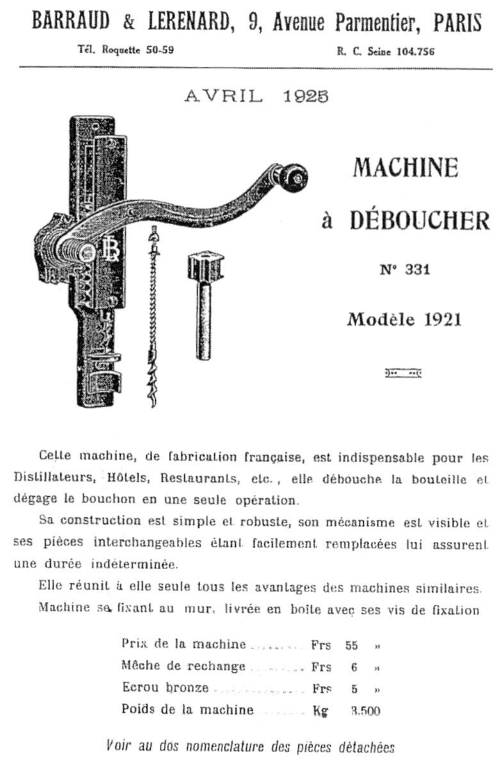

BARRAUD & LERENARD, 9, Avenue Parmentier, PARIS

Tél. Roquette 50-59 R. C. Seine 104.756

AVRIL 1925

MACHINE

à DÉBOUCHER

N° 331

Modèle 1921

Cette machine, de fabrication française, est indispensable pour les Distillateurs, Hôtels, Restaurants, etc., elle débouche la bouteille et dégage le bouchon en une seule opération.

Sa construction est simple et robuste, son mécanisme est visible et ses pièces interchangeables étant facilement remplacées lui assurent une durée indéterminée.

Elle réunit à elle seule tous les avantages des machines similaires.

Machine se fixant au mur, livrée en boite avec ses vis de fixation

Prix de la machine	Frs	55 »
Mèche de rechange	Frs	6 »
Ecrou bronze	Frs	5 »
Poids de la machine	Kg	3.500

Voir au dos nomenclature des pièces détachées

NAME:	**BL** (marked)
TRADEMARK:	BL
OTHER MARKS:	MARQUE DEPOSEE
NOTICE:	trade mark
I.D. #:	**B08.1.2**
INVENTOR & DATE:	no French patent found
REGISTRATION #:	
CIRCA:	1920 - 1930?
FREQUENCY:	
MANUFACTURER:	Barraud & Lerenard
MATERIAL:	cast iron
FINISH:	blue/gray paint
COMMENTS:	This example has a pressed on crank handle and a cast loop to hold the end of the spring.

NAME: **BL** (marked)
TRADEMARK: BL
OTHER MARKS: none
NOTICE: no MARQUE DEPOSEE mark
I.D. #: **B08.1.3**
INVENTOR & DATE: no French patent found
REGISTRATION #:
CIRCA: 1920 - 1930?
FREQUENCY:
MANUFACTURER: Barraud & Lerenard
MATERIAL: cast iron
FINISH: blue/gray paint
COMMENTS: This example has a pressed on crank handle and a cast loop to hold the end of the spring.

NAME: **BL** (marked)
TRADEMARK: BL
OTHER MARKS: MARQUE DEPOSEE
NOTICE: trade marked version
I.D. #: **B08.2.1**
INVENTOR & DATE: no French patent found
REGISTRATION #:
CIRCA: 1930? - 1940?
FREQUENCY:
MANUFACTURER: Barraud & Lerenard
MATERIAL: cast iron
FINISH: white paint, nickel cover
COMMENTS: This is a later, lower cost version of the BL.

NAME:	**BL** (unmarked)
TRADEMARK:	none
OTHER MARKS:	none
NOTICE:	thumb piece
I.D. #:	**B08.3.1**
INVENTOR & DATE:	no patent or registration found
REGISTRATION #:	
CIRCA:	1900? - 1940?
FREQUENCY:	
MANUFACTURER:	unknown
MATERIAL:	cast iron
FINISH:	none visible
COMMENTS:	This is a clamp mount version of the BL, possibly an Italian adaptation as the clamp mount frame is massive and the thumb piece is a typical Italian style.

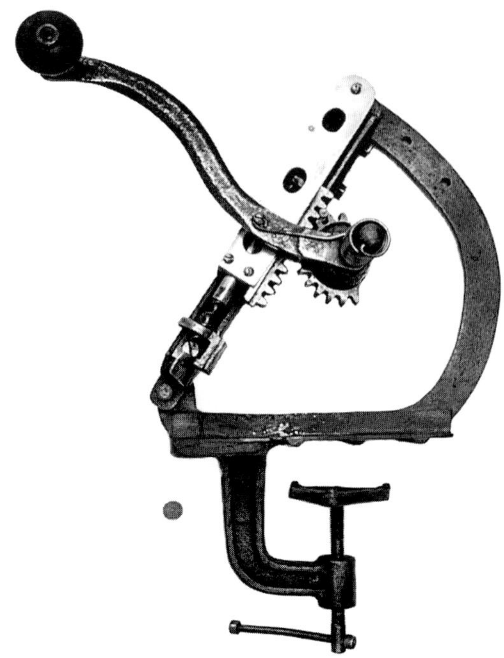

NAME:	**BLITZ** (not inspected)
TRADEMARK:	not inspected
OTHER MARKS:	not inspected
NOTICE:	clamp mount version
I.D. #:	**B09.1.1**
INVENTOR & DATE:	no German patent or registration found
REGISTRATION #:	
CIRCA:	1912? - 1930?
FREQUENCY:	
MANUFACTURER:	Arcade Manufacturing Co. ?
MATERIAL:	cast iron
FINISH:	not inspected
COMMENTS:	It is not known whether this is a private label YANKEE No 1 from Gilchrist, or a German copy.

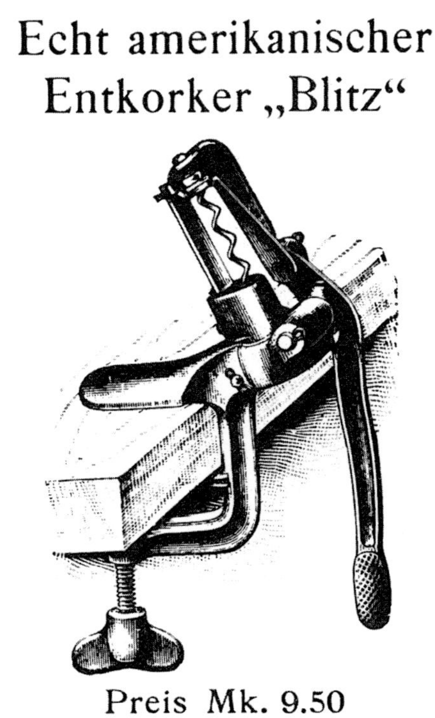

NAME:	**BLITZ** (not inspected)
TRADEMARK:	not inspected
OTHER MARKS:	not inspected
NOTICE:	wall mount version
I.D. #:	**B09.2.1**
INVENTOR & DATE:	no German patent or registration found
REGISTRATION #:	
CIRCA:	1912? - 1930?
FREQUENCY:	
MANUFACTURER:	Arcade Manufacturing Co. ?
MATERIAL:	cast iron
FINISH:	not inspected
COMMENTS:	It is not known whether this is a private label YANKEE No 2 from Gilchrist, or a German copy.

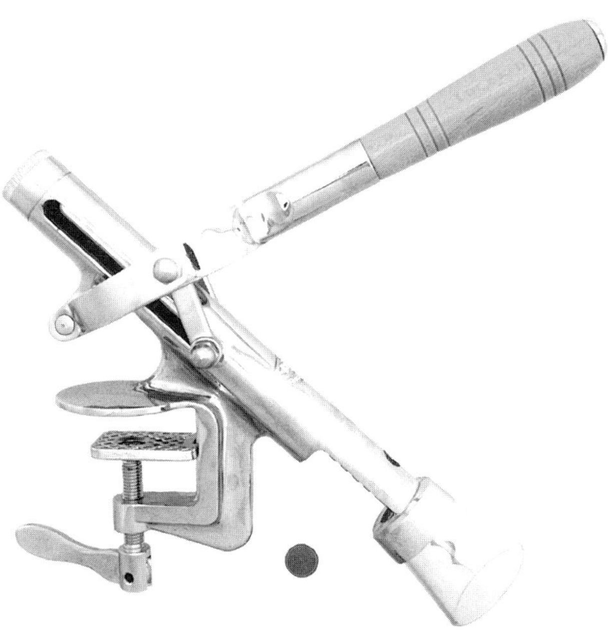

NAME:	**BOJ** (marked)
TRADEMARK:	none
OTHER MARKS:	EIBAR - ESPANA
NOTICE:	gold colored finish variant *B10.1.2*, wall mount versions, silver colored variant *B10.2.1*, gold colored variant *B10.2.2*.
I.D. #:	**B10.1.1**
INVENTOR & DATE:	no Spanish patent or registration found
REGISTRATION #:	
CIRCA:	1990? - ?
FREQUENCY:	
MANUFACTURER:	B. Olaneta Juaristi, S. A.
MATERIAL:	zinc ?
FINISH:	silver colored.
COMMENTS:	This is a modern version of the DON.

NAME: **BORDEAUX** (not marked)
TRADEMARK: none
OTHER MARKS: none
NOTICE:
I.D. #: **B11.1.1**
INVENTOR & DATE: no French patent or registration found
REGISTRATION #:
CIRCA: 1890? - 1910?
FREQUENCY:
MANUFACTURER: Barraud & Lerenard ?
MATERIAL: cast iron
FINISH: paint
COMMENTS: This 1898 advertising shows an early B&L corkscrew on a wooden stand. An example in the wine museum in Bordeaux was not marked.

NAME: **BRODERNE HERRMANN** (marked)
TRADEMARK: EJAB
OTHER MARKS: M26, A-B STOCKHOLM
NOTICE: cast bottle neck rest,
I.D. #: **B12.1.1**
INVENTOR & DATE: no Swedish patent or registration found
REGISTRATION #:
CIRCA: 1900? - 1940?
FREQUENCY:
MANUFACTURER: Eskilstuna Järnmanufaktur Aktiebolag
MATERIAL: cast iron
FINISH: brown lacquer and nickel
COMMENTS: A Swedish version of the ACME manufactured by EJAB for Broderne Herrmann, this corkscrew could also be purchased with a separate custom clamp mount. M26 is also found on the neck rest version of the Swedish QUICK & EASY.

NAME: **BRODERNE HERRMANN** (unmarked)

TRADEMARK: EJAB

OTHER MARKS: none

NOTICE: bottle lip only

I.D. #: **B12.2.1**

INVENTOR & DATE: no Swedish patent or registration found

REGISTRATION #:

CIRCA: 1900? - 1940?

FREQUENCY:

MANUFACTURER: Eskilstuna Järnmanufaktur Aktiebolag

MATERIAL: cast iron

FINISH: brown lacquer and nickel

COMMENTS: This ia a Swedish version of the ACME manufactured by EJAB for Broderne Herrmann; the mechanism in both versions contains some very nice, tiny ball bearings.

NAME: **BULL-DOG** (not inspected)

No. 91.

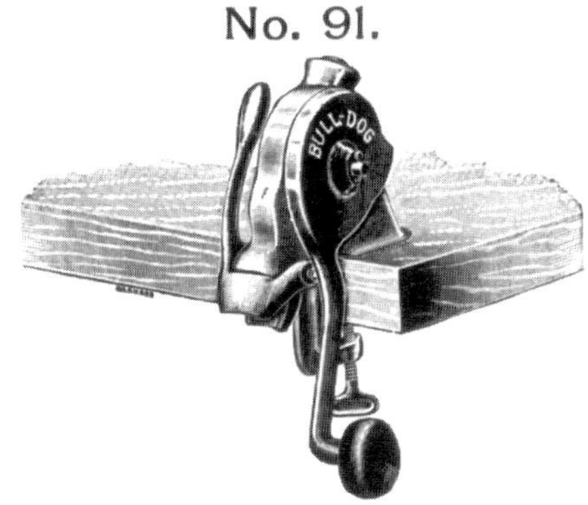

Patented in U. S. A. Feb. 27, 1894, July 23, 1895 and April 7, 1896.
Foreign Patents Granted and Patents Pending.

WALKER'S

"BULL DOG"

Cork Puller.

With Bottle Holder.

IMPROVED FOR 1901.

TRADEMARK: not inspected

OTHER MARKS: not inspected

NOTICE: bottle clasp, version No. 90 without the bottle clasp *B13.2.1*

I.D. #: **B13.1.1**

INVENTOR & DATE: E. Walker Jun 11, 1901

REGISTRATION #: P 676,013

CIRCA: 1900 - 1901?

FREQUENCY:

MANUFACTURER: Erie Specialty Co.

MATERIAL: cast iron

FINISH: nickel

COMMENTS: This was found in a 1901 Walker catalog.

NAME:	**CEDON** (not inspected)
TRADEMARK:	not inspected
OTHER MARKS:	not inspected
NOTICE:	top mount, tube cap
I.D. #:	**C01.1.1**
INVENTOR & DATE:	no German patent or registration found
REGISTRATION #:	
CIRCA:	1910? - 1930?
FREQUENCY:	
MANUFACTURER:	Frings & Co. o. H. G.
MATERIAL:	cast iron
FINISH:	not inspected
COMMENTS:	This 1913 advertising shows a German version of the DON with a flat end cap and no finial. It is curious that so few have ever been found.

Entkorkmaschine Cedon

	Gewicht	
	netto	brutto
1 St.	2,6 kg	4 kg
6 St.	16 kg	22 kg

NAME:	**CEDON** (marked)
TRADEMARK:	none
OTHER MARKS:	MADE IN W. GERMANY
NOTICE:	silver color finish variant *C01.2.1*
I.D. #:	**C01.2.2**
INVENTOR & DATE:	no German patent or registration found
REGISTRATION #:	
CIRCA:	1950? - 1990?
FREQUENCY:	
MANUFACTURER:	Frings & Co. o. H. G.
MATERIAL:	zinc ?
FINISH:	gold color
COMMENTS:	This is a modern version of the DON.

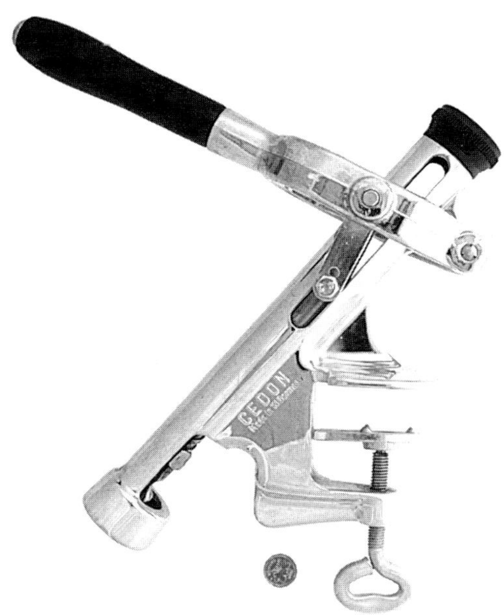

NAME:	"1893" **CHAMPION** (marked)
TRADEMARK:	none
OTHER MARKS:	none
NOTICE:	
I.D. #:	**C03.1.1**
INVENTOR & DATE:	no US patent or registration found
REGISTRATION #:	
CIRCA:	1890? - 1894?
FREQUENCY:	
MANUFACTURER:	American
MATERIAL:	cast iron
FINISH:	nickel
COMMENTS:	As there is in this 1893 advertisement, the plate marked CHAMPION is missing on the known example. This mechanism is a mounted version of the 1862 Russel mechanism. An "1893 CHAMPION" designation is used to differentiate it from all of the other CHAMPIONs.

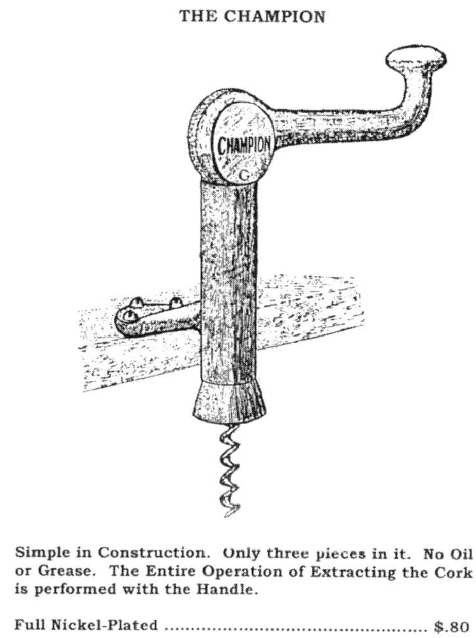

NAME:	**CHAMPION** (marked)
TRADEMARK:	none
OTHER MARKS:	PAT. PENDING
NOTICE:	early thumb piece, handle
I.D. #:	**C04.1.1**
INVENTOR & DATE:	PAT. PENDING
REGISTRATION #:	
CIRCA:	1896 - 1899
FREQUENCY:	
MANUFACTURER:	Arcade Manufacturing Co.
MATERIAL:	cast iron
FINISH:	nickel
COMMENTS:	This PAT PENDING CHAMPION has a very crude casting without the wire or string cutter.

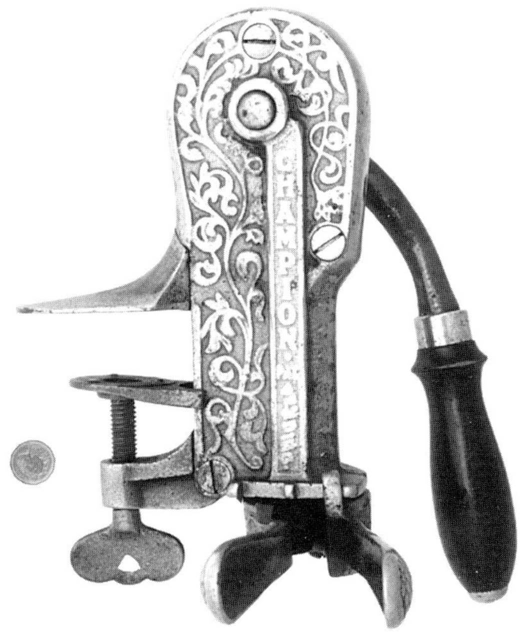

NAME: **CHAMPION** (marked)

TRADEMARK: none

OTHER MARKS: PAT. PENDING

NOTICE: early thumb piece, handle

I.D. #: **C04.1.2**

INVENTOR & DATE: PAT. PENDING

REGISTRATION #:

CIRCA: 1896 - 1899

FREQUENCY:

MANUFACTURER: Arcade Manufacturing Co.

MATERIAL: cast iron

FINISH: nickel

COMMENTS: This is another example of a very early PAT PENDING CHAMPION with no wire or string cutter and a very crude casting.

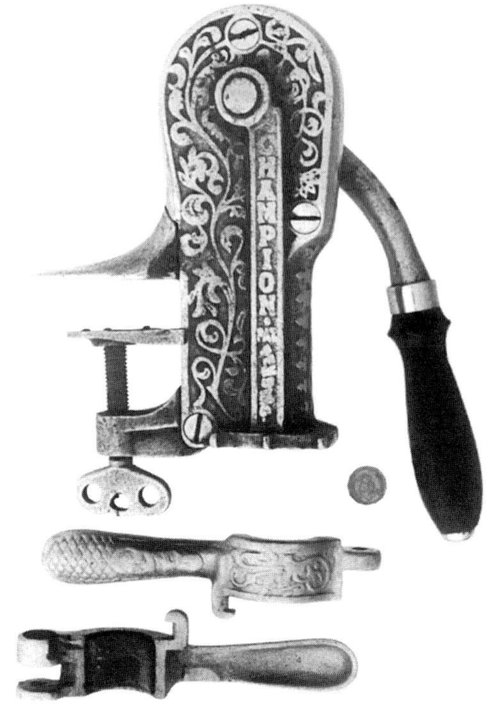

NAME: **CHAMPION** (marked)

TRADEMARK: none

OTHER MARKS: PAT. PENDING

NOTICE: early thumb piece, handle, tuscan bronze finish variant *C04.1.4*

I.D. #: **C04.1.3**

INVENTOR & DATE: PAT. PENDING

REGISTRATION #:

CIRCA: 1896 - 1899

FREQUENCY:

MANUFACTURER: Arcade Manufacturing Co.

MATERIAL: cast iron

FINISH: nickel

COMMENTS: As found in this 1897 advertising, this early CHAMPION has a wire or string cutter, the final handle shape and an early Arcade thumb piece.

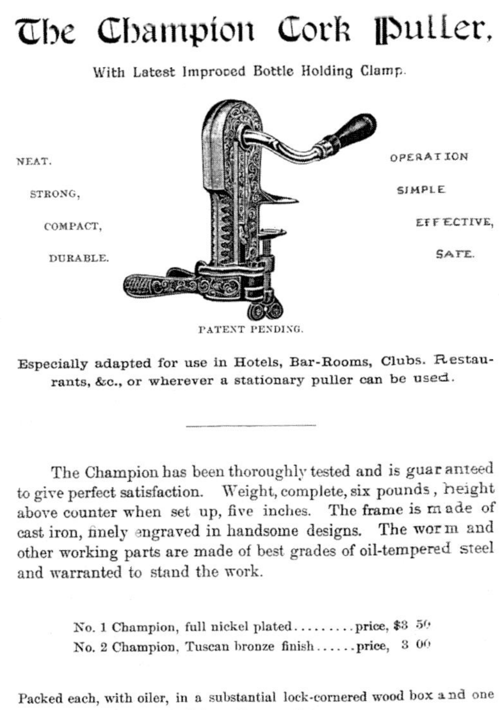

NAME: **CHAMPION** (marked)
TRADEMARK: none
OTHER MARKS: PAT. PENDING
NOTICE: thumb piece, handle
I.D. #: **C04.1.4**
INVENTOR & DATE: PAT. PENDING
REGISTRATION #:
CIRCA: 1896 - 1899
FREQUENCY:
MANUFACTURER: Arcade Manufacturing Co.
MATERIAL: cast iron
FINISH: nickel
COMMENTS: This is the patent pending CHAMPION with the final version of the thumb piece, wire cutter and handle.

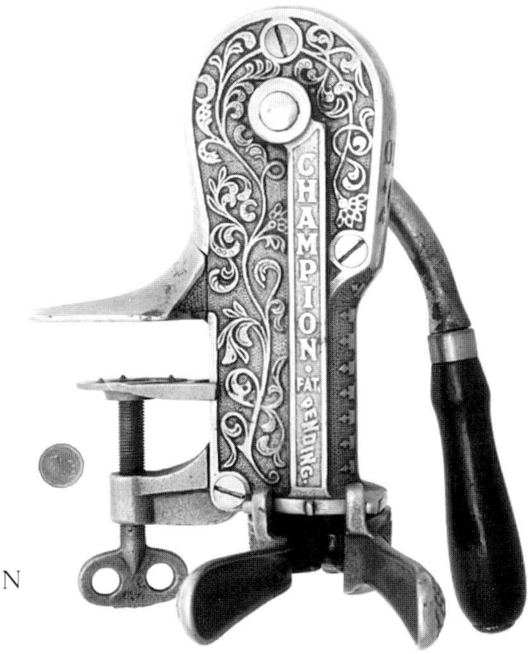

NAME: **CHAMPION** (marked)
TRADEMARK: none
OTHER MARKS: PAT SEPT 7 1897, DES. PAT JUNE 9 1896.
NOTICE: finish
I.D. #: **C04.2.1**
INVENTOR & DATE: M. Redlinger Jun 09,1896 and C. Morgan Mar 14, 1899
REGISTRATION #: DES 25,607 and P 620,949
CIRCA: 1896? - 1920?
FREQUENCY:
MANUFACTURER: Arcade Manufacturing Co.
MATERIAL: cast iron
FINISH: nickel
COMMENTS: This is the patented version of the CHAMPION. The design patent for the CHAMPION case was granted in 1896. The 1897 patent marked on the case was for the mechanism in the ARCADE.

NAME:	**CHAMPION** (marked)
TRADEMARK:	none
OTHER MARKS:	PAT SEPT 7 1897, DES. PAT JUNE 9 1896.
NOTICE:	it is very rare to find this finish intact
I.D. #:	**C04.2.2**
INVENTOR & DATE:	M. Redlinger Jun 09,1896 and C. Morgan Mar 14, 1899
REGISTRATION #:	DES 25,607 and P 620,949
CIRCA:	1896? - 1920?
FREQUENCY:	
MANUFACTURER:	Arcade Manufacturing Co.
MATERIAL:	cast iron
FINISH:	tuscan bronze
COMMENTS:	The actual Morgan 1899 patent for the CHAMPION mechanism was never marked on the case.

NAME:	**CHAMPION** (marked)
TRADEMARK:	none
OTHER MARKS:	REG US PAT OFF, ARCADE MFG. CO, MADE IN USA
NOTICE:	handle, decoration
I.D. #:	**C04.3.1**
INVENTOR & DATE:	M. Redlinger Jun 09,1896 and C. Morgan Mar 14, 1899
REGISTRATION #:	DES 25,607 and P 620,949
CIRCA:	1925? - 1935?
FREQUENCY:	
MANUFACTURER:	Arcade Manufacturing Co.
MATERIAL:	cast iron
FINISH:	nickel
COMMENTS:	This art deco style CHAMPION has a crank handle.

NAME: **CHAMPION** (marked)
TRADEMARK: none
OTHER MARKS: REG US PAT OFF, ARCADE MFG. CO, MADE IN USA
NOTICE: handle, decoration
I.D. #: **C04.3.2**
INVENTOR & DATE: M. Redlinger Jun 09,1896 and C. Morgan Mar 14, 1899
REGISTRATION #: DES 25,607 and P 620,949
CIRCA: 1925? - 1935?
FREQUENCY: 
MANUFACTURER: Arcade Manufacturing Co.
MATERIAL: cast iron
FINISH: chrome
COMMENTS: This is another art deco CHAMPION, with a standard Arcade handle.

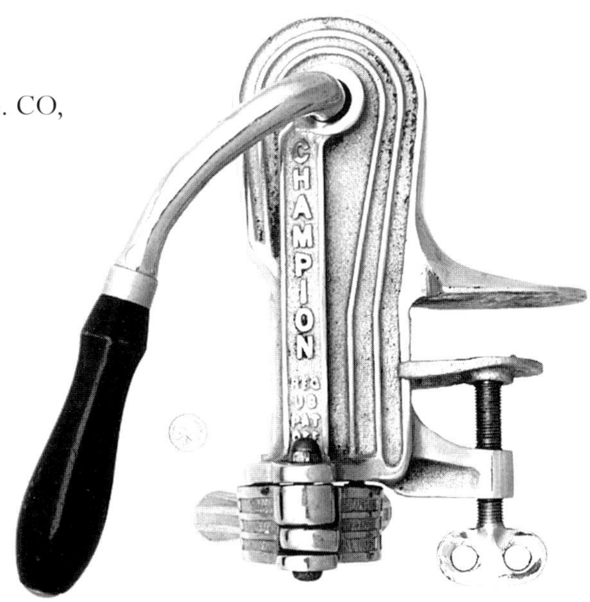

NAME: **CHAMPION** (marked)
TRADEMARK: none
OTHER MARKS: MADE IN USA
NOTICE:
I.D. #: **C04.4.1**
INVENTOR & DATE: M. Redlinger Jun 09,1896 and C. Morgan Mar 14, 1899
REGISTRATION #: DES 25,607 and P 620,949
CIRCA: 1910 - 1940?
FREQUENCY: 
MANUFACTURER: Arcade Manufacturing Co.
MATERIAL: cast iron
FINISH: nickel
COMMENTS: This is the made in USA version of the CHAMPION.

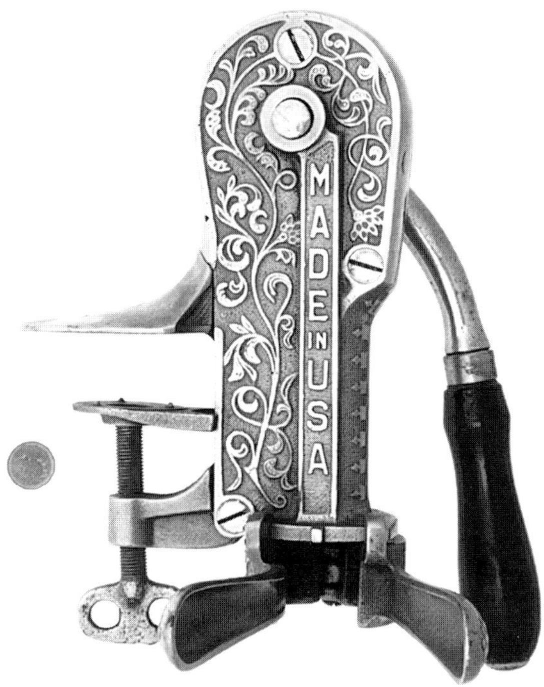

NAME: **CHAMPION** (marked)
TRADEMARK: none
OTHER MARKS: MADE IN USA
NOTICE: thumb piece
I.D. #: **C04.4.2**
INVENTOR & DATE: M. Redlinger Jun 09,1896 and C. Morgan Mar 14, 1899
REGISTRATION #: DES 25,607 and P 620,949
CIRCA: 1910 - 1940?
FREQUENCY:
MANUFACTURER: Arcade Manufacturing Co.
MATERIAL: cast iron
FINISH: nickel
COMMENTS: This is the same as **C04.4.1**, but with a thumb piece normally found on the PIX. Possibly it is a corkscrew made for Albert Pick, before the PIX frame was designed and patented.

NAME: **CHAMPION** (marked)
TRADEMARK: none
OTHER MARKS: PATENT PENDING, CENTENNIAL 1897 - 1997, ROGAR RICHMOND VA
NOTICE: nickel finish variant *C04.5.1*
I.D. #: **C04.5.2**
INVENTOR & DATE: PAT APL
REGISTRATION #:
CIRCA: 1997 - present
FREQUENCY:
MANUFACTURER: Asian for Rogar International Corp.
MATERIAL: not cast iron
FINISH: sterling silver
COMMENTS: This is the modern centennial version of the CHAMPION.

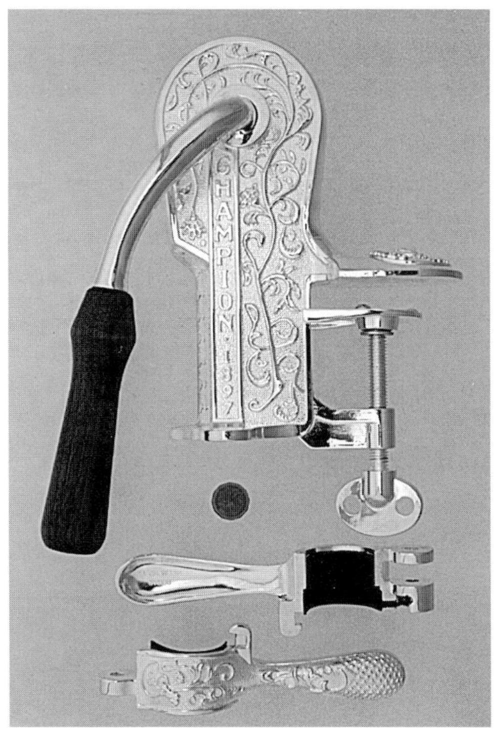

NAME: **CLIPPER, THE** (unmarked)

TRADEMARK: none

OTHER MARKS: none

NOTICE: Arcade thumbscrew and clamp plate, US screw threads, data from an existing example

I.D. #: **C05.1.1**

INVENTOR & DATE: no registration found

REGISTRATION #:

CIRCA: 1902? - ?

FREQUENCY:

MANUFACTURER: Arcade Manufacturing Co.

MATERIAL: cast iron

FINISH: none visible

COMMENTS: This advertisement dates from 1902; see *MECHANISMS* for additional information.

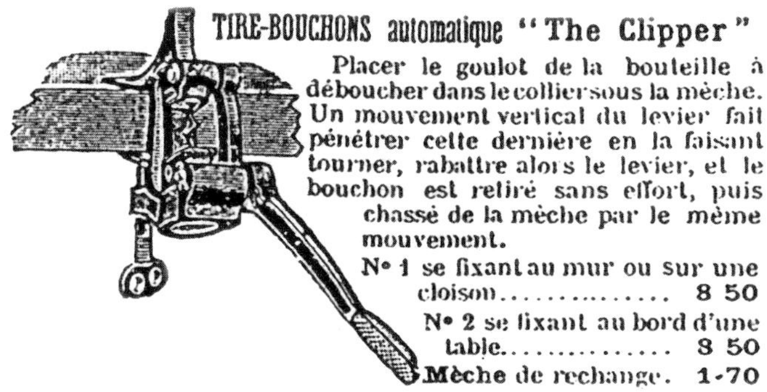

NAME: **CLIPPER, THE** (unmarked)

TRADEMARK: none

OTHER MARKS: none

NOTICE: wall mount

I.D. #: **C05.2.1**

INVENTOR & DATE: no registration found

REGISTRATION #:

CIRCA: 1902? - ?

FREQUENCY:

MANUFACTURER: Arcade Manufacturing Co.

MATERIAL: cast iron

FINISH: black paint

COMMENTS: An upside down "L" shaped wire on the left side catches the worm-nut; one could say that the wire "clips" the worm carrier and nut together.

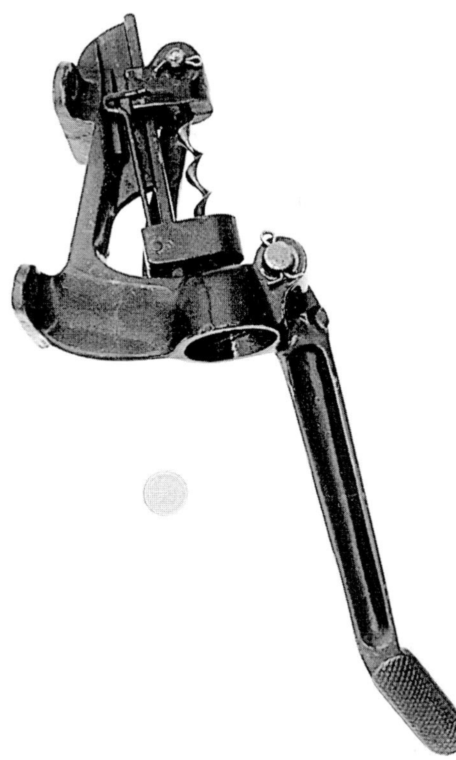

NAME:	**COLUMBIA** (not inspected)
TRADEMARK:	not inspected
OTHER MARKS:	not inspected
NOTICE:	three different finishes, coffee bronze finish variants *C09.1.2*, japanned finish variants *C09.1.3*
I.D. #:	**C09.1.1**
INVENTOR & DATE:	R. Gilchrist Jul 05, 1892
REGISTRATION #:	P 478545
CIRCA:	1891? - 1892?
FREQUENCY:	(corkscrew symbol)
MANUFACTURER:	Gilchrist Mfg. Co. or possibly The Guarranty Manufacturing Co.
MATERIAL:	cast iron
FINISH:	nickel
COMMENTS:	Gilchrist's third stem-nut patent with an optional wall or clamp mount.

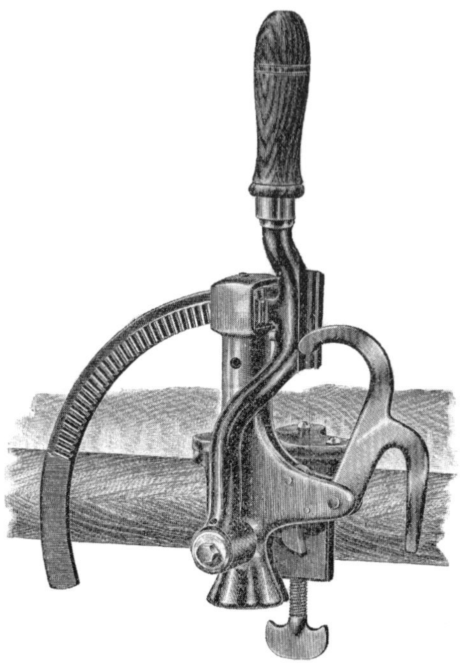

NAME:	**CROWN, THE** (not inspected)
TRADEMARK:	not inspected
OTHER MARKS:	not inspected
NOTICE:	
I.D. #:	**C06.1.1**
INVENTOR & DATE:	no British patent or registration found
REGISTRATION #:	
CIRCA:	1894? - 1898?
FREQUENCY:	(corkscrew symbol)
MANUFACTURER:	Arcade Manufacturing Co.
MATERIAL:	cast iron
FINISH:	nickel
COMMENTS:	This 1897 advertisement shows the English name for Gilchrist's MIDGET. It is doubtful that this corkscrew would have been manufactured in England or marked CROWN.

No. 558.—The Crown

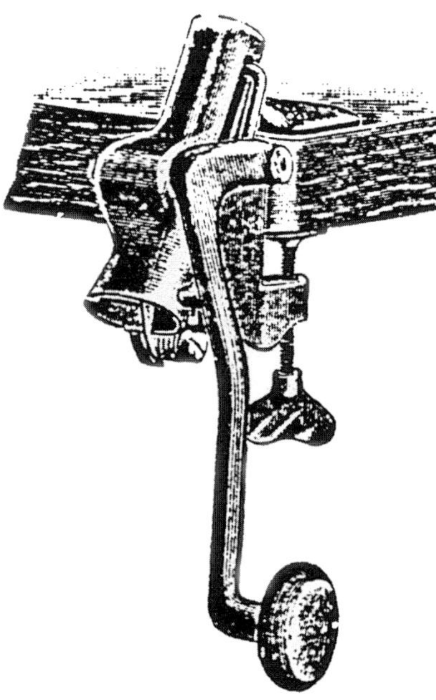

Nickel Plated, 12/6

NAME:	**CRYSTAL PALACE** (not inspected)
TRADEMARK:	not inspected
OTHER MARKS:	not inspected
NOTICE:	
I.D. #:	**C07.1.1**
INVENTOR & DATE:	H. Sanders Nov 04, 1865
REGISTRATION #:	LP 2,844
CIRCA:	1865? - 1895?
FREQUENCY:	(1 symbol)
MANUFACTURER:	British
MATERIAL:	cast iron
FINISH:	polished steel
COMMENTS:	An 1895 advertisement shows the first British automatic bar corkscrew. This was a very expensive machine, selling for many times the price of an ECLIPSE. This patent expired in 1872.

NAME:	**CYKLOP** (marked)
TRADEMARK:	not inspected
OTHER MARKS:	DRGM
NOTICE:	wire neck rest, Gilchrist style thumb piece, green paint variant *C08.1.2*
I.D. #:	**C08.1.1**
INVENTOR & DATE:	presumably G. Frings Mar 30, 1925
REGISTRATION #:	DRGM 926,839
CIRCA:	1925? -1940?
FREQUENCY:	(3 symbols)
MANUFACTURER:	FRINGS & CO. o. H. G.
MATERIAL:	cast iron
FINISH:	nickel
COMMENTS:	This advertisement shows the first version of this German manufactured corkscrew.

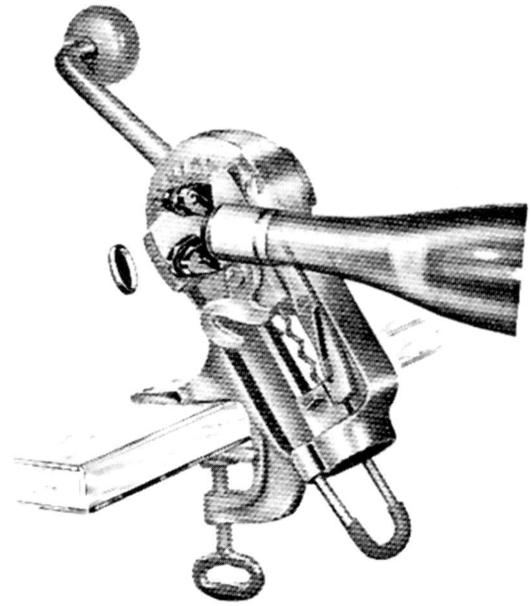

CYKLOP
mit Kapsel-Abschneider
with bottle cup cutter
avec coupoir de capsules à bouteilles

NAME:	**CYKLOP** (marked)
TRADEMARK:	not inspected
OTHER MARKS:	not inspected
NOTICE:	wire neck rest, German thumb piece, foil cutter, green paint variant *C08.2.2*
I.D. #:	**C08.2.1**
INVENTOR & DATE:	presumably G. Frings Mar 30, 1925
REGISTRATION #:	DRGM 926,839
CIRCA:	1925? -1940?
FREQUENCY:	
MANUFACTURER:	FRINGS & CO. o. H. G.
MATERIAL:	cast iron
FINISH:	nickel
COMMENTS:	This is the foil cutter version of the wire neck rest CYKLOP.

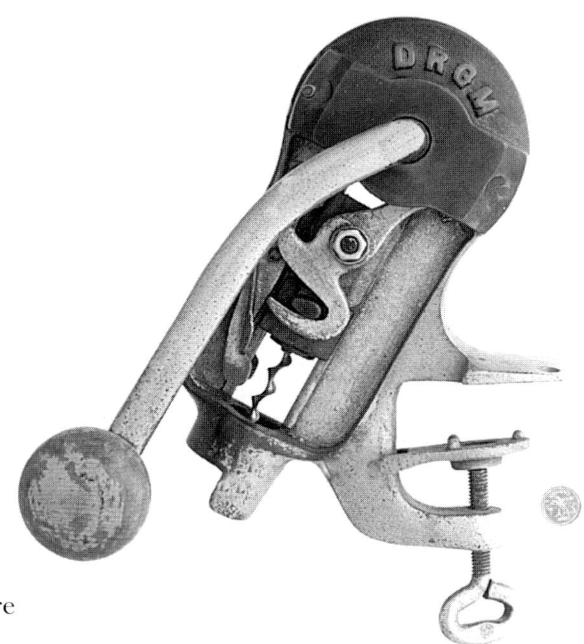

NAME:	**CYKLOP** (marked)
TRADEMARK:	**(K)** on thumb piece
OTHER MARKS:	DRGM
NOTICE:	cast bottle lip
I.D. #:	**C08.3.1**
INVENTOR & DATE:	presumably G. Frings Mar 30, 1925
REGISTRATION #:	DRGM 926,839
CIRCA:	1925? -1940?
FREQUENCY:	
MANUFACTURER:	FRINGS & CO. o. H. G.
MATERIAL:	cast iron
FINISH:	nickel
COMMENTS:	This is a later version of this German manufactured corkscrew with the wire neck rest replaced by a cast neck rest.

NAME: **CYKLOP** (marked)

TRADEMARK: **(K)** on thumb piece

OTHER MARKS: DRGM

NOTICE: 1990 - present version of the CYKLOP is ID# is ***C08.5.1.***

I.D. #: **C08.4.1**

INVENTOR & DATE: presumably G. Frings Mar 30, 1925

REGISTRATION #: DRGM 926,839

CIRCA: 1970 -1990?

FREQUENCY:

MANUFACTURER: FRINGS & CO. o. H. G.

MATERIAL: cast iron

FINISH: nickel

COMMENTS: This is the foil cutter version of the cast neck rest CYKLOP. DRGM was not marked on the latest version of the CYKLOP produced after about 1990.

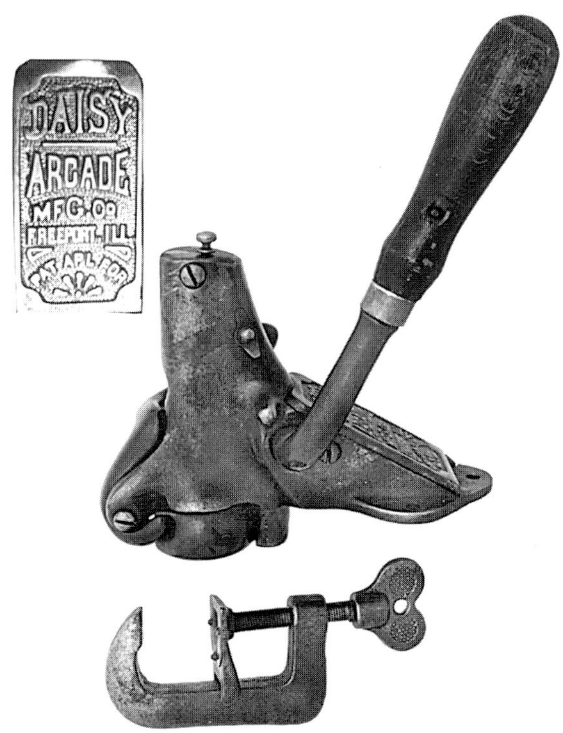

NAME: **DAISY** (marked)

TRADEMARK: none

OTHER MARKS: PAT. APL. FOR.

NOTICE: pinned handle, flat topped frame, advertising plate out of scale

I.D. #: **D01.1.1**

INVENTOR & DATE: C. Morgan, application filed Sep 12, 1894

REGISTRATION #: P 532,575

CIRCA: 1893? - 1895?

FREQUENCY:

MANUFACTURER: Arcade Manufacturing Co.

MATERIAL: cast iron

FINISH: nickel

COMMENTS: This is the pre-patent model; the early custom clamp is very hard to find.

NAME:	**DAISY** (marked)
TRADEMARK:	none
OTHER MARKS:	PAT. JAN 15, 1895
NOTICE:	data from an existing example
I.D. #:	**D01.1.2**
INVENTOR & DATE:	C. Morgan Jan 15, 1895
REGISTRATION #:	P 532,575
CIRCA:	1895? - 1897?
FREQUENCY:	
MANUFACTURER:	Arcade Manufacturing Co.
MATERIAL:	cast iron
FINISH:	nickel
COMMENTS:	As found in this 1895 advertisement, the first model of the DAISY did not have a scroll decoration on the case.

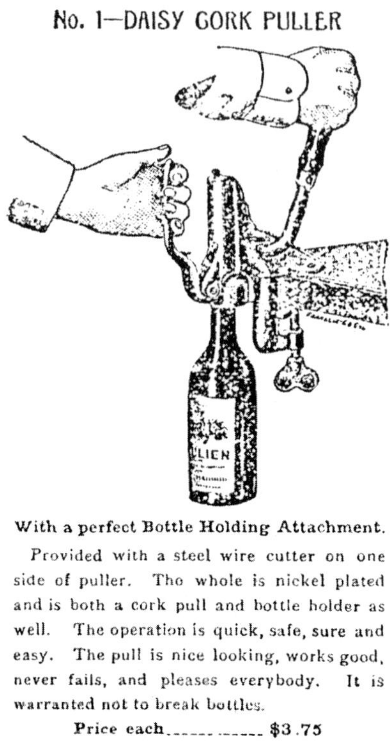

NAME:	**DAISY, THE** (marked)
TRADEMARK:	none
OTHER MARKS:	PAT NOV 12, 1895, PAT JAN 15, 1895 on advertising plate
NOTICE:	round top on the frame, scroll decoration, bolted handle, advertising plate out of scale
I.D. #:	**D02.1.1**
INVENTOR & DATE:	C. Morgan Nov 12 1895
REGISTRATION #:	P 532,575
CIRCA:	1897? - 1913?
FREQUENCY:	
MANUFACTURER:	Arcade Manufacturing Co.
MATERIAL:	cast iron
FINISH:	nickel
COMMENTS:	The brass oil cap screw seen on the top and the later custom clamp are very hard to find.

NAME: **DION** (marked)
TRADEMARK: not inspected
OTHER MARKS: not inspected
NOTICE: silver color finish variant *D03.1.1*
I.D. #: **D03.1.2**
INVENTOR & DATE: no patent or registration found
REGISTRATION #:
CIRCA: 1995? - 2000
FREQUENCY:
MANUFACTURER: Asia for Franmara ?
MATERIAL: zinc ?
FINISH: brass colored
COMMENTS: This is a modern version of the DON.

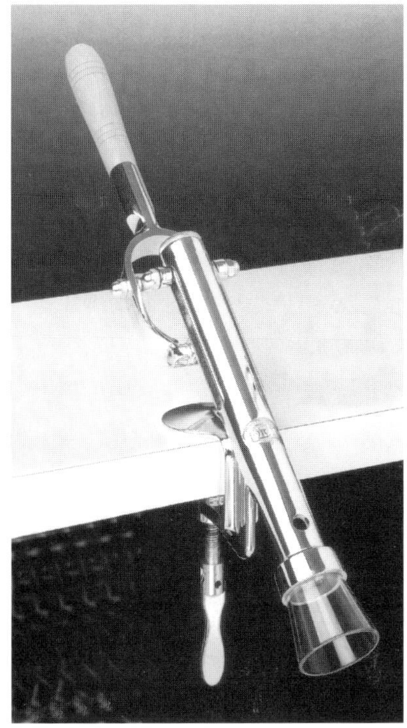

NAME: **DON** (not inspected)
TRADEMARK: not inspected
OTHER MARKS: not inspected
NOTICE: thumb piece, a removable throat is shown in this advertising, top mount version *D04.2.1*
I.D. #: **D04.1.1**
INVENTOR & DATE:
REGISTRATION #:
CIRCA: 1903? -1912?
FREQUENCY:
MANUFACTURER: presumably Samuel Mason Ltd.
MATERIAL: brass
FINISH: nickel
COMMENTS: This 1912 Farrow & Jackson advertisement appears to show a small version of the MERRITT named DON, with a screw-in throat and a scalloped base, like the SUN.

"DON"
Nickel plated on Brass
To clamp on counter as shown—*or* with plate to screw on counter

NAME:	**DON** (marked)
TRADEMARK:	sun
OTHER MARKS:	none
NOTICE:	clamp mount, short finial, top mount version *D04.4.1*
I.D. #:	**D04.3.1**
INVENTOR & DATE:	C. Chambers Aug 20, 1903
REGISTRATION #:	LP 18,006
CIRCA:	1903 -1905?
FREQUENCY:	
MANUFACTURER:	Samuel Mason Ltd.
MATERIAL:	brass
FINISH:	nickel
COMMENTS:	This is presumably the first version of the DON as patented by Chambers.

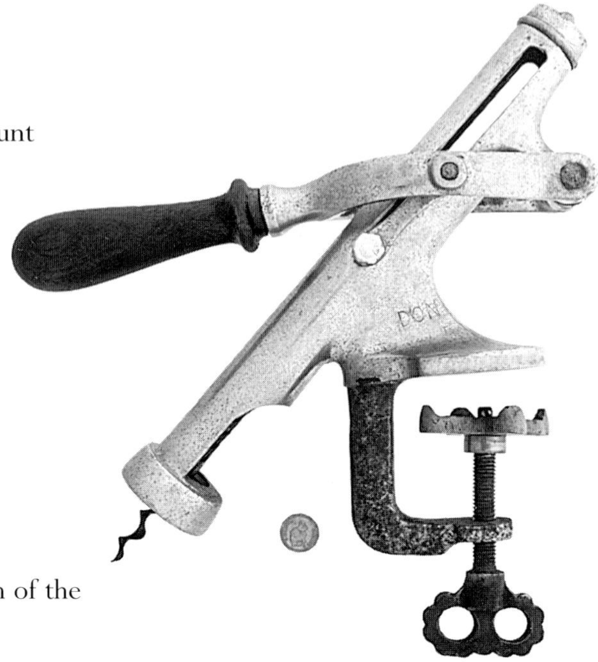

NAME:	**DON, THE** (marked)
TRADEMARK:	hand & star
OTHER MARKS:	G&C, CHAMBERS PATENT, 18006/03, W. G. EDMONDS & CO. DUBLIN
NOTICE:	name on the clamp frame, longer finial, slender side links
I.D. #:	**D05.1.1**
INVENTOR & DATE:	C. Chambers Aug 20, 1903
REGISTRATION #:	LP 18,006
CIRCA:	1905?-1920?
FREQUENCY:	
MANUFACTURER:	Gaskell & Chambers Ltd.
MATERIAL:	brass
FINISH:	nickel
COMMENTS:	–

NAME:	**DON, THE** (marked)
TRADEMARK:	hand & star
OTHER MARKS:	none
NOTICE:	finial, slender side links, top mount
I.D. #:	**D05.2.1**
INVENTOR & DATE:	C. Chambers Aug 20, 1903
REGISTRATION #:	LP 18,006
CIRCA:	1910?-1920?
FREQUENCY:	[2 frequency symbols]
MANUFACTURER:	Gaskell
MATERIAL:	brass
FINISH:	nickel
COMMENTS:	This Gaskell advertising dates to 1910.

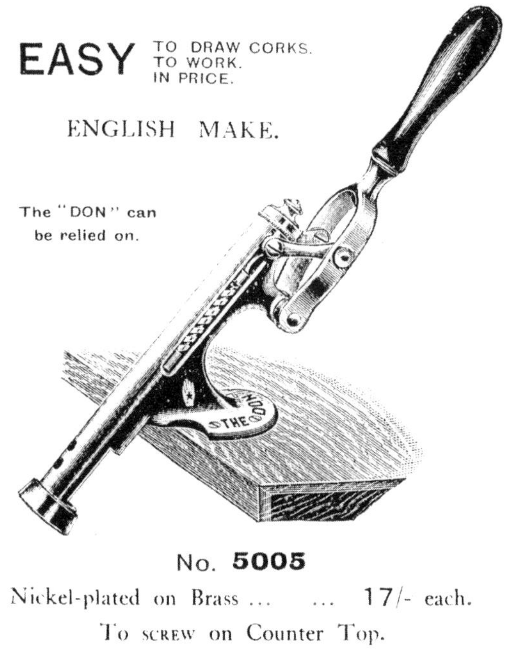

NAME:	**DON, THE** (marked)
TRADEMARK:	optic
OTHER MARKS:	CHAMBERS PATENT
NOTICE:	optic trade mark, scalloped side links
I.D. #:	**D05.3.1**
INVENTOR & DATE:	C. Chambers Aug 20, 1903
REGISTRATION #:	LP 18,006
CIRCA:	1920?-1927?
FREQUENCY:	[5 frequency symbols]
MANUFACTURER:	Gaskell & Chambers Ltd.
MATERIAL:	brass
FINISH:	nickel
COMMENTS:	This later Gaskell & Chambers version has no NAME on the clamp frame.

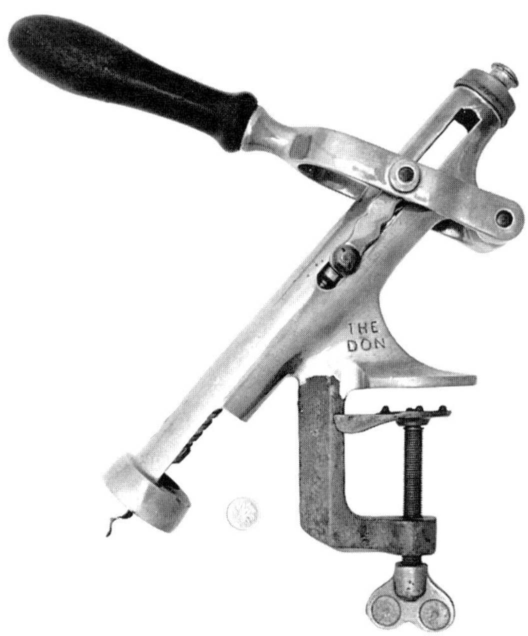

NAME:	**DON, THE** (marked)
TRADEMARK:	not inspected
OTHER MARKS:	CHAMBERS PATENT
NOTICE:	scalloped side links, top mount
I.D. #:	**D05.4.1**
INVENTOR & DATE:	C. Chambers Aug 20, 1903
REGISTRATION #:	LP 18,006
CIRCA:	1920?-1927?
FREQUENCY:	
MANUFACTURER:	Gaskell & Chambers Ltd.
MATERIAL:	brass
FINISH:	nickel
COMMENTS:	The top mount versions appear to be much harder to find than the clamp mount versions.

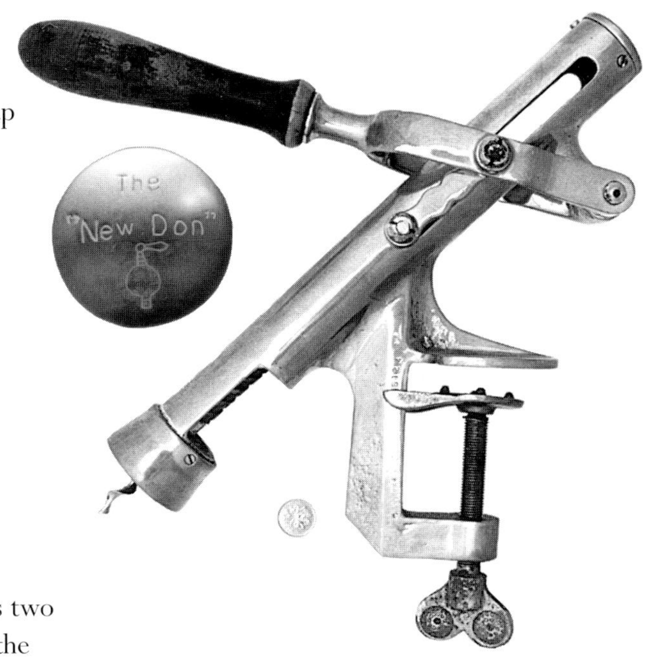

NAME:	**DON, THE NEW** (marked)
TRADEMARK:	optic
OTHER MARKS:	G&C
NOTICE:	clamp mount, throat and tube cap fastened on with screws
I.D. #:	**D06.1.1**
INVENTOR & DATE:	no English patent or registration found
REGISTRATION #:	
CIRCA:	1930?-1940?
FREQUENCY:	
MANUFACTURER:	Gaskell & Chambers Ltd.
MATERIAL:	brass
FINISH:	nickel
COMMENTS:	This last version of the DON has two internal guide rods, rather than the single guide rod found in the earlier DONs. The marks are found on the tube cap.

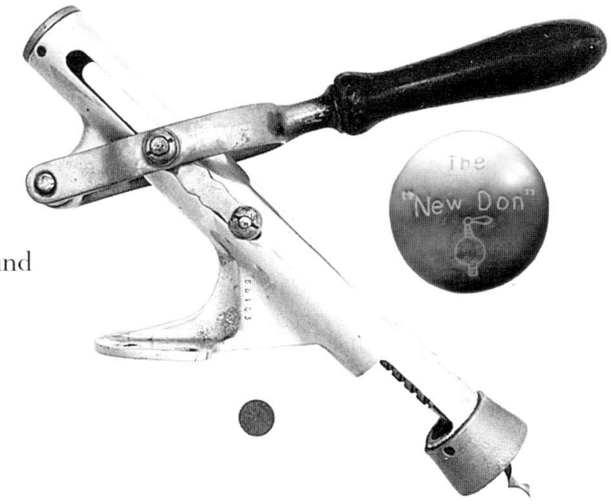

NAME: **DON, THE NEW** (marked)

TRADEMARK: optic

OTHER MARKS: G&C

NOTICE: top mount, the tube cap is always marked THE NEW DON

I.D. #: **D06.2.1**

INVENTOR & DATE: no English patent or registration found

REGISTRATION #:

CIRCA: 1930?-1963?

FREQUENCY:

MANUFACTURER: Gaskell & Chambers Ltd.

MATERIAL: aluminum body, brass fittings

FINISH: copper colored?

COMMENTS: Traces of copper show on both the aluminum and brass.

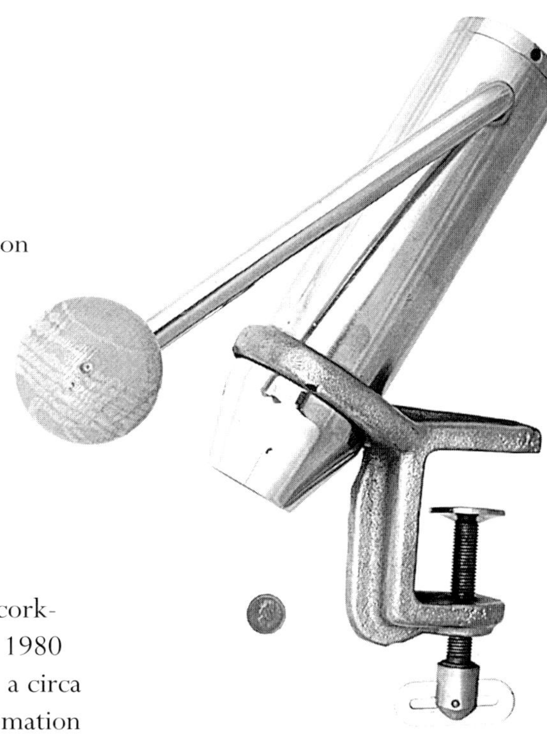

NAME: **DREKO** (marked)

TRADEMARK: DREKO

OTHER MARKS: MADE IN GDR

NOTICE: marked DREKO only *D07.1.2*, unmarked version *D07.1.3*

I.D. #: **D07.1.1**

INVENTOR & DATE: no E. German patent or registration found

REGISTRATION #:

CIRCA: 1960? - 1970?

FREQUENCY:

MANUFACTURER: Drehteile und Korkenzieher

MATERIAL: machined steel

FINISH: chrome

COMMENTS: This is the only East German bar corkscrew known; there is also a circa 1980 version marked DREKO only and a circa 1990 unmarked version. No information is available on the frequency of any specifically marked variant.

NAME: **ECLIPSE** (unmarked)
TRADEMARK: none
OTHER MARKS: none
NOTICE: the three bolts fastening the case cover all face the same way, straight throat bars

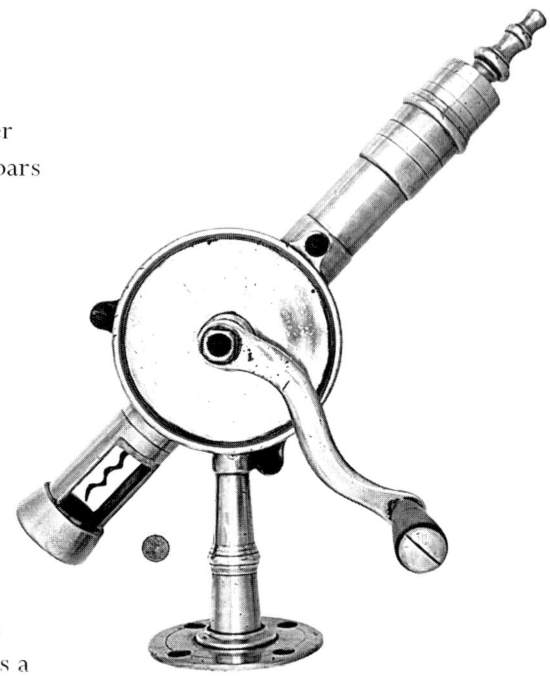

I.D. #: **E01.1.1**
INVENTOR & DATE: F. Marwood Mar 26, 1885
REGISTRATION #: LP 3,871
CIRCA: 1885? - 1900?
FREQUENCY:
MANUFACTURER: presumably Samuel Mason Ltd.
MATERIAL: brass
FINISH: nickel
COMMENTS: This is assumed to be an early version because reversing two of the bolts was a better design, allowing for more thread depth in the thicker metal. The NAME is usually on a brass tag soldered to the base; it may have come off.

NAME: **ECLIPSE** (marked)
TRADEMARK: sun
OTHER MARKS: none
NOTICE: curved throat bars, no slot in the screw holding the handle on

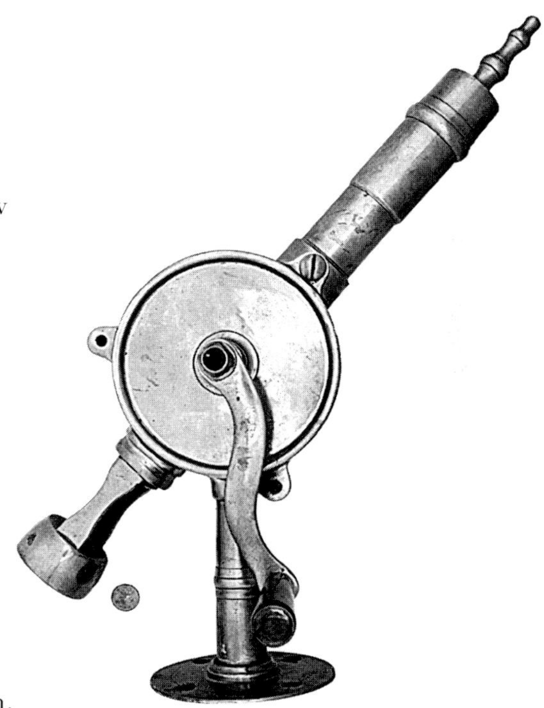

I.D. #: **E01.1.2**
INVENTOR & DATE: F. Marwood Mar 26, 1885
REGISTRATION #: LP 3,871
CIRCA: 1885? - 1910?
FREQUENCY:
MANUFACTURER: Samuel Mason Ltd.
MATERIAL: brass
FINISH: nickel
COMMENTS: The ECLIPSE is probably the only bar corkscrew that had a left handed worm.

NAME:	**ECLIPSE** (not inspected)
TRADEMARK:	hand & star
OTHER MARKS:	not inspected
NOTICE:	brass finish variant *E01.1.4*
I.D. #:	**E01.1.3**
INVENTOR & DATE:	F. Marwood Mar 26, 1885
REGISTRATION #:	LP 3,871
CIRCA:	1910? - 1920?
FREQUENCY:	
MANUFACTURER:	Gaskell
MATERIAL:	brass
FINISH:	nickel
COMMENTS:	Some versions of the ECLIPSE were sold in both nickel plated and polished brass versions.

NAME:	**ECLIPSE** (not inspected)
TRADEMARK:	not inspected
OTHER MARKS:	not inspected
NOTICE:	an unusual ECLIPSE with straight crank arm
I.D. #:	**E01.1.5**
INVENTOR & DATE:	no patent or registration found
REGISTRATION #:	
CIRCA:	1900? - 1940?
FREQUENCY:	
MANUFACTURER:	possibly Italian
MATERIAL:	brass
FINISH:	not inspected
COMMENTS:	The worm appears to be right handed and the tube case appears to be considerably shorter than on a standard ECLIPSE.

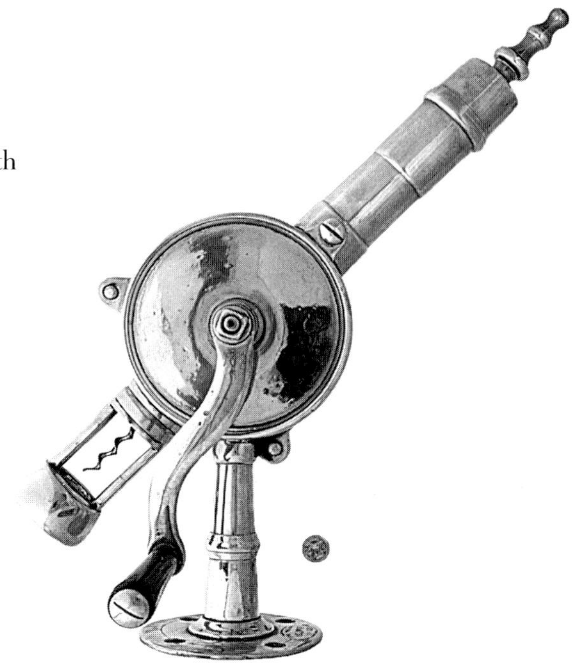

NAME: **ECLIPSE, THE PATENT** (marked)
TRADEMARK: none
OTHER MARKS: none
NOTICE: straight throat bars, handle held on with a screw
I.D. #: **E02.1.1**
INVENTOR & DATE: F. Marwood Mar 26, 1885
REGISTRATION #: LP 3,871
CIRCA: 1885? - 1905?
FREQUENCY:
MANUFACTURER: presumably Samuel Mason Ltd.
MATERIAL: brass
FINISH: nickel
COMMENTS: No information is available on the frequency of any specifically named versions of the ECLIPSE.

Nickel-plated, 50/-

NAME: **ECLIPSE, THE ORIGINAL** (marked)
TRADEMARK: not inspected
OTHER MARKS: not inspected
NOTICE: there is a corkscrew marked like this, but the source has been lost
I.D. #: **E03.1.1**
INVENTOR & DATE: F. Marwood Mar 26, 1885
REGISTRATION #: LP 3,871
CIRCA: 1910? - 1927?
FREQUENCY:
MANUFACTURER: presumably Gaskell & Chambers Ltd.
MATERIAL: brass
FINISH: nickel
COMMENTS: The ECLIPSE is often advertised as the ROTARY ECLIPSE, but there is no evidence that any were marked as such.

NAME:	**ELECTROPULL** (marked)
TRADEMARK:	not inspected
OTHER MARKS:	not inspected
NOTICE:	a prototype for Franmara
I.D. #:	**E04.1.1**
INVENTOR & DATE:	no US patent or registration found
REGISTRATION #:	
CIRCA:	2001
FREQUENCY:	
MANUFACTURER:	unknown
MATERIAL:	aluminum
FINISH:	
COMMENTS:	This corkscrew went into production early in 2001.

NAME:	**ÉLÉGANT, L'** (marked)
TRADEMARK:	none
OTHER MARKS:	1900 L. van Genechten - Con?? - ??ur - ???- Bruxelle?,1898 DESIGN
NOTICE:	bottle lip version, advertising plate out of scale
I.D. #:	**E05.1.1**
INVENTOR & DATE:	E. Walker Apr 07, 1896
REGISTRATION #:	P 557,734
CIRCA:	1900?
FREQUENCY:	
MANUFACTURER:	Erie Specialty Mfg. Co.
MATERIAL:	cast iron
FINISH:	nickel
COMMENTS:	This is a private label version of Walker's QUICK & EASY.

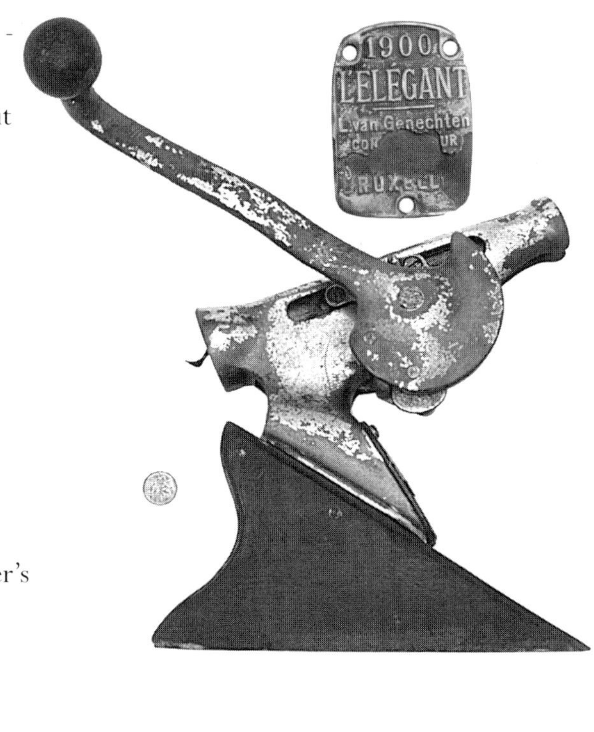

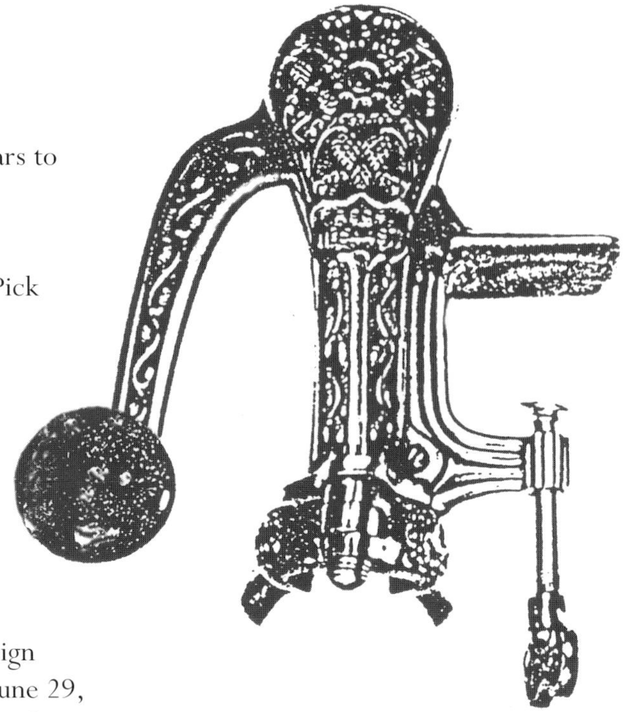

NAME:	**EMPIRE** (marked)
TRADEMARK:	not inspected
OTHER MARKS:	REG NO 544,977
NOTICE:	hop vine motif, clamp plate appears to be a replacement
I.D. #:	**E06.1.1**
INVENTOR & DATE:	R. Gilchrist Sep 03, 1894 and A. Pick Feb 08, 1895
REGISTRATION #:	LP 16,777 and LP 2,825
CIRCA:	1909?-?
FREQUENCY:	
MANUFACTURER:	Gaskell or Samuel Mason Ltd.
MATERIAL:	cast iron
FINISH:	nickel
COMMENTS:	544,977 is the decorative case design registration number received on June 29, 1909 by the Gunn Caster Co. Ltd. of Birmingham.

NAME:	**ENTERPRISE NO 113** (marked)
TRADEMARK:	none
OTHER MARKS:	ENTERPRISE MFG. Co. PHILA. PA USA
NOTICE:	clamp mount
I.D. #:	**E07.1.1**
INVENTOR & DATE:	presumably J. Hurley Sep 07, 1886
REGISTRATION #:	P 348,743
CIRCA:	1886? - 1908?
FREQUENCY:	
MANUFACTURER:	Enterprise Mfg. Co.
MATERIAL:	cast iron
FINISH:	black paint, gold letters
COMMENTS:	This appears to be an improved version of the Hurley patent; see *MECHANISMS* for additional comments.

NAME: **ENTERPRISE N0. 111** (marked)
TRADEMARK: none
OTHER MARKS: ENTERPRISE MFG. Co, PHILA. PA USA, PAT APL'D FOR
NOTICE: top mount
I.D. #: **E07.2.1**
INVENTOR & DATE: presumably J. Hurley Sep 07, 1886
REGISTRATION #: P 348,743
CIRCA: 1886?
FREQUENCY:
MANUFACTURER: Enterprise Mfg. Co.
MATERIAL: cast iron
FINISH: black paint, gold letters
COMMENTS: It is not known if this patent application was referring to Hurley's application; see *MECHANISMS* for additional comments.

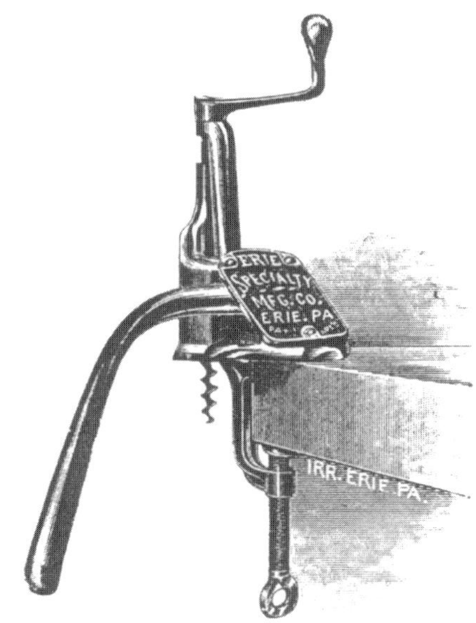

20, Erie, Full Nickel plated
25, " " " with Clamp
Extra Screws for Samson or Erie Cork Pullers

NAME: **ERIE** (marked)
TRADEMARK: none
OTHER MARKS: ERIE SPECIALTY MFG. CO. ERIE. PA
NOTICE:
I.D. #: **E08.1.1**
INVENTOR & DATE: E. Walker May 19, 1891
REGISTRATION #: P 452,625
CIRCA: 1890? - 1894?
FREQUENCY:
MANUFACTURER: Erie Specialty Mfg. Co.
MATERIAL: cast iron
FINISH: nickel
COMMENTS: As found in this 1894 advertisement, this is a very early name for THE WALKER.

NAME: **ESKILSTUNA** (marked)

TRADEMARK: EJAB

OTHER MARKS: E.J.A.B., M26

NOTICE: cast bottle neck rest, advertising plate out of scale

I.D. #: **E13.2.1**

INVENTOR & DATE: no Swedish patent or registration found

REGISTRATION #:

CIRCA: unknown

FREQUENCY:

MANUFACTURER: Eskilstuna Järnmanufaktur Aktiebolag

MATERIAL: cast iron

FINISH: brown lacquer

COMMENTS: This is a Swedish version of the QUICK & EASY; **M26** is found on another Swedish corkscrew that had a cast bottle neck rest.

NAME: **ESKILSTUNA** (marked)

TRADEMARK: EJAB

OTHER MARKS: E.J.A.B.

NOTICE: bottle lip only, advertising plate out of scale

I.D. #: **E13.2.2**

INVENTOR & DATE: no Swedish patent or registration found

REGISTRATION #:

CIRCA: unknown

FREQUENCY:

MANUFACTURER: Eskilstuna Järnmanufaktur Aktiebolag

MATERIAL: cast iron

FINISH: brown lacquer

COMMENTS: This Swedish version of the QUICK & EASY had a cast bottle lip.

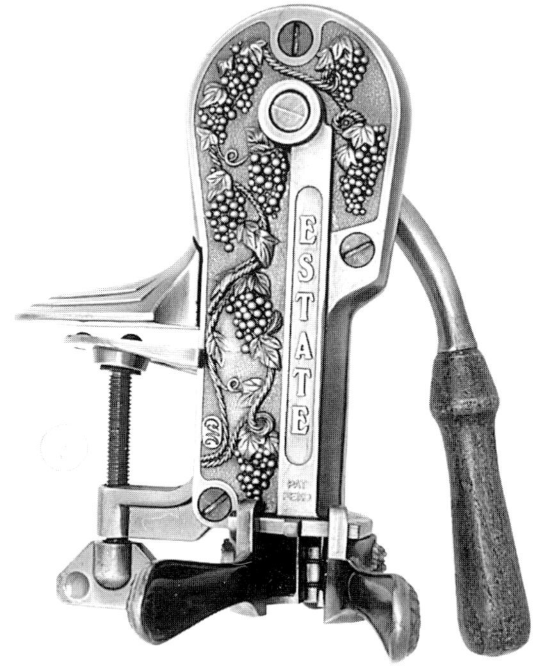

NAME: **ESTATE** (marked)
TRADEMARK: none
OTHER MARKS: PAT PEND, CM
NOTICE:
I.D. #: **E09.1.1**
INVENTOR & DATE: PAT APL
REGISTRATION #:
CIRCA: 1960? -1997?
FREQUENCY:
MANUFACTURER: Asian for Rogar International Corp.
MATERIAL: aluminum
FINISH: gold anodized
COMMENTS: This corkscrew had a CHAMPION mechanism, but is no longer in production.

NAME: **ESTATE** (unmarked)
TRADEMARK: none
OTHER MARKS: none
NOTICE: material, handle
I.D. #: **E09.2.1**
INVENTOR & DATE: no patent or registration found
REGISTRATION #:
CIRCA: 1960?
FREQUENCY:
MANUFACTURER: American ?
MATERIAL: brass
FINISH: brass
COMMENTS: This is a very well made, unmarked brass corkscrew with the ESTATE case decorations. Possibly the original plan was to sell a brass version.

NAME:	**EXHIBITION** (not inspected)
TRADEMARK:	not inspected
OTHER MARKS:	not inspected
NOTICE:	
I.D. #:	**E10.1.1**
INVENTOR & DATE:	W. Vaughan Aug 15, 1887
REGISTRATION #:	LP 11,104
CIRCA:	1887? - 1900?
FREQUENCY:	
MANUFACTURER:	presumably Samuel Mason Ltd.
MATERIAL:	brass
FINISH:	nickel
COMMENTS:	As found in this 1895 Farrow & Jackson advertisement, it is possibly a private label version of the ACME manufactured for Farrow & Jackson by Mason.

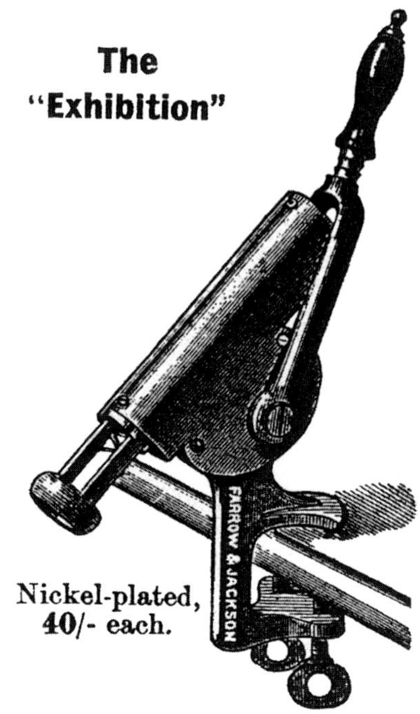

NAME:	**EXPRESS, THE** (marked)
TRADEMARK:	none
OTHER MARKS:	E. COANEY & Co. DALE END BIRMINGHAM, PATENT, 1898 DESIGN
NOTICE:	advertising plate out of scale
I.D. #:	**E11.1.1**
INVENTOR & DATE:	E. Walker Apr 07, 1896
REGISTRATION #:	P 557,734
CIRCA:	1898 - 1910?
FREQUENCY:	
MANUFACTURER:	Erie Specialty Co.
MATERIAL:	cast iron
FINISH:	nickel
COMMENTS:	Shown in this advertisement is a British private label name for the QUICK & EASY.

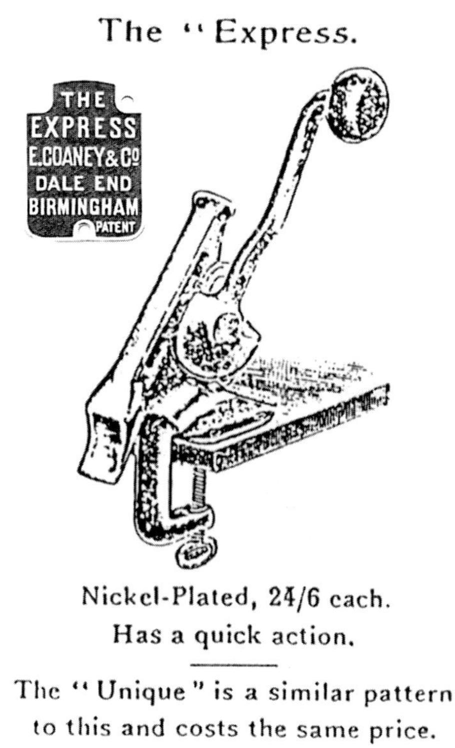

NAME: **EXTRACTEE** (not inspected)
TRADEMARK: not inspected
OTHER MARKS: not inspected
NOTICE: cork catching tray under the clamp
I.D. #: **E12.1.1**
INVENTOR & DATE: A. Baumgarten Apr 01, 1902
REGISTRATION #: P 696,399
CIRCA: 1902? - 1905?
FREQUENCY:
MANUFACTURER: presumably Manning Bowman & Co.
MATERIAL: cast iron
FINISH: not inspected
COMMENTS: This 1905 advertisement shows a version of the PULLMEE with a cork catching bin.

EXTRACTEE CORK EXTRACTOR

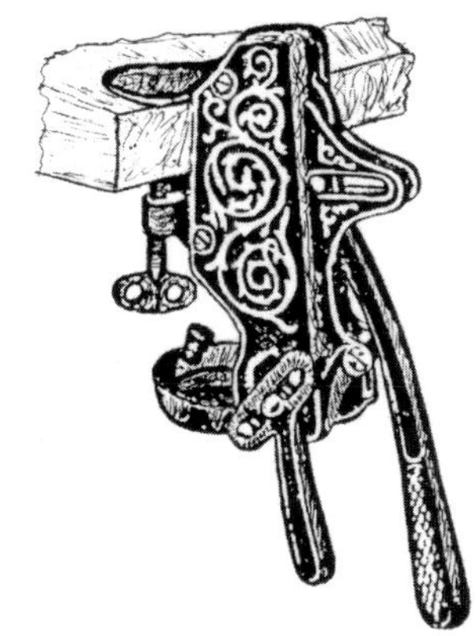

This machine has all the qualities of the "Shomee". It has the same style of bottle grasp and works in the same manner except that it pulls the cork free from the bottle, depositing it in the receptacle back of the puller. This is a strictly high grade, perfect working machine and is guaranteed to be satisfactory in every detail.
Price .... $ 3.50 each

NAME: **FALEAU** (marked)
TRADEMARK: not inspected
OTHER MARKS: not inspected
NOTICE: handle finial
I.D. #: **F01.1.1**
INVENTOR & DATE: no patent or registration found
REGISTRATION #:
CIRCA: 1910? - ?
FREQUENCY:
MANUFACTURER: unknown
MATERIAL: brass
FINISH: not inspected
COMMENTS: This is a version of the DON, by an unknown manufacturer.

NAME:	**FAMLEE** (marked)
TRADEMARK:	none
OTHER MARKS:	PAT. APL. FOR, MERIDEN CONN. USA.
NOTICE:	
I.D. #:	**F02.1.1**
INVENTOR & DATE:	A. Baumgarten applied for Aug 20, 1900
REGISTRATION #:	P 675,051
CIRCA:	1900? - 1905?
FREQUENCY:	
MANUFACTURER:	Manning Bowman & Co.
MATERIAL:	cast iron
FINISH:	nickel
COMMENTS:	This is a PULLMEE mechanism, without the bottle clasp.

NAME:	**FAMLEE** (marked)
TRADEMARK:	none
OTHER MARKS:	not inspected
NOTICE:	bottle clasp
I.D. #:	**F02.2.1**
INVENTOR & DATE:	A. Baumgarten applied for Aug 20, 1900
REGISTRATION #:	P 675,051
CIRCA:	1900? - 1905?
FREQUENCY:	
MANUFACTURER:	Manning Bowman & Co.
MATERIAL:	cast iron
FINISH:	nickel
COMMENTS:	This 1905 advertisement shows a bottle clasp version of the FAMLEE.

FAMLEE CORK EXTRACTOR

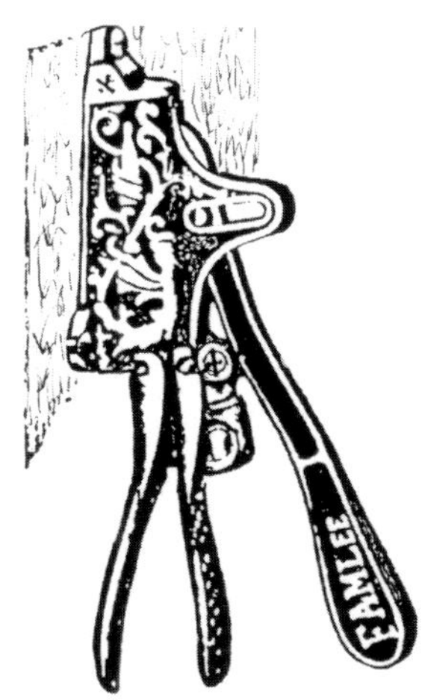

A household gem. With one up and down pull, the cork is extracted with the greatest ease and stripped from the screw, leaving machine ready for another cork to be extracted.
Price .... $ 1.50 each

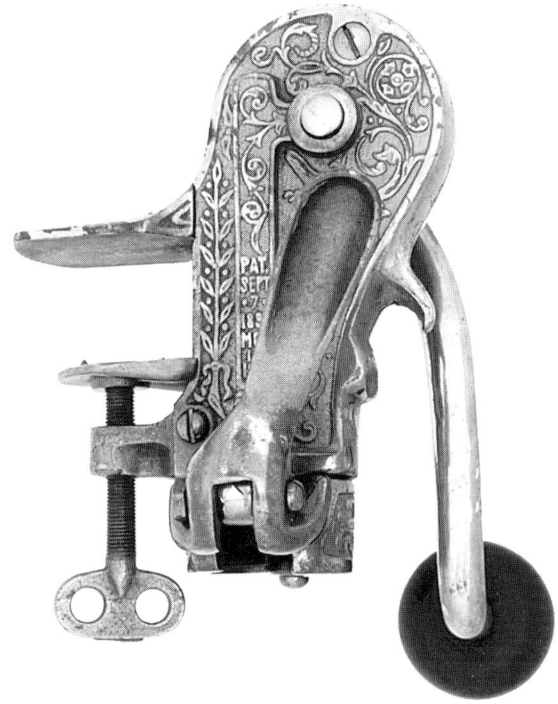

NAME: **FAVORITE** (marked)
TRADEMARK: none
OTHER MARKS: PAT SEPT 07 1897, MAR 14 1899
NOTICE: single lever bottle clasp, like a DAISY bottle clasp
I.D. #: **F03.1.1**
INVENTOR & DATE: C. Morgan Mar 14, 1899
REGISTRATION #: P 620,949
CIRCA: 1900? - 1913?
FREQUENCY:
MANUFACTURER: Arcade Manufacturing Co.
MATERIAL: cast iron
FINISH: nickel
COMMENTS: This was a shorter modified version of the CHAMPION mechanism, in a new case. It is presumed to be a very early version of the FAVORITE due to it having hand made brass components in the mechanism.

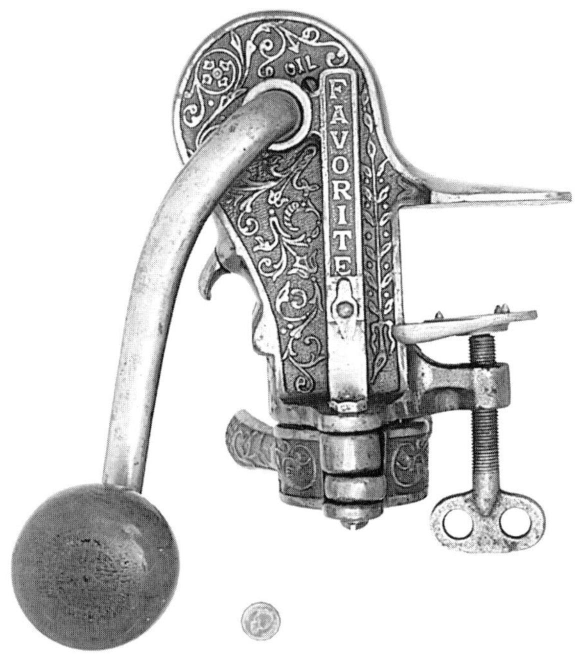

NAME: **FAVORITE** (marked)
TRADEMARK: none
OTHER MARKS: none
NOTICE: patent date not marked
I.D. #: **F03.2.1**
INVENTOR & DATE: C. Morgan Mar 14, 1899
REGISTRATION #: P 620,949
CIRCA: 1900? - 1923?
FREQUENCY:
MANUFACTURER: Arcade Manufacturing Co.
MATERIAL: cast iron
FINISH: nickel
COMMENTS: This was the version with a cap lifter cast into the frame and standard bottle clasps. It is presumed to be an early version due to some brass components in the mechanism.

NAME:	**FAVORITE** (marked)
TRADEMARK:	none
OTHER MARKS:	PAT SEPT 07 1897, MAR 14 1899
NOTICE:	bottle clasp, no cap lifter
I.D. #:	**F03.3.1**
INVENTOR & DATE:	C. Morgan Mar 14, 1899
REGISTRATION #:	P 620,949
CIRCA:	1900? - 1913?
FREQUENCY:	
MANUFACTURER:	Arcade Manufacturing Co.
MATERIAL:	cast iron
FINISH:	nickel
COMMENTS:	This version has no cap lifter, but this example had cast iron production components in the mechanism.

NAME:	**FAVORITE** (marked)
TRADEMARK:	none
OTHER MARKS:	none
NOTICE:	finish
I.D. #:	**F03.3.2**
INVENTOR & DATE:	C. Morgan Mar 14, 1899
REGISTRATION #:	P 620,949
CIRCA:	1900? - 1923?
FREQUENCY:	
MANUFACTURER:	Arcade Manufacturing Co.
MATERIAL:	cast iron
FINISH:	arcadian bronze finish
COMMENTS:	This 1913 Arcade advertisement shows the arcadian bronze finish version.

Arcade Cork Pullers

The Favorite

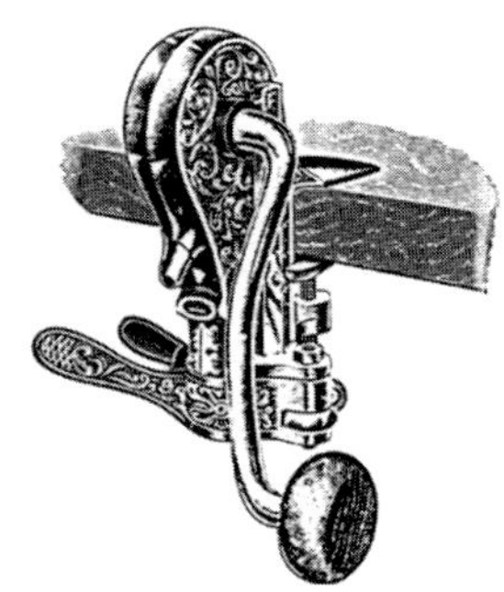

A cork puller which will remove crown seals, as well as pull corks, is something of a novelty, but the Favorite has this and many other features.

It is so constructed that the working parts are below the counter.

The method of operation gives a powerful, rapid stroke.

It contains improvements which are the result of many years of experience in producing cork pulling machines.

No. 1. Nickel plated finish.

No. 2. Arcadian bronze finish

PACKING

Each puller in a wooden box; ½ dozen in a heavy shipping case.

Case weight, net 33 pounds, gross 57 pounds.

Case measurements, 22x15x11 inches

NAME: **5th AVENUE** (marked)
TRADEMARK: none
OTHER MARKS: FRARY, PATENT APD FOR
NOTICE: black japanned finish variant *F04.1.2*, the Jappaned variant is
I.D. #: **F04.1.1**
INVENTOR & DATE: no patent or registration found
REGISTRATION #:
CIRCA: 1888 - 1890
FREQUENCY:
MANUFACTURER: Meriden Malleable Iron Co.
MATERIAL: cast iron
FINISH: nickel
COMMENTS: Collectors commonly call this corkscrew THE FRARY, but there are other corkscrews marked FRARY. The hanging apparatus is known as "the bird" to collectors. The beak was used to break wire or string and the teeth inside of it were used to hold the cork while it was being stripped.

NAME: **5th AVENUE** (marked)
TRADEMARK: none
OTHER MARKS: FRARY, PATENT APD FOR
NOTICE: cork grip
I.D. #: **F04.2.1**
INVENTOR & DATE: no patent or registration found
REGISTRATION #:
CIRCA: 1888 - 1890
FREQUENCY:
MANUFACTURER: Meriden Malleable Iron Co.
MATERIAL: cast iron
FINISH: nickel
COMMENTS: This version has a cork holding grip attached to the frame, replacing the bird.

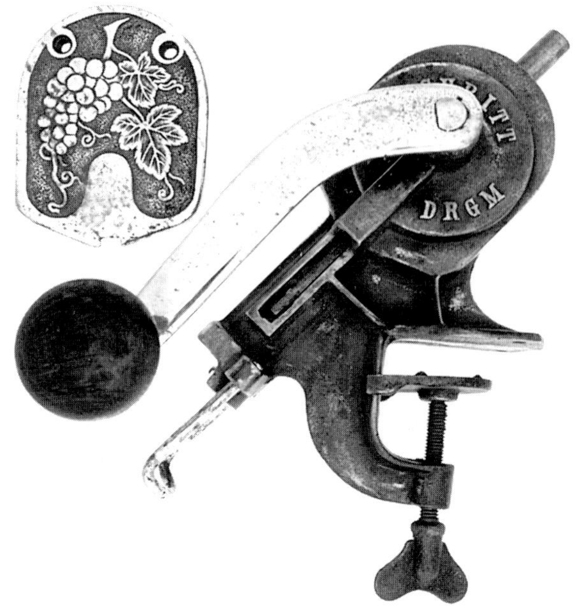

NAME: **FORTSCHRITT** (marked)
TRADEMARK: HMK
OTHER MARKS: DRGM, HMK
NOTICE: DRGM, decorative case cover plate out of scale
I.D. #: **F05.1.1**
INVENTOR & DATE: no German registration found
REGISTRATION #: DRGM
CIRCA: 1925? - 1935?
FREQUENCY:
MANUFACTURER: German
MATERIAL: cast iron
FINISH: nickel and black paint
COMMENTS: FORTSCHRITT translates as "progress"; see *MECHANISMS* for additional information.

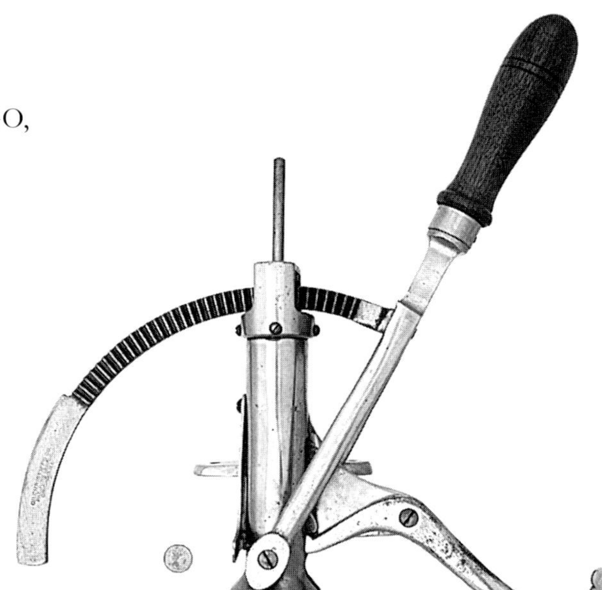

NAME: **GILCHRIST** (marked)
TRADEMARK: none
OTHER MARKS: GILCHRIST M'F'G CO, CHICAGO, ILL, PAT. JUNE 19, 1888
NOTICE:
I.D. #: **G01.1.1**
INVENTOR & DATE: R. Gilchrist Oct 30, 1888
REGISTRATION #: P 392,116
CIRCA: 1888? - ?
FREQUENCY:
MANUFACTURER: Gilchrist Mfg. Co.
MATERIAL: cast iron
FINISH: nickel
COMMENTS: Gilchrist's second stem-nut patent. There is no evidence that Gilchrist manufactured other products, so it is possible that he was a distributor using the word "manufacturer" in his company name.

NAME:	**GRAPE, LE** (marked)
TRADEMARK:	none
OTHER MARKS:	none
NOTICE:	
I.D. #:	**G02.1.1**
INVENTOR & DATE:	no patent or registration found
REGISTRATION #:	
CIRCA:	1995? - 1998 ?
FREQUENCY:	
MANUFACTURER:	Taiwanese
MATERIAL:	zinc ?
FINISH:	brass colored
COMMENTS:	This is a modern version of the CHAMPION. The one example inspected did not work and there appeared to have been a mistake in copying the design. It is no longer in production.

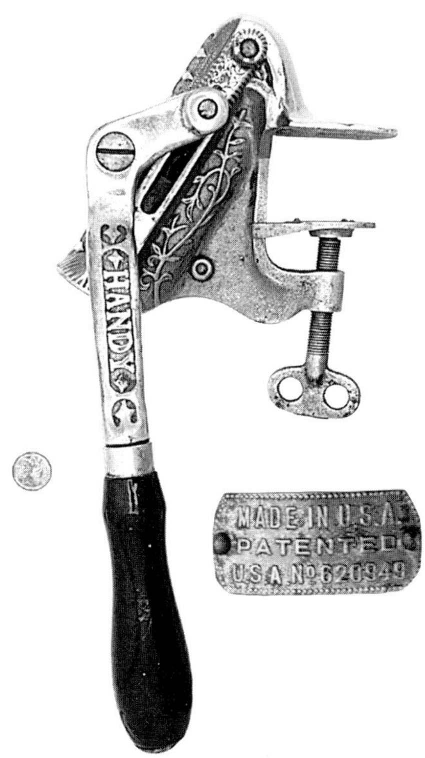

NAME:	**HANDY** (marked)
TRADEMARK:	none
OTHER MARKS:	MAR 14, 1899
NOTICE:	clamp mount
I.D. #:	**H01.1.1**
INVENTOR & DATE:	H. Tscherning May 19, 1903
REGISTRATION #:	P 728,519
CIRCA:	1903? - 1923?
FREQUENCY:	
MANUFACTURER:	Arcade Manufacturing Co.
MATERIAL:	cast iron
FINISH:	nickel
COMMENTS:	Advertised as the No. 100, the mechanism had only a partial connection to the CHAMPION patent date marked on this example. In this mechanism the worm-nut contains a spring loaded latch which clips into the worm carrier.

NAME: **HANDY** (marked)
TRADEMARK: not inspected
OTHER MARKS: not inspected
NOTICE: wall mount
I.D. #: **H01.2.1**
INVENTOR & DATE: H. Tscherning May 19, 1903
REGISTRATION #: P 728,519
CIRCA: 1903? - 1923?
FREQUENCY:
MANUFACTURER: Arcade Manufacturing Co.
MATERIAL: cast iron
FINISH: nickel
COMMENTS: As found in Arcade's 1913 advertisement, this is a smaller, shorter version of Tscherning's patent. As no STANDARD has been found with Tscherning's original mechanism, it is probable that the HANDY mechanism was developed shortly after the STANDARD was introduced, and replaced it.

Arcade Cork Pullers

The Handy No. 105

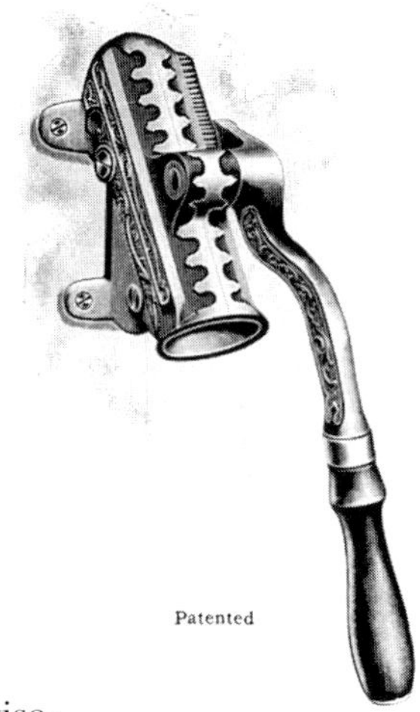

The wall attachment of this puller adds much to the convenience and power of operation.

The same simple method of construction is used as in the No. 100.

Every puller is thoroughly tested before it is sent out.

Heavily nickel plated.

PACKING

Each puller is packed in a box, 1 dozen in a strong case.

Case weight, net 35 lbs., gross 63 lbs.

Case measurements, 24x13x13 inches.

NAME: **HEKTOR** (not inspected)
TRADEMARK: not inspected
OTHER MARKS: not inspected
NOTICE: Arcade "vine & leaf" decoration, Gilchrist thumb piece
I.D. #: **H02.1.1**
INVENTOR & DATE: G. Frings, probably Nov 04, 1925
REGISTRATION #: DRGM 930,900
CIRCA: 1925? - 1933?
FREQUENCY:
MANUFACTURER: Frings & Co. o. H. G.
MATERIAL: cast iron
FINISH: nickel
COMMENTS: As found in this advertisement, it is not clear that this corkscrew was marked. This may be an illustration previously used for the HERO NO5. It is missing the latching link improvement discussed in *MECHANISMS,* but the advertising claims DRGM.

Entkorkmaschine Hektor
mit Stahlführung D. R. G. M. vernickelt RM **18.**–
Reservekorkenzieher RM **1.50**

NAME: **HEKTOR** (marked)
TRADEMARK: **(K)** on thumb piece
OTHER MARKS: internal component numbers preceded by **F**
NOTICE: German thumb piece
I.D. #: **H02.1.2**
INVENTOR & DATE: G. Frings, probably Nov 04, 1925
REGISTRATION #: DRGM 930,900
CIRCA: 1925? - 1933?
FREQUENCY:
MANUFACTURER: Frings & Co. o. H. G.
MATERIAL: cast iron
FINISH: nickel
COMMENTS: This is a German manufactured corkscrew with the "vine & leaf" decoration. All HEKTORs included rocker arm and latching link improvements to the HERO NO5 mechanism; see *MECHANISMS* for additional information. This may be the corkscrew shown in H02.1.1 advertising.

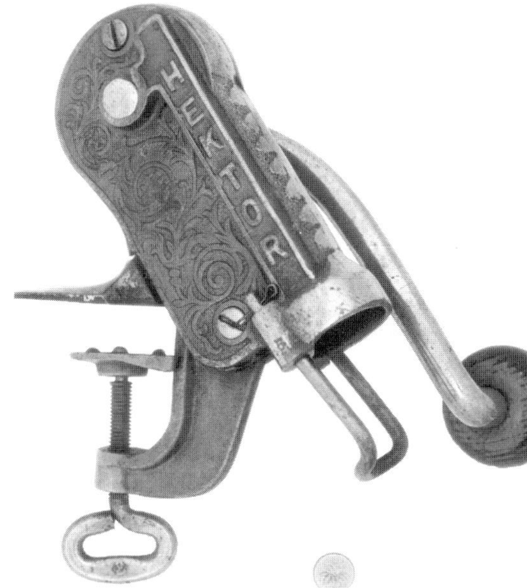

NAME: **HEKTOR** (marked)
TRADEMARK: none
OTHER MARKS: internal component numbers preceded by **F**
NOTICE: top mount version
I.D. #: **H02.2.1**
INVENTOR & DATE: G. Frings, probably Nov 04, 1925
REGISTRATION #: DRGM 930,900
CIRCA: 1925? - 1933?
FREQUENCY:
MANUFACTURER: Frings & Co. o. H. G.
MATERIAL: cast iron
FINISH: nickel
COMMENTS: This experimental top mount HEKTOR was modified in the factory from a clamp mount, before it was nickel plated.

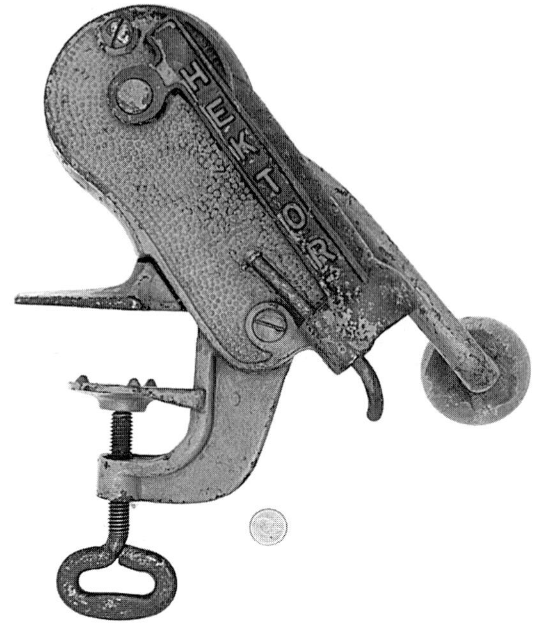

NAME: **HEKTOR** (marked)
TRADEMARK: **(K)** on thumb piece
OTHER MARKS: internal component numbers preceded by **F**
NOTICE: nickel plated finish variant *H02.3.1*
I.D. #: **H02.3.2**
INVENTOR & DATE: G. Frings, probably Nov 04, 1925
REGISTRATION #: DRGM 930,900
CIRCA: 1925? - 1940?
FREQUENCY:
MANUFACTURER: Frings & Co. o. H. G.
MATERIAL: cast iron
FINISH: green paint
COMMENTS: This stipple patterned case decorated version is presumed to be later.

NAME: **HEKTOR 1** (marked)
TRADEMARK: **(K)** on thumb piece
OTHER MARKS: F. u C., internal component numbers preceded by **F**
NOTICE: restored example, green painted finish variant *H03.1.2*
I.D. #: **H03.1.1**
INVENTOR & DATE: G. Frings, probably Nov 04, 1925
REGISTRATION #: DRGM 930,900
CIRCA: 1940? - 1950?
FREQUENCY:
MANUFACTURER: Frings & Co. o. H. G.
MATERIAL: cast iron
FINISH: nickel
COMMENTS: The **F. u C.** mark is "Frings and Co." The wire neck rest was only used on the HEKTOR and HEKTOR 1.

NAME: **HEKTOR 1** (marked)

TRADEMARK: **(K)** on thumb piece

OTHER MARKS: BCM, internal component numbers preceded by **F**

NOTICE: foil cutter version of the HECTOR 1

I.D. #: **H03.2.1**

INVENTOR & DATE: G. Frings, probably Nov 04, 1925

REGISTRATION #: DRGM 930,900

CIRCA: 1940? - 1950?

FREQUENCY: 

MANUFACTURER: Frings & Co. o. H. G.

MATERIAL: cast iron

FINISH: green paint

COMMENTS: The significance of the **BCM** mark is unknown, however both the HEKTOR 1 & HEKTOR 2 foil cutter versions are marked this way.

NAME: **HEKTOR 2** (marked)

TRADEMARK: **(K)** on thumb piece

OTHER MARKS: internal component numbers preceded by **F**

NOTICE: cast neck rest

I.D. #: **H04.1.1**

INVENTOR & DATE: G. Frings, probably Nov 04, 1925

REGISTRATION #: DRGM 930,900

CIRCA: 1940? - 1980?

FREQUENCY: 

MANUFACTURER: Frings & Co. o. H. G.

MATERIAL: cast iron

FINISH: nickel

COMMENTS: This is the grape leaf decorated version.

NAME:	**HEKTOR 2** (marked)
TRADEMARK:	none
OTHER MARKS:	BCM, internal component numbers preceded by **F**
NOTICE:	foil cutter, stipple case, cast neck rest
I.D. #:	**H04.2.1**
INVENTOR & DATE:	G. Frings, probably Nov 04, 1925
REGISTRATION #:	DRGM 930,900
CIRCA:	1950 - 1980?
FREQUENCY:	
MANUFACTURER:	Frings & Co. o. H. G.
MATERIAL:	cast iron
FINISH:	nickel
COMMENTS:	The significance of the **BCM** mark is unknown, however both the HEKTOR 1 & HEKTOR 2 with foil cutters are marked **BCM** beside the foil cutter.

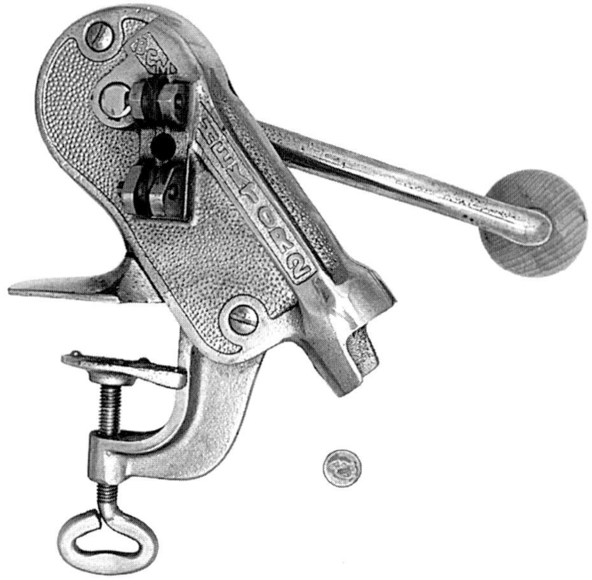

NAME:	**HEKTOR 3** (marked)
TRADEMARK:	none
OTHER MARKS:	internal component numbers preceded by **F**
NOTICE:	no foil cutter version, cast neck rest
I.D. #:	**H05.1.1**
INVENTOR & DATE:	G. Frings, probably Nov 04, 1925
REGISTRATION #:	DRGM 930,900
CIRCA:	1980? - 2001?
FREQUENCY:	
MANUFACTURER:	Frings & Co. o. H. G.
MATERIAL:	cast iron
FINISH:	nickel
COMMENTS:	The square freestanding clamp plate is probably not original.

NAME: **HEKTOR 3** (marked)
TRADEMARK: none
OTHER MARKS: HEKTOR 3
NOTICE: foil cutter version, cast neck rest
I.D. #: **H05.2.1**
INVENTOR & DATE: G. Frings, probably Nov 04, 1925
REGISTRATION #: DRGM 930,900
CIRCA: 1980? - 2001?
FREQUENCY:
MANUFACTURER: Frings & Co. o. H. G.
MATERIAL: cast iron
FINISH: nickel
COMMENTS:

NAME: **HELIOS** (marked)
TRADEMARK: none
OTHER MARKS: none
NOTICE: unusual thumb piece, clamp plate
I.D. #: **H06.1.1**
INVENTOR & DATE: G. Frings, probably Nov 04, 1925
REGISTRATION #: DRGM 930,900
CIRCA: 1930? - 1940?
FREQUENCY:
MANUFACTURER: Erste Mainzer Metallkapsel-Fabrik ?
MATERIAL: cast iron
FINISH: nickel
COMMENTS: The HELIOS is presumed to have not been manufactured by Frings due to the crude “vine & leaf” decoration and a different shaped hook on the latching link. It was advertised as DRGM, but not marked as such.

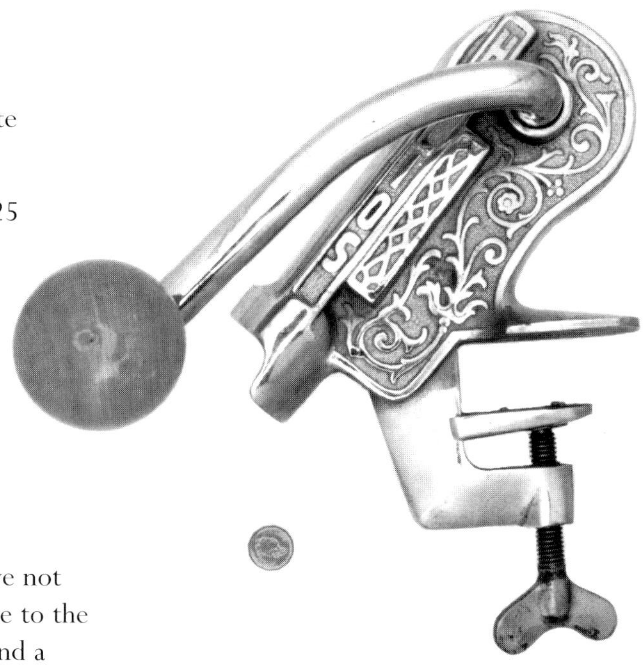

NAME:	**HENVI** (marked)
TRADEMARK:	none
OTHER MARKS:	none
NOTICE:	all aluminum except for the worm, nuts and bolts and the operating arm shaft
I.D. #:	**H07.1.1**
INVENTOR & DATE:	no patent or registration found
REGISTRATION #:	
CIRCA:	
FREQUENCY:	
MANUFACTURER:	Europe
MATERIAL:	aluminum
FINISH:	clear anodized
COMMENTS:	This is a completely redesigned aluminum version of the QUICK & EASY with case decorations similar to the ALEXANDERWERK; the manufacturer is unknown.

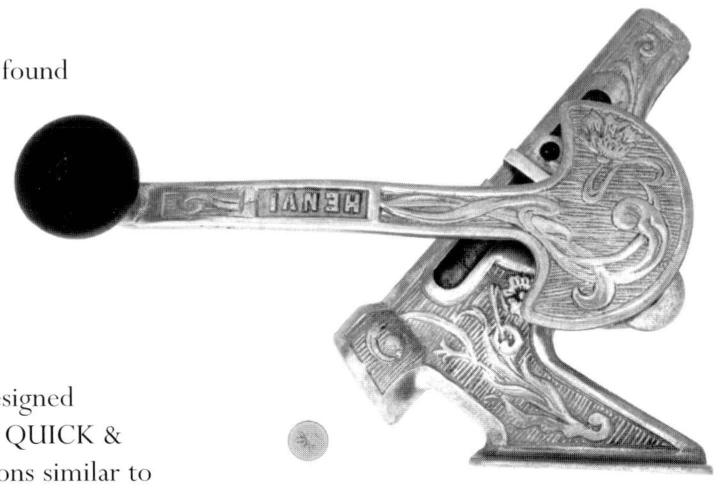

NAME:	**HERO NO5** (marked)
TRADEMARK:	none
OTHER MARKS:	MADE IN USA
NOTICE:	the patent was for the wire neck rest
I.D. #:	**H08.1.1**
INVENTOR & DATE:	R. Gilchrist Jun 14, 1904
REGISTRATION #:	DRP 162,930
CIRCA:	1904?-1913?
FREQUENCY:	
MANUFACTURER:	Arcade Manufacturing Co.
MATERIAL:	cast iron
FINISH:	nickel
COMMENTS:	An inclined version of the YANKEE NO6, the HERO was sold in Germany and became the basis for other heroes such as HEKTOR and HELIOS. By about 1913 the HERO was being copied in Germany.

NAME:	**HGB 7** (not inspected)
TRADEMARK:	not inspected
OTHER MARKS:	not inspected
NOTICE:	black and gold finish variant *H09.1.2*
I.D. #:	**H09.1.1**
INVENTOR & DATE:	R. Gilchrist Jun 14, 1904
REGISTRATION #:	DRP 162,930
CIRCA:	1913 - 1920?
FREQUENCY:	
MANUFACTURER:	Helmut Gebel
MATERIAL:	cast iron
FINISH:	nickel
COMMENTS:	This advertisement dates to 1936; possibly this is only an alternative marketing name for the BISON No 6 and no marked versions existed.

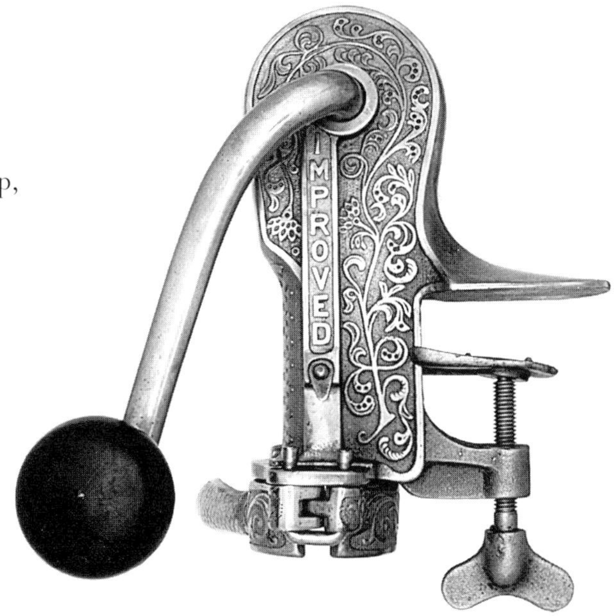

NAME:	**IMPROVED** (marked)
TRADEMARK:	none
OTHER MARKS:	none
NOTICE:	Gilchrist thumb piece, bottle clasp, crank handle
I.D. #:	**I01.1.1**
INVENTOR & DATE:	R. Gilchrist Jun 19, 1906
REGISTRATION #:	P 823,678
CIRCA:	1906? -1913?
FREQUENCY:	
MANUFACTURER:	Arcade Manufacturing Co.
MATERIAL:	cast iron
FINISH:	nickel
COMMENTS:	This is a predecessor to Gilchrist's YANKEE NO6 mechanism, in a CHAMPION case; the patent is for the bottle clasp mechanism.

NAME: **INFANTA no 8** (marked)

TRADEMARK: none

OTHER MARKS: Pat. Jan. 1st 95.

NOTICE: a mounted version of the THOMASON mechanism

I.D. #: **I02.1.1**

INVENTOR & DATE: H. Williams Jan 01, 1895

REGISTRATION #: P 531,670

CIRCA: 1895 - ?

FREQUENCY:

MANUFACTURER: presumably Meriden Malleable Iron Co.

MATERIAL: cast iron

FINISH: nickel

COMMENTS: This 1895 advertisement shows the first version with a nut holding the crank arm on and no hole or clip in the front of the frame, as per the patent drawing and claim.

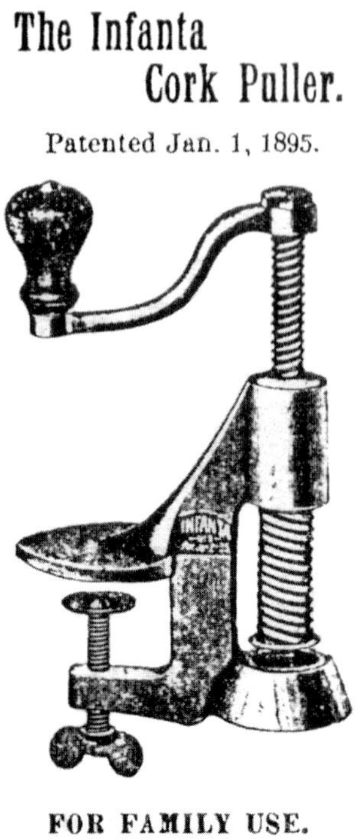

NAME: **INFANTA no 8** (marked)

TRADEMARK: none

OTHER MARKS: Pat. Jan. 1st 95.

NOTICE: hole in the front of the frame, notch in the screw thread just above the frame

I.D. #: **I02.1.2**

INVENTOR & DATE: H. Williams Jan 01, 1895

REGISTRATION #: P 531,670

CIRCA: 1896? - ?

FREQUENCY:

MANUFACTURER: presumably Meriden Malleable Iron Co.

MATERIAL: cast iron

FINISH: nickel

COMMENTS: This was an interim solution with a spring and ball bearing inserted into the rear of the frame which engaged a notch cut into a thread in the outer screw.

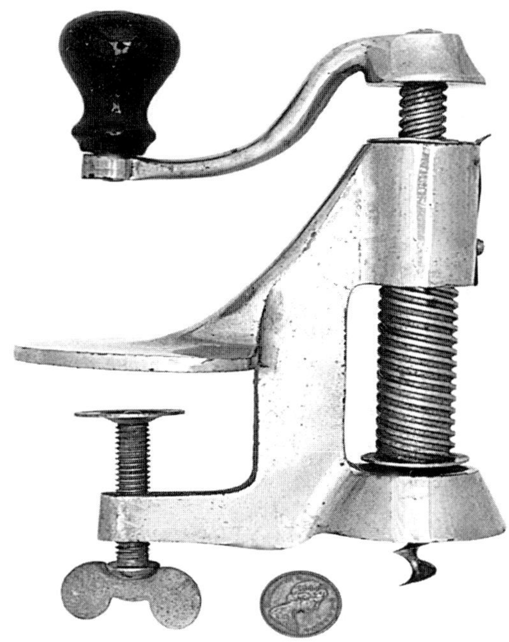

NAME: **INFANTA no 8** (unmarked)

TRADEMARK: none

OTHER MARKS: none

NOTICE: clip and screw on the front of the frame, the crank is fixed by a screw, marked version is *I02.2.1*

I.D. #: **I02.2.2**

INVENTOR & DATE: H. Williams Jan 01, 1895

REGISTRATION #: P 531,670

CIRCA: 1897? - ?

FREQUENCY:

MANUFACTURER: presumably Meriden Malleable Iron Co.

MATERIAL: cast iron

FINISH: nickel

COMMENTS: Assumed to be the final version, where the clip, inserted in a cut channel, captured the outer screw, holding it down thus preventing it from being dragged up by the inner screw. The marked version **I02.2.1** would be

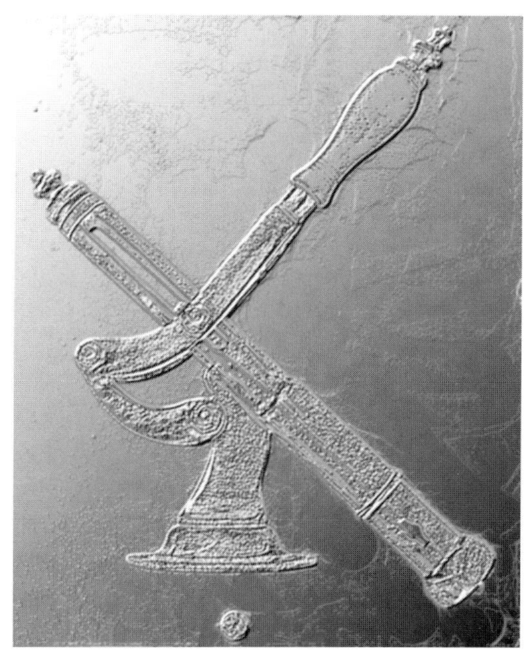

NAME: **INVICTA** (marked)

TRADEMARK: not inspected

OTHER MARKS: L. LUMLEY & CO. LTD. LONDON.

NOTICE: no photo available

I.D. #: **I03.1.1**

INVENTOR & DATE: no English patent or registration found

REGISTRATION #:

CIRCA: 1900? - ?

FREQUENCY:

MANUFACTURER: British

MATERIAL: brass

FINISH: not inspected

COMMENTS: This corkscrew is a private label version of the British RAPID.

Echt amerikanischer
Invincible-Entkorker

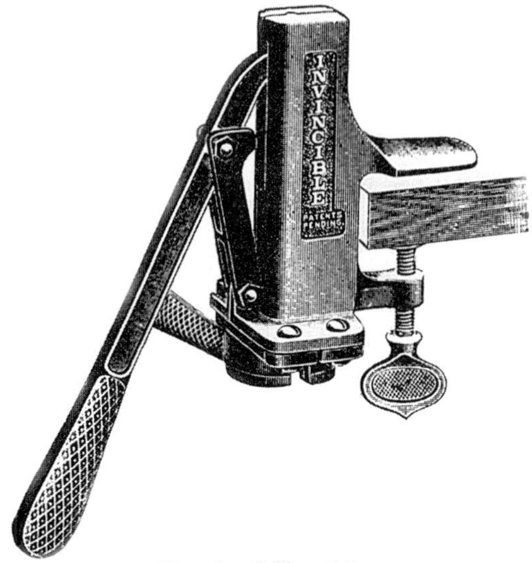

Preis Mk. 15.—

NAME:	**INVINCIBLE** (marked)
TRADEMARK:	not inspected
OTHER MARKS:	PATENTS PENDING
NOTICE:	operating lever, thumb piece, bottle clasps
I.D. #:	**I04.1.1**
INVENTOR & DATE:	no patent or registration found
REGISTRATION #:	
CIRCA:	1900? - ?
FREQUENCY:	
MANUFACTURER:	American ?
MATERIAL:	cast iron
FINISH:	not inspected
COMMENTS:	In this advertisement for an unknown corkscrew, the operating lever looks like a Baumgarten design, the bottle clasps something like Gilchrist; the thumb piece would indicate Bradley & Hubbard as the manufacturer. See AJAX.

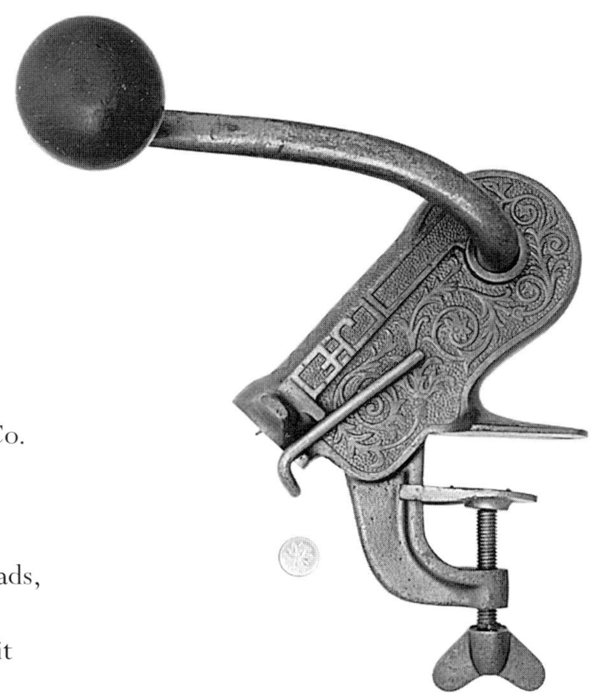

NAME:	**JHE** (marked)
TRADEMARK:	none
OTHER MARKS:	none
NOTICE:	not quite a Gilchrist thumb piece
I.D. #:	**J01.1.1**
INVENTOR & DATE:	R. Gilchrist Jun 14, 1904
REGISTRATION #:	DRP 162,930
CIRCA:	1905? - ?1913
FREQUENCY:	
MANUFACTURER:	presumably Arcade Manufacturing Co.
MATERIAL:	cast iron
FINISH:	no trace remaining
COMMENTS:	This corkscrew has USA screw threads, Arcade "vine & leaf" pattern, screw mounted crank handle; presumably it was a US made private label for the European market.

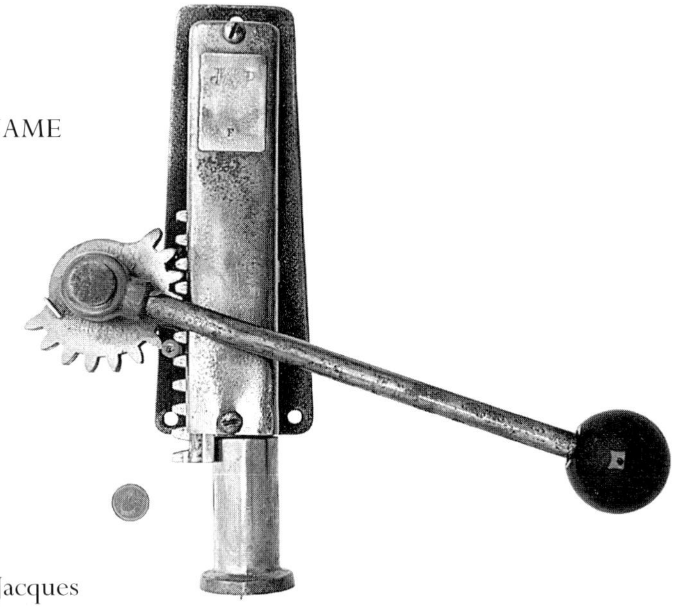

NAME: **JP f** (marked)
TRADEMARK: none
OTHER MARKS: none
NOTICE: rather crude hand stamped NAME
I.D. #: **J03.1.1**
INVENTOR & DATE: no French patent or registration found
REGISTRATION #:
CIRCA: 1920? - 1940?
FREQUENCY:
MANUFACTURER: France ?
MATERIAL: cast iron, brass
FINISH: no trace remaining
COMMENTS: Could "JP" over "f" indicate Jacques Perille, France?

The Jubilee

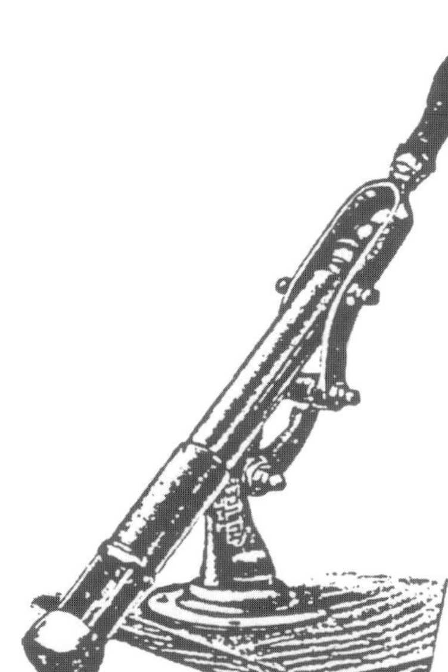

Very strong and well nickel-plated to screw on counter, **35/-**

NAME: **JUBILEE, THE** (not inspected)
TRADEMARK: not inspected
OTHER MARKS: not inspected
NOTICE: open throat
I.D. #: **J04.1.1**
INVENTOR & DATE: no English patent or registration found
REGISTRATION #:
CIRCA: 1896? -1897?
FREQUENCY:
MANUFACTURER: presumably Samuel Mason Ltd.
MATERIAL: brass
FINISH: nickel
COMMENTS: As found in this 1897 T. Heath advertisement this is possibly a private label RAPID for Heath.

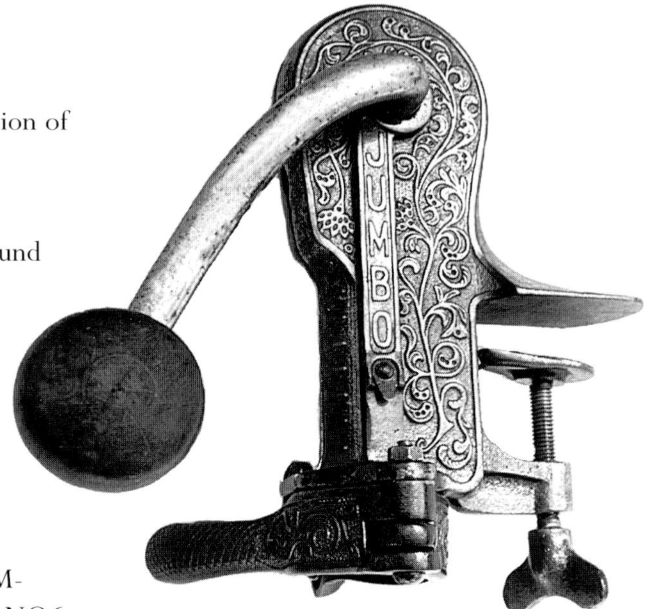

NAME:	**JUMBO** (marked)
TRADEMARK:	none
OTHER MARKS:	none
NOTICE:	Gilchrist thumb piece, early version of his bottle clasp
I.D. #:	**J05.1.1**
INVENTOR & DATE:	no USA patent or registration found
REGISTRATION #:	
CIRCA:	1900? - 1905?
FREQUENCY:	
MANUFACTURER:	Arcade Manufacturing Co.
MATERIAL:	cast iron
FINISH:	nickel
COMMENTS:	This predecessor to Gilchrist's IMPROVED has the early YANKEE NO6 mechanism in a CHAMPION case. The bottle clasp is also a predecessor to his patented bottle clasp. P. T. Barnum popularized the name "Jumbo" in about 1890.

NAME:	**JUPP** (not inspected)
TRADEMARK:	not inspected
OTHER MARKS:	not inspected
NOTICE:	no illustration available
I.D. #:	**J06.1.1**
INVENTOR & DATE:	no German patent or registration found
REGISTRATION #:	
CIRCA:	1900? - ?
FREQUENCY:	
MANUFACTURER:	Helmut Gebel
MATERIAL:	cast iron
FINISH:	not inspected
COMMENTS:	This NAME was mentioned in an article by Helmut Gebel who said "it was like the BISON-HEBE".

NAME:	**KING, THE** (marked)
TRADEMARK:	none
OTHER MARKS:	THE KING, MAISON RUBEN, 17 RUE HEYVAERT, BRUXELLES
NOTICE:	the wooden base with the Ruben plate is not shown, an aluminum stem carrier, metric screw threads
I.D. #:	**K01.1.1**
INVENTOR & DATE:	no Belgian patent or registration found
REGISTRATION #:	
CIRCA:	1923? - ?
FREQUENCY:	
MANUFACTURER:	Maison Ruben ?
MATERIAL:	brass
FINISH:	nickel
COMMENTS:	Presumably manufactured by the makers of the TITAN; it is not known which king is being referred to.

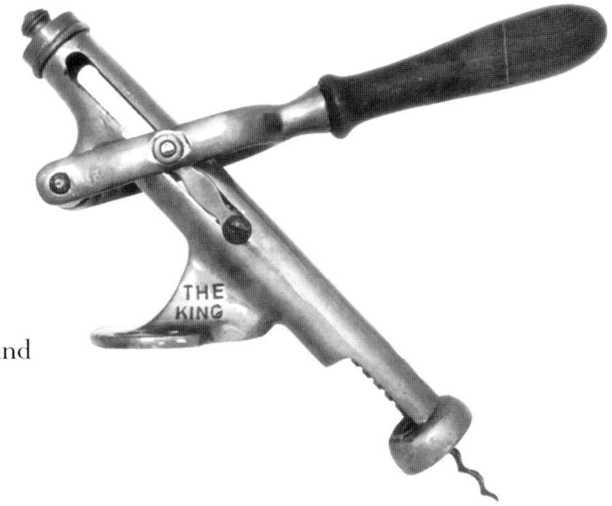

NAME:	**KING, THE** (marked)
TRADEMARK:	not inspected
OTHER MARKS:	not inspected
NOTICE:	shown with and without the advertising plate, advertising plate version *K02.2.1*
I.D. #:	**K02.1.1**
INVENTOR & DATE:	R. Gilchrist Aug 12, 1902
REGISTRATION #:	LP 17,752
CIRCA:	1901? - 1910?
FREQUENCY:	
MANUFACTURER:	Gaskell
MATERIAL:	cast iron
FINISH:	nickel
COMMENTS:	A British advertising plate version of Gilchrist's MODERN, very similar to the advertising plate version of the YANKEE No 2; it was a slightly modified version of THE REX.

NAME:	**LEVER** (unmarked)
TRADEMARK:	none
OTHER MARKS:	HURLEY, ERIE, PA
NOTICE:	marks are cast into the barrel, no advertising plate, frame slightly larger and heavier than the wire breaker version
I.D. #:	**L03.1.1**
INVENTOR & DATE:	D. Hurley Oct 25, 1887
REGISTRATION #:	P 372,266
CIRCA:	1886? - 1887?
FREQUENCY:	
MANUFACTURER:	American
MATERIAL:	cast iron
FINISH:	traces of gold paint
COMMENTS:	This patent by Daniel Hurley (rather than John) was not assigned to the F. F. Adams Company.

NAME:	**LEVER** (unmarked)
TRADEMARK:	none
OTHER MARKS:	none
NOTICE:	data from an unmarked version of L03.1.1, no advertising plate
I.D. #:	**L03.1.2**
INVENTOR & DATE:	D. Hurley Oct 25, 1887
REGISTRATION #:	P 372,266
CIRCA:	1887 - 1900?
FREQUENCY:	
MANUFACTURER:	American
MATERIAL:	cast iron
FINISH:	nickel
COMMENTS:	This 1895 advertisement shows the patented version; LEVER is a great name for this corkscrew.

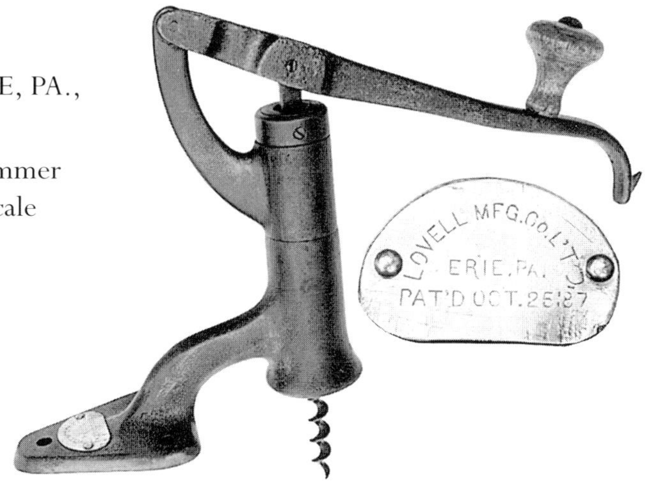

NAME: **LEVER** (unmarked)
TRADEMARK: none
OTHER MARKS: LOVELL MFG. Co. L'T'D', ERIE, PA., PAT'D OCT. 25.87
NOTICE: operating lever wire breaker, slimmer barrel, advertising plate out of scale
I.D. #: **L03.1.3**
INVENTOR & DATE: D. Hurley Oct 25, 1887
REGISTRATION #: P 372,266
CIRCA: 1887 - 1900?
FREQUENCY:
MANUFACTURER: Lovell Mfg. Co.
MATERIAL: cast iron
FINISH: nickel
COMMENTS: Presumed to be a slightly later version, this has a wire breaker on the end of the operating lever.

NAME: **LINDSTROM, P. F.** (marked)
TRADEMARK: not inspected
OTHER MARKS: PATENT, STOCKHOLM
NOTICE: weighing in at 14 kg with 144 different components
I.D. #: **L06.1.1**
INVENTOR & DATE: P. F. Lindstrom Feb 24, 1870
REGISTRATION #: not found
CIRCA: 1870? - 1875 ?
FREQUENCY:
MANUFACTURER: Swedish
MATERIAL: cast iron
FINISH: black paint
COMMENTS: The very first automatic bar corkscrew, whose production costs would have limited their sale. A. Muir patented a copy of this corkscrew in both England and the USA.

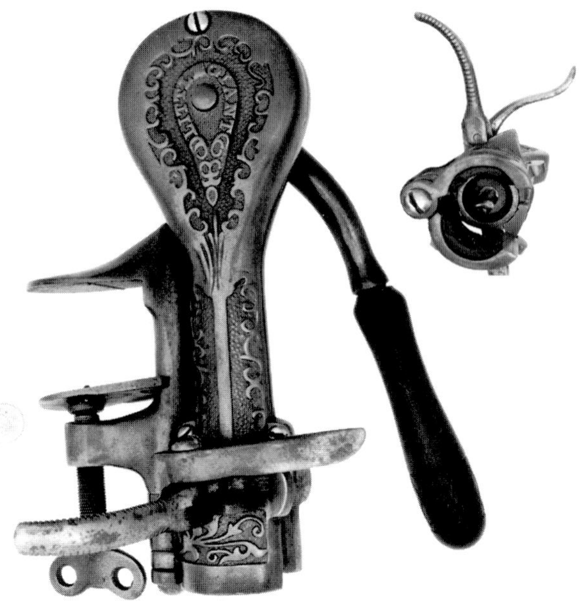

NAME: **LITTLE GIANT** (marked)

TRADEMARK: none

OTHER MARKS: PAT APD FOR

NOTICE: ARCADE style frame decorations and BEAUMONT style thumb piece

I.D. #: **L07.1.1**

INVENTOR & DATE: J. Rogginger, application filed Sep 13, 1900

REGISTRATION #: P 676,205

CIRCA: 1900

FREQUENCY:

MANUFACTURER: Arcade Manufacturing Co.

MATERIAL: cast iron

FINISH: nickel

COMMENTS: This was manufactured as shown in the patent drawing. The basic worm-nut mechanism would have infringed on Arcade's patent.

NAME: **LITTLE QUICKER** (marked)

TRADEMARK: none

OTHER MARKS: PATENTED JULY 23, 1895 - APR. 7, 1896, PAT'S PENDING

NOTICE: only one slot in the case, stud on the inside of the bottle clasp lever, advertising plate out of scale

I.D. #: **L04.1.1**

INVENTOR & DATE: E. Walker, Nov 03, 1899

REGISTRATION #: P 64,722

CIRCA: 1899? -1905?

FREQUENCY:

MANUFACTURER: Erie Specialty Co.

MATERIAL: cast iron

FINISH: nickel

COMMENTS: On this version, a stud on the bottle clasp handle catches and releases the worm nut. The only patent found that was specific to this corkscrew is the 1899 Canadian patent.

NAME: **LITTLE QUICKER** (marked)

TRADEMARK: none

OTHER MARKS: PATENTED JULY 23, 1895, PAT'S PENDING

NOTICE: only one slot in the frame, lever sticking out through the bottle neck rest, advertising plate out of scale

I.D. #: **L04.2.1**

INVENTOR & DATE: no applicable US patent or registration found

REGISTRATION #:

CIRCA: 1895? -1900?

FREQUENCY:

MANUFACTURER: Erie Specialty Co.

MATERIAL: cast iron

FINISH: nickel

COMMENTS: On this version, a lever is bent around and up through the throat. When a bottle is placed on the neck rest, the lever lifts the swinging plate, which releases the worm nut.

NAME: **LITTLE QUICKER** (marked)

TRADEMARK: none

OTHER MARKS: PATENTED JULY 23, 1895, PAT'S PENDING

NOTICE: two slots in the frame allowing an external lever to release the worm nut, advertising plate out of scale

I.D. #: **L04.3.1**

INVENTOR & DATE: E. Walker, May 15, 1900

REGISTRATION #: P 649,498

CIRCA: 1896 - 1900?

FREQUENCY:

MANUFACTURER: Erie Specialty Co.

MATERIAL: cast iron

FINISH: nickel

COMMENTS: As with the QUICK & EASY, the bottle clasp was very fragile and is often missing, leaving an empty mounting hole in the left side of the throat.

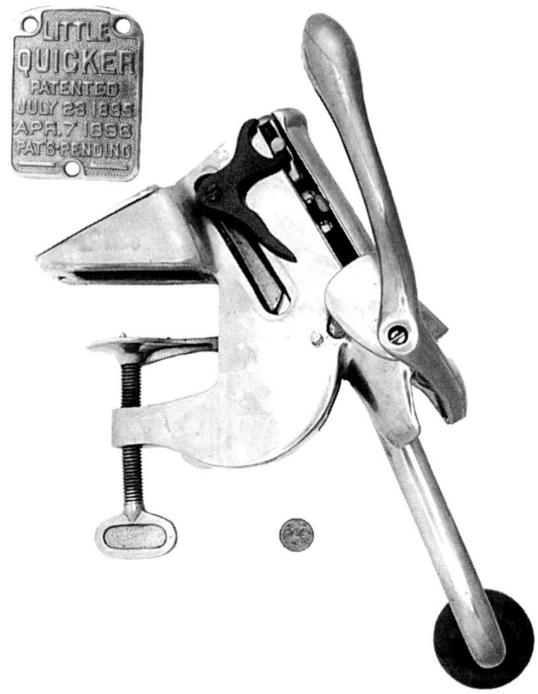

NAME:	**LITTLE QUICKER** (marked)
TRADEMARK:	none
OTHER MARKS:	PATENTED JULY 23, 1895 - APR. 7, 1896, PAT'S PENDING
NOTICE:	a completely restored example, both internally and externally, advertising plate out of scale
I.D. #:	**L04.4.1**
INVENTOR & DATE:	E. Walker, May 15, 1900
REGISTRATION #:	P 649,498
CIRCA:	1896 - 1900?
FREQUENCY:	
MANUFACTURER:	Erie Specialty Co.
MATERIAL:	cast iron
FINISH:	nickel
COMMENTS:	It has the same mechanism as **L04.3.1**, but this version is complete with the bottle clasp.

"The Luxury"

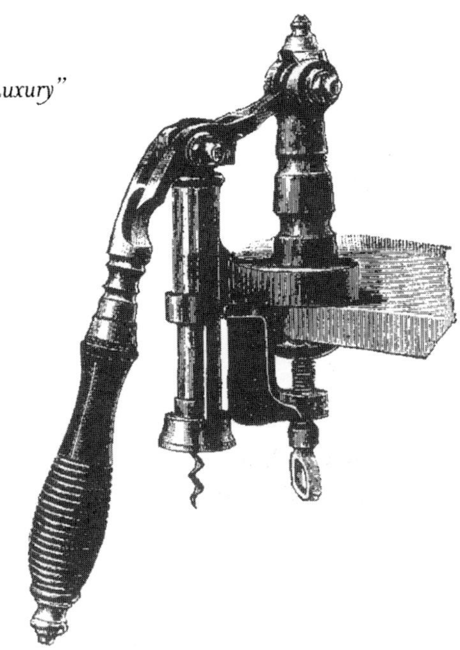

NAME:	**LUXURY** (not inspected)
TRADEMARK:	not inspected
OTHER MARKS:	not inspected
NOTICE:	vertical version
I.D. #:	**L05.1.1**
INVENTOR & DATE:	W. Vaughan May 05, 1896
REGISTRATION #:	LP 9,519
CIRCA:	1896 - ?
FREQUENCY:	
MANUFACTURER:	English
MATERIAL:	not inspected
FINISH:	not inspected
COMMENTS:	This has a British worm-nut mechanism.

NAME: **LUXURY** (not inspected)
TRADEMARK: not inspected
OTHER MARKS: not inspected
NOTICE: inclined version
I.D. #: **L05.2.1**
INVENTOR & DATE: W. Vaughan May 05, 1897
REGISTRATION #: LP 9,519
CIRCA: 1896 - ?
FREQUENCY:
MANUFACTURER: English
MATERIAL: not inspected
FINISH: not inspected
COMMENTS: This has a British worm-nut mechanism.

"The Luxury"

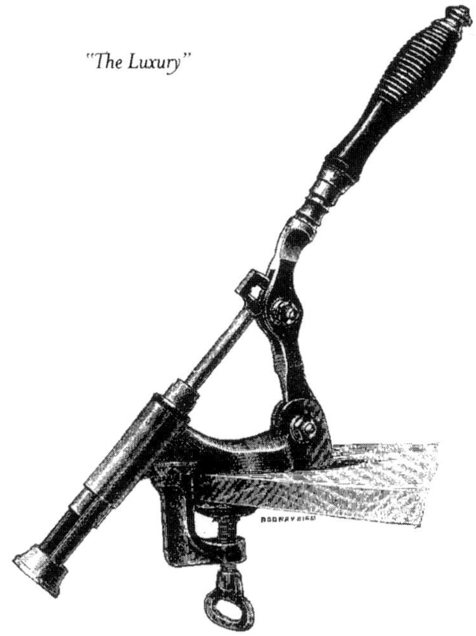

NAME: **MERIDEN** (not inspected)
TRADEMARK: not inspected
OTHER MARKS: not inspected
NOTICE: appears to have a rack driven worm-nut mechanism
I.D. #: **M01.1.1**
INVENTOR & DATE: no US patent or registration found
REGISTRATION #:
CIRCA: 1894 - ?
FREQUENCY:
MANUFACTURER: Meriden Malleable Iron Co.
MATERIAL: cast iron
FINISH: nickel
COMMENTS: The illustration was extremely poor in this 1894 advertisement. It would appear that a long protuberance on the crank arm engaged a stud on the worm-nut, pushing the worm-nut down to strip the cork.

MERIDEN CORK PULL No. 48

One of the best Cork Pulls for Hotels, Cafes and Club use. Avoids many of the defective points of construction in other patterns, has great strength, easy power and lasting qualities. Is nickel plated and provided with clamp.

Price each $3.25

NAME:	**MERRITT, THE** (unmarked)
TRADEMARK:	none
OTHER MARKS:	PAT. APLD. FOR
NOTICE:	thumb piece, brass finish variant *M02.1.2*
I.D. #:	**M02.1.1**
INVENTOR & DATE:	C. Chambers, application filed Mar 20, 1888
REGISTRATION #:	LP 4,564
CIRCA:	Mar 1888 - Jan 1889
FREQUENCY:	
MANUFACTURER:	presumably Samuel Mason Ltd.
MATERIAL:	brass or bronze
FINISH:	none
COMMENTS:	This prototype or very early MERRITT, without the Merritt name marked on it, has a clamp frame of brass rather than iron and an Italian style thumb piece. It is the only known example of a British bar corkscrew marked to indicate that a patent had been applied for. The patent was accepted Jan 22, 1889.

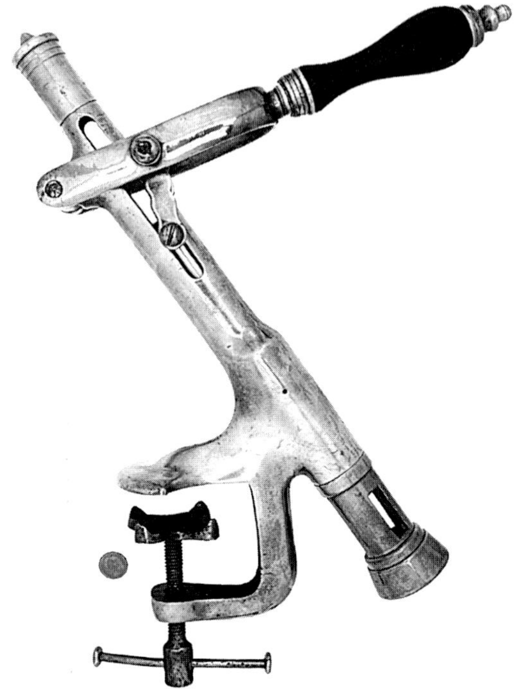

NAME:	**MERRITT, THE** (marked)
TRADEMARK:	none
OTHER MARKS:	none
NOTICE:	cast iron clamp, thumb piece
I.D. #:	**M02.2.1**
INVENTOR & DATE:	C. Chambers Mar 20, 1888
REGISTRATION #:	LP 4,564
CIRCA:	1890? - 1900?
FREQUENCY:	
MANUFACTURER:	presumably Samuel Mason Ltd.
MATERIAL:	brass
FINISH:	nickel
COMMENTS:	The thumb piece probably indicates an early version.

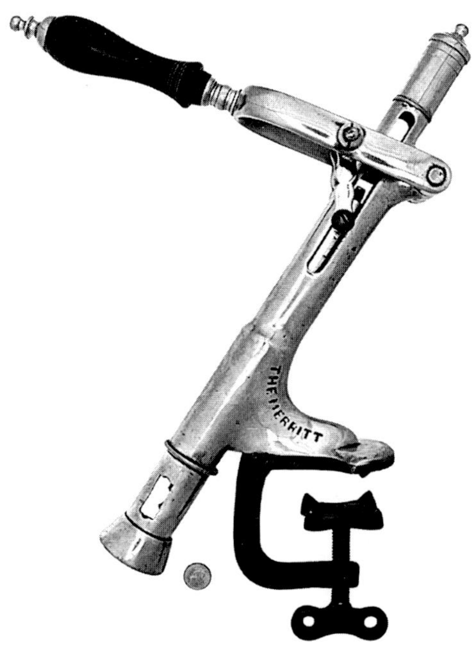

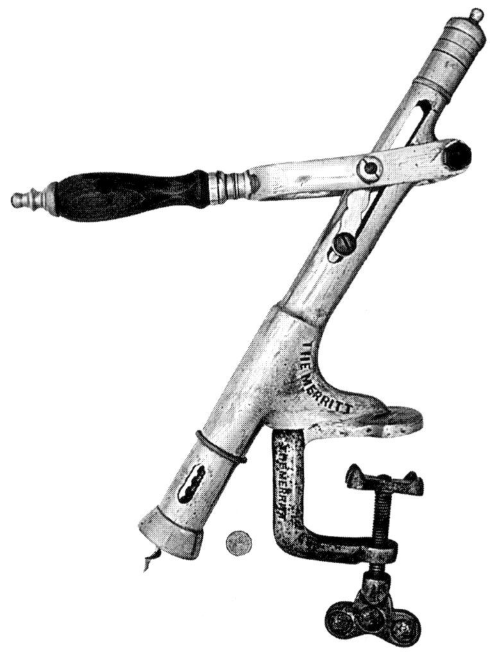

NAME: **MERRITT, THE** (marked)
TRADEMARK: hand & star
OTHER MARKS: CHAMBERS PATENT
NOTICE: brass finish variant *M02.3.2*
I.D. #: **M02.3.1**
INVENTOR & DATE: C. Chambers Mar 20, 1888
REGISTRATION #: LP 4,564
CIRCA: 1900 - 1920?
FREQUENCY:
MANUFACTURER: Gaskell
MATERIAL: brass
FINISH: nickel
COMMENTS: **MERRITT** is cast into both the iron clamp frame and the brass frame.

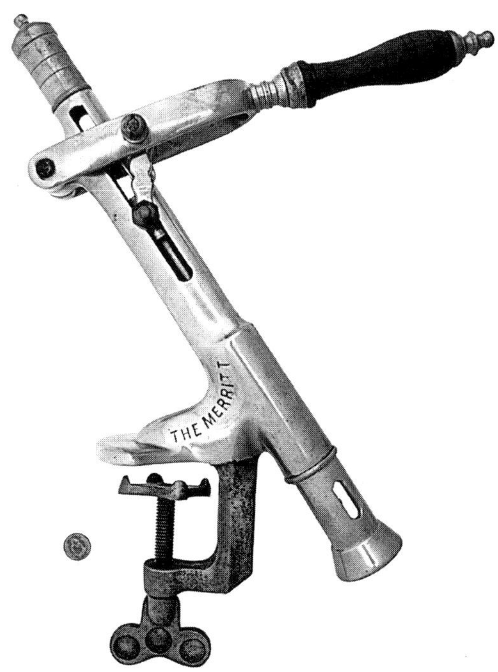

NAME: **MERRITT, THE** (marked)
TRADEMARK: optic
OTHER MARKS: CHAMBERS PATENT, G&C
NOTICE: brass finish variant *M02.3.4*
I.D. #: **M02.3.3**
INVENTOR & DATE: C. Chambers Mar 20, 1888
REGISTRATION #: LP 4,564
CIRCA: 1925?-?
FREQUENCY:
MANUFACTURER: Gaskell & Chambers Ltd.
MATERIAL: brass
FINISH: nickel
COMMENTS: A later version; most of these cork-screws have only traces of nickel plating remaining.

NAME:	**MERRITT, THE** (marked)
TRADEMARK:	hand & star
OTHER MARKS:	CHAMBERS PATENT
NOTICE:	brass finish variant *M02.4.2*
I.D. #:	**M02.4.1**
INVENTOR & DATE:	C. Chambers Mar 20, 1888
REGISTRATION #:	LP 4,564
CIRCA:	1900 - 1920?
FREQUENCY:	
MANUFACTURER:	Gaskell
MATERIAL:	brass
FINISH:	nickel
COMMENTS:	This top mount version has slight differences in finials and throat decoration.

NAME:	**MERRITT, THE** (marked)
TRADEMARK:	optic
OTHER MARKS:	CHAMBERS PATENT
NOTICE:	brass finish variant *M02.5.2*
I.D. #:	**M02.5.1**
INVENTOR & DATE:	C. Chambers Mar 20, 1888
REGISTRATION #:	LP 4,564
CIRCA:	1925?-?
FREQUENCY:	
MANUFACTURER:	Gaskell & Chambers Ltd.
MATERIAL:	brass
FINISH:	nickel
COMMENTS:	This top mount version has slight differences in finials and throat decoration.

NAME:	**MIDGET** (unmarked)
TRADEMARK:	none
OTHER MARKS:	none
NOTICE:	clamp mount version
I.D. #:	**M03.1.1**
INVENTOR & DATE:	no US patent or registration found
REGISTRATION #:	
CIRCA:	1893? - 1898?
FREQUENCY:	
MANUFACTURER:	Arcade Manufacturing Co.
MATERIAL:	cast iron
FINISH:	nickel
COMMENTS:	This 1893 advertising shows the first two cycle, very small, Gilchrist corkscrew which may pre-date the ARCADE. This corkscrew mechanism is similar to the much later YANKEE No 1 mechanism in that a stud on the operating lever released the worm-nut. On the examples examined, the brass nut was filled with the standard babbitt.

NAME:	**MIDGET** (unmarked)
TRADEMARK:	none
OTHER MARKS:	none
NOTICE:	wall mount version
I.D. #:	**M03.2.1**
INVENTOR & DATE:	no US patent or registration found
REGISTRATION #:	
CIRCA:	1893? - 1898?
FREQUENCY:	
MANUFACTURER:	Arcade Manufacturing Co.
MATERIAL:	cast iron
FINISH:	nickel
COMMENTS:	MIDGETs have a metal clip to hold a beer bottle lip; both the worm-nut and the lip catch were released by the operating lever. It is curious that Gilchrist did not patent this mechanism in the USA, but that he did patent a different style of bottle clasp for it in 1905. The complete MIDGET with the later bottle clasp was patented by A. Pick in England in 1896 and in Germany by A. Pick and H. Bisseker of Birmingham in 1897.

NAME: **MILANO** (marked)
TRADEMARK: not inspected
OTHER MARKS: not inspected
NOTICE: handle, thumb piece
I.D. #: **M04.1.1**
INVENTOR & DATE: no Italian patent or registration found
REGISTRATION #:
CIRCA: 1895 ? - 1910?
FREQUENCY:
MANUFACTURER: Italian ?
MATERIAL: cast iron
FINISH: nickel
COMMENTS: Because of the typical Italian style thumb piece it is assumed that this corkscrew was made in Italy rather than being a private label version of the CHAMPION.

NAME: **MODERN, THE** (marked)
TRADEMARK: none
OTHER MARKS: none
NOTICE:
I.D. #: **M05.1.1**
INVENTOR & DATE: R. Gilchrist Jun 25, 1907
REGISTRATION #: P 857,992
CIRCA: 1901 - 1920?
FREQUENCY:
MANUFACTURER: Arcade Manufacturing Co.
MATERIAL: cast iron
FINISH: nickel
COMMENTS: This 1902 advertisement shows a decorative version of the YANKEE No 2 with only very slight modifications to the original YANKEE mechanism.

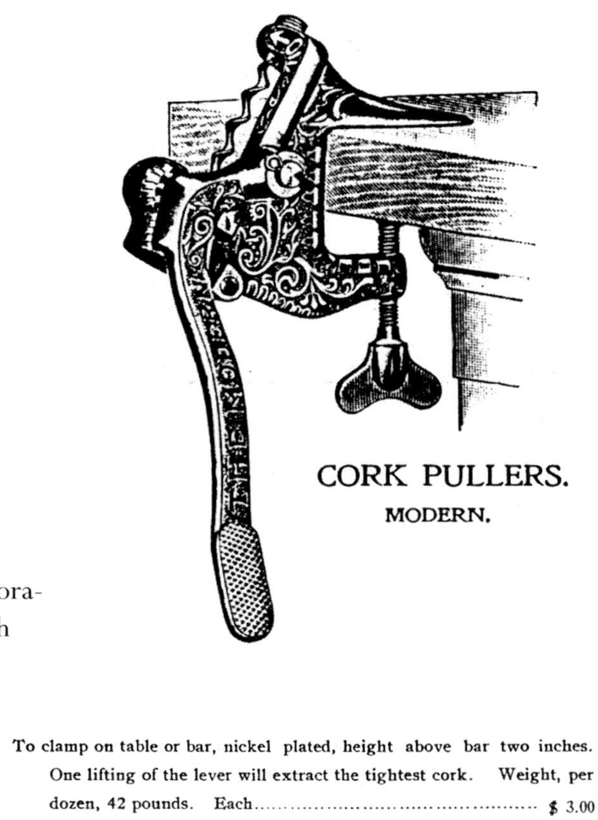

NAME:	**MODERN, THE** (marked)	
TRADEMARK:	none	
OTHER MARKS:	none	
NOTICE:	crank handle, advertising plate out of scale	
I.D. #:	**M05.1.2**	
INVENTOR & DATE:	R. Gilchrist Jun 25, 1907	
REGISTRATION #:	P 857,992	
CIRCA:	1901 - 1920?	
FREQUENCY:		
MANUFACTURER:	Arcade Manufacturing Co.	
MATERIAL:	cast iron	
FINISH:	nickel	
COMMENTS:	Possibly the crank handle was implemented for the European market.	

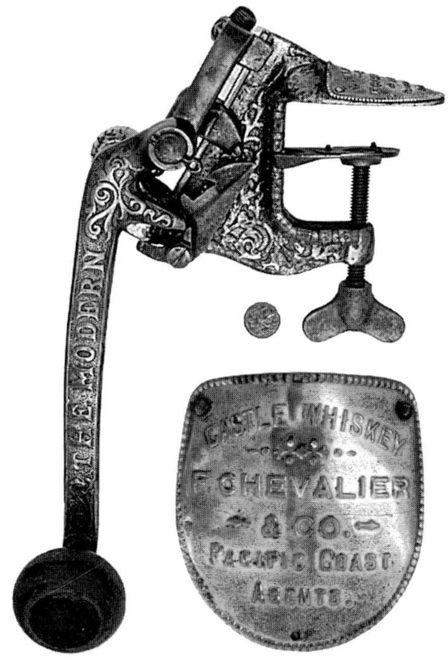

NAME:	**MODERN, THE** (marked)	
TRADEMARK:	none	
OTHER MARKS:	none	
NOTICE:	wall mount version	
I.D. #:	**M05.2.1**	
INVENTOR & DATE:	R. Gilchrist Jun 25, 1907	
REGISTRATION #:	P 857,992	
CIRCA:	1901 - 1920?	
FREQUENCY:		
MANUFACTURER:	Arcade Manufacturing Co.	
MATERIAL:	cast iron	
FINISH:	nickel	
COMMENTS:	This is a decorative version of the YANKEE No 1.	

NAME: **MODERN, U.S.** (marked)
TRADEMARK: none
OTHER MARKS: none
NOTICE: name
I.D. #: **M06.1.1**
INVENTOR & DATE: R. Gilchrist Jun 25, 1907
REGISTRATION #: P 857,992
CIRCA: 1901 - 1920?
FREQUENCY:
MANUFACTURER: Arcade Manufacturing Co.
MATERIAL: cast iron
FINISH: nickel
COMMENTS: Possibly "US" was added so that it could be imported into Europe, where the country of origin had to be marked on the product.

NAME: **MONTEREY** (marked)
TRADEMARK: not inspected
OTHER MARKS: not inspected
NOTICE: no photograph available
I.D. #: **M07.1.1**
INVENTOR & DATE: not inspected
REGISTRATION #:
CIRCA:
FREQUENCY:
MANUFACTURER: Arcade Manufacturing Co.
MATERIAL: cast iron
FINISH: not inspected
COMMENTS: It was reported as "looking like a CHAMPION, but was marked MONTEREY".

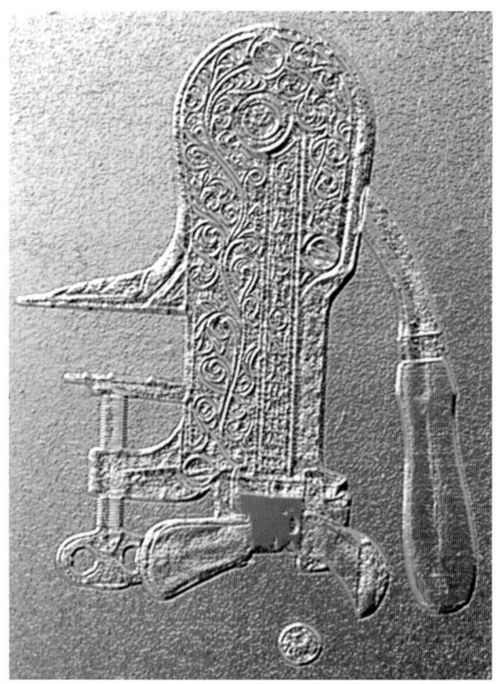

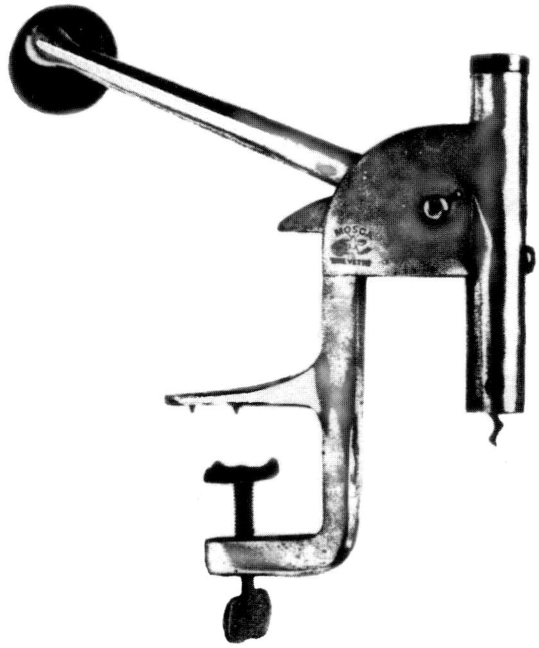

NAME:	**MOSCA** (marked)
TRADEMARK:	FLY
OTHER MARKS:	T??E VET?? (difficult to read)
NOTICE:	Mason style thumb piece and clamp, missing bottle-pushing sleeve
I.D. #:	**M08.1.1**
INVENTOR & DATE:	no Italian patent or registration found
REGISTRATION #:	
CIRCA:	1890? - 1900?
FREQUENCY:	[corkscrew symbol]
MANUFACTURER:	American, British or Mosca in Italy?
MATERIAL:	cast iron
FINISH:	not inspected
COMMENTS:	The illustration is not good, but this is a version of the US RAPID. It is not known if this was a private label manufactured in the USA, a Gaskell or an Italian product.

One dozen in a box.

New Century Cork Puller. Easy Working. Nickel-Plated . . . Per Dozen $33 00

NAME:	**NEW CENTURY** (marked)
TRADEMARK:	none
OTHER MARKS:	none
NOTICE:	the name should make this relatively easy to date
I.D. #:	**N01.1.1**
INVENTOR & DATE:	R. Gilchrist Jun 25, 1907
REGISTRATION #:	P 857,992
CIRCA:	1899 - 1902?
FREQUENCY:	[corkscrew symbol])
MANUFACTURER:	Arcade Manufacturing Co.
MATERIAL:	cast iron
FINISH:	nickel
COMMENTS:	This 1902 advertising shows a private label version of THE MODERN.

NAME:	**NEW ENGLAND** (marked)
TRADEMARK:	none
OTHER MARKS:	none
NOTICE:	found in Sweden, clamp plate, bushings and tapered pins are not standard
I.D. #:	**N02.1.1**
INVENTOR & DATE:	no Swedish patent or registration found
REGISTRATION #:	
CIRCA:	1901 - 1920?
FREQUENCY:	
MANUFACTURER:	Arcade Manufacturing Co. ?
MATERIAL:	cast iron
FINISH:	nickel
COMMENTS:	The US cotter pins normally found on this corkscrew have been replaced. Possibly this was imported as components and then "improved" and assembled. This can result in a new "country of origin" designation, greatly reducing the import duty.

NAME:	**NEW ERA** (marked)
TRADEMARK:	none
OTHER MARKS:	WILLIAMSONS, PAT JAN 15, 1895 - SEPT 7 1897- MAR 14 1889
NOTICE:	the name should make this relatively easy to date
I.D. #:	**N03.1.1**
INVENTOR & DATE:	C. Morgan May 19, 1903
REGISTRATION #:	P 728,806
CIRCA:	1901? - 1903?
FREQUENCY:	
MANUFACTURER:	Arcade Manufacturing Co.
MATERIAL:	cast iron
FINISH:	nickel
COMMENTS:	Lots of patent dates are marked, but not the applicable one, on this private label PHOENIX 30 made for Williamsons by Arcade. For additional comments see PHOENIX.

NAME:	**NEW ERA** (marked)
TRADEMARK:	none
OTHER MARKS:	WILLIAMSONS, PAT NOV 12, 1895 - SEPT 7 1897- MAR 14 1889
NOTICE:	bottle clasp
I.D. #:	**N03.2.1**
INVENTOR & DATE:	C. Morgan May 19, 1903
REGISTRATION #:	P 728,806
CIRCA:	1901? - 1903?
FREQUENCY:	
MANUFACTURER:	Arcade Manufacturing Co.
MATERIAL:	cast iron
FINISH:	nickel
COMMENTS:	This is a vertical version of the PHOENIX 30 with bottle clasps. Presumably the NOV 12, 1895 patent date is a typo, thus this would be the earlier version.

NAME:	**OK** (marked)
TRADEMARK:	not inspected
OTHER MARKS:	M. J. ORDI & CO LTD. DUBLIN
NOTICE:	probably a replacement clamp plate
I.D. #:	**O01.1.1**
INVENTOR & DATE:	S. Mason Oct 30, 1902
REGISTRATION #:	LP 23,675
CIRCA:	1902 - ?
FREQUENCY:	
MANUFACTURER:	Samuel Mason Ltd.
MATERIAL:	brass
FINISH:	nickel
COMMENTS:	This is a private label version of the A1.

NAME:	**PARK BREW CO** (marked)
TRADEMARK:	none
OTHER MARKS:	none
NOTICE:	
I.D. #:	**P01.1.1**
INVENTOR & DATE:	R. Gilchrist Jun 25, 1907
REGISTRATION #:	P 857,992
CIRCA:	1901? - ?
FREQUENCY:	
MANUFACTURER:	Arcade Manufacturing Co.
MATERIAL:	cast iron
FINISH:	nickel
COMMENTS:	This is a private label version of the YANKEE No 1.

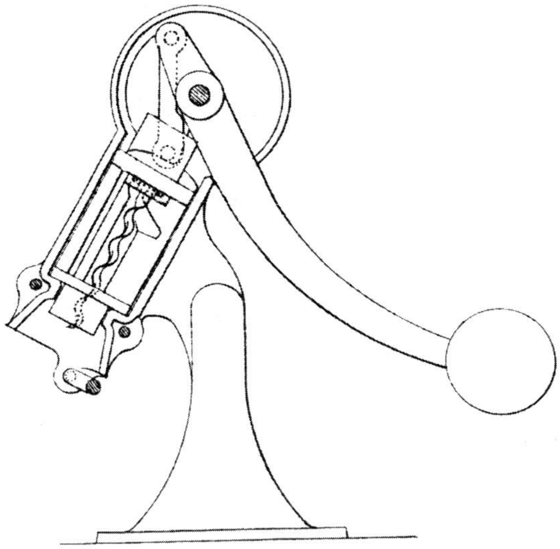

NAME:	**PÉLICAN, LE** (not inspected)
TRADEMARK:	not inspected
OTHER MARKS:	not inspected
NOTICE:	a worm-nut mechanism, painted variant *P02.1.2*
I.D. #:	**P02.1.1**
INVENTOR & DATE:	E. Sitbon Mar 11, 1922
REGISTRATION #:	SGDG 537,989
CIRCA:	1921 - 1926?
FREQUENCY:	
MANUFACTURER:	d' Acier Poli
MATERIAL:	not inspected
FINISH:	nickel
COMMENTS:	This is a patent drawing; there is also a 1922 French advertisement.

NAME: **PERFECT** (marked)
TRADEMARK: not inspected
OTHER MARKS: not inspected
NOTICE: thumb piece, top mount version *P03.2.1*
I.D. #: **P03.1.1**
INVENTOR & DATE: no French patent or registration found
REGISTRATION #:
CIRCA: 1903?
FREQUENCY:
MANUFACTURER: Ernest Martenet ?
MATERIAL: brass
FINISH: nickel
COMMENTS: This advertisement is by Ernest Martenet, makers of the PERFECT lazy tongs. The Swiss style thumb piece might indicate a private label version of the DON made for Martenet. The top mount version was marked, so it is assumed that the clamp mount version was also marked.

NAME: **PHOENIX 20** (marked)
TRADEMARK: none
OTHER MARKS: PAT NOV 12 1895, SEPT 7 1897, MAR 14 1889
NOTICE: operating lever swings over parallel to the counter top
I.D. #: **P04.1.1**
INVENTOR & DATE: C. Morgan May 19, 1903
REGISTRATION #: P 728,806
CIRCA: 1901? - 1903?
FREQUENCY:
MANUFACTURER: Arcade Manufacturing Co.
MATERIAL: cast iron
FINISH: nickel
COMMENTS: Presumably the NOV 12, 1895 patent date is a typo, as this patent was for the second DAISY patent and had nothing to do with this corkscrew. These are all marked PHOENIX on the handle, but the specific model number may or may not have been marked on the clamp frame.

NAME:	**PHOENIX 30** (marked)
TRADEMARK:	none
OTHER MARKS:	PAT NOV 12 1895, SEPT 7 1897. MAR 14 1889
NOTICE:	same mechanism as the PHOENIX 20, but with a vertical operating lever
I.D. #:	**P05.1.1**
INVENTOR & DATE:	C. Morgan May 19, 1903
REGISTRATION #:	P 728,806
CIRCA:	1901? - 1923?
FREQUENCY:	
MANUFACTURER:	Arcade Manufacturing Co.
MATERIAL:	cast iron
FINISH:	nickel
COMMENTS:	The numbers 20,30,etc., in this series are sometimes found cast into the clamp frame.

NAME:	**PHOENIX 40** (marked)
TRADEMARK:	none
OTHER MARKS:	PAT JAN 15 1895, SEPT 7 1897, MAR 14 1889
NOTICE:	bottle clasp version of the PHOENIX 20
I.D. #:	**P04.2.1**
INVENTOR & DATE:	H. Tscherning May 19, 1903
REGISTRATION #:	P 728,517
CIRCA:	1901? - 1903?
FREQUENCY:	
MANUFACTURER:	Arcade Manufacturing Co.
MATERIAL:	cast iron
FINISH:	nickel
COMMENTS:	Arcade has corrected the patent date typo found in **P04.1.1**; still it is only closer to the real patent date.

NAME: **PHOENIX 50** (marked)
TRADEMARK: none
OTHER MARKS: PAT NOV 12 1895, SEPT 7 1897, MAR 14 1889
NOTICE: wall mount version of the PHOENIX 30
I.D. #: **P05.2.1**
INVENTOR & DATE: C. Morgan May 19, 1903
REGISTRATION #: P 728,806
CIRCA: 1901? - 1903?
FREQUENCY:
MANUFACTURER: Arcade Manufacturing Co.
MATERIAL: cast iron
FINISH: nickel
COMMENTS: Arcade has not marked the pertinent patent date on any of the PHOENIXs.

NAME: **PHOENIX 60** (marked)
TRADEMARK: none
OTHER MARKS: not inspected
NOTICE: bottle clasp version of the PHOENIX 30
I.D. #: **P05.3.1**
INVENTOR & DATE: H. Tscherning May 19, 1903
REGISTRATION #: P 728,517
CIRCA: 1901? - 1903?
FREQUENCY:
MANUFACTURER: Arcade Manufacturing Co.
MATERIAL: cast iron
FINISH: nickel
COMMENTS: The very delicate bottle clasp was part of H. Tscherning's 1903 patent.

Arcade Cork Pullers

The Phœnix No. 60

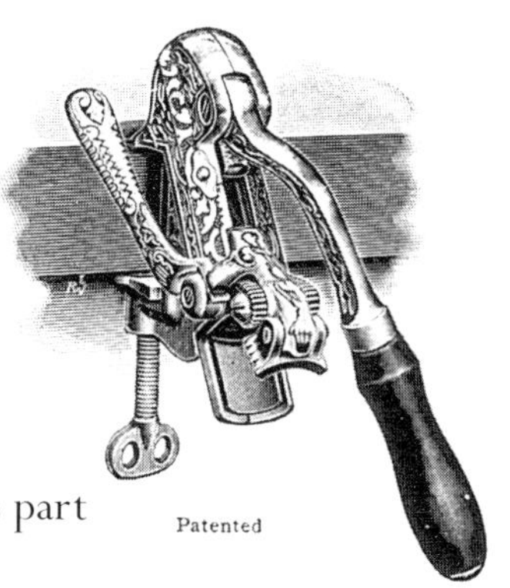

The arrangement of both levers of the No. 60 is most convenient, and as a result a rapid and powerful action is obtained.
All working parts are below the counter.
The puller is built to stand many years of hard service.
Finished with heavy nickel plate, highly polished.

PACKING

Each puller is packed in a wooden box, 1 dozen in a strong shipping case.
Case weight, net 42 pounds, gross 76 pounds. Case measurements, 28x14x12 inches.

NAME:	**PHOENIX 100** (marked)
TRADEMARK:	none
OTHER MARKS:	not inspected
NOTICE:	wall mount version of the PHOENIX 60
I.D. #:	**P05.4.1**
INVENTOR & DATE:	H. Tscherning May 19, 1903
REGISTRATION #:	P 728,517
CIRCA:	1901? - 1903?
FREQUENCY:	
MANUFACTURER:	Arcade Manufacturing Co.
MATERIAL:	cast iron
FINISH:	nickel
COMMENTS:	Due to the clasp lever being very slender cast iron, very few intact bottle clasps will be found.

The Phœnix No. 100

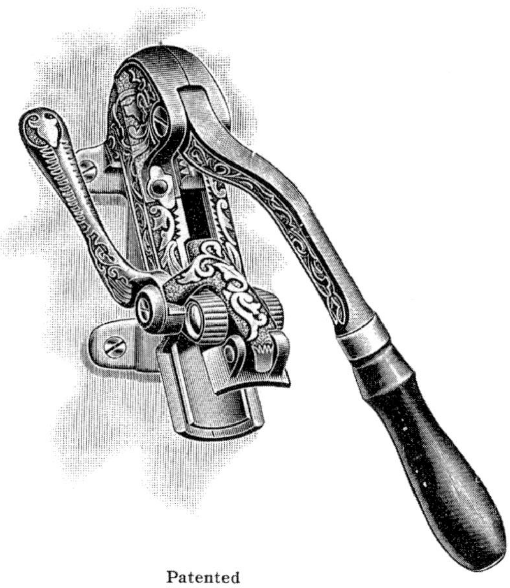

Patented

NAME:	**PHR** (marked)
TRADEMARK:	none
OTHER MARKS:	none
NOTICE:	decorative cast iron clamp plate, thumb piece
I.D. #:	**P06.1.1**
INVENTOR & DATE:	G. Frings, presumably Nov 04, 1925
REGISTRATION #:	DRGM 930,900
CIRCA:	1925? - ?
FREQUENCY:	
MANUFACTURER:	Paul Hammerschmidt
MATERIAL:	cast iron
FINISH:	black and gold paint
COMMENTS:	Despite its fine condition this is possibly an early, or first, version of the grapevine decorated PHR.

NAME: **PHR** (marked)
TRADEMARK: **(K)** on thumb piece
OTHER MARKS:
NOTICE: aluminum paint finish variant *P06.2.2*
I.D. #: **P06.2.1**
INVENTOR & DATE: G. Frings, presumably Nov 04, 1925
REGISTRATION #: DRGM 930,900
CIRCA: 1940 - ?
FREQUENCY: 
MANUFACTURER: Paul Hammerschmidt
MATERIAL: cast iron
FINISH: nickel
COMMENTS: This is a stipple patterned version of the PHR.

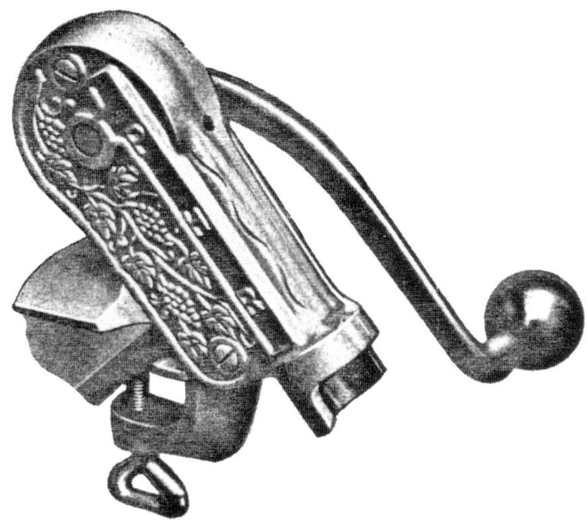

NAME: **PHR** (marked)
TRADEMARK: not inspected
OTHER MARKS: not inspected
NOTICE: ball handle, aluminum paint finish variant *P06.3.2*
I.D. #: **P06.3.1**
INVENTOR & DATE: G. Frings, presumably Nov 04, 1925
REGISTRATION #: DRGM 930,900
CIRCA: 1949? - 1990?
FREQUENCY: 
MANUFACTURER: Paul Hammerschmidt
MATERIAL: cast iron
FINISH: nickel
COMMENTS: This advertisement shows a relatively modern West German version of the earlier grapevine PHR.

NAME: **PIX** (marked)
TRADEMARK: none
OTHER MARKS: ALBERT PICK & CO. CHICAGO USA
NOTICE: PIX cast into one clamp handle
I.D. #: **P07.1.1**
INVENTOR & DATE: C. Morgan Aug 24, 1915
REGISTRATION #: DES 47,755
CIRCA: 1915 - 1920?
FREQUENCY:
MANUFACTURER: Arcade Manufacturing Co.
MATERIAL: cast iron
FINISH: nickel
COMMENTS: This is a private label version of the CHAMPION made for Albert Pick. Morgan's design patent was for the case shape.

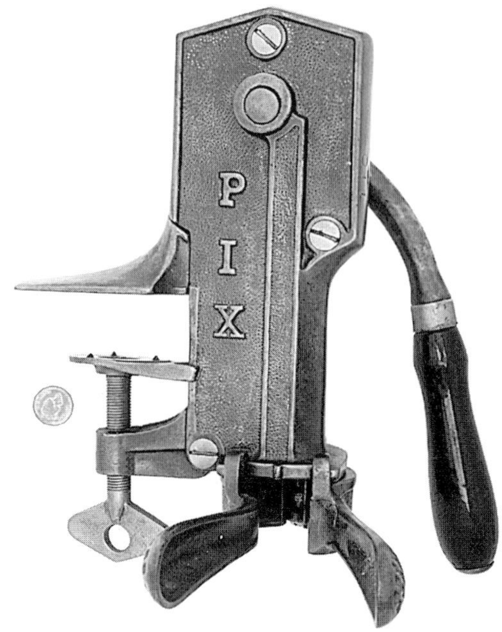

NAME: **PIX** (marked)
TRADEMARK: none
OTHER MARKS: ALBERT PICK & CO. CHICAGO USA
NOTICE: crank handle
I.D. #: **P07.1.2**
INVENTOR & DATE: C. Morgan Aug 24, 1915
REGISTRATION #: DES 47,755
CIRCA: 1915 - 1920?
FREQUENCY:
MANUFACTURER: Arcade Manufacturing Co.
MATERIAL: cast iron
FINISH: nickel
COMMENTS: PIX is not cast into the bottle clasp, as in other examples.

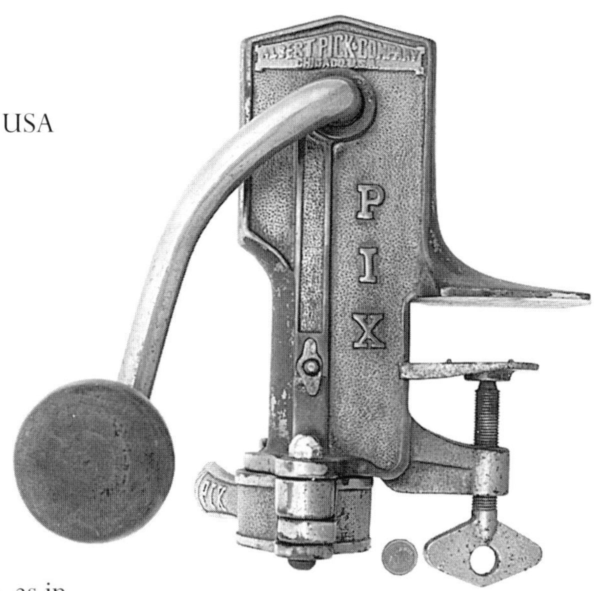

NAME:	**PIX** (marked)
TRADEMARK:	none
OTHER MARKS:	ALBERT PICK & CO. CHICAGO USA
NOTICE:	crank handle, finish
I.D. #:	**P07.1.3**
INVENTOR & DATE:	C. Morgan Aug 24, 1915
REGISTRATION #:	DES 47,755
CIRCA:	1915 - 1920?
FREQUENCY:	
MANUFACTURER:	Arcade Manufacturing Co.
MATERIAL:	cast iron
FINISH:	bronze
COMMENTS:	The PIXs all have the diamond shape thumb piece shown.

NAME:	**PRESTO** (marked)
TRADEMARK:	(G)
OTHER MARKS:	Bte SGDG
NOTICE:	
I.D. #:	**P08.1.1**
INVENTOR & DATE:	P. Wintenberger Jul 16, 1934
REGISTRATION #:	SGDG 771,129
CIRCA:	1932 - ?
FREQUENCY:	
MANUFACTURER:	French
MATERIAL:	cast iron
FINISH:	gray/green paint
COMMENTS:	This was manufactured as shown in the patent drawing.

NAME:	**PRESTO** (marked)
TRADEMARK:	none
OTHER MARKS:	Bte SGDG
NOTICE:	spring added
I.D. #:	**P08.1.2**
INVENTOR & DATE:	P. Wintenberger Jul 16, 1934
REGISTRATION #:	SGDG 771,129
CIRCA:	1932 - ?
FREQUENCY:	
MANUFACTURER:	French
MATERIAL:	cast iron
FINISH:	blue paint
COMMENTS:	This is presumed to be a later version, as the frame is extended above the mounting lugs to allow for a spring assisted cork pull.

NAME:	**PULLMEE** (marked)
TRADEMARK:	none
OTHER MARKS:	MANNING BOWMAN & CO, CHICAGO, ILL, PAT May 28, 1901, MADE IN USA
NOTICE:	wrong address marked for Manning Bowman
I.D. #:	**P09.1.1**
INVENTOR & DATE:	A. Baumgarten May 28, 1901 and May 07, 1907
REGISTRATION #:	P 675,051 and P 853,151
CIRCA:	1907? - ?
FREQUENCY:	
MANUFACTURER:	Manning Bowman & Co.
MATERIAL:	cast iron
FINISH:	nickel
COMMENTS:	This style of bottle clasp was patented in 1907 by Baumgarten.

NAME:	**PULLMEE** (marked)
TRADEMARK:	none
OTHER MARKS:	ALBERT PICK & CO, CHICAGO, ILL, PAT MAY 28, 1901, MADE IN USA
NOTICE:	bottle clasp with spring
I.D. #:	**P09.1.2**
INVENTOR & DATE:	A. Baumgarten May 28, 1901 and May 07, 1907
REGISTRATION #:	P 675,051 and P 853,151
CIRCA:	1907 - ?
FREQUENCY:	
MANUFACTURER:	Manning Bowman & Co.
MATERIAL:	cast iron
FINISH:	bronze paint
COMMENTS:	This is a private label version for Albert Pick.

NAME:	**PULLMEE** (marked)
TRADEMARK:	none
OTHER MARKS:	FREEPORT NOVELTY CO. FREEPORT, ILL USA, PAT. APL'D FOR
NOTICE:	manufacturer's name
I.D. #:	**P09.2.1**
INVENTOR & DATE:	A. Baumgarten May 28,1901
REGISTRATION #:	P 675,051
CIRCA:	1900 - ?
FREQUENCY:	
MANUFACTURER:	Freeport Novelty Co.
MATERIAL:	cast iron
FINISH:	nickel
COMMENTS:	This is presumably the first version manufactured by Baumgarten's company.

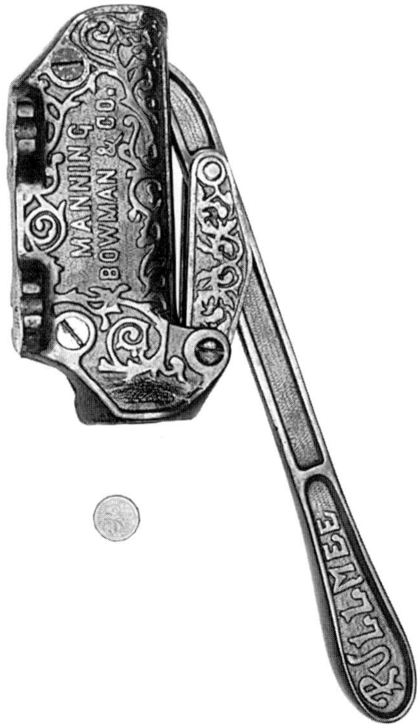

NAME: **PULLMEE** (marked)

TRADEMARK: none

OTHER MARKS: MANNING BOWMAN & CO. MERIDEN, CONN. U. S. A., PAT. APL'D FOR

NOTICE: a very early version

I.D. #: **P09.2.2**

INVENTOR & DATE: A. Baumgarten May 28,1901

REGISTRATION #: P 675,051

CIRCA: 1900 - ?

FREQUENCY:

MANUFACTURER: Manning Bowman & Co.

MATERIAL: cast iron

FINISH: nickel

COMMENTS: Baumgarten's wall mount PULLMEEs incorporated the SHOMEE mechanism, without a bottle clasp; both patents were received on the same day.

NAME: **PULLMEE** (marked)

TRADEMARK: none

OTHER MARKS: LIVERPOOL ENGLAND, ENG. PAT. NO. 6224. 1900, MADE IN USA

NOTICE: English patent dates, made in the USA

I.D. #: **P09.2.3**

INVENTOR & DATE: A. Baumgarten May 28,1901

REGISTRATION #: P 675,051

CIRCA: 1901 - ?

FREQUENCY:

MANUFACTURER: presumably Manning Bowman & Co.

MATERIAL: cast iron

FINISH: nickel

COMMENTS: "Made in USA" was stamped into a small metal disk riveted to the case.

NAME: **PUNTIGAM BRAUEREI** (marked)
TRADEMARK: none
OTHER MARKS: none
NOTICE: clamp plate, crude Gilchrist style thumb piece
I.D. #: **P10.1.1**
INVENTOR & DATE: no Austrian patent or registration found
REGISTRATION #:
CIRCA: 1900?
FREQUENCY:
MANUFACTURER: Austrian ?
MATERIAL: cast iron
FINISH: none visible
COMMENTS: On this very crudely cast version of the CHAMPION, the bottle clasps have an elliptical raised design.

NAME: **PUNTIGAM BRAUEREI** (marked)
TRADEMARK: none
OTHER MARKS: none
NOTICE: Arcade style thumb piece
I.D. #: **P10.1.2**
INVENTOR & DATE: no Austrian patent or registration found
REGISTRATION #:
CIRCA: 1900?
FREQUENCY:
MANUFACTURER: Austrian ?
MATERIAL: cast iron
FINISH: none visible
COMMENTS: The bottle clasps on this version have an Arcade style "vine & leaf" pattern.

NAME:	**QUICK** (not inspected)
TRADEMARK:	none
OTHER MARKS:	not inspected
NOTICE:	
I.D. #:	**Q01.1.1**
INVENTOR & DATE:	R. Gilchrist Jun 14, 1904
REGISTRATION #:	DRP 162,930
CIRCA:	1905? - 1940?
FREQUENCY:	
MANUFACTURER:	German ?
MATERIAL:	cast iron
FINISH:	nickel
COMMENTS:	A private label HERO NO5, as seen in this advertisement; it is not clear that this corkscrew is marked.

Echt amerikanischer Entkorker „Quick“

Preis Mk. 12.—

NAME:	**QUICK & EASY** (marked)
TRADEMARK:	none
OTHER MARKS:	PAT. FEB 27 94
NOTICE:	almost vertical frame, advertising plate out of scale
I.D. #:	**Q02.1.1**
INVENTOR & DATE:	E. Walker Feb 27, 1894
REGISTRATION #:	P 515,412
CIRCA:	1894?
FREQUENCY:	
MANUFACTURER:	Erie Specialty Co.
MATERIAL:	cast iron
FINISH:	nickel
COMMENTS:	This first version of the QUICK & EASY has a single roller pin; presumably not many were produced, as Walker applied for a patent on an improved design seven months later.

NAME: **QUICK & EASY** (unmarked)

TRADEMARK: none

OTHER MARKS: 1895 DESIGN, [QUANDT BREWING CO. TROY, N.Y. on advertising plate, but no QUICK & EASY name]

NOTICE: 1895 design, no yoke, advertising plate out of scale

I.D. #: **Q03.1.1**

INVENTOR & DATE: E. Walker Jul 23,1895

REGISTRATION #: P 543,224

CIRCA: 1895?

FREQUENCY:

MANUFACTURER: Erie Specialty Co.

MATERIAL: cast iron

FINISH: nickel

COMMENTS: This improved version of the QUICK & EASY includes the cast lip and two roller pins in the operating arm's semi-disk; 1895 DESIGN is marked inside the semi-disk.

NAME: **QUICK & EASY** (marked)

TRADEMARK: none

OTHER MARKS: PAT. FEB 27 94, 1896 DESIGN

NOTICE: 1896 design, advertising plate out of scale

I.D. #: **Q03.1.2**

INVENTOR & DATE: E. Walker Apr 07, 1896

REGISTRATION #: P 557,734

CIRCA: 1896?

FREQUENCY:

MANUFACTURER: Erie Specialty Co.

MATERIAL: cast iron

FINISH: nickel

COMMENTS: The 1896 patent included adding a yoke to the corkscrew carrier and this bottle clasp which was rather delicate; it is rarely found, leaving two empty attachment holes in the throat. The custom counter clamp shown is extremely hard to find.

NAME: **QUICK & EASY** (marked)
TRADEMARK: none
OTHER MARKS: 1897 DESIGN
NOTICE: 1897 design
I.D. #: **Q03.1.3**
INVENTOR & DATE: E. Walker Apr 07, 1896
REGISTRATION #: P 557,734
CIRCA: 1897?
FREQUENCY:
MANUFACTURER: Erie Specialty Co.
MATERIAL: cast iron
FINISH: nickel
COMMENTS: The 1897 design was not a new patent; it consisted of slight changes to the spacing of the two roller pins in the operating arm. The design date is found cast into the inside of the semi-disk on the operating arm.

NAME: **QUICK & EASY** (marked)
TRADEMARK: none
OTHER MARKS: PAT. FEB 27' 94 JULY 23' 95, IN USA and EUROPE, 1898 DESIGN
NOTICE: first version of the 1898 design, advertising plate out of scale
I.D. #: **Q03.1.4**
INVENTOR & DATE: E. Walker Apr 07, 1896
REGISTRATION #: P 557,734
CIRCA: 1898 - 1901?
FREQUENCY:
MANUFACTURER: Erie Specialty Co.
MATERIAL: cast iron
FINISH: nickel
COMMENTS: This 1898 version of the QUICK & EASY includes the final spacing changes for the two roller pins. It still has the two bottle clasp mounting holes in the throat and three mounting screws for the advertising plate.

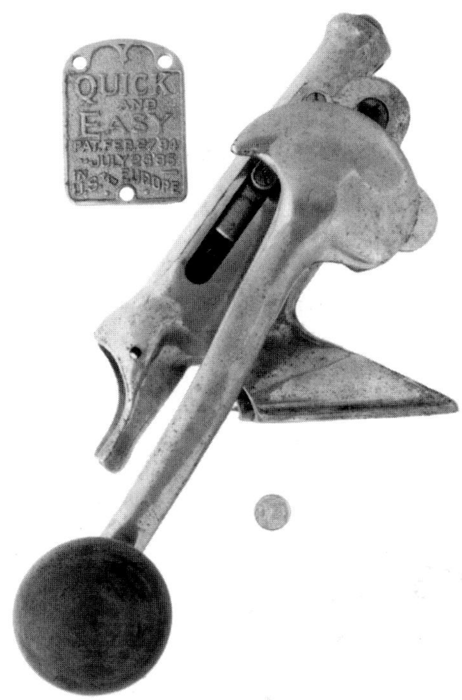

NAME:	**QUICK & EASY** (marked)
TRADEMARK:	none
OTHER MARKS:	PAT. FEB 27' 94 JULY 23' 95, IN USA and EUROPE, 1898 DESIGN
NOTICE:	later version of the 1898 design, advertising plate out of scale
I.D. #:	**Q03.1.5**
INVENTOR & DATE:	E. Walker Apr 07, 1896
REGISTRATION #:	P 557,734
CIRCA:	1901? - 1920?
FREQUENCY:	
MANUFACTURER:	Erie Specialty Co.
MATERIAL:	cast iron
FINISH:	nickel
COMMENTS:	Presumably about the time Walker applied for the patent on his new bottle clasp design, he discontinued the mounting holes in the throat. Around this time the advertising plate was changed to require only two mounting screws.

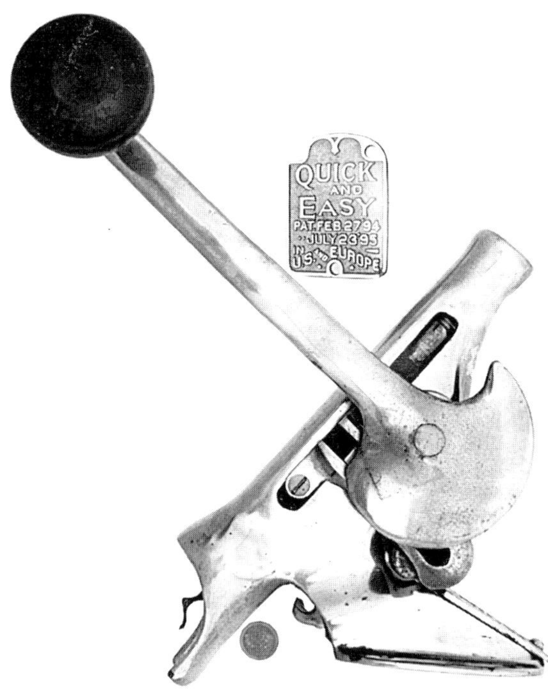

NAME:	**QUICK & EASY** (marked)
TRADEMARK:	none
OTHER MARKS:	PAT. FEB 27' 94 JULY 23' 95, IN USA and EUROPE, 1898 DESIGN
NOTICE:	big bottle clasp, advertising plate out of scale
I.D. #:	**Q03.2.1**
INVENTOR & DATE:	E. Walker Apr 07, 1896 and Nov 11, 1902
REGISTRATION #:	P 557,734 and P 713,540
CIRCA:	1902? - ?
FREQUENCY:	
MANUFACTURER:	Erie Specialty Co.
MATERIAL:	cast iron
FINISH:	nickel
COMMENTS:	This version of the QUICK & EASY included Walker's massive, complex and no doubt expensive bottle clasp.

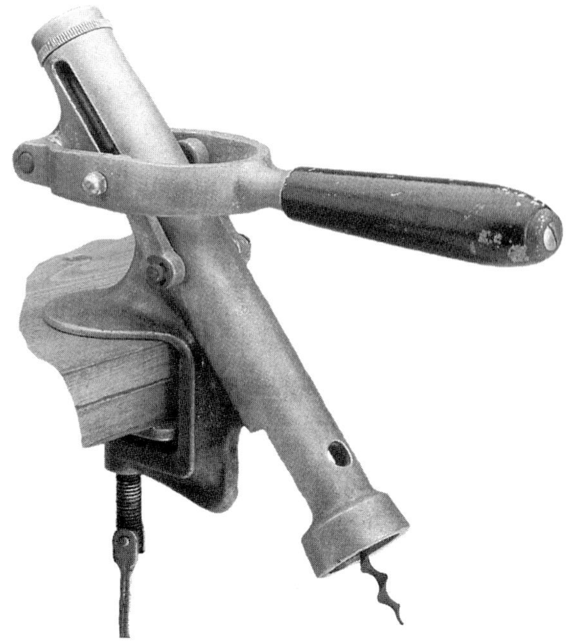

NAME: **RAPID** (marked)

TRADEMARK: none

OTHER MARKS: SWISS MADE

NOTICE:

I.D. #: **R01.1.1**

INVENTOR & DATE: no Swiss patent or registration found

REGISTRATION #:

CIRCA: 1930 - 1940?

FREQUENCY:

MANUFACTURER: Swiss

MATERIAL: cast iron

FINISH: not inspected

COMMENTS: This is presumed to be an early version of the Swiss RAPID.

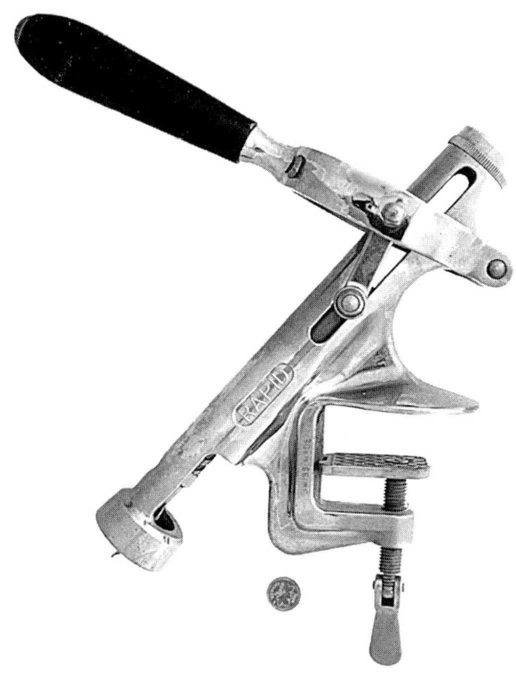

NAME: **RAPID** (marked)

TRADEMARK: none

OTHER MARKS: SWISS MADE, INCA 2906 A3

NOTICE: gold colored finish variant *R01.2.2*

I.D. #: **R01.2.1**

INVENTOR & DATE: no Swiss patent or registration found

REGISTRATION #:

CIRCA: 1950? - 1990?

FREQUENCY:

MANUFACTURER: Swiss

MATERIAL: zinc ?

FINISH: nickel

COMMENTS: This modern Swiss version of the DON is sometimes found with a plastic throat extender to guide the bottle.

NAME:	**RAPID** (marked)
TRADEMARK:	none
OTHER MARKS:	PATENTED APR 21, 1891
NOTICE:	flat brass nut on the handle, not marked MADE IN USA on frame, advertising plate out of scale
I.D. #:	**R02.1.1**
INVENTOR & DATE:	H. Williams Apr 21, 1891
REGISTRATION #:	P 450,957
CIRCA:	1891 - ?
FREQUENCY:	
MANUFACTURER:	Meriden Malleable Iron Co.
MATERIAL:	cast iron
FINISH:	nickel
COMMENTS:	This is presumably an earlier version of the US RAPID. This one has SCOVILL, MADE IN USA, 7331 stamped into the brass ferrule. Scovill manufactured non-ferrous metal products, so it would seem that Meriden Malleable purchased the ferrule from them.

NAME:	**RAPID** (marked)
TRADEMARK:	none
OTHER MARKS:	PATENTED APR 21, 91, MADE IN USA
NOTICE:	finish, typical round nut on the handle
I.D. #:	**R02.1.2**
INVENTOR & DATE:	H. Williams Apr 21, 1891
REGISTRATION #:	P 450,957
CIRCA:	1895? - ?
FREQUENCY:	
MANUFACTURER:	Meriden Malleable Iron Co.
MATERIAL:	cast iron
FINISH:	copper
COMMENTS:	A slightly later version with MADE IN USA very lightly <u>hand</u> <u>stamped</u> into the frame.

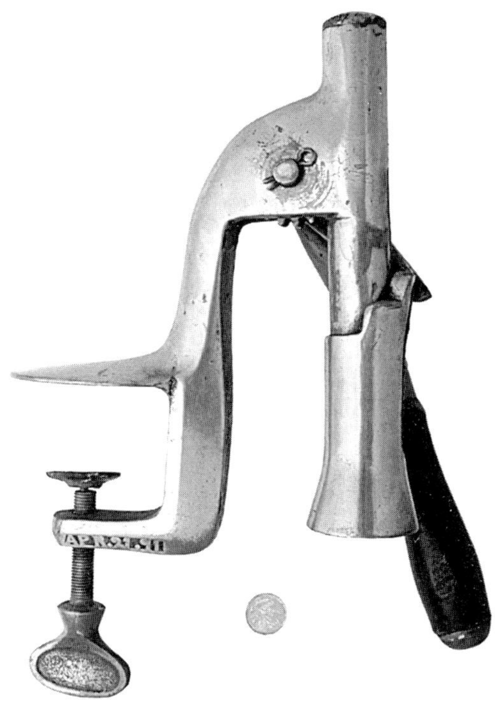

NAME:	**RAPID** (not inspected)
TRADEMARK:	none
OTHER MARKS:	not inspected
NOTICE:	the standard nickel plated version of *R02.1.2*
I.D. #:	**R02.1.3**
INVENTOR & DATE:	H. Williams Apr 21, 1891
REGISTRATION #:	P 450,957
CIRCA:	1910? - ?
FREQUENCY:	
MANUFACTURER:	Meriden Malleable Iron Co.
MATERIAL:	cast iron
FINISH:	nickel
COMMENTS:	As found in a 1910 Gaskell advertisement, with this kind of help from your distributor, who needs enemies?

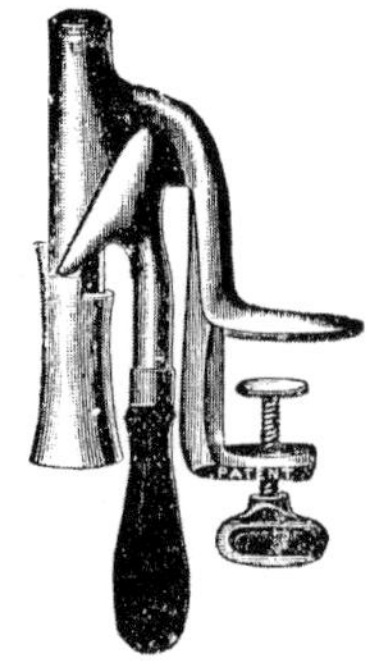

No. **5018**
"Rapid" Cork Drawer.
14/- each.

The "Rapid" is an American made Cork Drawer, nickel-plated on cast-iron, and is supplied at purchaser's own risk ; no responsibility taken for breakage, etc.

For reliable Cork Drawers of OUR OWN MAKE see pages 200 to 205.

NAME:	**RAPID** (marked)
TRADEMARK:	none
OTHER MARKS:	PATENTED APR 21, 91, MADE IN USA
NOTICE:	thumb piece, marking
I.D. #:	**R02.1.4**
INVENTOR & DATE:	H. Williams Apr 21, 1891
REGISTRATION #:	P 450,957
CIRCA:	1910? - ?
FREQUENCY:	
MANUFACTURER:	Bradley & Hubbard Mfg. Co.
MATERIAL:	cast iron
FINISH:	nickel
COMMENTS:	This later version has a pointed thumb piece and MADE IN USA cast into the frame. Presumably this is a Bradley & Hubbard thumb piece design.

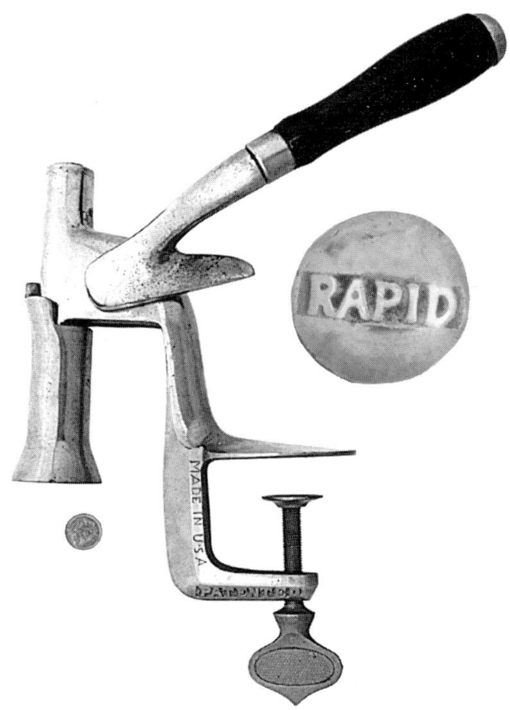

NAME: **RAPID** (marked)
TRADEMARK: none
OTHER MARKS: PATENTED APR 21, 1891, MADE IN USA
NOTICE: bottle clasp version
I.D. #: **R02.2.1**
INVENTOR & DATE: H. Williams Apr 21, 1891
REGISTRATION #: P 450,957
CIRCA: 1910? - ?
FREQUENCY:
MANUFACTURER: Bradley & Hubbard Mfg. Co.
MATERIAL: cast iron
FINISH: nickel
COMMENTS: It is doubtful that this bottle clasp version of Williams' RAPID was very effective.

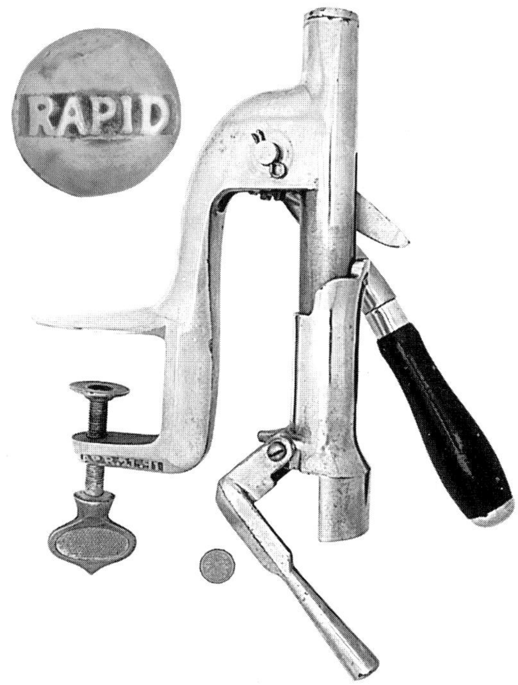

NAME: **RAPID** (not inspected)
TRADEMARK: none
OTHER MARKS: not inspected
NOTICE: not inspected
I.D. #: **R02.3.1**
INVENTOR & DATE: H. Williams Apr 21, 1891
REGISTRATION #: P 450,957
CIRCA: 1891? - 1894?
FREQUENCY:
MANUFACTURER: Meriden Malleable Iron Co.
MATERIAL: cast iron
FINISH: nickel
COMMENTS: The top mount version of the US RAPID is shown in an 1894 advertisement; later RAPID advertising did not mention this version.

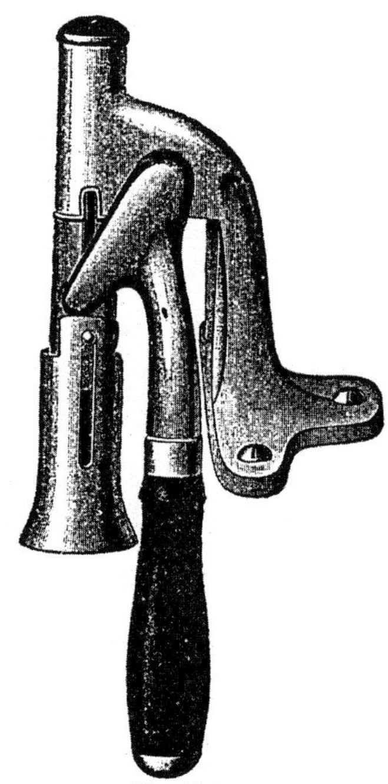

No. 27.

THE RAPID.

Full Nickel-plated.

No. 27, Without Clamp,	-	each,	$3 50
28, With "		"	4 00
Extra Cork Screws,	-	per dozen,	2 40

The "Rapid" cuts the Wires and draws the Cork of any ordinary Ale, Wine or Mineral Water Bottle with one movement.

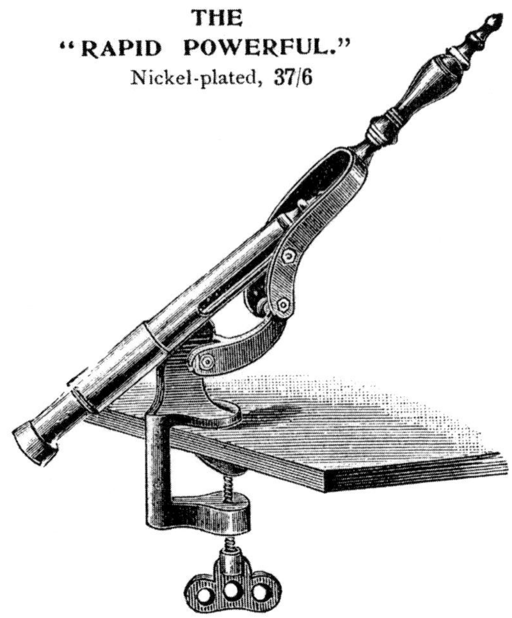

NAME: **RAPID POWERFUL,THE**
(not inspected)

TRADEMARK: not inspected

OTHER MARKS: not inspected

NOTICE: not inspected

I.D. #: **R03.1.1**

INVENTOR & DATE: no English patent or registration found

REGISTRATION #:

CIRCA: 1890? - ?

FREQUENCY:

MANUFACTURER: presumably Samuel Mason Ltd.

MATERIAL: brass

FINISH: nickel

COMMENTS: As shown in this 1895 advertisement, it is not known if this was a marked example or whether POWERFUL was a marketing name.

NAME: **RAPID, THE** (marked)

TRADEMARK: none

OTHER MARKS: LOFTUS LONDON

NOTICE: single fulcrum link attached to the pedestal

I.D. #: **R04.1.1**

INVENTOR & DATE: no English patent or registration found

REGISTRATION #:

CIRCA: 1896? - 1910?

FREQUENCY:

MANUFACTURER: presumably Samuel Mason Ltd.

MATERIAL: brass

FINISH: nickel

COMMENTS: The British RAPID is not a Deacle patent; there is no known patent for this style of lever operating a stem-nut.

NAME:	**RAPID, THE** (unmarked)	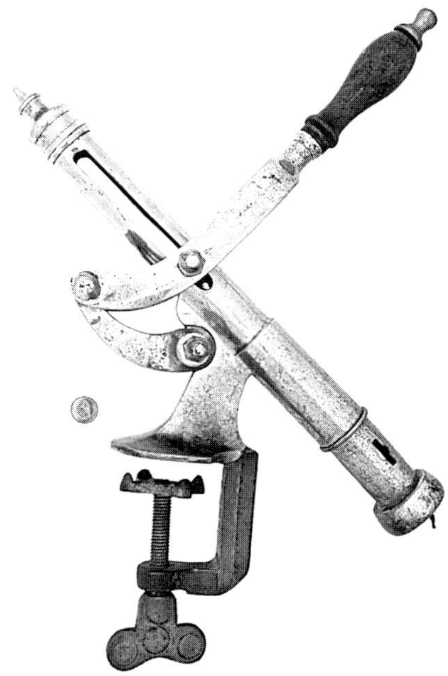
TRADEMARK:	optic	
OTHER MARKS:	G&C	
NOTICE:	not original handle finial	
I.D. #:	**R04.1.2**	
INVENTOR & DATE:	no English patent or registration found	
REGISTRATION #:		
CIRCA:	1920? - 1930?	
FREQUENCY:		
MANUFACTURER:	Gaskell & Chambers Ltd.	
MATERIAL:	brass	
FINISH:	nickel	
COMMENTS:	The G&C trademark is found only on the bottom of the clamp plate.	

NAME:	**RAPID, THE** (marked)	
TRADEMARK:	none	
OTHER MARKS:	LOFTUS LONDON	
NOTICE:	top mount version	
I.D. #:	**R04.2.1**	
INVENTOR & DATE:	no English patent or registration found	
REGISTRATION #:		
CIRCA:	1896? - 1910?	
FREQUENCY:		
MANUFACTURER:	presumably Samuel Mason Ltd.	
MATERIAL:	brass	
FINISH:	nickel	
COMMENTS:	This is assumed to have been manufactured by Mason for distribution by Loftus.	

NAME: **RAPID (THE RAPID CORK DRAWER)** (marked)

TRADEMARK: not inspected

OTHER MARKS: PARNALL & SONS, NARROW WINE St, BRISTOL, shown out of scale

NOTICE: handle finial, top mount

I.D. #: **R07.2.1**

INVENTOR & DATE: no English patent or registration found

REGISTRATION #:

CIRCA: 1890? - ?

FREQUENCY:

MANUFACTURER: presumably Samuel Mason Ltd.

MATERIAL: brass

FINISH: nickel

COMMENTS: Presumably PARNALL & SONS were a distributor.

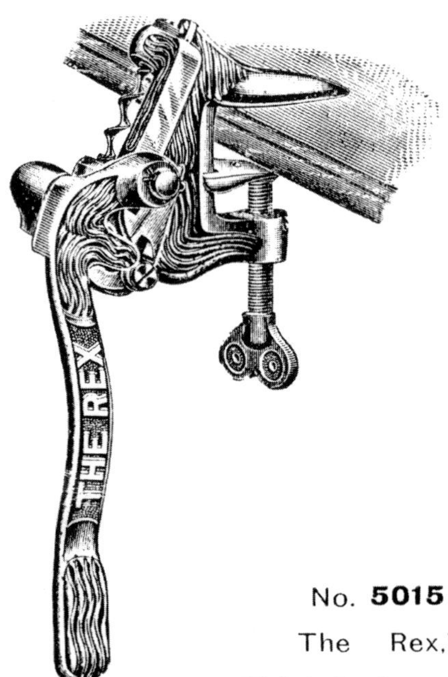

No. **5015**
The Rex."
Nickel-plated ... 7/6

NAME: **REX, THE** (marked)

TRADEMARK: not inspected

OTHER MARKS: not inspected

NOTICE:

I.D. #: **R08.1.1**

INVENTOR & DATE: R. Gilchrist Aug 12, 1902

REGISTRATION #: LP 17,752

CIRCA: 1901? - 1910?

FREQUENCY:

MANUFACTURER: Gaskell

MATERIAL: cast iron

FINISH: nickel

COMMENTS: This is a British version of Gilchrist's MODERN.

NAME: **RIMO** (marked)

TRADEMARK: **(K)** on thumb piece

OTHER MARKS: internal component numbers preceded by **F**

NOTICE: clamp plate missing

I.D. #: **R05.1.1**

INVENTOR & DATE: G. Frings, probably Nov 04, 1925

REGISTRATION #: DRGM 930,900

CIRCA: 1920? - 1940?

FREQUENCY:

MANUFACTURER: FRINGS & CO. o. H. G.

MATERIAL: cast iron

FINISH: nickel

COMMENTS: This is a private label version of the grape leaf decorated HEKTOR 2.

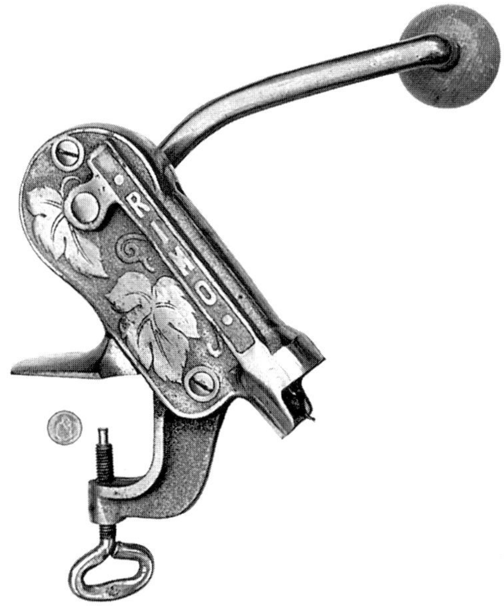

NAME: **RITZ, THE** (marked)

TRADEMARK: none

OTHER MARKS: PATENT 18 ?—?, ?—?SE (mostly worn away)

NOTICE: clamp plate missing, thumb piece, RAPID style linkage

I.D. #: **R09.1.1**

INVENTOR & DATE: C. Chambers Aug 20, 1903

REGISTRATION #: LP 18,006

CIRCA: 1903? - ?

FREQUENCY:

MANUFACTURER: Samuel Mason Ltd.

MATERIAL: brass

FINISH: nickel

COMMENTS: A DON mechanism with a RAPID style frame and linkage.

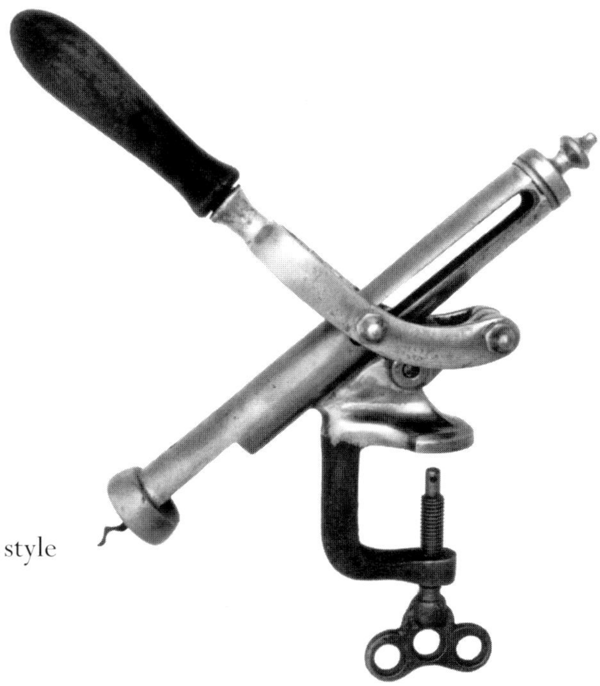

NAME:	**ROTHCHILD NO 7** (marked)
TRADEMARK:	none
OTHER MARKS:	none
NOTICE:	
I.D. #:	**R06.1.1**
INVENTOR & DATE:	R. Gilchrist Apr 08, 1913
REGISTRATION #:	P 1,058,361
CIRCA:	1907? - ?
FREQUENCY:	
MANUFACTURER:	Arcade Manufacturing Co.
MATERIAL:	cast iron
FINISH:	nickel
COMMENTS:	This is a private label version of Gilchrist's YANKEE NO7.

NAME:	**SACHS, DRUDEN** (marked)
TRADEMARK:	none
OTHER MARKS:	PAT SEPT 7, 86, DAYTON, OH
NOTICE:	mechanism very similar to the ENTERPRISE, advertising plate out of scale
I.D. #:	**S23.1.1**
INVENTOR & DATE:	J. Hurley Sep 07, 1886
REGISTRATION #:	P 348,743
CIRCA:	1886 - ?
FREQUENCY:	
MANUFACTURER:	Sachs, Druden & Co. ?
MATERIAL:	cast iron
FINISH:	nickel
COMMENTS:	This is the only known example of this corkscrew to have been manufactured almost identical to the original patent drawings; see *MECHANISMS* for additional information.

NAME: **SAFETY** (marked)

TRADEMARK: sun

OTHER MARKS: S. MASON, cast into the thumb piece

NOTICE:

I.D. #: **S01.1.1**

INVENTOR & DATE: R. Gilchrist Sep 03, 1894 and A. Pick Feb 08, 1895

REGISTRATION #: LP 16,777 and LP 2,825

CIRCA: 1906? - 1910?

FREQUENCY: 

MANUFACTURER: Samuel Mason Ltd.

MATERIAL: cast iron

FINISH: nickel

COMMENTS: Gilchrist's patent for the ARCADE worm-nut mechanism and Pick's patent for the bottle clasp would have expired by this date. Possibly this was manufactured only for Farrow & Jackson, as no other distributor advertising has been found.

NAME: **SAFETY** (marked)

TRADEMARK: sun

OTHER MARKS: FARROW & JACKSON LTD LONDON

NOTICE: right side same as *S01.1.1*

I.D. #: **S01.1.2**

INVENTOR & DATE: R. Gilchrist Sep 03, 1894 and A. Pick Feb 08, 1895

REGISTRATION #: LP 16,777 and LP 2,825

CIRCA: 1906? - 1910?

FREQUENCY: 

MANUFACTURER: Samuel Mason Ltd.

MATERIAL: cast iron

FINISH: nickel

COMMENTS: This is a private label version manufactured for Farrow & Jackson by Mason.

NAME: **SAFETY** (marked)
TRADEMARK: sun
OTHER MARKS: none
NOTICE: top mount version
I.D. #: **S01.2.1**
INVENTOR & DATE: R. Gilchrist Sep 03, 1894 and A. Pick Feb 08, 1895
REGISTRATION #: LP 16,777 and LP 2,825
CIRCA: 1906? - 1910?
FREQUENCY:
MANUFACTURER: Samuel Mason Ltd.
MATERIAL: cast iron
FINISH: nickel
COMMENTS: The bottle clasps have been removed to show the decorative pattern.

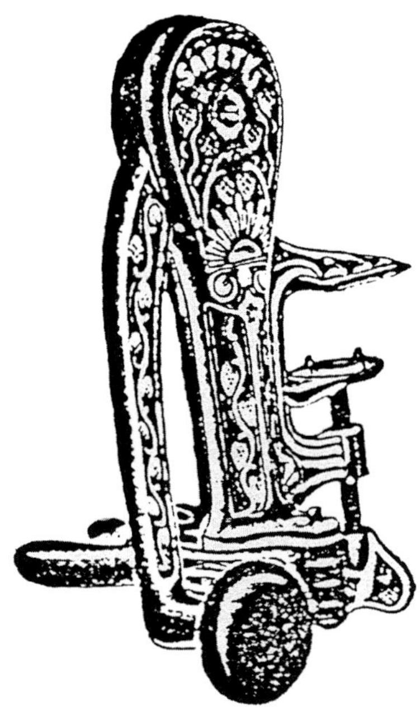

"SAFETY"
To clamp on Counter

NAME: **SAFETY** (marked)
TRADEMARK: sun
OTHER MARKS: none
NOTICE: ribbed edges on the frame and frame clamp plate
I.D. #: **S02.1.1**
INVENTOR & DATE: R. Gilchrist Sep 03, 1894 and A. Pick Feb 08, 1895
REGISTRATION #: LP 16,777 and LP 2,825
CIRCA: 1906? - 1910?
FREQUENCY:
MANUFACTURER: Samuel Mason Ltd.
MATERIAL: cast iron
FINISH: nickel
COMMENTS: Farrow & Jackson advertised this ribbed, hop leaf patterned SAFETY in 1912. There are Gaskell & Chambers ORIGINAL SAFETY advertisements warning "Beware of Imitations".

NAME: **SAFETY** (marked)
TRADEMARK: sun
OTHER MARKS: none
NOTICE: top mount version
I.D. #: **S02.2.1**
INVENTOR & DATE: R. Gilchrist Sep 03, 1894 and A. Pick Feb 08, 1895
REGISTRATION #: LP 16,777 and LP 2,825
CIRCA: 1906? - 1910?
FREQUENCY:
MANUFACTURER: Samuel Mason Ltd.
MATERIAL: cast iron
FINISH: nickel
COMMENTS: This unusual ribbing on the edges of the case is also found on the SUNOID; these decorative ribs would have been difficult to cast.

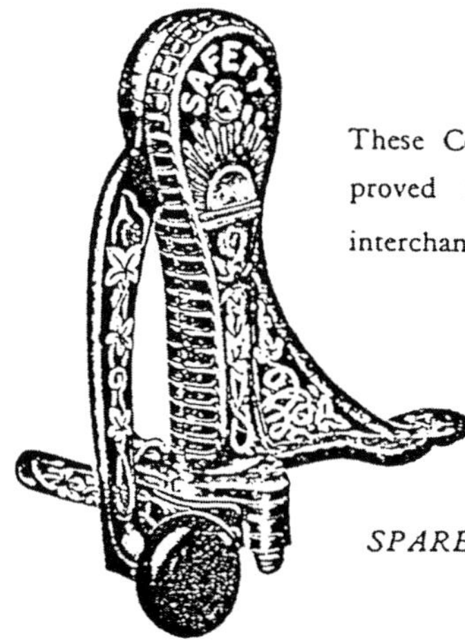

These Cork Drawers are cast by improved methods and all parts are interchangeable and of the very best materials

SPARE PARTS IN STOCK

" SAFETY "
With Plate to screw on Counter

NAME: **SAFETY, ORIGINAL** (marked)
TRADEMARK: hand & star
OTHER MARKS: MADE IN ENGLAND, REG No 543083, TRADE MARK (GASKELL inside the case and bottle grips)
NOTICE: the registered design was for the frame decorations
I.D. #: **S03.1.1**
INVENTOR & DATE: R. Gilchrist Sep 03, 1894 and A. Pick Feb 08, 1895 and Gaskell & Chambers
REGISTRATION #: LP 16,777 and LP 2,825 and REG 543,083
CIRCA: 1909?-1937?
FREQUENCY:
MANUFACTURER: Gaskell
MATERIAL: cast iron
FINISH: nickel
COMMENTS: The registered design for the case of the ORIGINAL SAFETY was in effect from 1909 - 1924.

NAME: **SAFETY, ORIGINAL** (marked)

TRADEMARK: hand & star

OTHER MARKS: MADE-IN-ENGLAND, TRADE MARK (GASKELL inside the case and bottle grips)

NOTICE: brass version

I.D. #: **S03.1.2**

INVENTOR & DATE: R. Gilchrist Sep 03, 1894 and A. Pick Feb 08, 1895 and Gaskell & Chambers

REGISTRATION #: LP 16,777 and LP 2,825 and REG 543,083

CIRCA: 1909?-1937?

FREQUENCY:

MANUFACTURER: Gaskell

MATERIAL: brass

FINISH: nickel

COMMENTS: Only one example of advertising for the brass ORIGINAL SAFETY has been found; this one is from 1908.

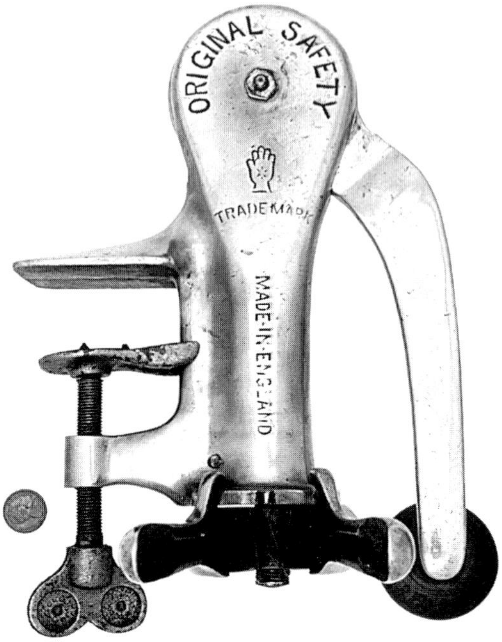

NAME: **SAFETY, ORIGINAL** (marked)

TRADEMARK: hand & star

OTHER MARKS: MADE IN ENGLAND, REG No 543083, TRADE MARK (GASKELL inside the case and bottle grips)

NOTICE: top mount version

I.D. #: **S03.2.1**

INVENTOR & DATE: R. Gilchrist Sep 03, 1894 and A. Pick Feb 08, 1895 and Gaskell & Chambers

REGISTRATION #: LP 16,777 and LP 2,825 and REG 543,083

CIRCA: 1909?-1924?

FREQUENCY:

MANUFACTURER: Gaskell

MATERIAL: cast iron

FINISH: nickel

COMMENTS: Worm nuts wore out quickly; Chambers patented a longer wearing worm-nut for the SAFETY and the SIMPLE in 1911.

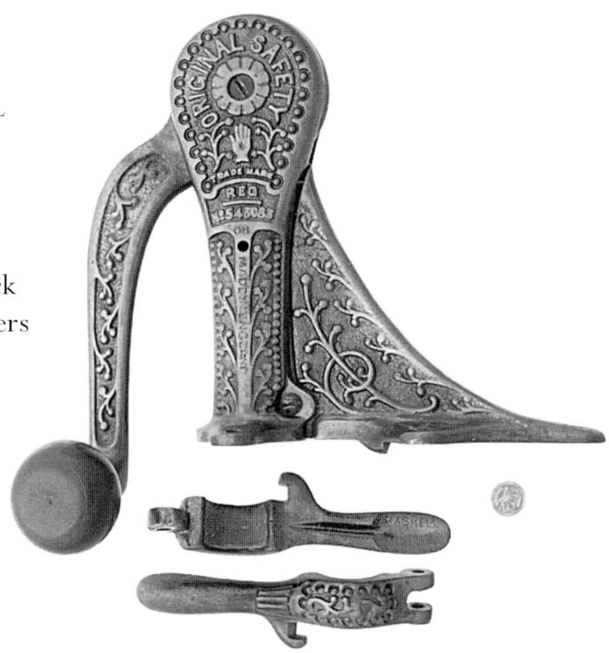

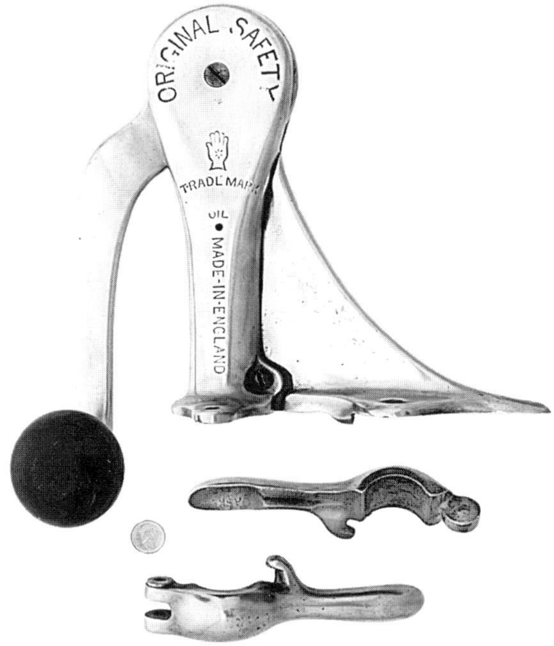

NAME:	**SAFETY, ORIGINAL** (marked)
TRADEMARK:	hand & star
OTHER MARKS:	MADE-IN-ENGLAND, REG 543083, TRADE MARK (GASKELL inside the case and bottle grips)
NOTICE:	top mount version
I.D. #:	**S03.2.2**
INVENTOR & DATE:	R. Gilchrist Sep 03, 1894 and A. Pick Feb 08, 1895 and Gaskell & Chambers
REGISTRATION #:	LP 16,777 and LP 2,825 and REG 543,083
CIRCA:	1909?-1924?
FREQUENCY:	
MANUFACTURER:	Gaskell
MATERIAL:	brass
FINISH:	nickel
COMMENTS:	Worm nuts wore out quickly; Chambers patented a longer wearing worm-nut for the SAFETY and SIMPLE in 1911.

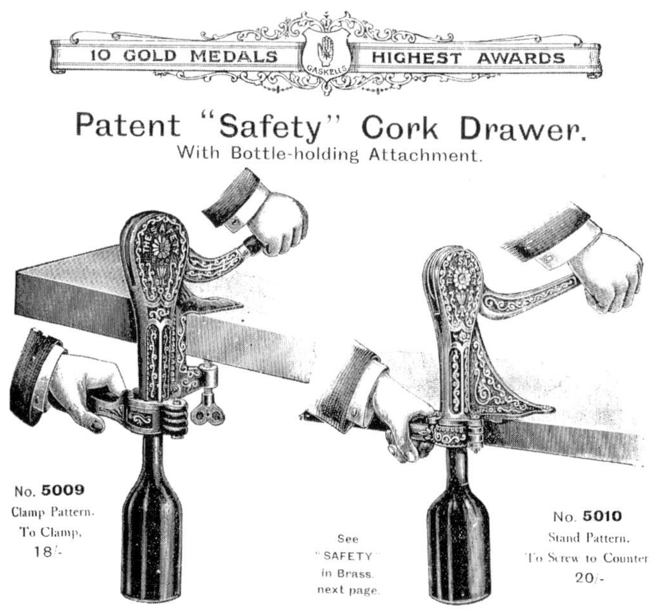

NAME:	**SAFETY, THE** (marked)
TRADEMARK:	not inspected
OTHER MARKS:	not inspected
NOTICE:	handle, thumb piece, case decoration, top mount version *S04.2.1*
I.D. #:	**S04.1.1**
INVENTOR & DATE:	R. Gilchrist Sep 03, 1894 and A. Pick Feb 08, 1895
REGISTRATION #:	LP 16,777 and LP 2,825
CIRCA:	1895? - 1896?
FREQUENCY:	
MANUFACTURER:	English or American ?
MATERIAL:	cast iron
FINISH:	nickel
COMMENTS:	This Gaskell advertisement shows THE SAFETY with an ARCADE style handle, thumb piece, bottle clasp and case decoration. It is not known if this version was manufactured as shown, or, if so, whether it was manufactured by Arcade or by Gaskell.

NAME: **SAFETY, THE**

TRADEMARK: hand & star

OTHER MARKS: PATENT 16777

NOTICE: marked internal, Gaskells, hand & star, top mount version *S05.2.1*

I.D. #: **S05.1.1**

INVENTOR & DATE: R. Gilchrist Sep 03, 1894 and A. Pick Feb 08, 1895

REGISTRATION #: LP 16,777 and LP 2,825

CIRCA: 1895? - 1909?

FREQUENCY:

MANUFACTURER: Gaskell

MATERIAL: cast iron

FINISH: nickel

COMMENTS: This is the first version that we know for sure was manufactured in England. Gilchrist patented this design in 1894; one year later Pick patented the bottle clasps for the SAFETY.

NAME: **SAFETY, THE** (not inspected)

TRADEMARK: hand & star

OTHER MARKS: PATENT

NOTICE: name, brass, top mount nickel variant *S05.2.2*, brass finished variants, clamp mount *S05.2.3*, top mount *S05.2.4*.

I.D. #: **S05.2.1**

INVENTOR & DATE: R. Gilchrist Sep 03, 1894 and A. Pick Feb 08, 1895

REGISTRATION #: LP 16,777 and LP 2,825

CIRCA: 1895? - 1910

FREQUENCY:

MANUFACTURER: Gaskell

MATERIAL: brass

FINISH: nickel

COMMENTS: The corkscrew shown in this advertisement for a brass THE SAFETY have not been found.

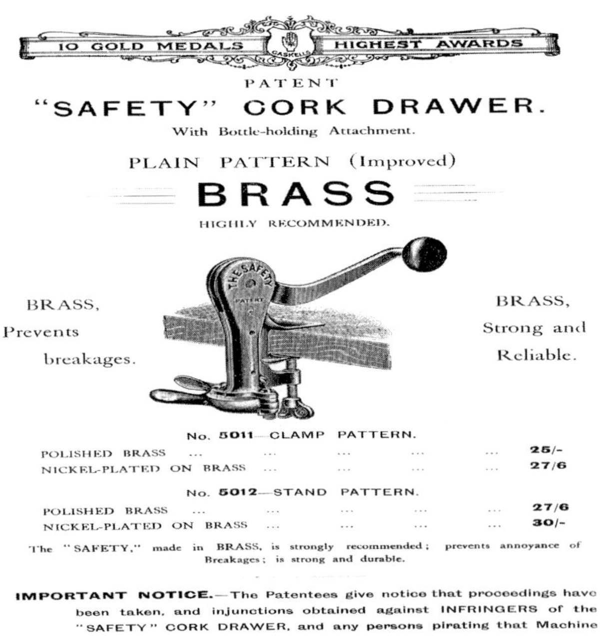

NAME:	**SAMSON** (unmarked)
TRADEMARK:	none
OTHER MARKS:	THE F. F. ADAMS CO, ERIE PA U.S.A., PATd OCT 5 86
NOTICE:	long smooth wooden handle as seen in one advertisement, advertising plate out of scale
I.D. #:	**S06.1.1**
INVENTOR & DATE:	J. Hurley Oct 05, 1886
REGISTRATION #:	P 350,308
CIRCA:	1886? - 1901?
FREQUENCY:	
MANUFACTURER:	F. F. Adams Co.
MATERIAL:	cast iron
FINISH:	nickel
COMMENTS:	This frame has the standard base mounting plate. SAMSON is also found spelled SAMPSON in some USA advertising between 1893 and 1901.

NAME:	**SAMSON** (unmarked)
TRADEMARK:	none
OTHER MARKS:	THE F. F. ADAMS CO, ERIE PA U.S.A., PATd OCT 5 86
NOTICE:	square back base plate
I.D. #:	**S06.1.2**
INVENTOR & DATE:	J. Hurley Oct 05, 1886
REGISTRATION #:	P 350,308
CIRCA:	1886? - 1901?
FREQUENCY:	
MANUFACTURER:	F. F. Adams Co.
MATERIAL:	cast iron
FINISH:	nickel
COMMENTS:	The base mounting plate has a squared-off back, rather than the standard version. The two screws fixing the wire breaker on the SAMSON were designed to penetrate into the path of the cork, keeping it from turning during the unwinding of the worm crank.

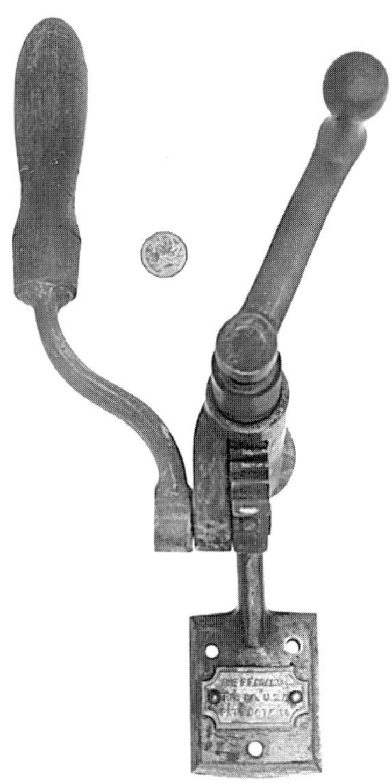

NAME: **SAMSON** (unmarked)

TRADEMARK: none

OTHER MARKS: THE BISHOP & BABCOCK Co, CLEVELAND OH, PATd OCT. 5. 86.

NOTICE: wooden handle, advertising plate, no wire breaker, advertising plate out of scale

I.D. #: **S06.1.3**

INVENTOR & DATE: J. Hurley Oct 05, 1886

REGISTRATION #: P 350,308

CIRCA: 1886? - 1901?

FREQUENCY:

MANUFACTURER: F. F. Adams Co.

MATERIAL: cast iron

FINISH: nickel

COMMENTS: This handle is the most common one seen in advertising, however there is not enough data available to associate this name plate specifically with this handle shape. The wire breaker is very often missing on these corkscrews.

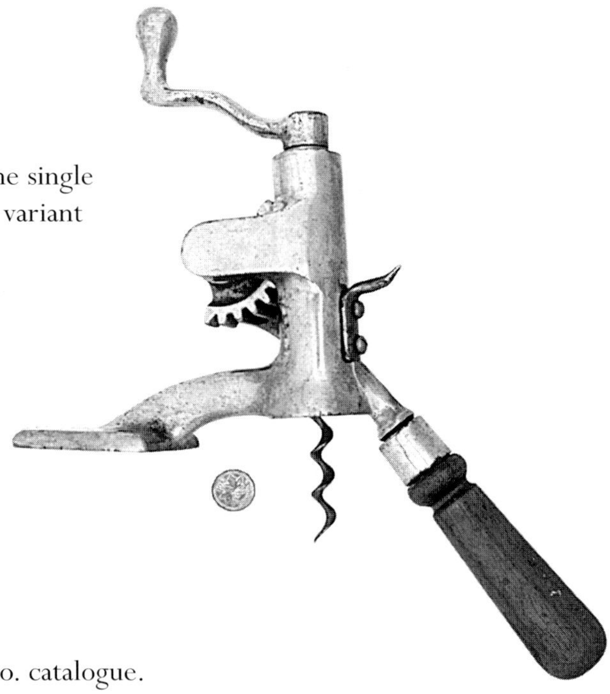

NAME: **SAMSON** (unmarked)

TRADEMARK: none

OTHER MARKS: no advertising plate or holes for mounting same

NOTICE: operating lever and pinion cast as one single piece, speed worm, standard worm variant *S06.2.1*

I.D. #: **S06.2.2**

INVENTOR & DATE: J. Hurley Oct 05, 1886

REGISTRATION #: P 350,308

CIRCA: 1901? - 1908?

FREQUENCY:

MANUFACTURER: Erie Specialty Co.

MATERIAL: cast iron

FINISH: nickel

COMMENTS: As found in a 1901 Erie Specialty Co. catalogue. The SAMSON appears to have been produced by a number of manufacturers over the years, this version by Walker may have been the last.

NAME:	**SCHNELL** (not inspected)
TRADEMARK:	not inspected
OTHER MARKS:	not inspected
NOTICE:	computer generated image
I.D. #:	**S07.1.1**
INVENTOR & DATE:	A. Flach May 23, 1894
REGISTRATION #:	DRGM 26,576
CIRCA:	1894? - ?
FREQUENCY:	
MANUFACTURER:	German ?
MATERIAL:	cast iron
FINISH:	not inspected
COMMENTS:	This is an inclined version of H. Williams 1891 patent for the US RAPID.

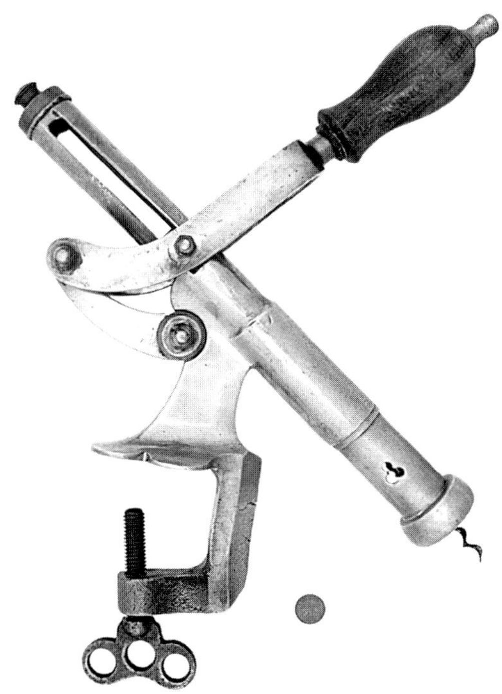

NAME:	**SHAMROCK** (unmarked)
TRADEMARK:	none
OTHER MARKS:	none
NOTICE:	Mason thumb piece, cracked brass clamp frame
I.D. #:	**S08.1.1**
INVENTOR & DATE:	no English patent or registration found
REGISTRATION #:	
CIRCA:	1900? - 1910?
FREQUENCY:	
MANUFACTURER:	presumably Samuel Mason Ltd.
MATERIAL:	brass
FINISH:	nickel
COMMENTS:	This is presumably a SHAMROCK prototype, due to the brass clamp bracket and no method of fixing a clamp plate. The non-standard handle and tube finial could be original or replacements.

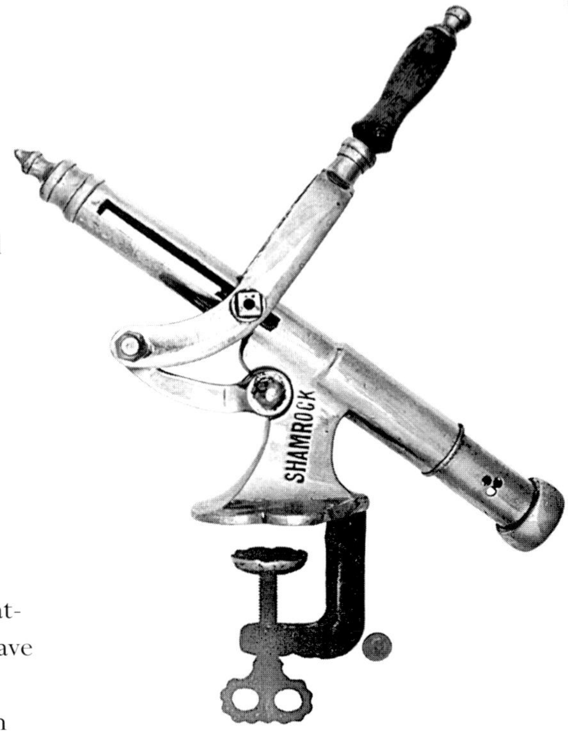

NAME: **SHAMROCK** (marked)
TRADEMARK: none
OTHER MARKS: none
NOTICE: Mason thumb piece
I.D. #: **S08.1.2**
INVENTOR & DATE: no English patent or registration found
REGISTRATION #:
CIRCA: 1900? - 1910?
FREQUENCY:
MANUFACTURER: Samuel Mason Ltd.
MATERIAL: brass
FINISH: nickel
COMMENTS: No one appears to have patented the single link from the frame to the operating lever, so the SHAMROCK could have been made anytime after about 1890; presumably it was a private label for an Irish distributor.

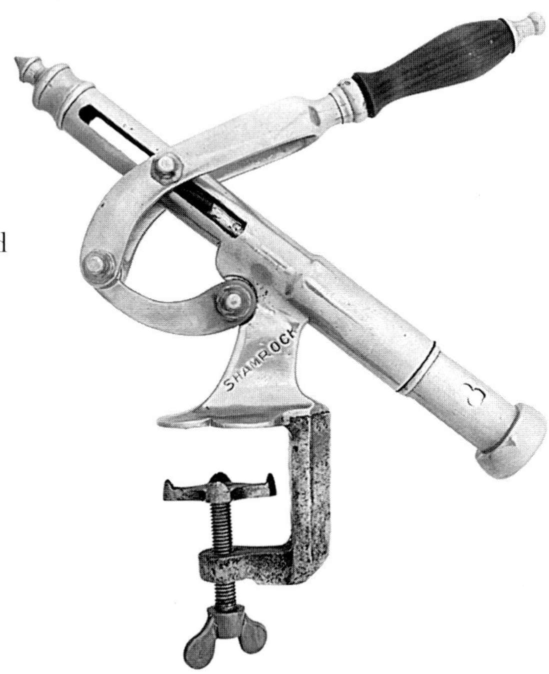

NAME: **SHAMROCK** (marked)
TRADEMARK: hand & star
OTHER MARKS: none
NOTICE: G&C clamp plate
I.D. #: **S08.1.3**
INVENTOR & DATE: no English patent or registration found
REGISTRATION #:
CIRCA: 1910? - 1920?
FREQUENCY:
MANUFACTURER: Gaskell
MATERIAL: brass
FINISH: nickel
COMMENTS: The thumb piece is a replacement and the operating lever is installed upside down.

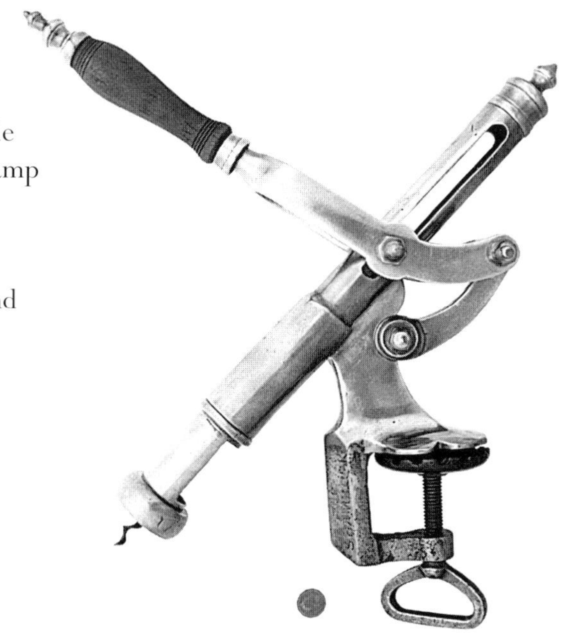

NAME: **SHAMROCK, THE** (marked)

TRADEMARK: none

OTHER MARKS: none

NOTICE: no hole pattern in the throat, probable Mason clamp plate, NAME on the clamp frame

I.D. #: **S09.1.1**

INVENTOR & DATE: no English patent or registration found

REGISTRATION #:

CIRCA: 1885? - 1900?

FREQUENCY:

MANUFACTURER: presumably Samuel Mason Ltd.

MATERIAL: brass

FINISH: brass

COMMENTS: The SHAMROCK is a RAPID with a scalloped frame clamp plate. This version has an unusual thumb piece and yoke; elaborate handle finials are found on older Mason pieces.

NAME: **SHOMEE** (marked)

TRADEMARK: none

OTHER MARKS: MANNING BOWMAN & CO, MERIDEN, CONN. U.S.A., PAT. APLD. FOR, SHORT, LONG

NOTICE: thumb piece, manufacturer's name

I.D. #: **S10.1.2**

INVENTOR & DATE: Baumgarten, application filed Feb 02, 1900

REGISTRATION #: P 675,032

CIRCA: 1900? - 1901?

FREQUENCY:

MANUFACTURER: Manning Bowman & Co.

MATERIAL: cast iron

FINISH: nickel

COMMENTS: Baumgarten used a number of different foundries after he left Arcade, resulting in slightly different thumb pieces. The SHORT, LONG switch allowed the operator to partially pull a cork.

NAME: **SHOMEE** (marked)
TRADEMARK: none
OTHER MARKS: PAT MAY 28 1901, NOVELTY LINE, THE STOVER MFG. Co., FREEPORT ILL USA
NOTICE: clamp plate missing
I.D. #: **S10.1.3**
INVENTOR & DATE: A. Baumgarten May 28, 1901
REGISTRATION #: P 675,032
CIRCA: 1901? - 1905?
FREQUENCY:
MANUFACTURER: The Stover Mfg. Co.
MATERIAL: cast iron
FINISH: nickel
COMMENTS: Baumgarten's involvement with Stover appears to have been very short.

NAME: **SHOMEE** (marked)
TRADEMARK: none
OTHER MARKS: MANNING BOWMAN & CO, MERIDEN, CONN. U.S.A., PAT MAY 28 1901
NOTICE: thumb piece, manufacturer
I.D. #: **S10.1.4**
INVENTOR & DATE: A. Baumgarten May 28, 1901
REGISTRATION #: P 675,032
CIRCA: 1900 ?
FREQUENCY:
MANUFACTURER: Manning Bowman & Co.
MATERIAL: cast iron
FINISH: nickel
COMMENTS: This is the patented version of **S10.1.2**.

NAME:	**SHOMEE** (marked)
TRADEMARK:	none
OTHER MARKS:	ENG. PAT. NO. 6224. 1900, LIVERPOOL ENGLAND, MADE IN USA
NOTICE:	thumb piece, manufacturers
I.D. #:	**S10.1.5**
INVENTOR & DATE:	A. Baumgarten May 28, 1901
REGISTRATION #:	P 675,032
CIRCA:	1900? - ?
FREQUENCY:	
MANUFACTURER:	presumably Manning Bowman & Co.
MATERIAL:	cast iron
FINISH:	nickel
COMMENTS:	English patent date marked, but manufactured in the USA; SHOMEE was always cast into the bottle clasps.

NAME:	**SHOMEE** (marked)
TRADEMARK:	none
OTHER MARKS:	ALBERT PICK & CO. CHICAGO ILL, PAT MAY 28 1901
NOTICE:	thumb piece, name
I.D. #:	**S10.1.6**
INVENTOR & DATE:	A. Baumgarten May 28, 1901
REGISTRATION #:	P 675,032
CIRCA:	1901? - 1905?
FREQUENCY:	
MANUFACTURER:	presumably Manning Bowman & Co.
MATERIAL:	cast iron
FINISH:	nickel
COMMENTS:	This is a private label version for Albert Pick.

NAME:	**SHOMEE** (marked)	
TRADEMARK:	none	
OTHER MARKS:	FREEPORT NOVELTY CO, FREEPORT ILL USA, PAT. APLD. FOR.	
NOTICE:	wall mount with bottle clasp	
I.D. #:	**S10.2.1**	
INVENTOR & DATE:	Baumgarten, application filed Feb 02, 1900	
REGISTRATION #:	P 675,032	
CIRCA:	1900?	
FREQUENCY:		
MANUFACTURER:	Freeport Novelty Co.	
MATERIAL:	cast iron	
FINISH:	nickel	
COMMENTS:	Presumably the first version, this would have been manufactured in Baumgarten's foundry.	

NAME:	**SHOMEE** (marked)
TRADEMARK:	none
OTHER MARKS:	ALBERT PICK & CO. CHICAGO ILL, PAT MAY 28 1901
NOTICE:	wall mount
I.D. #:	**S10.2.6**
INVENTOR & DATE:	A. Baumgarten May 28, 1901
REGISTRATION #:	P 675,032
CIRCA:	1901? - ?
FREQUENCY:	
MANUFACTURER:	presumably Manning Bowman & Co.
MATERIAL:	cast iron
FINISH:	none visible
COMMENTS:	A private label version for A. Pick. This is possibly a prototype as no decorations have been cast into the operating lever or the clasp lever.

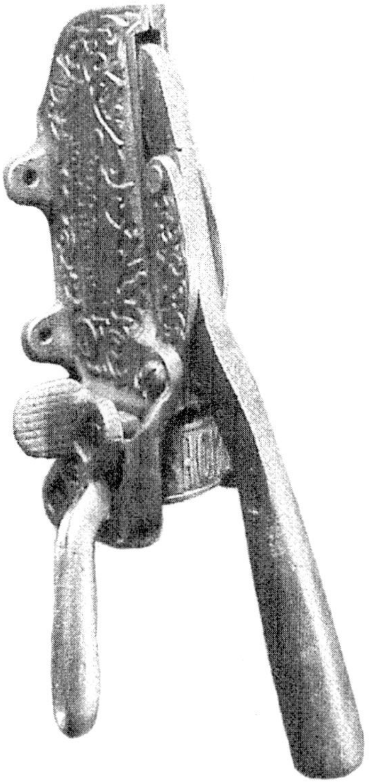

NAME:	**SIMPLE, THE** (marked)
TRADEMARK:	hand & star
OTHER MARKS:	PATENT 16777, GASKELL marked internally
NOTICE:	no bottle clasp
I.D. #:	**S11.1.1**
INVENTOR & DATE:	R. Gilchrist Sep 03, 1894
REGISTRATION #:	LP 16,777
CIRCA:	1894? - 1910?
FREQUENCY:	
MANUFACTURER:	Gaskell
MATERIAL:	cast iron
FINISH:	nickel
COMMENTS:	A British version of the ARCADE, possibly first produced before the bottle clasp was patented in 1895. The frame decoration is very similar to that shown in the **S4.1.1** advertising.

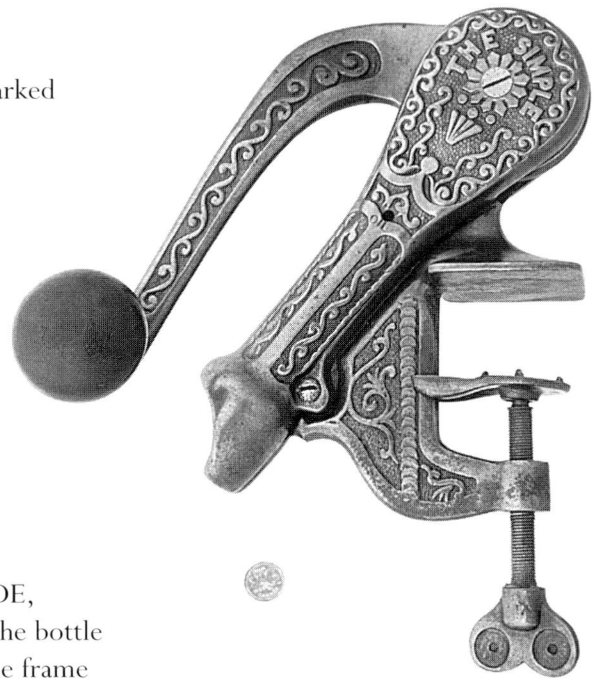

NAME:	**SIMPLEX, THE** (marked)
TRADEMARK:	none
OTHER MARKS:	PAT JAN 26 94
NOTICE:	this mechanism is somewhat similar to the German 1904 L. Kummer patent
I.D. #:	**S12.1.1**
INVENTOR & DATE:	H. Cliff 1894
REGISTRATION #:	no US registration found
CIRCA:	1894- ?
FREQUENCY:	
MANUFACTURER:	almost certainly Manning Bowman & Co.
MATERIAL:	cast iron
FINISH:	nickel
COMMENTS:	A curious patent date as Cliff was from Chicago but there is no known US patent. While Cliff patented this mechanism in France, Germany and England, none of those patents were filed for or received on this date.

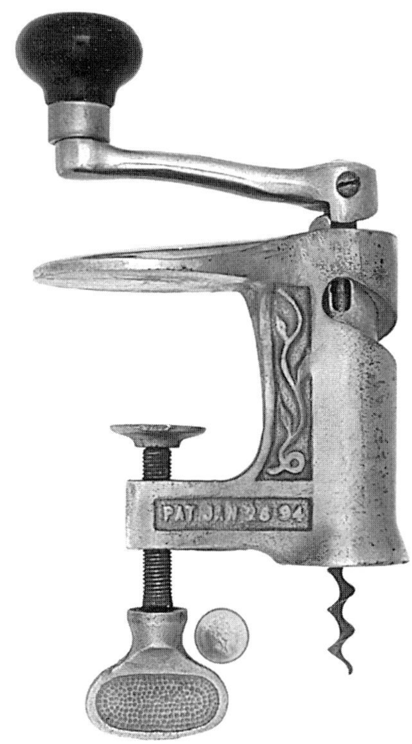

NAME:	**SIMPLEX** (not inspected)
TRADEMARK:	not inspected
OTHER MARKS:	not inspected
NOTICE:	NAME only, at the bottom of the advertisement shown
I.D. #:	**S13.1.1**
INVENTOR & DATE:	not inspected
REGISTRATION #:	
CIRCA:	1895?
FREQUENCY:	
MANUFACTURER:	unknown
MATERIAL:	not inspected
FINISH:	not inspected
COMMENTS:	As mentioned at the bottom of this 1895 advertisement, this SIMPLEX is far too expensive to be THE SIMPLEX.

The "MERRITT."

Nickel-plated .. 39/–, Brass ... 35/–

Also the "**Simplex**" Machine at same prices.

NAME:	**SISTEMA** (marked)
TRADEMARK:	not inspected
OTHER MARKS:	F. R. SUCESORES, GIJON
NOTICE:	
I.D. #:	**S14.1.1**
INVENTOR & DATE:	no Spanish patent or registration found
REGISTRATION #:	
CIRCA:	1920?
FREQUENCY:	
MANUFACTURER:	F. R. Sucesores
MATERIAL:	brass
FINISH:	white paint
COMMENTS:	This rack and pinion mechanism is very similar to the ALFREDO type.

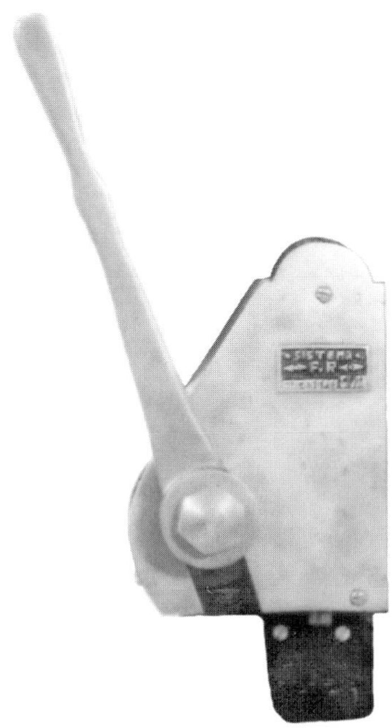

NAME: **SLAM, THE** (marked)

TRADEMARK: optic

OTHER MARKS: CHAMBERS PATENT

NOTICE: single link, top mount version *S15.2.1*

I.D. #: **S15.1.1**

INVENTOR & DATE: C. Chambers Aug 20, 1903

REGISTRATION #: LP 18,006

CIRCA: 1920? -1930?

FREQUENCY:

MANUFACTURER: Gaskell & Chambers Ltd.

MATERIAL: brass

FINISH: nickel

COMMENTS: This is a later, lower cost version of the single link RAPID style, utilizing the DON mechanism. The patent referred to would be for the DON mechanism. A top mount version would be .

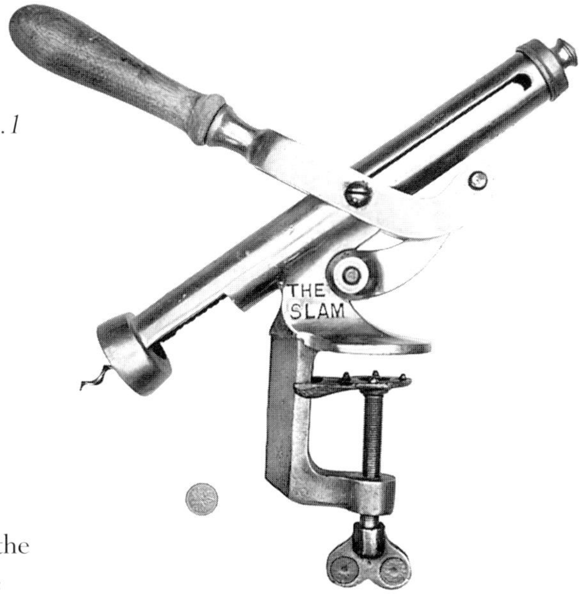

NAME: **SÖNNERGRENS, EDV.** (marked)

TRADEMARK: none

OTHER MARKS: EDV. SÖNNERGRENS, GOTEBORG, PATENT NR 43176

NOTICE: a computer generated image, used to restore the missing part of the casting

I.D. #: **S23.1.1**

INVENTOR & DATE: E. Sönnergrens May 16, 1916

REGISTRATION #: P 43,176

CIRCA: 1916? - ?

FREQUENCY:

MANUFACTURER: Swedish

MATERIAL: cast iron

FINISH: not inspected

COMMENTS: This is missing some parts, but is a great old Swedish corkscrew. The fascinating story of its rediscovery is available from the Helix Scandinavica collectors club.

NAME:	**STANDARD** (marked)
TRADEMARK:	none
OTHER MARKS:	none
NOTICE:	
I.D. #:	**S16.1.1**
INVENTOR & DATE:	H. Tscherning May 19, 1903
REGISTRATION #:	P 728,519
CIRCA:	1903? - 1913?
FREQUENCY:	
MANUFACTURER:	Arcade Manufacturing Co.
MATERIAL:	cast iron
FINISH:	nickel
COMMENTS:	This is the full sized version of Tscherning's patent, which involved a spring loaded latch on the worm-nut to lock it to the worm carrier.

The Standard No. 25

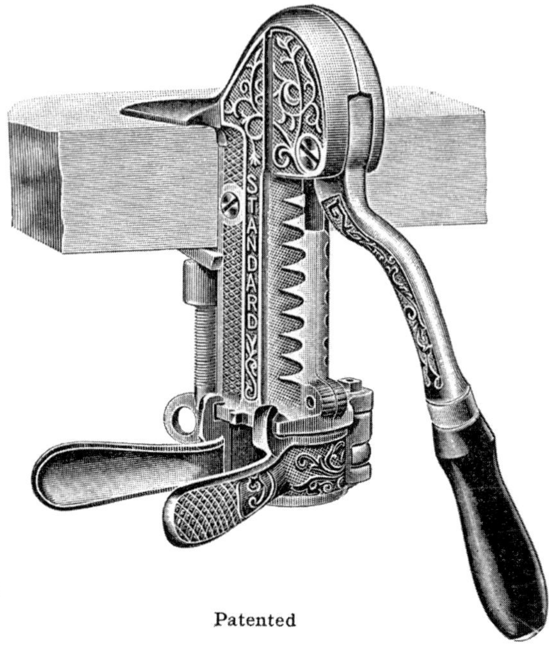

Patented

NAME:	**STANDARD** (marked)
TRADEMARK:	none
OTHER MARKS:	none
NOTICE:	wall mount
I.D. #:	**S16.2.1**
INVENTOR & DATE:	H. Tscherning May 19, 1903
REGISTRATION #:	P 728,519
CIRCA:	1903? - 1913?
FREQUENCY:	
MANUFACTURER:	Arcade Manufacturing Co.
MATERIAL:	cast iron
FINISH:	nickel
COMMENTS:	This Arcade advertisement dates to 1913.

Arcade Cork Pullers

The Standard No. 26

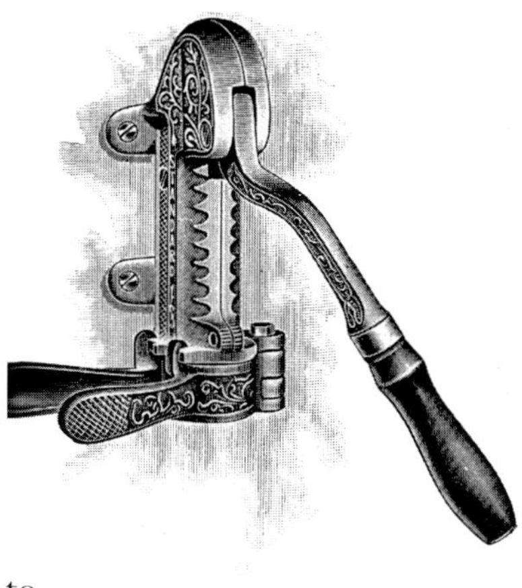

Patented

This puller is designed to be fastened to the wall or the refrigerator.

It is built for heavy work, and will last a lifetime.

It is handsomely finished in the highest quality of nickel plate.

A reliable puller for the saloon trade.

PACKING

Each puller is packed in a wooden box, 1 dozen in a strong case.

Case weight, net 26 lbs., gross 68 lbs. Case measurements, 30x17x13 inches.

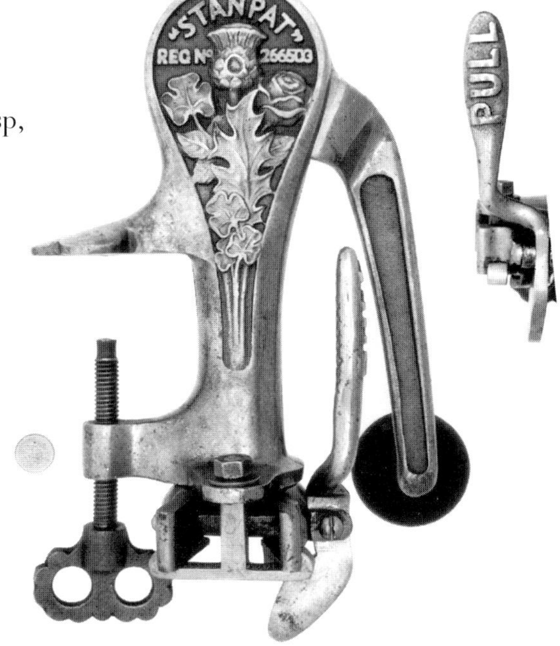

NAME: **STANPAT** (marked)

TRADEMARK: none

OTHER MARKS: REG No. 266503

NOTICE: unknown style of single lever bottle clasp, Mason thumb piece

I.D. #: **S17.1.1**

INVENTOR & DATE: British registration number is not for a corkscrew case design

REGISTRATION #: REG 288,503

CIRCA: 1893? - 1895?

FREQUENCY:

MANUFACTURER: presumably Samuel Mason Ltd.

MATERIAL: brass

FINISH: nickel

COMMENTS: This pre-production sample was designed for show only, as all of the components including screws and bolts were made of nickel plated brass, except for the worm, link rod and one bolt and spring in the bottle clasp. Presumably it was made in the time period between the 1894 SAFETY patent and the 1895 SAFETY bottle clasp patent. Possibly the name and registration number were made up just to show the client how it might look in production.

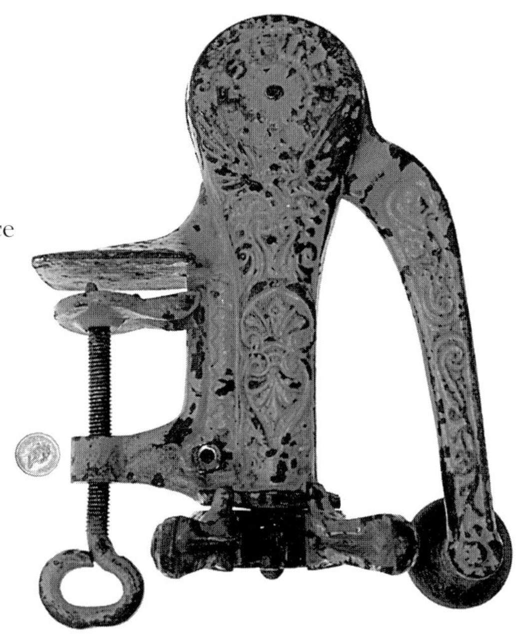

NAME: **STEINER, F** (marked)

TRADEMARK: none

OTHER MARKS: KARLSTHAL, CSR

NOTICE: very crude case casting, 1/4" shorter than the ALEXANDERWERK, thumb piece

I.D. #: **S18.1.1**

INVENTOR & DATE: no patent or registration found

REGISTRATION #:

CIRCA: 1895? - 1900 ?

FREQUENCY:

MANUFACTURER: American

MATERIAL: cast iron

FINISH: red paint

COMMENTS: This is the same case decoration as found on the ALEXANDERWERK.
It appears to have been made in the USA, but not by Arcade. This is the earliest known example of what later became the standard German thumb piece.

NAME: **SULLIVAN** (unmarked)
TRADEMARK: none
OTHER MARKS: none
NOTICE: hole pattern in the operating lever handle, shown out of scale
I.D. #: **S19.1.1**
INVENTOR & DATE: W. Redlich Aug 12, 1884
REGISTRATION #: P 303,400
CIRCA: 1884? - 1896?
FREQUENCY:
MANUFACTURER: Meriden Malleable Iron Co.
MATERIAL: cast iron
FINISH: nickel
COMMENTS: This is a top mount version of the SULLIVAN, without the decorative frame design; it is possibly the one shown in the advertisement **S19.1.2.**

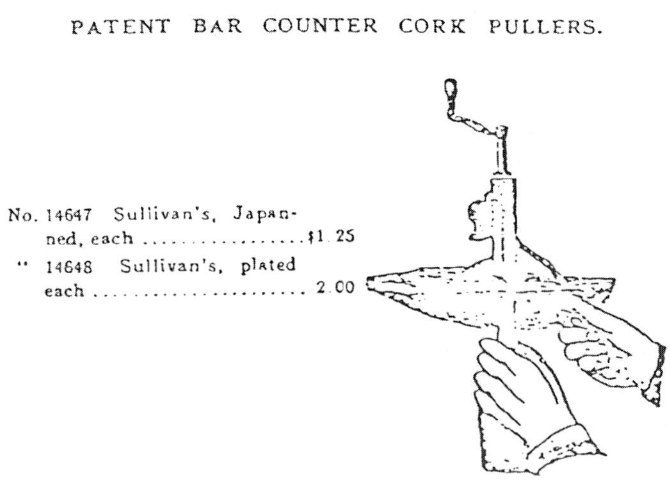
PATENT BAR COUNTER CORK PULLERS.

No. 14647 Sullivan's, Japanned, each $1.25
" 14648 Sullivan's, plated each 2.00

NAME: **SULLIVAN** (unmarked)
TRADEMARK: none
OTHER MARKS: not inspected
NOTICE:
I.D. #: **S19.1.2**
INVENTOR & DATE: W. Redlich Aug 12, 1884
REGISTRATION #: P 303,400
CIRCA: 1884? - 1896?
FREQUENCY:
MANUFACTURER: Meriden Malleable Iron Co.
MATERIAL: cast iron
FINISH: japanned
COMMENTS: The text was repaired, but not the illustration, in this 1896 advertisement.

NAME:	**SULLIVAN** (unmarked)
TRADEMARK:	none
OTHER MARKS:	none
NOTICE:	M&M thumb piece
I.D. #:	**S19.2.1**
INVENTOR & DATE:	W. Redlich Aug 12, 1884
REGISTRATION #:	P 303,400
CIRCA:	1884? - 1896?
FREQUENCY:	
MANUFACTURER:	Meriden Malleable Iron Co.
MATERIAL:	cast iron
FINISH:	nickel
COMMENTS:	This has the same grape motif as the marked SULLIVAN, but this example is unmarked.

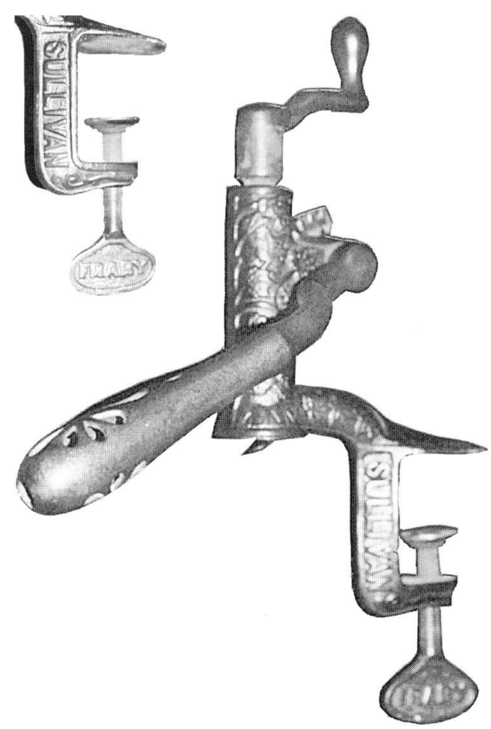

NAME:	**SULLIVAN** (marked)
TRADEMARK:	none
OTHER MARKS:	FRARY'S, FRARY
NOTICE:	this is a wide rack and pinion mechanism
I.D. #:	**S19.3.1**
INVENTOR & DATE:	W. Redlich Aug 12, 1884
REGISTRATION #:	P 303,400
CIRCA:	1888 - 1890
FREQUENCY:	
MANUFACTURER:	Meriden Malleable Iron Co.
MATERIAL:	cast iron
FINISH:	nickel
COMMENTS:	All of the SULLIVANs have the identical complex pattern piercing the cast iron handle, thus it is almost certain that they were all made in the same foundry.

NAME: **SUN** (marked)
TRADEMARK: none
OTHER MARKS: S. MASON, cast into the thumb piece
NOTICE: throat
I.D. #: **S20.1.1**
INVENTOR & DATE: C. Chambers Mar 26, 1888
REGISTRATION #: LP 4,564
CIRCA: 1888? - 1903?
FREQUENCY:
MANUFACTURER: Samuel Mason Ltd.
MATERIAL: brass
FINISH: nickel
COMMENTS: This looks like a DON, but it is a small version of the MERRITT with a removable throat.

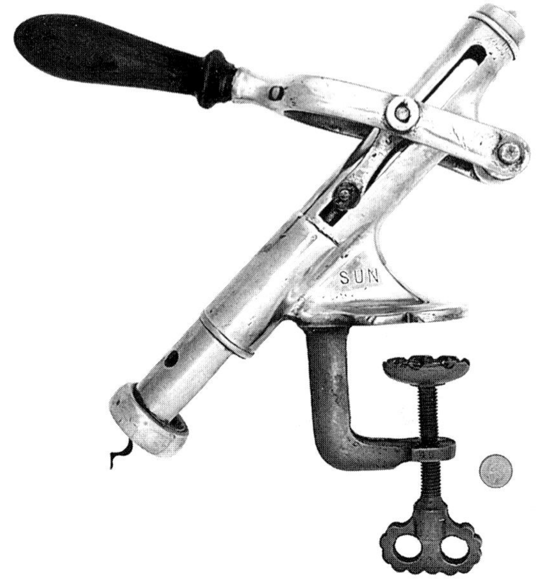

NAME: **SUNOID** (marked)
TRADEMARK: sun
OTHER MARKS: S. MASON cast in the thumb piece
NOTICE: ribbed edges on case and frame
I.D. #: **S21.1.1**
INVENTOR & DATE: R. Gilchrist Sep 03, 1894 and A. Pick Feb 08, 1895
REGISTRATION #: LP 16,777 and LP 2,825
CIRCA: 1910? - 1913?
FREQUENCY:
MANUFACTURER: Samuel Mason Ltd.
MATERIAL: cast iron
FINISH: nickel
COMMENTS: The link between many Mason corkscrews is that he did like adding "oid". The missing clamp plate may be a "U" type; his normal plate does not fit. Mason's SUN trademark was part of the frame decoration. The original SAFETY patents would have expired.

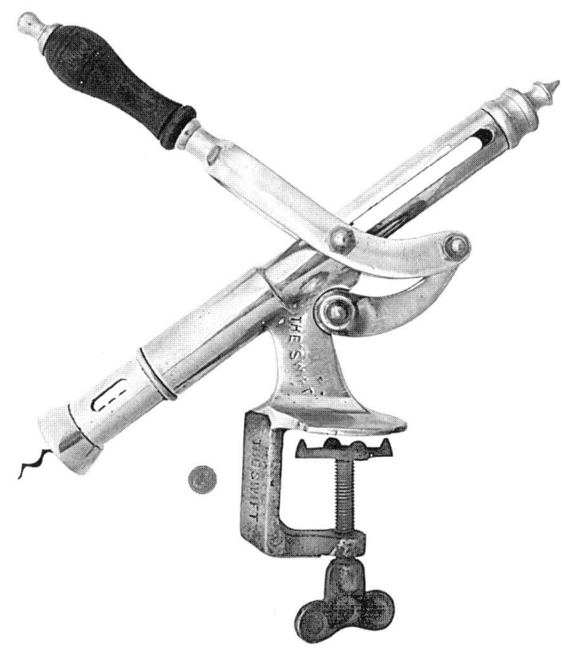

NAME: **SWIFT, THE** (marked)

TRADEMARK: both optic and hand & star

OTHER MARKS: none

NOTICE: brass finish variant *S22.1.2*

I.D. #: **S22.1.1**

INVENTOR & DATE: no English patent or registration found

REGISTRATION #:

CIRCA: 1920? - 1925?

FREQUENCY:

MANUFACTURER: Gaskell & Chambers Ltd.

MATERIAL: brass

FINISH: nickel

COMMENTS: The name is cast into the clamp frame and the pedestal of this private label British RAPID.

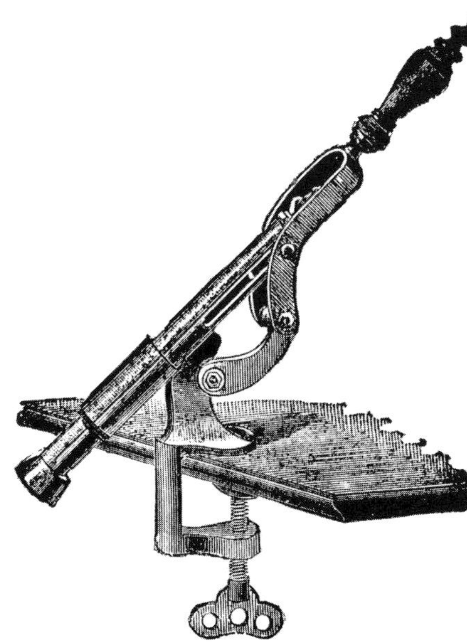

No. **5008**—The "Swift."
Nickel-plated on Brass ... 30/- each.
Polished Brass ... ... 28/- „
On Stand or with Adjustable Clamp.
When ordering say Stand or Clamp.

NAME: **SWIFT, THE** (not inspected)

TRADEMARK: not inspected

OTHER MARKS: not inspected

NOTICE: top mount advertised, brass finish variant *S22.2.2*

I.D. #: **S22.2.1**

INVENTOR & DATE: no English patent or registration found

REGISTRATION #:

CIRCA: 1902?-1920?

FREQUENCY:

MANUFACTURER: Gaskell

MATERIAL: brass

FINISH: nickel

COMMENTS: This corkscrew was advertised by James Heeley in 1909 and Gaskell in 1910.

NAME:	**SWIFT, THE** (marked)
TRADEMARK:	hand & star
OTHER MARKS:	none
NOTICE:	thumb piece
I.D. #:	**S22.3.1**
INVENTOR & DATE:	no English patent or registration found
REGISTRATION #:	
CIRCA:	1910?
FREQUENCY:	
MANUFACTURER:	Gaskell
MATERIAL:	brass
FINISH:	nickel
COMMENTS:	This thumb piece looks like, but is not, the standard Mason thumb piece; possibly it is a Gaskell & Chambers version made shortly after Mason was purchased. A top mounted SWIFT would be .

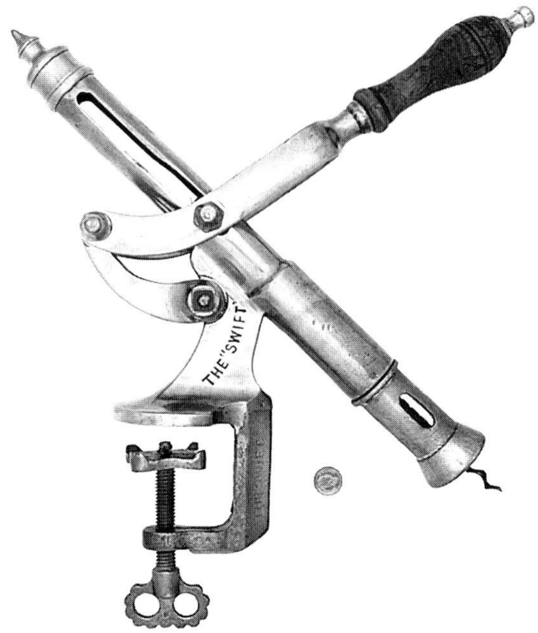

NAME:	**TITAN** (marked)
TRADEMARK:	none
OTHER MARKS:	none
NOTICE:	short finial, no throat holes, small frame differences
I.D. #:	**T01.1.1**
INVENTOR & DATE:	no Belgian patent or registration found
REGISTRATION #:	
CIRCA:	1903? - ?
FREQUENCY:	
MANUFACTURER:	Belgian ?
MATERIAL:	cast iron
FINISH:	nickel
COMMENTS:	This cast iron version of the DON has metric nuts and bolts. No information is available on the frequency of each specific variant.

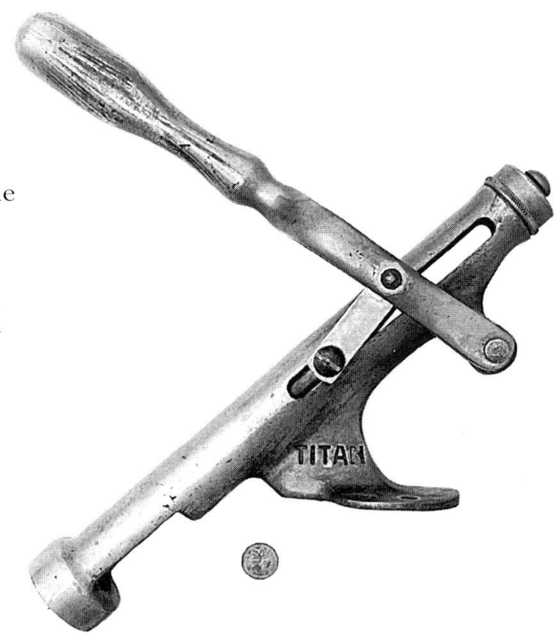

NAME:	**TITAN** (marked)
TRADEMARK:	none
OTHER MARKS:	none
NOTICE:	long finial, two hole throat, no nuts on the side links
I.D. #:	**T01.1.2**
INVENTOR & DATE:	no Belgian patent or registration found
REGISTRATION #:	
CIRCA:	1903? - ?
FREQUENCY:	
MANUFACTURER:	Belgian ?
MATERIAL:	cast iron
FINISH:	nickel
COMMENTS:	This cast iron version of the DON has metric nuts and bolts. Presumably these were made in Belgium.

NAME:	**TITAN** (marked)
TRADEMARK:	none
OTHER MARKS:	MAISON RUBEN, 17 RUE HEYVAERT, BRUXELLES
NOTICE:	long finial, two hole throat, advertising plate out of scale
I.D. #:	**T01.1.3**
INVENTOR & DATE:	no Belgian patent or registration found
REGISTRATION #:	
CIRCA:	1930? - ?
FREQUENCY:	
MANUFACTURER:	Belgian ?
MATERIAL:	cast iron
FINISH:	chrome
COMMENTS:	This is a later version, as chrome only started to became popular around 1930. Helmut Gebel in a 1932 article states that mounted corkscrews were being manufactured in Belgium. This corkscrew may not be the original one on this base.

NAME: **TRIUMPH, THE** (marked)

TRADEMARK: none

OTHER MARKS: PAT. APL'D. FOR

NOTICE: the early version, advertising plate out of scale

I.D. #: **T02.1.1**

INVENTOR & DATE: J. Schermack, application filed Dec 03, 1900

REGISTRATION #: P 683,004

CIRCA: 1900? - 1901?

FREQUENCY:

MANUFACTURER: Arcade Manufacturing Co.

MATERIAL: cast iron

FINISH: nickel

COMMENTS: There are slight differences in the frame castings between the two TRIUMPHs shown.

NAME: **TRIUMPH, THE** (unmarked)

TRADEMARK: none

OTHER MARKS: ARCADE MFG. CO. FREEPORT, ILL

NOTICE: data from an existing example

I.D. #: **T02.1.2**

INVENTOR & DATE: J. Schermack Sep 17, 1901

REGISTRATION #: P 683,004

CIRCA: 1900? - 1913?

FREQUENCY:

MANUFACTURER: Arcade Manufacturing Co.

MATERIAL: cast iron

FINISH: nickel

COMMENTS: This Arcade catalog illustration dates to 1913.

The Triumph

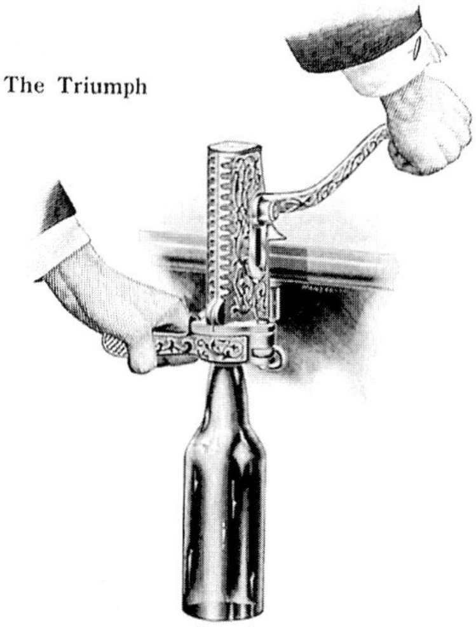

Patented

In producing the Triumph Cork Puller we have made the interior action on an entirely new principle. There is no lost motion, and a full, direct stroke is the result.

One action of the lever draws the cork front the bottle and ejects the cork from the worm.

The construction is such that a new worm may be placed in the puller without removing the side plates.

It is carefully finished and will last for years.

PACKING

Each puller in a wooden box; ½ dozen in a strong shipping case.
Case weight, net 31 pounds, gross 59 pounds.

NAME: **UNIQUE, 1898** (marked)

TRADEMARK: none

OTHER MARKS: PAT'D IN AMERICA & EUROPE, AMERICAN MANUFACTURE, 1898 DESIGN

NOTICE: offset operating arm, advertising plate out of scale

I.D. #: **U01.1.1**

INVENTOR & DATE: E. Walker Apr 07, 1896

REGISTRATION #: P 557,734

CIRCA: 1898? - ?

FREQUENCY:

MANUFACTURER: Erie Specialty Co.

MATERIAL: cast iron

FINISH: nickel

COMMENTS: The 1898 QUICK & EASY sold under the UNIQUE name in England. Most UNIQUEs have a straight operating arm rather than the offset one found on the QUICK & EASY.

NAME: **UNIQUE, NEW** (marked)

TRADEMARK: none

OTHER MARKS: PAT'D IN AMERICA & EUROPE, AMERICAN MANUFACTURE, 1898 DESIGN

NOTICE: bolt attached crank handle, a later design with two hole mounted advertising plate, advertising plate out of scale

I.D. #: **U02.1.1**

INVENTOR & DATE: E. Walker Apr 07, 1896

REGISTRATION #: P 557,734

CIRCA: 1900? - 1913?

FREQUENCY:

MANUFACTURER: Erie Specialty Co.

MATERIAL: cast iron

FINISH: nickel

COMMENTS: The American crank handles were press fitted onto a sleeve on the operating arm; Europe preferred the much sturdier method of attaching the crank handle with a bolt.

NAME:	**UNIQUE, NEW** (marked)
TRADEMARK:	none
OTHER MARKS:	PAT'D IN AMERICA & EUROPE, AMERICAN MANUFACTURE,1898 DESIGN
NOTICE:	advertising plate out of scale
I.D. #:	**U02.2.1**
INVENTOR & DATE:	E. Walker Apr 07, 1896
REGISTRATION #:	P 557,734
CIRCA:	1900? - 1913?
FREQUENCY:	
MANUFACTURER:	Erie Specialty Co.
MATERIAL:	cast iron
FINISH:	nickel
COMMENTS:	It is not known what the advantage was to only have a bottle lip, rather than the far more common neck rest.

NAME:	**UNIQUE, THE** (marked)
TRADEMARK:	none
OTHER MARKS:	PAT. ALOWED, AMERICAN MANUFACTURE
NOTICE:	the unusual crank handle appears to be original, advertising plate out of scale
I.D. #:	**U03.1.1**
INVENTOR & DATE:	E. Walker Feb 27, 1894
REGISTRATION #:	P 515,412
CIRCA:	1894? - 1895?
FREQUENCY:	
MANUFACTURER:	Erie Specialty Co.
MATERIAL:	cast iron
FINISH:	nickel
COMMENTS:	This first version of the QUICK & EASY sold under the UNIQUE name in England.

NAME:	**UNIQUE, THE** (marked)
TRADEMARK:	hand & star
OTHER MARKS:	BRITISH MANUFACTURE, BRITISH MAKE
NOTICE:	brass frame, cast iron arm, advertising plate out of scale
I.D. #:	**U04.1.1**
INVENTOR & DATE:	E. Walker Apr 07, 1896
REGISTRATION #:	LP 7,409
CIRCA:	1909? - 1920?
FREQUENCY:	
MANUFACTURER:	Gaskell
MATERIAL:	brass with iron crank arm
FINISH:	nickel
COMMENTS:	The later version of the 1898 QUICK & EASY manufactured by Gaskell & Chambers in England was marked BRITISH MAKE inside the semi-disk.

NAME:	**UNIQUE** (unmarked)
TRADEMARK:	none
OTHER MARKS:	none
NOTICE:	a William Morris inspired case design, no advertising plate
I.D. #:	**U05.1.1**
INVENTOR & DATE:	E. Walker Apr 07, 1896 & Nov 11, 1902
REGISTRATION #:	P 557,734 & P 713,540
CIRCA:	1902? - ?
FREQUENCY:	
MANUFACTURER:	Erie Specialty Co.
MATERIAL:	cast iron
FINISH:	nickel
COMMENTS:	This unique UNIQUE incorporates Walker's 1902 bottle clasp patent; the clamp plate is not original.

NAME:	**VAMPIR** (marked)
TRADEMARK:	none
OTHER MARKS:	none
NOTICE:	wire neck rest installed upside down?
I.D. #:	**V01.1.1**
INVENTOR & DATE:	no German patent or registration found
REGISTRATION #:	
CIRCA:	1950? - 1960?
FREQUENCY:	
MANUFACTURER:	German
MATERIAL:	cast aluminum
FINISH:	green paint
COMMENTS:	This style of thumb piece is normally found on Italian corkscrews. It is possible that the neck rest was designed "upside down" such that the lip support worked in opposition to the neck support.

NAME:	**VICTOR JR.** (marked)
TRADEMARK:	none
OTHER MARKS:	none
NOTICE:	
I.D. #:	**V02.1.1**
INVENTOR & DATE:	R. Gilchrist Jun 25, 1907
REGISTRATION #:	P 857,992
CIRCA:	1910 - ?
FREQUENCY:	
MANUFACTURER:	Arcade Manufacturing Co.
MATERIAL:	cast iron
FINISH:	nickel
COMMENTS:	This is a version of YANKEE No 1 with a cap lifter on the front of the frame.

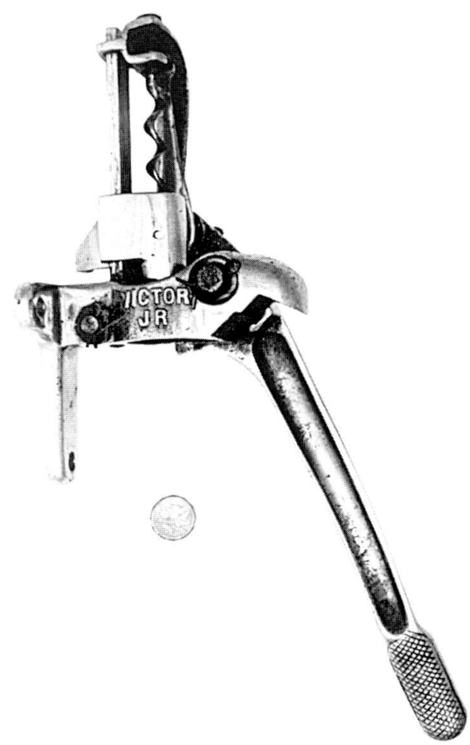

NAME:	**VICTOR, THE PATENT** (marked)
TRADEMARK:	none
OTHER MARKS:	not inspected
NOTICE:	not inspected
I.D. #:	**V03.1.1**
INVENTOR & DATE:	S. Mason Feb 20, 1890
REGISTRATION #:	LP 2,725
CIRCA:	1890? - 1900?
FREQUENCY:	
MANUFACTURER:	Samuel Mason Ltd.
MATERIAL:	brass
FINISH:	nickel
COMMENTS:	The advertising plate contains advertising for JAMES SIMPSON & SONS whiskey.

No. P 2218—The "Victor" Cork Drawer. (Patent.)

The quickest Machine ever invented, and the easiest. Working parts cannot get out of order with fair usage. Will last a lifetime.
Nickel-plated, ... 52/6 each.

NAME:	**VICTOR, THE** (marked)
TRADEMARK:	not inspected
OTHER MARKS:	not inspected
NOTICE:	not inspected
I.D. #:	**V03.1.2**
INVENTOR & DATE:	S. Mason Feb 20, 1890
REGISTRATION #:	LP 2,725
CIRCA:	1890? - 1900?
FREQUENCY:	
MANUFACTURER:	Samuel Mason Ltd.
MATERIAL:	brass
FINISH:	nickel
COMMENTS:	The advertising dates to 1898. Part of Mason's patent was for the advertising space on the side of the corkscrew; no information is available on the frequency of a specifically named version.

NAME: **VIKTORIA** (not inspected)
TRADEMARK: not inspected
OTHER MARKS: not inspected
NOTICE: not inspected
I.D. #: **V04.1.1**
INVENTOR & DATE: A. D'Avis Oct 11, 1900 and Mar 09, 1908
REGISTRATION #: DRGM 144,035 and 351,906
CIRCA: 1900? - 1920?
FREQUENCY:
MANUFACTURER: Erste Mainzer Metallkapsel-Fabrik ?
MATERIAL: cast iron
FINISH: not inspected
COMMENTS: This corkscrew was designed to be used in a winery to disgorge sparkling wine, not to be used in a bar.

Degorgier-Entkorker „Viktoria"
Mk. 55.—

NAME: **VINTNER** (marked)
TRADEMARK: none
OTHER MARKS: PATENT PENDING
NOTICE:
I.D. #: **V05.1.1**
INVENTOR & DATE: no US patent or registration found
REGISTRATION #:
CIRCA: 1970? - 1998?
FREQUENCY:
MANUFACTURER: Asian for Rogar International Corp.
MATERIAL: brass
FINISH: brass
COMMENTS: This modern version of the CHAMPION was not in production after 1998.

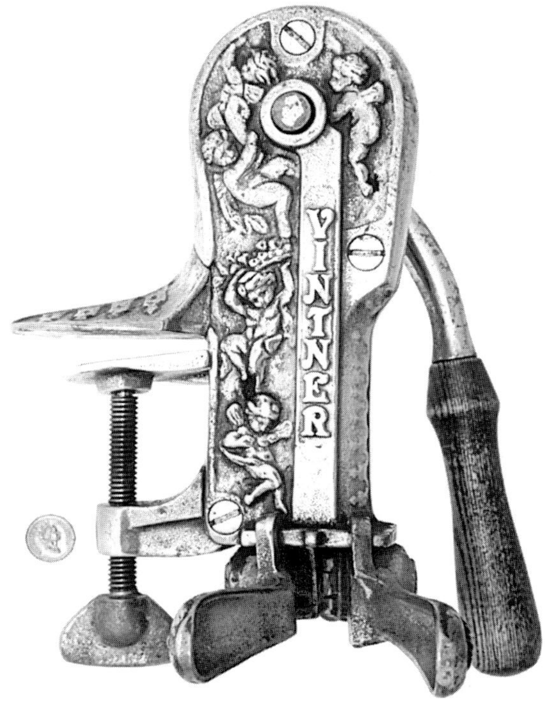

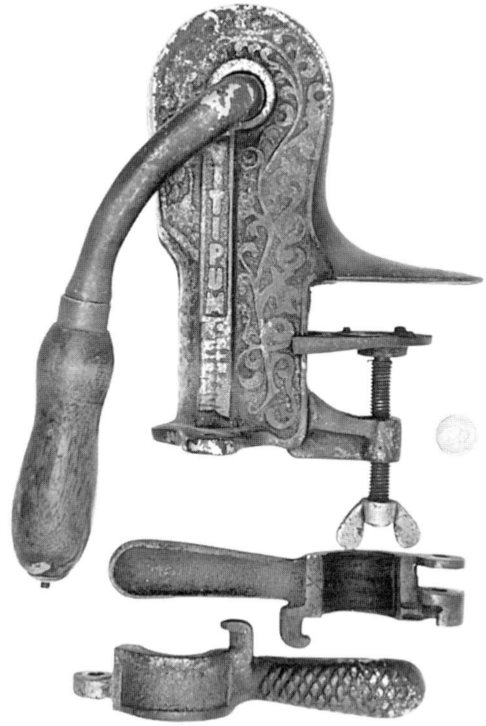

NAME: **VITIPUM** (marked)

TRADEMARK: none

OTHER MARKS: MARCO REG. INDUSTRIA ARGENTINA

NOTICE: replacement thumb piece, handle nut missing

I.D. #: **V06.1.1**

INVENTOR & DATE: no Argentinean patent or registration found

REGISTRATION #:

CIRCA: 1900? - 1940?

FREQUENCY:

MANUFACTURER: Argentinean ?

MATERIAL: cast iron

FINISH: nickel

COMMENTS: This appears to be an Argentinean manufactured version of the CHAMPION.

The Walker Automatic Cork Pull

This is a new principle for operating cork pulls. The entire machine is built to be an ornament as well as a useful article. By turning the handle forward the screw enters the cork, and by reversing it the cork is pulled and afterwards thrown off from the screw. machine stands at an angle and is 11 inches tall when fastened to the counter. The clamp extends 4 inches below; is fitted with both clamp and screws, so that either or both can be used as wanted for fastening. The operation of the screw inside the machine is so different from the method usually employed in operating cork pulls that it is comparatively indestructible, and there is no soft babbiting to soon wear out. While these machines are, a little more expensive in price, they are so durable that they will soon pay for themselves in not needing repairs of any kind.

Price each $5.50

NAME: **WALKER AUTOMATIC, THE** (marked)

TRADEMARK: none

OTHER MARKS: ERIE SPECIALTY MFG. CO, ERIE, PA. U.S.A., PAT FEB 27'84

NOTICE:

I.D. #: **W01.1.1**

INVENTOR & DATE: E. Walker Feb 27, 1894

REGISTRATION #: P 515,411

CIRCA: 1893? - 1894?

FREQUENCY:

MANUFACTURER: Erie Specialty Mfg. Co.

MATERIAL: cast iron

FINISH: nickel

COMMENTS: In one advertisement this very expensive machine was listed at $10.00 when equivalent bar corkscrews on the same page were selling in the $2.50 - $3.50 range.

NAME: **WALKER, THE** (unmarked)

TRADEMARK: none

OTHER MARKS: ERIE SPECIALTY CO, MAKERS, ERIE, PA USA

NOTICE: collar under the crank, advertising plate out of scale

I.D. #: **W02.1.1**

INVENTOR & DATE: E. Walker May 19, 1891

REGISTRATION #: P 452,625

CIRCA: 1889? -1891?

FREQUENCY:

MANUFACTURER: Erie Specialty Co.

MATERIAL: cast iron

FINISH: nickel

COMMENTS: This is the first version of THE WALKER, with the collar as shown in the patent drawing. This corkscrew may have been sold under the ERIE name.

NAME: **WALKER, THE** (marked)

TRADEMARK: none

OTHER MARKS: MFT'D BY ERIE SPECIALTY M'F'G Co, ERIE, PA USA , PAT AL'D

NOTICE: a restored example, advertising plate out of scale

I.D. #: **W02.1.2**

INVENTOR & DATE: E. Walker, application filed May 01, 1889

REGISTRATION #: P 452,625

CIRCA: 1889? - 11891?

FREQUENCY:

MANUFACTURER: Erie Specialty Mfg. Co.

MATERIAL: cast iron

FINISH: nickel

COMMENTS: This corkscrew is also known to some collectors as the "beaver tail".

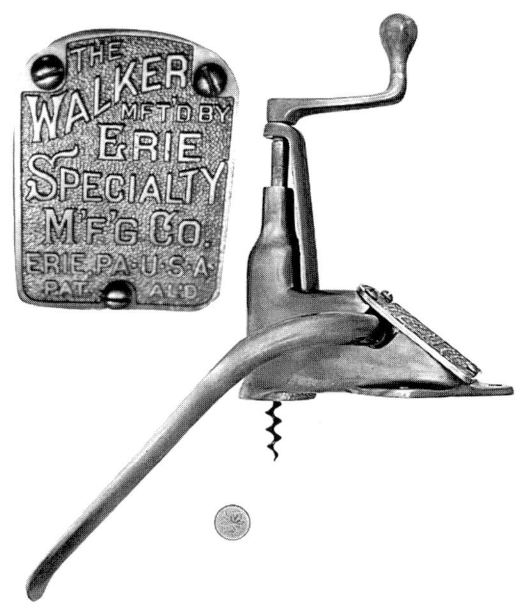

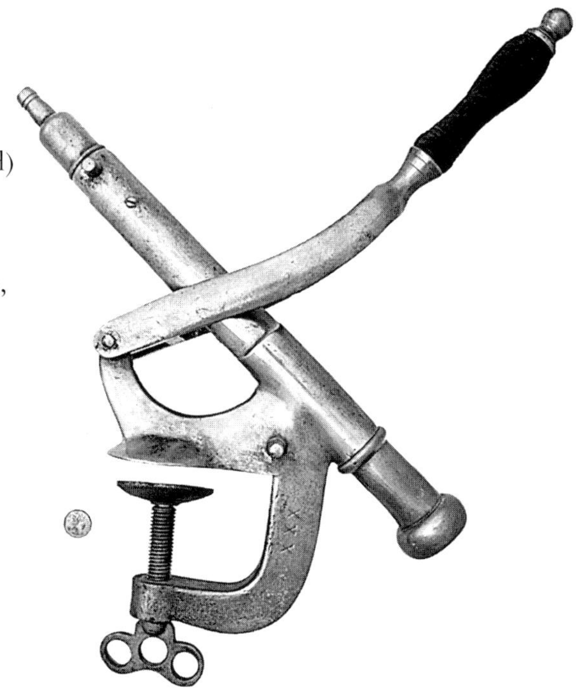

NAME: **XXX** (marked)

TRADEMARK: none

OTHER MARKS: W. CURTIS & SONS 108 (hand stamped)

NOTICE: the stem nut mechanism is connected through a slot in the bottom of the frame, Mason style thumb piece

I.D. #: **X01.1.1**

INVENTOR & DATE: J. Haslam Jan 30, 1889

REGISTRATION #: LP 1,640

CIRCA: 1889? - 1890?

FREQUENCY:

MANUFACTURER: presumably Samuel Mason Ltd.

MATERIAL: brass

FINISH: brass

COMMENTS: Very much a prototype, possibly the **XXX** would have been replaced with a name if it had gone into production; however XXX does fit well with the whisky bottle finial. This is the first known brass example of Mason's three hole thumb piece.

NAME: **YANKEE** (unmarked)

TRADEMARK: none

OTHER MARKS: none

NOTICE: silver finish variant *Y01.1.2*

I.D. #: **Y01.1.1**

INVENTOR & DATE: R. Gilchrist Jun 25, 1907

REGISTRATION #: P 857,992

CIRCA: 1901? - ?

FREQUENCY:

MANUFACTURER: Arcade Manufacturing Co. or Gilchrist Mfg. Co.

MATERIAL: cast iron

FINISH: nickel

COMMENTS: As found in this undated advertising, this unmarked curved wall bracket style also had a slightly longer handle. Advertised in 1902, these may be the first versions of the YANKEE No 1 and YANKEE No 2.

NAME:	**YANKEE** (unmarked)
TRADEMARK:	none
OTHER MARKS:	none
NOTICE:	wall bracket
I.D. #:	**Y01.1.3**
INVENTOR & DATE:	R. Gilchrist Jun 25, 1907
REGISTRATION #:	P 857,992
CIRCA:	1901? - ?
FREQUENCY:	
MANUFACTURER:	Arcade Manufacturing Co. or Gilchrist Mfg. Co. ?
MATERIAL:	cast iron
FINISH:	black paint
COMMENTS:	The only advertising found for this version was directly from Gilchrist, implying that initially he was the manufacturer and distributor.

NAME:	**YANKEE N<u>o</u> 1., THE** (marked)
TRADEMARK:	none
OTHER MARKS:	BRITISH MADE
NOTICE:	
I.D. #:	**Y01.2.1**
INVENTOR & DATE:	R. Gilchrist Aug 12, 1902
REGISTRATION #:	LP 17,752
CIRCA:	1901? - ?
FREQUENCY:	
MANUFACTURER:	Gaskell
MATERIAL:	cast iron
FINISH:	nickel
COMMENTS:	This is a British manufactured version of the YANKEE N<u>o</u> 1.

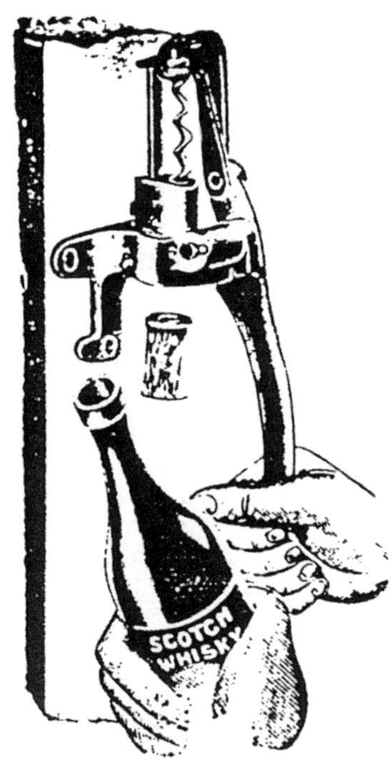

"YANKEE," No. 1.
Nickel Plated ...
To screw to wall...

NAME:	**YANKEE No 1, THE** (marked)
TRADEMARK:	none
OTHER MARKS:	none
NOTICE:	
I.D. #:	**Y01.3.1**
INVENTOR & DATE:	R. Gilchrist Jun 25, 1907
REGISTRATION #:	P 857,992
CIRCA:	1901? - ?
FREQUENCY:	
MANUFACTURER:	Arcade Manufacturing Co.
MATERIAL:	cast iron
FINISH:	nickel
COMMENTS:	This is the low cost wall mount version, for home use.

NAME:	**YANKEE No 2** (marked)
TRADEMARK:	none
OTHER MARKS:	none
NOTICE:	
I.D. #:	**Y02.1.1**
INVENTOR & DATE:	R. Gilchrist Jun 25, 1907
REGISTRATION #:	P 857,992
CIRCA:	1901? - ?
FREQUENCY:	
MANUFACTURER:	Arcade Manufacturing Co.
MATERIAL:	cast iron
FINISH:	nickel
COMMENTS:	This is the clamp mount version of the YANKEE No 1.

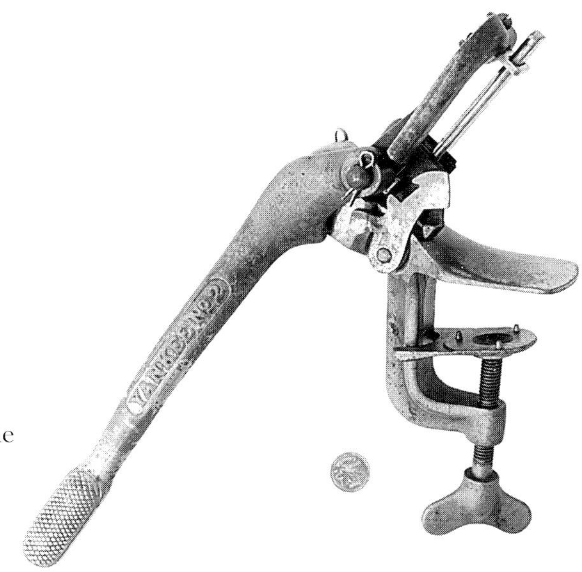

NAME: **YANKEE N<u>o</u> 2.** (marked)
TRADEMARK: hand & star
OTHER MARKS:
NOTICE: Gaskell thumb piece
I.D. #: **Y02.1.2**
INVENTOR & DATE: R. Gilchrist Aug 12, 1902
REGISTRATION #: LP 17,752
CIRCA: 1901? - 1920?
FREQUENCY:
MANUFACTURER: Gaskell
MATERIAL: cast iron
FINISH: nickel
COMMENTS: The YANKEE N<u>o</u> 2 was also made in Britain; this version has a hand & star trade mark cast into the clamp plate.

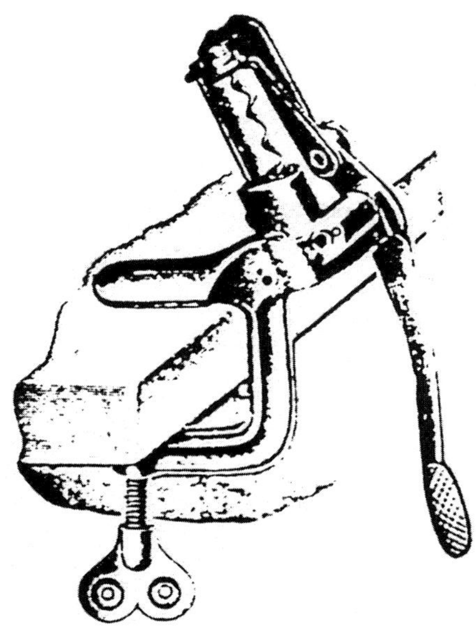

" YANKEE," No. 2.
Nickel Plated ...
To clamp ...

NAME: **YANKEE N<u>o</u> 2.** (marked)
TRADEMARK: G&C
OTHER MARKS: BRITISH MADE, G&C
NOTICE: Gaskell thumb piece
I.D. #: **Y02.1.3**
INVENTOR & DATE: R. Gilchrist Aug 12, 1902
REGISTRATION #: LP 17,752
CIRCA: 1901? - ?
FREQUENCY:
MANUFACTURER: Gaskell
MATERIAL: cast iron
FINISH: nickel
COMMENTS: This is a later British version of Gilchrist's YANKEE N<u>o</u> 2.

NAME: **YANKEE N<u>o</u> 2** (marked)

TRADEMARK: none

OTHER MARKS:

NOTICE: a second example of an advertising plate is shown out of scale

I.D. #: **Y02.2.1**

INVENTOR & DATE: R. Gilchrist Jun 25, 1907

REGISTRATION #: P 857,992

CIRCA: 1901? - ?

FREQUENCY:

MANUFACTURER: Arcade Manufacturing Co.

MATERIAL: cast iron

FINISH: nickel

COMMENTS: This advertising plate version of the YANKEE N<u>o</u> 2 incorporated an advertising plate riveted to a flange on the clamp frame; an alternate advertising plate is shown.

NAME: **YANKEE NO6** (marked)

TRADEMARK: none

OTHER MARKS: YANKEE 6

NOTICE:

I.D. #: **Y03.1.1**

INVENTOR & DATE: R. Gilchrist Jun 19, 1906 and Apr 08, 1913

REGISTRATION #: P 823,678 and P 1,058,361

CIRCA: 1904? - 1919?

FREQUENCY:

MANUFACTURER: Arcade Manufacturing Co.

MATERIAL: cast iron

FINISH: nickel

COMMENTS: The 1906 patent was for the bottle clasp design. The mechanism patent was filed in 1904 showing the YANKEE NO7 mechanism, which is a "flipped over" version of the YANKEE NO6 mechanism.

NAME: **YANKEE NO6** (marked)
TRADEMARK: none
OTHER MARKS: YANKEE 6
NOTICE: Arcade bronze finish
I.D. #: **Y03.1.2**
INVENTOR & DATE: R. Gilchrist Jun 19, 1906 and Apr 08, 1913
REGISTRATION #: P 823,678 and P 1,058,361
CIRCA: 1904? - 1919?
FREQUENCY:
MANUFACTURER: Arcade Manufacturing Co.
MATERIAL: cast iron
FINISH: Arcade bronze
COMMENTS: Other than his first corkscrew, Gilchrist never marked his corkscrews with the patent dates. Gilchrist's bottle clasps were attached with a "U" clamp vs. Arcade's single bolt attachment.

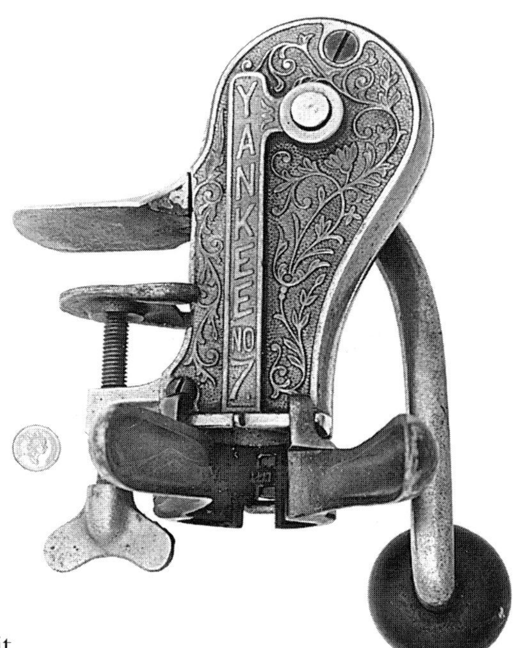

NAME: **YANKEE NO7.** (marked)
TRADEMARK: none
OTHER MARKS: none
NOTICE:
I.D. #: **Y04.1.1**
INVENTOR & DATE: R. Gilchrist Apr 25, 1905 and Jun 19, 1906 and Apr 08, 1913
REGISTRATION #: DES 37,417 and P 823,678 and P 1,058,361
CIRCA: 1904? - 1919?
FREQUENCY:
MANUFACTURER: Arcade Manufacturing Co.
MATERIAL: cast iron
FINISH: nickel
COMMENTS: The YANKEE NO7 is the YANKEE NO6 mechanism "flipped over" so that it would fit into Arcade's FAVORITE case. The case decoration design patent was received in 1905, the bottle clasp patent in 1906 and the internal mechanism patent in 1913; the internal mechanism had been in the patent pending file since 1904.

NAME:	**YANKEE NO7.** (marked)
TRADEMARK:	none
OTHER MARKS:	none
NOTICE:	
I.D. #:	**Y04.1.2**
INVENTOR & DATE:	R. Gilchrist Apr 25, 1905 and Jun 19, 1906 and Apr 08, 1913
REGISTRATION #:	DES 37,417 and P 823,678 and P 1,058,361
CIRCA:	1904? - 1919?
FREQUENCY:	
MANUFACTURER:	Arcade Manufacturing Co.
MATERIAL:	cast iron
FINISH:	Arcade bronze
COMMENTS:	This advertisement shows Gilchrist promoting his self-centering bottle clasp; the bronze finish saved $.50 in 1909.

Style of No. 7.

Yankee Cork Puller and Re-Corker, With Self-Centering Bottle Holding Clamp. One in a box. $4.00

NAME:	**ZEUS** (marked)
TRADEMARK:	none
OTHER MARKS:	FRANMARA, SPAIN, UNCORKING MACHINE
NOTICE:	advertising plate out of scale, brass colored finish variant *Z01.1.2*
I.D. #:	**Z01.1.1**
INVENTOR & DATE:	no Spanish patent or registration found
REGISTRATION #:	
CIRCA:	1980? - 2001
FREQUENCY:	
MANUFACTURER:	Presumably B. Olaneta Juaristi, S. A.
MATERIAL:	zinc ?
FINISH:	nickel
COMMENTS:	This is a modern, wall mounted, version of the DON.

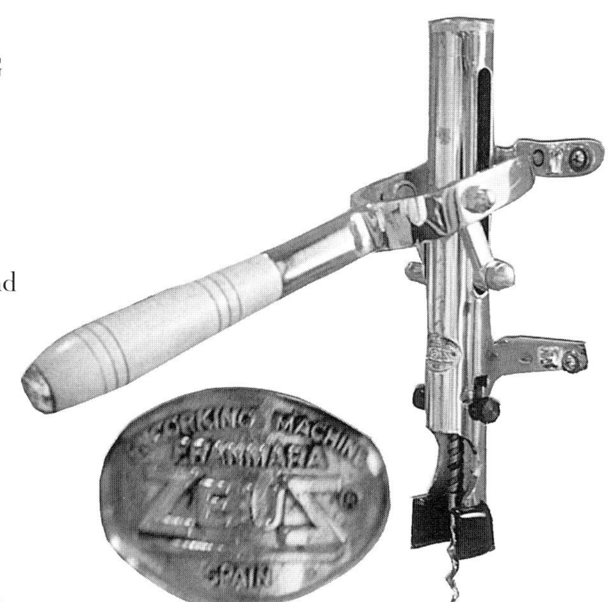

UNMARKED, NO-NAME FOUND SECTION

The corkscrews found on the following pages of the *IDENTIFICATION* Section have no NAME marked on them, and no NAME for corkscrews with a similar shape and mechanism has been found to date.

The NAME: used is the most pertinent information available. This information, in order of priority, includes the inventor's name, the manufacturer, the country it was manufactured or sold in, or, failing any of the above, unknown.

The temporary I. D. #: starts with the first letter of the NAME:, followed by 99. A permanent I. D. number will be allotted when a marked or advertised name is found.

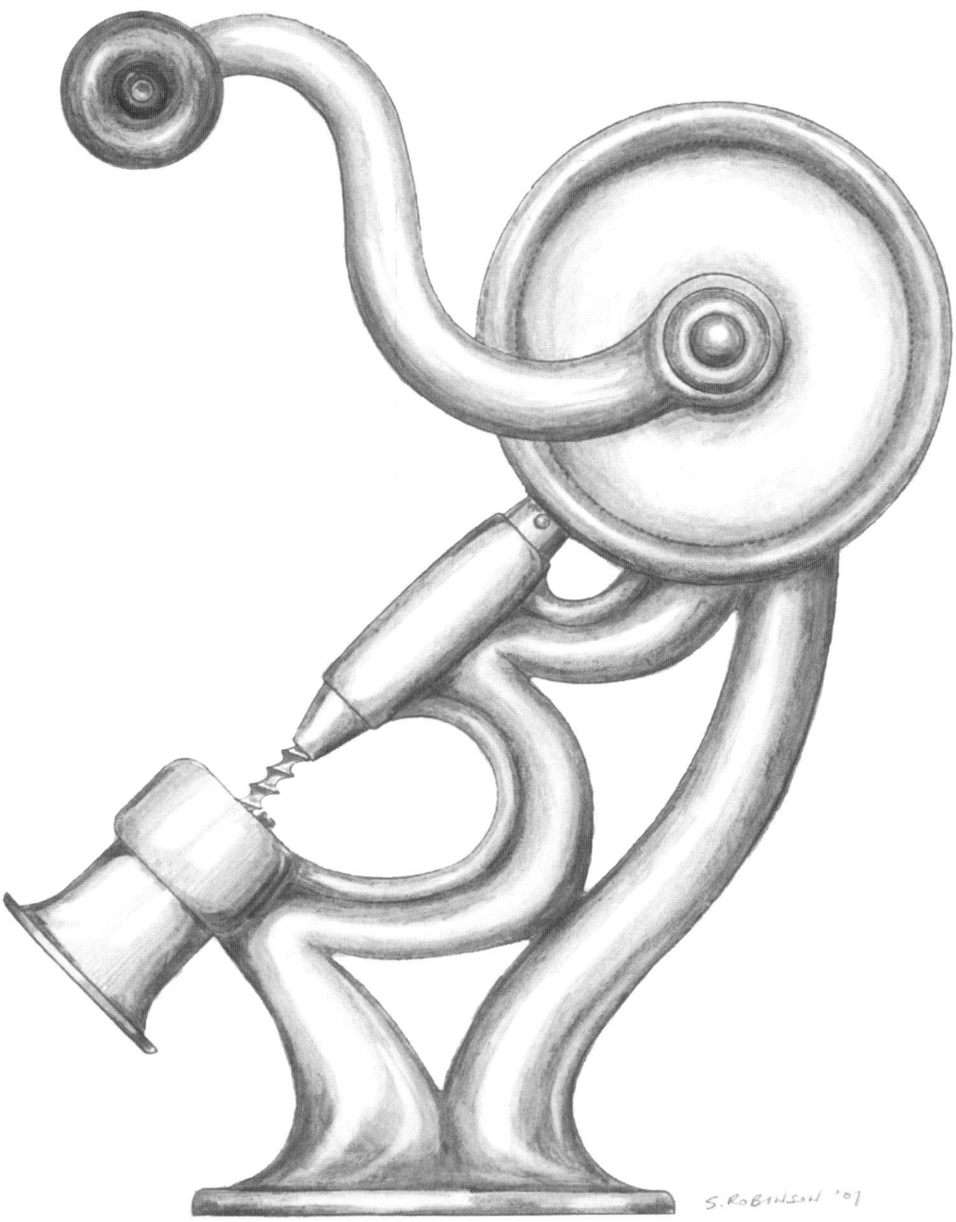

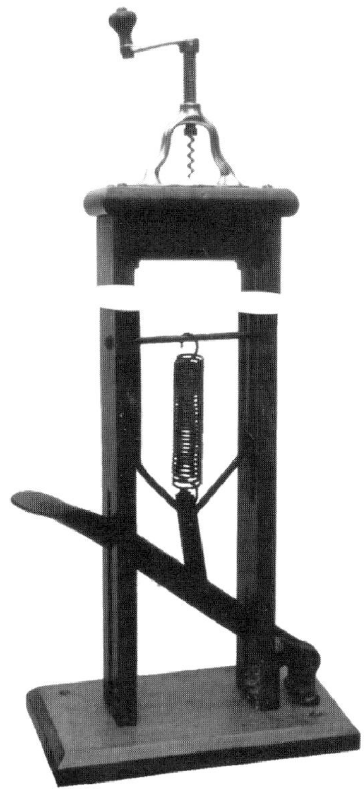

NAME:	**BLOESER** (unmarked, no name found)
TRADEMARK:	none
OTHER MARKS:	none
NOTICE:	See inside dust jacket for a complete picture
I.D. #:	**B99.2.1**
INVENTOR & DATE:	J. Bloeser Mar 16, 1886
REGISTRATION #:	P 337,921
CIRCA:	1886?
FREQUENCY:	
MANUFACTURER:	American
MATERIAL:	brass, cast iron and wood
FINISH:	
COMMENTS:	This mechanism works very well, allowing a cork to be pulled with great ease.

NAME:	**ENGLISH** (unmarked, no name found)
TRADEMARK:	none
OTHER MARKS:	none
NOTICE:	the loose collar on the stem has an internal spring keeping it from sliding down the stem
I.D. #:	**E99.3.1**
INVENTOR & DATE:	no English patent or registration found
REGISTRATION #:	
CIRCA:	1900?
FREQUENCY:	
MANUFACTURER:	English
MATERIAL:	cast iron
FINISH:	nickel
COMMENTS:	Possibly this is missing a cork gripper that was actuated by the crank arm; see *MECHANISMS* for additional information.

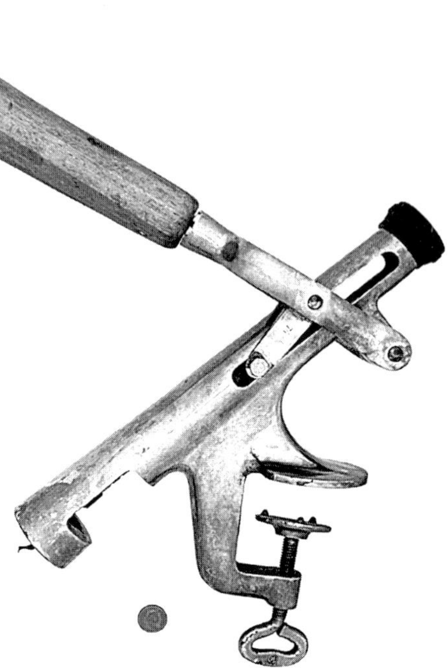

NAME: **FRINGS** (unmarked, no name found)
TRADEMARK: **(K)** on thumb piece
OTHER MARKS: clamp plate marked **F23**
NOTICE: operating lever handle not original
I.D. #: **F99.1.1**
INVENTOR & DATE: no German patent or registration found
REGISTRATION #:
CIRCA: 1920? - 1940?
FREQUENCY:
MANUFACTURER: FRINGS & CO. o. H. G.
MATERIAL: cast iron
FINISH: nickel
COMMENTS: This is a Frings manufactured version of the DON, probably one of his versions of the CEDON.

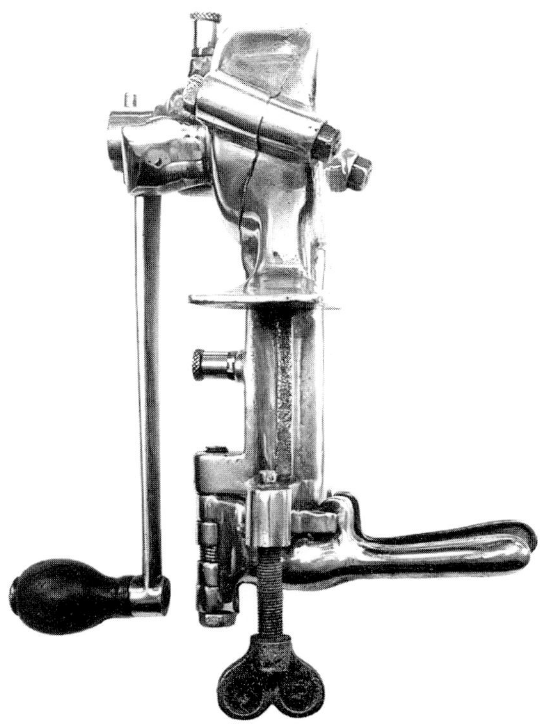

NAME: **GASKELL** (unmarked, no name found)
TRADEMARK: none
OTHER MARKS: indistinct, possibly ROTHERMAN'S or ROTHERBY'S; Coventry, R4
NOTICE: Gaskell thumb piece
I.D. #: **G99.4.1**
INVENTOR & DATE: no English patent or registration found
REGISTRATION #:
CIRCA: 1900?
FREQUENCY:
MANUFACTURER: Gaskell
MATERIAL: brass
FINISH: nickel
COMMENTS: This was not inspected internally; mechanism is unknown.

NAME:	**ITALIAN** (unmarked, no name found)
TRADEMARK:	not inspected
OTHER MARKS:	not inspected
NOTICE:	clamp mount
I.D. #:	**I99.1.1**
INVENTOR & DATE:	no Italian patent or registration found
REGISTRATION #:	
CIRCA:	1950? - ?
FREQUENCY:	
MANUFACTURER:	Italian ?
MATERIAL:	not inspected
FINISH:	not inspected
COMMENTS:	This is a frame and case for a rack and pinion driven mechanism.

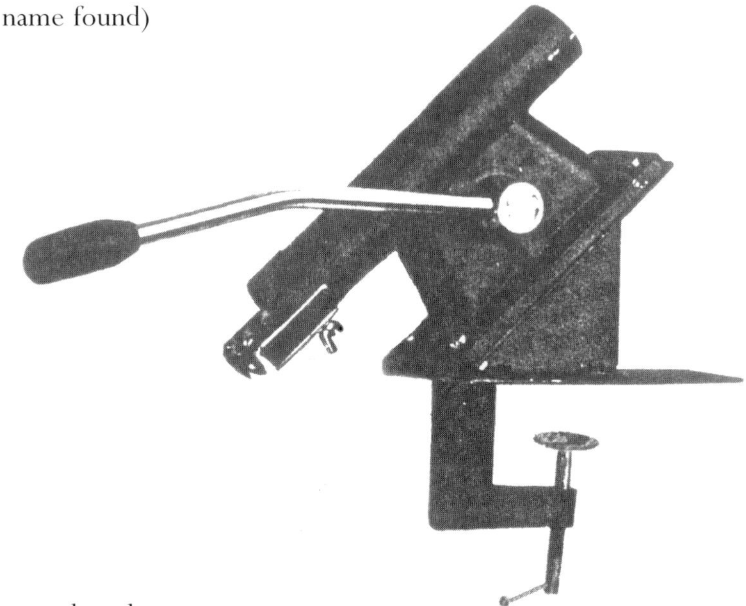

NAME:	**ITALIAN** (unmarked, no name found)
TRADEMARK:	not inspected
OTHER MARKS:	not inspected
NOTICE:	wall mount
I.D. #:	**I99.1.2**
INVENTOR & DATE:	no Italian patent or registration found
REGISTRATION #:	
CIRCA:	1950? - ?
FREQUENCY:	
MANUFACTURER:	Italian ?
MATERIAL:	not inspected
FINISH:	not inspected
COMMENTS:	This is a frame and case for a rack and pinion driven mechanism.

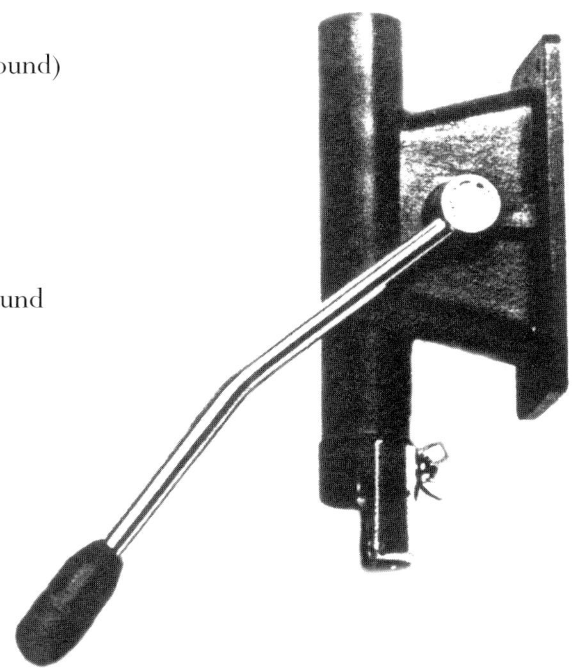

NAME:	**ITALIAN** (unmarked, no name found)
TRADEMARK:	not inspected
OTHER MARKS:	not inspected
NOTICE:	no bottle neck rest, corkscrew carrier protruding
I.D. #:	**199.2.1**
INVENTOR & DATE:	no Italian patent or registration found
REGISTRATION #:	
CIRCA:	?
FREQUENCY:	
MANUFACTURER:	Italian ?
MATERIAL:	not inspected
FINISH:	not inspected
COMMENTS:	It is hard to tell from this third generation copy of a photo, but this might be an Italian version of the QUICK & EASY. The corkscrew carrier appears to stick out much further than a Walker manufactured corkscrew.

NAME:	**ITALIAN** (unmarked, no name found)
TRADEMARK:	not inspected
OTHER MARKS:	not inspected
NOTICE:	corkscrew carrier mechanism
I.D. #:	**199.3.1**
INVENTOR & DATE:	no Italian patent or registration found
REGISTRATION #:	
CIRCA:	unknown
FREQUENCY:	
MANUFACTURER:	Italian ?
MATERIAL:	not inspected
FINISH:	not inspected
COMMENTS:	This appears to be an Italian wall mount corkscrew utilizing a corkscrew carrier mechanism.

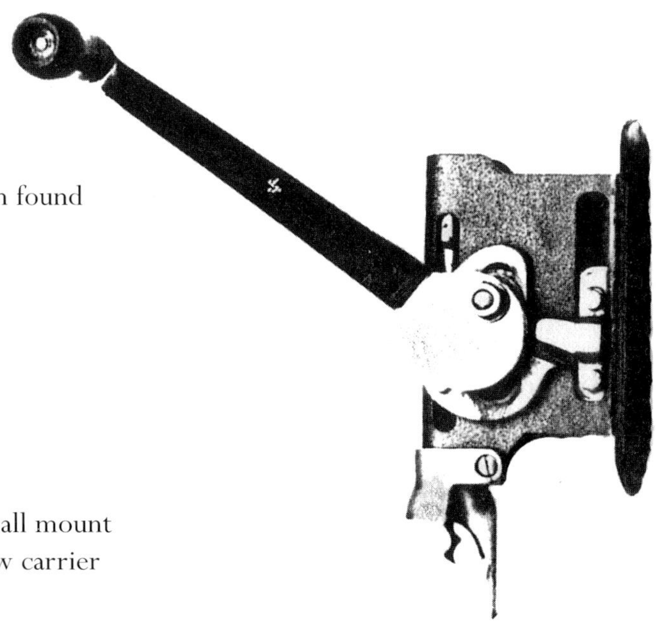

NAME:	**ITALIAN** (unmarked, no name found)
TRADEMARK:	not inspected
OTHER MARKS:	not inspected
NOTICE:	corkscrew carrier mechanism
I.D. #:	**I99.3.2**
INVENTOR & DATE:	no Italian patent or registration found
REGISTRATION #:	
CIRCA:	unknown
FREQUENCY:	
MANUFACTURER:	Italian ?
MATERIAL:	not inspected
FINISH:	not inspected
COMMENTS:	This appears to be another version of an Italian wall mount corkscrew utilizing a corkscrew carrier mechanism.

NAME:	**JUMA** (unmarked, no name found)
TRADEMARK:	none
OTHER MARKS:	none
NOTICE:	lever and link driven mechanism
I.D. #:	**J99.1.1**
INVENTOR & DATE:	no Spanish patent or registration found
REGISTRATION #:	
CIRCA:	1970?
FREQUENCY:	
MANUFACTURER:	JUMA
MATERIAL:	brass
FINISH:	white paint
COMMENTS:	not inspected

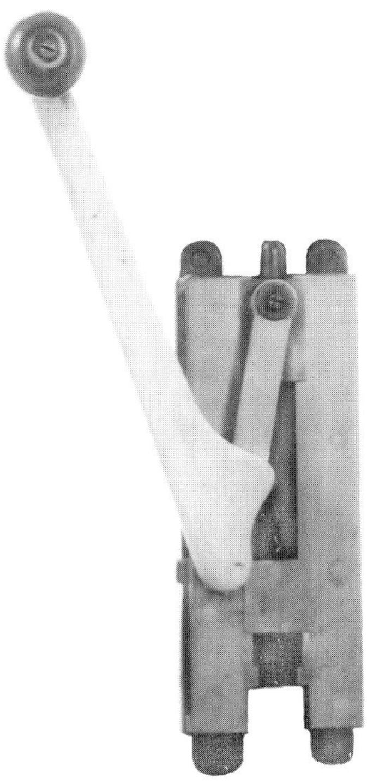

NAME:	**KRICHAU** (unmarked, no name found)
TRADEMARK:	none
OTHER MARKS:	PATENT (indistinct in gold paint)
NOTICE:	the worm can be set to penetrate to three different depths
I.D. #:	**K99.1.1**
INVENTOR & DATE:	N. Krichau Aug 20, 1886 in Germany
REGISTRATION #:	DRP 39,103
CIRCA:	1886? - 1910?
FREQUENCY:	
MANUFACTURER:	Stockholm, Sweden
MATERIAL:	cast iron
FINISH:	black and gold paint
COMMENTS:	A gear driven corkscrew, there are examples with different painted advertising or decorations. This machine can be set to pull the cork only part way out, by eleven 1/8" steps. The German patent appears to be the only record of this Swedish corkscrew; see *MECHANISMS* for additional information.

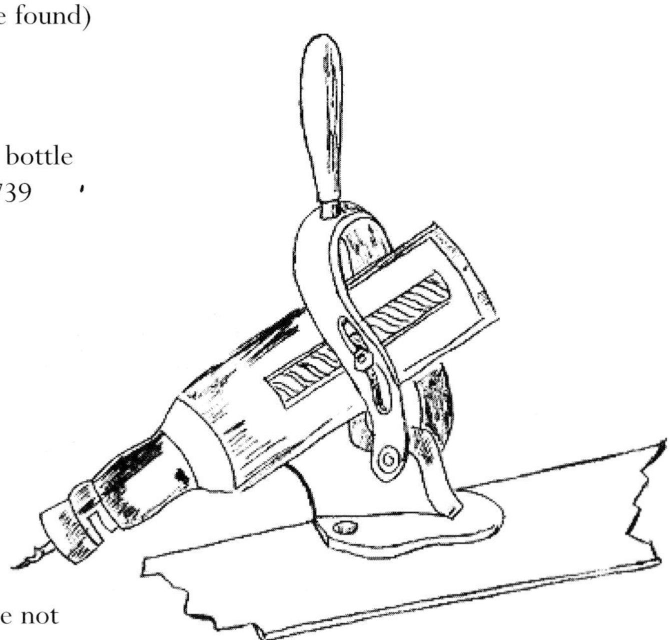

NAME:	**MASON** (unmarked, no name found)
TRADEMARK:	not inspected
OTHER MARKS:	not inspected
NOTICE:	this is a registered design for a bottle shaped version of the A1 or A739
I.D. #:	**M99.1.1**
INVENTOR & DATE:	S. Mason Jan 12, 1903
REGISTRATION #:	REG 403347
CIRCA:	1903?
FREQUENCY:	
MANUFACTURER:	probably not produced
MATERIAL:	not inspected
FINISH:	not inspected
COMMENTS:	Normally corkscrews that were not known to be produced or advertised are not listed but this was just too funky to leave out of the book.

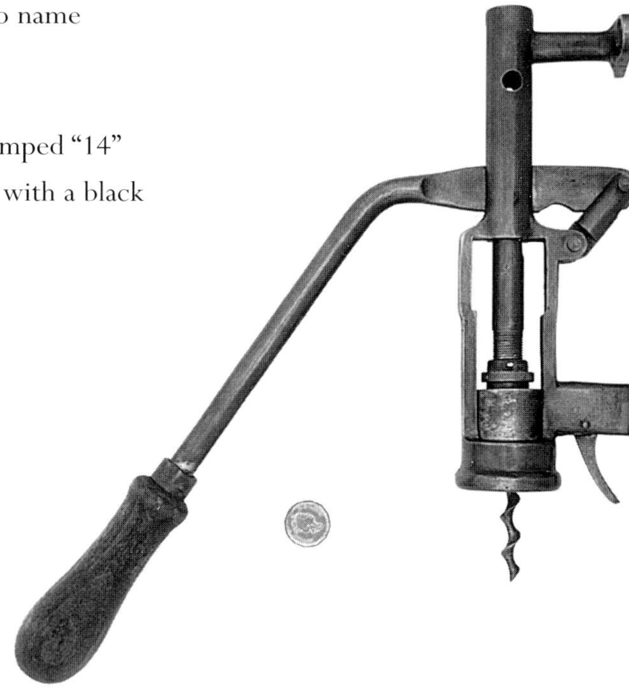

NAME: **McMASTER** (unmarked, no name found)

TRADEMARK: none

OTHER MARKS: various components hand stamped "14"

NOTICE: the original finish was nickel with a black painted handle

I.D. #: **M99.2.1**

INVENTOR & DATE: L. McMaster Jun 23, 1896

REGISTRATION #: P 562,645

CIRCA: 1885? - 1895?

FREQUENCY:

MANUFACTURER: Manning Bowman & Co. ?

MATERIAL: cast iron

FINISH: nickel

COMMENTS: In this wall mount version of the McMaster patent, the "trigger" behind the throat released the worm nut to allow the cork to be pulled; on the second pull of the lever the nut was captured and the cork stripped.

NAME: **MORGAN** (unmarked, no name found)

TRADEMARK: none

OTHER MARKS: PAT' APLD FOR

NOTICE: wire breaker hook at the top

I.D. #: **M99.3.1**

INVENTOR & DATE: C. Morgan applied for Apr 03, 1886

REGISTRATION #: P 390183

CIRCA: 1886? - ?

FREQUENCY:

MANUFACTURER: Arcade Manufacturing Co. ?

MATERIAL: cast iron

FINISH: nickel

COMMENTS: This patent was for the blade that split the cork off as it was cranked out of the bottle.

NAME:	**MORGAN** (unmarked, no name found)
TRADEMARK:	none
OTHER MARKS:	PAT' APLD FOR
NOTICE:	bottle lip holder added to the throat
I.D. #:	**M99.3.2**
INVENTOR & DATE:	C. Morgan applied for Apr 03, 1886
REGISTRATION #:	P 390183
CIRCA:	1886? - ?
FREQUENCY:	
MANUFACTURER:	Arcade Manufacturing Co. ?
MATERIAL:	cast iron
FINISH:	nickel
COMMENTS:	This is presumed to be the later version.

NAME:	**UNKNOWN** (unmarked, no name found)
TRADEMARK:	none
OTHER MARKS:	none
NOTICE:	
I.D. #:	**U99.1.1**
INVENTOR & DATE:	no patent or registration found
REGISTRATION #:	
CIRCA:	1903? - 1940?
FREQUENCY:	
MANUFACTURER:	unknown
MATERIAL:	cast iron
FINISH:	white paint
COMMENTS:	This is a stand mounted version of the DON. The screw threads are not metric screw threads; they appeared to be British Whitworth. Despite the "homemade" look, the throat and yoke must have been produced in a foundry.

NAME:	**UNKNOWN** (unmarked, no name found)
TRADEMARK:	none
OTHER MARKS:	none
NOTICE:	case decorations, thumb piece
I.D. #:	**U99.2.1**
INVENTOR & DATE:	no patent or registration found
REGISTRATION #:	
CIRCA:	1893 - 1900?
FREQUENCY:	
MANUFACTURER:	unknown
MATERIAL:	cast iron
FINISH:	nickel
COMMENTS:	This unmarked version of the ARCADE was presumably manufactured after the STEINER and before the ALEXANDERWERK.

NAME:	**UNKNOWN** (unmarked, no name found)
TRADEMARK:	none
OTHER MARKS:	none
NOTICE:	metric bolts, finial, scalloped side links, one hole in the throat
I.D. #:	**U99.3.1**
INVENTOR & DATE:	no patent or registration found
REGISTRATION #:	
CIRCA:	1932 - 1940?
FREQUENCY:	unknown
MANUFACTURER:	Helmut Gebel ?
MATERIAL:	brass
FINISH:	nickel
COMMENTS:	Marked versions of the BISON-DONAR are unknown; there is no proof that these were made by Helmut Gebel, but he claimed that they made an exact copy. The general size and shape, including the scalloped side links, are close to an exact copy.

NAME:	**UNKNOWN** (unmarked, no name found)
TRADEMARK:	none
OTHER MARKS:	none
NOTICE:	metric bolts, finial, straight thick side links, no hole in the throat
I.D. #:	**U99.4.1**
INVENTOR & DATE:	no patent or registration found
REGISTRATION #:	
CIRCA:	1932 - 1940?
FREQUENCY:	unknown, not marked
MANUFACTURER:	Belgian ?
MATERIAL:	brass
FINISH:	nickel
COMMENTS:	This is a copy of the DON mechanism with the heavy side links and general shape matching the TITAN case shape.

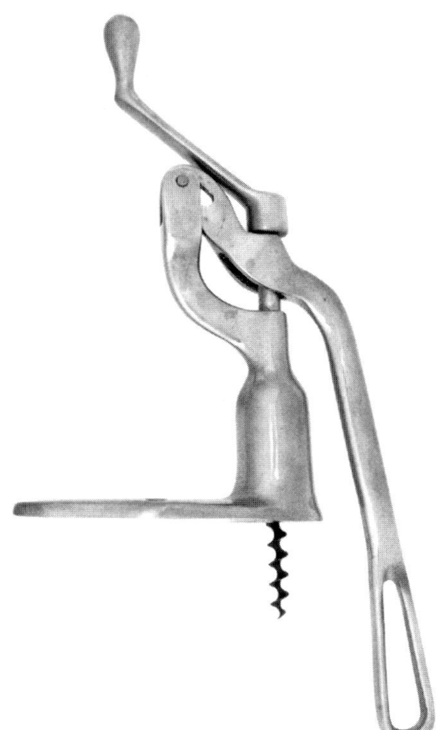

NAME:	**WALKER** (unmarked, no name found)
TRADEMARK:	none
OTHER MARKS:	none
NOTICE:	a restored example
I.D. #:	**W99.1.1**
INVENTOR & DATE:	E. Walker Feb 14, 1888
REGISTRATION #:	P 377,790
CIRCA:	1887? - ?
FREQUENCY:	
MANUFACTURER:	Erie Specialty Mfg. Co.
MATERIAL:	cast iron
FINISH:	nickel
COMMENTS:	This version has no custom clamp or cork gripping hook.

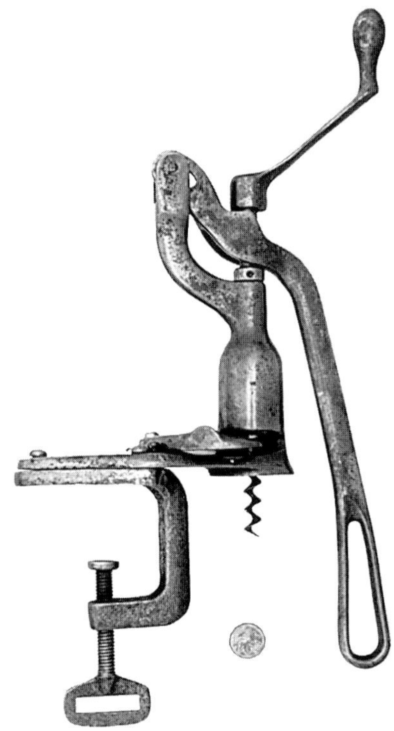

NAME:	**WALKER** (unmarked, no name found)
TRADEMARK:	none
OTHER MARKS:	none
NOTICE:	
I.D. #:	**W99.2.1**
INVENTOR & DATE:	E. Walker Feb 14, 1888
REGISTRATION #:	P 377,790
CIRCA:	1887? - ?
FREQUENCY:	
MANUFACTURER:	Erie Specialty Mfg. Co.
MATERIAL:	cast iron
FINISH:	nickel
COMMENTS:	The version has a custom clamp attached and a hook that gripped the cork when it was being stripped.

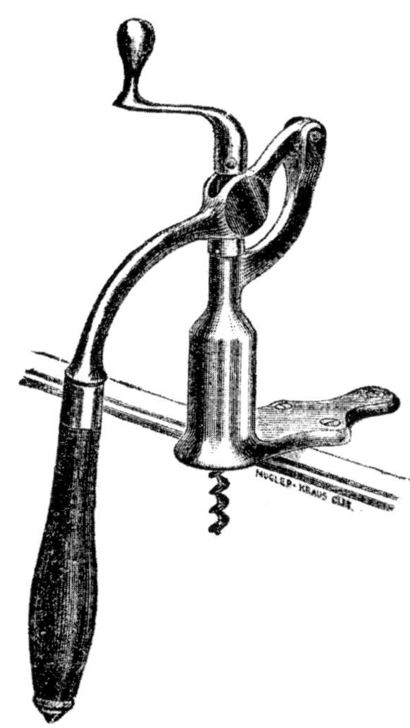

CORK PULLER,

Price, ... $2 50

NAME:	**WALKER** (unmarked, no name found)
TRADEMARK:	not inspected
OTHER MARKS:	not inspected
NOTICE:	operating lever handle
I.D. #:	**W99.3.1**
INVENTOR & DATE:	E. Walker Feb 14, 1888
REGISTRATION #:	P 377,790
CIRCA:	1887? - ?
FREQUENCY:	
MANUFACTURER:	Erie Specialty Mfg. Co.
MATERIAL:	cast iron
FINISH:	nickel
COMMENTS:	An unusual wooden handle is shown in this advertisement. It is probable that Walker sold this under the IMPROVED name.

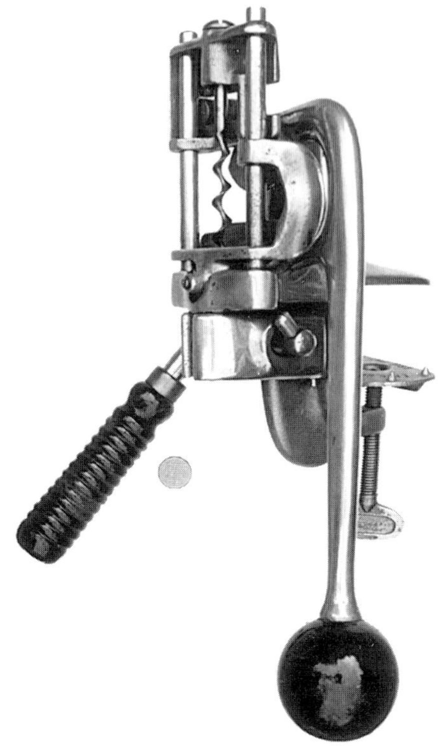

NAME:	**WALKER** (unmarked, no name found)
TRADEMARK:	none
OTHER MARKS:	ERIE SPECIALTY CO, ERIE PA, PAT FEB 27, 1894, JULY 23 1895
NOTICE:	
I.D. #:	**W99.4.1**
INVENTOR & DATE:	E. Walker Jul 07, 1910 and Mar 25, 1913
REGISTRATION #:	P 964,588 and P 1,057,021
CIRCA:	1907? - 1908?
FREQUENCY:	
MANUFACTURER:	Erie Specialty Co.
MATERIAL:	cast iron
FINISH:	nickel
COMMENTS:	The 1910 patent date is for the bottle clasp; both patents were applied for in 1907. Walker appears to have been studying Gilchrist's patent delaying methods.

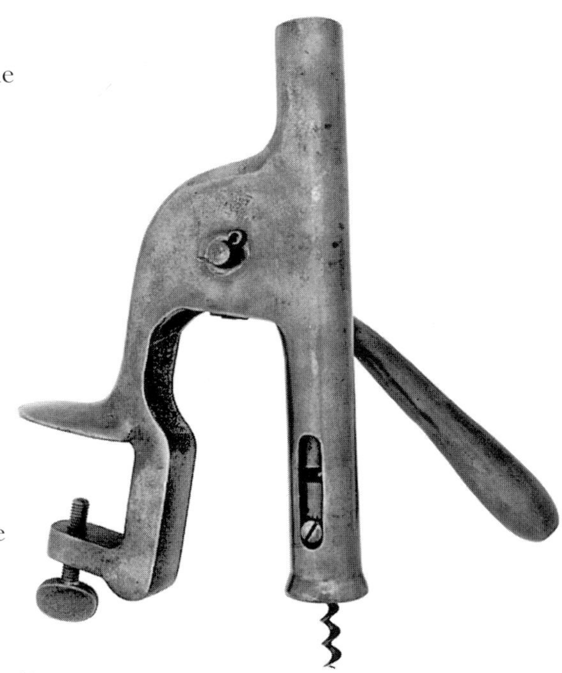

NAME:	**WILLIAMS** (unmarked, no name found)
TRADEMARK:	none
OTHER MARKS:	none
NOTICE:	no clamp plate or method of attaching one
I.D. #:	**W99.5.1**
INVENTOR & DATE:	H. Williams Feb 14, 1899
REGISTRATION #:	P 619,648
CIRCA:	1899? - ?
FREQUENCY:	
MANUFACTURER:	American
MATERIAL:	cast iron
FINISH:	none
COMMENTS:	This is assumed to be a prototype, as there is no method of fixing a clamp plate and no visible original finish. At first glance this looks like a US RAPID, but it is a later Williams patent. The internal mechanism can be swapped with the Barrett mechanism and they both still operate correctly. See *MECHANISMS* for additional information.

NAME: **ZERBINATO** (unmarked, no name found)

TRADEMARK: not inspected

OTHER MARKS: not inspected

NOTICE: older style of cast handle

I.D. #: **Z99.1.1**

INVENTOR & DATE: Leonard Zerbinato & Ennio Masin May 03, 1960

REGISTRATION #: P 604,312

CIRCA: 19060? - 1970?

FREQUENCY:

MANUFACTURER: Franco Cicogna & Co. ?

MATERIAL: cast iron?

FINISH: not inspected

COMMENTS: This appears to have the same mechanism as the other Z99 corkscrews, with two slots cut out of each side of the barrel, performing the same function as the channels cut inside the barrel of British stem-nut mechanisms.

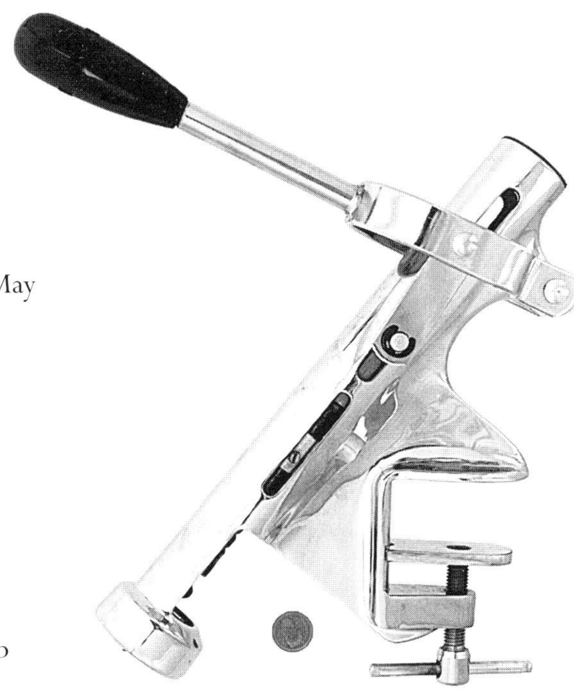

NAME: **ZERBINATO** (unmarked, no name found)

TRADEMARK: none

OTHER MARKS: none

NOTICE: red painted finish variant *Z99.2.2*

I.D. #: **Z99.2.1**

INVENTOR & DATE: Leonard Zerbinato & Ennio Masin May 03, 1960

REGISTRATION #: P 604,312

CIRCA: 1970? - present?

FREQUENCY:

MANUFACTURER: Franco Cicogna & Co. ?

MATERIAL: aluminum

FINISH: nickel

COMMENTS: This was a typical Italian style thumb piece.

NAME:	**ZERBINATO** (unmarked, no name found)
TRADEMARK:	none
OTHER MARKS:	none
NOTICE:	red painted finish variant *Z99.3.2*, green painted finish variant *Z99.3.3*
I.D. #:	**Z99.3.1**
INVENTOR & DATE:	Leonard Zerbinato & Ennio Masin May 03, 1960
REGISTRATION #:	P 604,312
CIRCA:	1970? - present
FREQUENCY:	
MANUFACTURER:	Franco Cicogna & Co. ?
MATERIAL:	aluminum
FINISH:	nickel
COMMENTS:	This is the wall mount version of *Z99.2.1*

Glossary

advertising plate – a plate, attached to the frame or used as a case cover, containing the name of the manufacturer, distributor or product

automatic corkscrew – a corkscrew that automatically strips the cork from the worm after the cork is removed from the bottle

babbitt – a whitish alloy of tin, antimony and copper, or a similar alloy, used as a bearing surface to reduce friction

barrel – a tube shaped case

beveled gear – a gear with a sloping edge, usually formed such that it will change the angle of drive by 90° when it meshes with a second gear

bottle clasp – a single lever or double handled clamping mechanism used to grip the neck of a bottle while the cork is being extracted

bottle clasp bolt – a bolt that attaches the bottle clasp mechanism to the frame

bottle clasp handles – a double lever mechanism made to be squeezed by the hand, activating the bottle clasping mechanism

bottle clasp jaw – a part of the bottle clasp mechanism that grips and holds the neck of the bottle, usually padded with rubber

bottle clasp lever – a single lever mechanism made to be pulled by the hand, activating the bottle clasp mechanism

bottle clasp lug – a projection on the bottle clasp jaw that keeps the jaw in alignment and centered around the bottle neck

bottle lip rest – a very short front flange on a throat that the lip of the bottle rests on

bottle neck rest – a projection on the bottom of a throat that a bottle neck rests on

cam – a projection on a wheel that changes circular motion into an irregular motion

cam surface – a raised projection on a surface that causes irregular motion or allows and prevents motion in a secondary device

case – an enclosure housing the corkscrew mechanism

case decoration – a decorative design cast into the case or the case cover

clamp bolt – a threaded shaft connecting the thumb piece to the lower clamp plate

clamp frame – a "U" shaped portion of the corkscrew frame that allows the corkscrew to be clamped to a counter top

clamp mount – a corkscrew designed to be clamped to a counter top

clamp plate – a plate on the end of the clamp bolt that grips the underside of a counter

clutch – a device in a machine for connecting or disconnecting the driving force

cork ejection slot – an opening in the underside of the throat that allows the cork to fall out of the barrel of the corkscrew

cork slicing blade – a blade fixed to the frame, such that it cuts the cork open as the cork is being withdrawn from the bottle

cork stripping – the act of unwinding the worm, out of the cork, after the cork has been removed from the bottle

corkscrew carrier – a cork extraction mechanism that contains both the worm carrier and worm-nut

crank – a part of a machine connected at right angles to a shaft to transmit motion

crank handle – a portion of the crank that is grasped in the hand

cross-over lever – a lever that has the worm attached between the fulcrum and the handle

dog – a device to hold or grip a mechanism

driving rack – a bar with teeth on one edge that fit into the teeth cut into a pinion, changing linear motion into circular motion

dual clamp mount – a corkscrew with twin clamping brackets

dual mount – a corkscrew frame designed to be clamp mounted or top mounted

ferrule – a metal ring or cap around the end of a wooden handle, designed to prevent the wood from splitting

finial – a threaded decorative end or finishing point on the corkscrew barrel or operating lever handle

frame – a supporting structure that the various corkscrew components and the mechanism case are attached to

frame clamp plate – a part of the frame that forms the upper clamp plate, which contacts the top of the counter

frame pivot point – the fulcrum on the frame that the operating lever, or the operating lever link, pivots on

front – the side of the corkscrew containing the throat, or the side facing away from the mount

guide-nut – a nut that causes the worm to move in and out as the shaft of the worm is turned clockwise or counter-clockwise; it also centers the worm over the cork

handle cap nut – a nut used to fix the wooden handle on to the operating arm

inclined frame – a frame that holds the corkscrew mechanism at an angle of about 45° to the counter top

keyway – a slot cut lengthwise into a shaft such that a gear, sliding on the shaft, can continue to provide circular driving force from any location on the shaft

latching link – a link containing a latch or hook at the lower end, such that it will catch the lug on a worm-nut, lifting it up

left side – the left side from the perspective of the corkscrew, when the throat is the front

link pivot point – the fulcrum on the frame, barrel or operating lever that the link pivots on

link rod – a link consisting of a rod

mounted corkscrew – a non-automatic corkscrew, often based on a mechanism found in a sideboard corkscrew with some type of mounting bracket attached

narrow rack – a shaft with a narrow band of rack teeth cut lengthwise into it

operating arm – an operating lever resembling the shape of an arm, with the fulcrum inside of the case, usually extending from the left side of the case

operating lever – a lever pivoted externally to the frame or case, usually centered over the barrel

operating lever pivot point – the fulcrum on the frame, barrel or link that the operating lever pivots on

operating lever yoke – the two arms of an operating lever joined together at the junction of the handle; most commonly found on corkscrews containing a stem-nut mechanism

pawl – a pivoted bar arranged to catch in the teeth of a ratchet wheel so as to prevent backwards movement

pedestal – a base on which a column stands

pinion – a small gear with teeth that fit into the teeth of a larger gear or rack

plunger – a cylinder that acts with a plunging motion

private label – a product labeled with the distributor's name rather than with the original manufacturer's name; often the external "look" of the product is modified to the distributor's specifications

rack and pinion – a mechanism that changes circular motion into linear motion

ratchet – a wheel with teeth that strike against a catch, fixed so that motion is permitted in one direction only

right side – the right side from the perspective of the corkscrew, when the throat is the front

roller pin – a short round stud enclosed by a metal band that acts as a bearing

screw-in throat – a throat threaded such that it can be turned into the barrel of a corkscrew

semi-disk – a partial disk

side links – the links connecting the stem carrier to the operating lever

single cycle – an automatic corkscrew mechanism that requires only one cycle of the operating arm to pull and eject the cork

snail face – a projection in the shape of a snail, with a flat surface and a curved surface

spindle – a rod that turns around, on which something turns

split case – a case that is constructed such that each half of the case is approximately the same size

stem – a rod connecting the worm to the driving mechanism

stem carrier bolt – a bolt that couples the operating lever or its links to the stem carrier

stem carrier rack – a stem carrier with rack teeth cut into it, such that the stem carrier is driven by a pinion

stem-nut – a nut that causes a threaded stem to turn when the stem is pushed or pulled through the nut

stud – a knob or short rod sticking out from a surface

threaded stem – a threaded rod connecting to the worm

throat – an opening in a corkscrew that the neck of the bottle is inserted into

throat hole pattern – a hole pattern cut into the top of a throat, used to identify the diameter and thread size of the threaded portion of a removable throat

thumb piece – the decorative end of a threaded rod, used to turn the clamp bolt

thumb rest – a projection on the left side of the case, used to hook the thumb over while holding the bottle in place

top mount – a corkscrew designed to be screwed or bolted to the top of a counter

transverse guide – a guide slot on a corkscrew carrier, which is engaged by a roller pin in the crank arm

tube cap – a cap on the upper end of the barrel of a corkscrew containing a stem-nut mechanism

tube case – a case in the shape of a tube, usually found on corkscrews containing a stem-nut mechanism

two cycle – an automatic corkscrew mechanism that requires two cycles of the operating arm to pull and eject the cork

vertical frame – a frame that holds the corkscrew mechanism at an angle of about 90° to the counter top

wall mount – a corkscrew designed to be screwed or bolted to a wall

wall mounting lugs – projections on the case shaped such that they can be used to fasten the case to a wall

wide rack – a shaft with rack teeth cut around the circumference

wire neck rest – a wire rod bent in a shape that will support the neck of a bottle

wire or string breaker – a blade or hook fixed to the corkscrew, such that it can be used to cut or break the string or wire holding the cork in the bottle

worm – a short continuously threaded shaft or screw that turns into the cork and pulls the cork from the bottle

worm carrier – a device that the worm is attached to, allowing the worm to turn freely

worm-nut – a nut that causes a worm to turn when the worm is pushed or pulled through the nut

worm-nut catch lug – a projection on a worm-nut formed such that the hook on a latching link can lift the worm-nut

Appendix 1
ADVERTISING & PARTS LISTS

Arcade Cork Pullers

The Phœnix No. 30

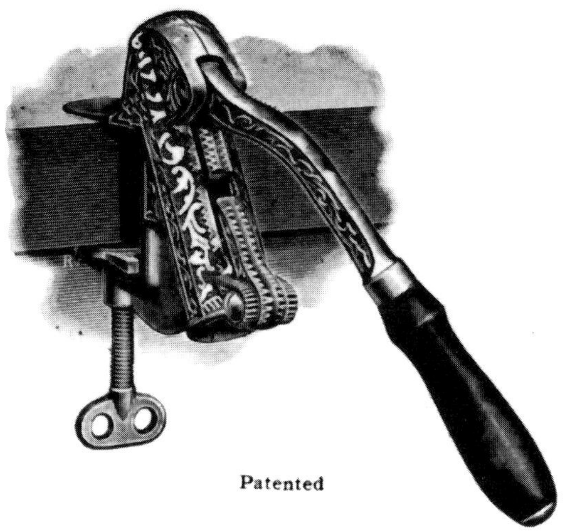

Patented

It is a great convenience to have the lever and all working parts of a puller below the counter.

In addition to this feature, the No. 30 has an action which is simple and powerful.

The price is very attractive.

Finished in heavy nickel plate.

PACKING

Each puller is packed in a wooden box, 1 dozen in a case.

Case weight, net 35 lbs., gross 65 lbs. Case measurements, 28x14x12 inches.

Separate Parts of No. 30 Phœnix Cork Puller

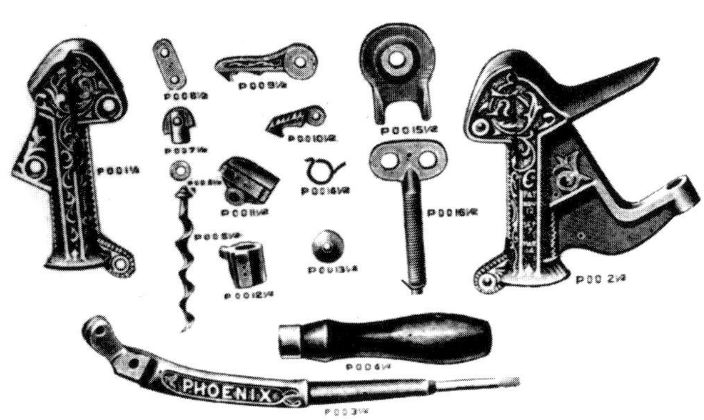

No.		Price.	No.		Price.
P 002½	Main Frame	$0.75	P 0010½	Small Hook	$0.10
P 001½	Minor Frame	.40	P 007½	Cap Nut	.10
P 003½	Operating Lever	.60	P 008½	Connecting Link	.10
P 004½	Wood Handle	.10	P 006½	Washer	.10
P 0011½	Upper Nut	.20	P 0014½	Steel Spring	.10
P 0012½	Lower Nut	.20	P 0015½	Washer	.10
P 005½	Worm or Screw	.50	P 0016½	Thumb Screw	.15
P 009½	Large Hook	.10	P 0013½	Washer	.10

In ordering give number of part wanted.

Advertising and parts lists

Advertising and parts lists are a good research source. Advertising can be misleading, as illustrations were expensive to produce, so they were used repeatedly over many years. In some cases, they were used by another manufacturer, resulting in no firm information on when a certain model changed or who produced it. For instance, the double clamp ACME was used in some advertising illustrations until at least 1921, thus they are combined with the generic ACME. Arcade used the same "patent pending" illustration of their CHAMPION in all of the catalogues they ever published. For this reason, on some corkscrews, the total range of years that a name was advertised is used. For instance, in the case of a SAFETY, it was not possible to reliably differentiate whether the advertising was for a model marked SAFETY, THE SAFETY or the ORIGINAL SAFETY, so they have all been included in the date range. The range of years over which a corkscrew may have been advertised is indicated in the "earliest found" and "latest found" columns. The "yes" indicates a parts list has been found.

Advertised Name	Version	Country	Earliest Found	Latest Found	.Parts list Found
A1		England	1926	1927	
ACME	clamp mount	England	1895	1927	
ACME	top mount	England	1898		
ADAMS		USA or Canada	1896		
AJAX		England	1895	1900	
AJAX		Germany	c. 1930		
AJAX 2		Germany	c. 1940		
ARCADE		USA or Canada	1897		
BACCHUS		USA or Canada	unknown		
BEAUMONT		USA or Canada	1899		
BISON 6		Germany	1932	1936	
BISON - DONAR		Germany	1932	1936	yes
BISON - HEBE		Germany	1932	1936	yes
BISON - UNIQUE		Germany	1932	1936	yes
BL		France	1902	1925	yes
BLITZ		Germany	1908		
BORDEAUX		England	1898	1900	
BULL-DOG		USA or Canada	1901		yes
CEDON	cast iron	Germany	c. 1930	c. 1950	yes
CEDON	later version	USA or Canada		2001	yes
CELLAR CONCEPTS		USA or Canada		2000	
CHAMPION	(1893)	USA or Canada	1893	1894	
CHAMPION	all	USA or Canada	1893	1923	yes
CLIPPER		France	1902		
COLUMBIA		USA or Canada	1891		
CROWN		England	1897	1898	
CRYSTAL PALACE		England	1895	1900	
CYKLOP	wire neck rest, foil cutter	Germany	c. 1930	c. 1950	
CYKLOP	cast neck rest	USA or Canada		2001	yes
DAISY		USA or Canada	1893	1923	yes
DION		USA or Canada		2001	yes
DON		England	1909	1927	

Advertised Name	Version	Country	Earliest Found	Latest Found	Parts list Found
DON	screw in throat	England	1912		
DON		Germany	c. 1933		
DREKO		East Germany		1990	
ECLIPSE		England	1895	1927	
ELECTROPULL		USA or Canada	2001	2001	
ENTERPRISE		USA or Canada	1896	1908	
ERIE		USA or Canada	1894		
ESTATE		USA or Canada	1983		yes
EXHIBITION		England	1895	1900	
EXPRESS		England	c. 1900-1920		
EXTRACTEE		USA or Canada	1905		
FAMLEE	with cork grip	USA or Canada	1905		
FAVORITE	with cap lifter	USA or Canada	1913	1923	
FORTSCHRITT		Germany	c. 1933		
HANDY		USA or Canada	1913	1923	yes
HEKTOR	vine and leaf decoration	Germany	c. 1930	c. 1933	
HEKTOR 1	vine and leaf decoration	Germany	c. 1940		
HEKTOR 2	foil cutter	Germany	c. 1950		
HEKTOR 2	grape leaf	Germany	c. 1940	c. 1950	
HEKTOR 3	both	Germany		2001	
HELIOS		Germany	c. 1933		
HERO NO5		Germany	1908		
HGB 7		Germany	1936		
INFANTA		USA or Canada	1895		
INVINCIBLE		Germany	1908		
JUBILEE		England	1897		
KING		England	1910		
LEVER		England	1895	1900	
MERIDEN		USA or Canada	1894		
MERRITT		England	1895	1927	
MIDGET		USA or Canada	1893		
MODERN		USA or Canada	1902		
MUIR's	(a copy of the Lindstrom patent)	England	1884	1885	
NEW CENTURY		USA or Canada	1902		
PELICAN		France	1922		
PHOENIX 20		USA or Canada	1913		yes
PHOENIX 30		USA or Canada	1902	1923	yes
PHOENIX 40		USA or Canada	1913		yes
PHOENIX 50		USA or Canada	1913		yes
PHOENIX 60		USA or Canada	1902	1913	yes
PHOENIX 100		USA or Canada	1913		yes
PHR	ball handle	West Germany	unknown		
QUICK		Germany	c. 1900 - 1920		
QUICK & EASY	1st version	USA or Canada	1893	1896	
QUICK & EASY	big bottle clamp	USA or Canada	1905	1907	
QUICK & EASY	all others	USA or Canada	1905	1909	yes

Advertised Name	Version	Country	Earliest Found	Latest Found	Parts list Found
RAPID	Swiss	USA or Canada	1983	1995	yes
RAPID	English	England	1896	1921	
RAPID	US	USA or Canada	1894	1908	yes
RAPID	"US, top mount"	USA or Canada	1894		
RAPID	US	England	1896	1910	
RAPID	US	Germany	1908		
RAPID POWERFUL		England	1895		
REX		England	1910		
SAFETY	brass	England	1908	1910	
SAFETY	ribbed case and frame	England	1912		yes
SAFETY	all others	England	1895	1937	yes
SAMPSON	(alternate spelling SAMSON)	USA or Canada	1893	1901	
SAMSON		USA or Canada	1894	1908	
SAMSON		England	1895		
SHAMROCK		England	1926		
SHOMEE		USA or Canada	1905		
SIMPLE		England	1908	1910	
SIMPLEX	(no illustration)	England	1894		
SLAM		England	1908		
STANDARD		USA or Canada	1913		yes
SULLIVAN		USA or Canada	1896		
SWIFT		England	1909	1927	
TRIUMPH		USA or Canada	1913		
UNIQUE	British	England	1909	1926	
UNIQUE, NEW		England	1909		
UNIQUE, NEW		Germany	c. 1933		
UNIQUE	all other versions	England	1895	1898	
UNIQUE	all other versions	Germany	1908		
VICTOR		England	1898		
VIKTORIA		Germany	1908	1933	
VINTNER		USA or Canada	1983		yes
WALKER, THE		USA or Canada	1901	1908	
WALKER AUTOMATIC		USA or Canada	1893	1901	yes
YANKEE		USA or Canada	1902	1913	
YANKEE		France	1908		
YANKEE No1 & No2		France	1902	1909	
YANKEE No1 & No2		England	1909	1927	
YANKEE NO6		USA or Canada	1905		
YANKEE NO6		England	1909		
YANKEE NO7		USA or Canada	1905	1909	
ZEUS		USA or Canada		2001	yes
1888 BARRETT		USA or Canada	1893	1894	

Sample parts lists

Arcade Cork Pullers

Champion Cork Puller Parts

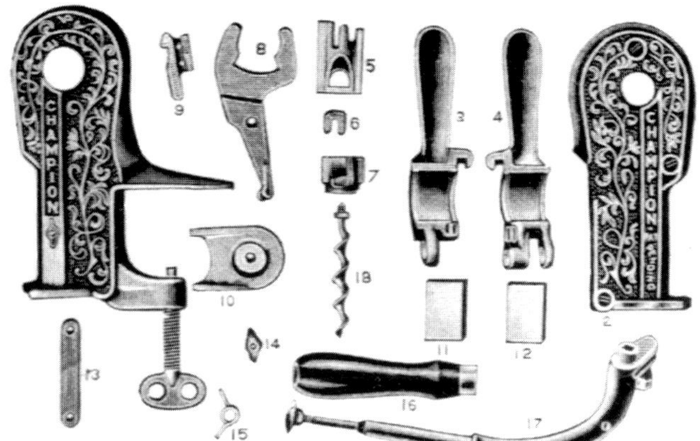

No.		Price.	No.		Price.
1	Right Frame	$1.00	10	Clamp Washer	$0.10
2	Left Frame	.75	11-12	Rubber Cushions (pair)	.10
3	Left Bottle Clamp	.30	13	Connecting Link	.10
4	Right Bottle Clamp	.30	14	Wire Stripper	.10
5	Upper Nut	.25	15	Steel Spring	.10
6	Brass Washer	.10	16	Wood Handle	.10
7	Lower Nut	.25	17	Operating Lever	.80
8	Rocker Arm	.10	18	Worm or Screw	.50
9	Lifting Hook	.10			

Daisy Cork Puller Parts

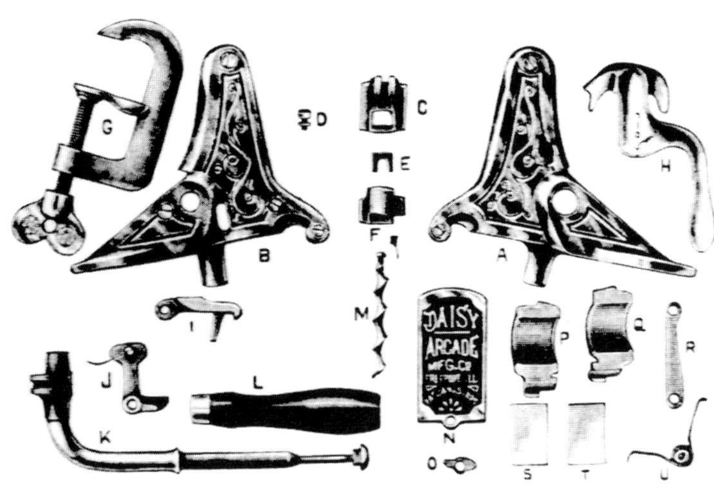

No.		Price.	No.		Price.
A	Right Frame	$1.00	K	Main Operating Lever	$0.75
B	Left Frame	1.00	L	Wood Handle	.10
C	Upper Nut	.25	M	Worm or Screw	.50
D	Cap Screw	.10	N	Name Plate	.10
E	Brass Washer	.10	O	Wire Stripper	.10
F	Lower Nut	.25	P	Left Bottle Clasp	.10
G	Screw Clamp	.50	Q	Right Bottle Clasp	.10
H	Bottle Holding Lever	.50	R	Connecting Link	.10
I	Hook	.10	S & T	Rubber Cushions (pair)	.10
J	Spring Holder	.15	U	Steel Spring	.10

Separate Parts of No. 100 Handy Cork Puller

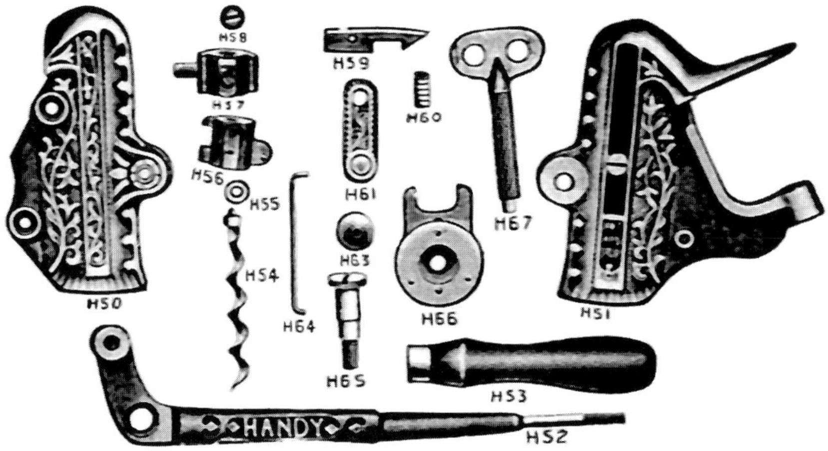

No.		Price.	No.		Price.
H 51	Main Frame	$0.75	H 59	Hook	$0.10
H 50	Minor Frame	.40	H 60	Steel Stud	.10
H 52	Operating Lever	.60	H 61	Connecting Link	.10
H 53	Wood Handle	.10	H 64	Wire Rod	.10
H 54	Worm	.10	H 63	Washer	.10
H 55	Washer	.10	H 65	Screw Head Bolt	.20
H 56	Lower Nut	.20	H 66	Washer	.10
H 57	Upper Nut	.20	H 67	Thumb Screw	.20
H 58	Set Screw	.10			

Separate Parts of Phœnix No. 40 Cork Puller

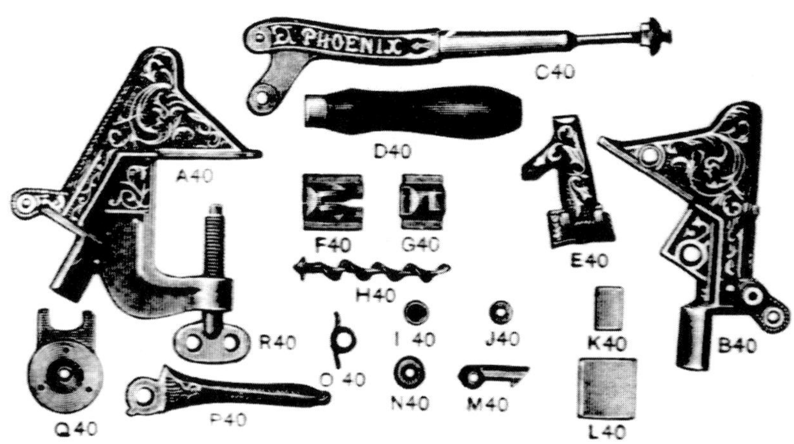

No.		Price.	No.		Price.
A 40	Main Frame	$1.00	J 40	Washer	$0.10
B 40	Minor Frame	.75	K 40	Rubber Cushion	.10
C 40	Operating Lever	.75	L 40	Rubber Cushion	.10
D 40	Wood Handle	.10	M 40	Small Hook	.10
E 40	Bottle Clasp	.25	N 40	Washer	.10
F 40	Upper Nut	.25	O 40	Tempered Steel Stripper	.10
G 40	Lower Nut	.25	P 40	Bottle Holding Lever	.50
H 40	Worm or Screw	.50	Q 40	Thumb Screw Washer	.10
I 40	Washer	.10	R 40	Thumb Screw	.20

Separate Parts of No. 60 Phœnix Cork Puller

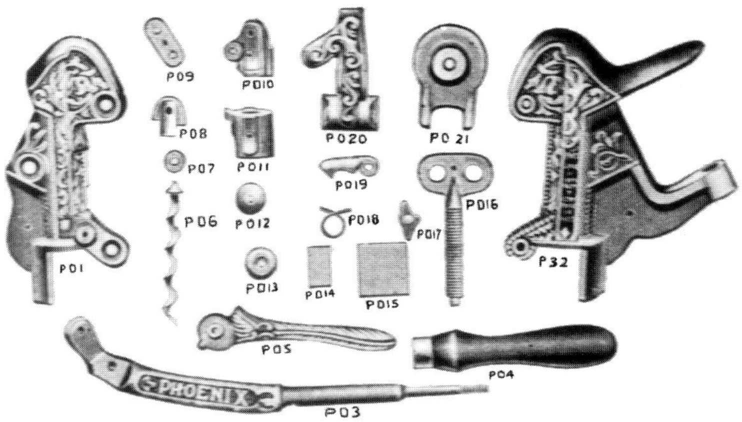

No.		Price.
P 02	Main Frame	$1.00
P 01	Minor Frame	.75
P 03	Main Operating Lever	.75
P 05	Bottle Holding Lever	.50
P 04	Wood Handle	.10
P 010	Upper Nut	.25
P 011	Lower Nut	.25
P 020	Bottle Clamp	.25
P 016	Thumb Screw	.20
P 09	Connecting Link	.10
P 08	Cap Nut	.15

No.		Price.
P 06	Worm	$0.50
P 015	Rubber Cushion	.10
P 014	Rubber Cushion	.05
P 019	Small Hook	.10
P 018	Tempered Steel Spring	.10
P 017	Steel Wire Stripper	.10
P 07	Washer	.10
P 012	Washer	.10
P 013	Washer	.10
P 021	Washer	.10

Separate Parts of No. 25 Standard Cork Puller

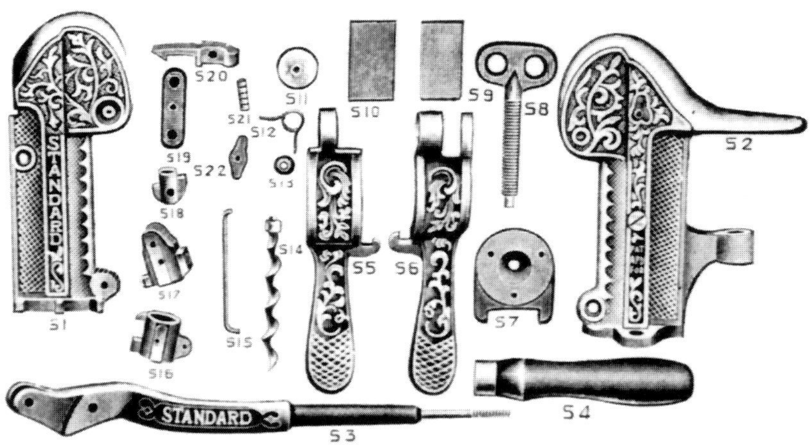

No.		Price.
S 2	Main Frame	$1.00
S 1	Minor Frame	.75
S 6	Bottle Clamp, right	.30
S 5	Bottle Clamp, left	.30
S 17	Upper Nut	.25
S 16	Lower Nut	.25
S 3	Operating Lever	.80
S 4	Wood Handle	.10
S 14	Worm or Screw	.50
S 9 & S 10	Rubber Cushions (pair)	.10
S 8	Thumb Screw	.20

No.		Price.
S 7	Thumb Screw Washer	$0.10
S 19	Connecting Link	.10
S 20	Hook	.10
S 18	Cap Nut	.10
S 11	Washer	.10
S 12	Steel Spring	.10
S 15	Wire Rod	.10
S 22	Steel Wire Stripper	.10
S 13	Washer	.10
S 21	Steel Stud	.10

Entkorkmaschinen

Bison-Donar

Die massive Qualitätsmaschine für jede Beanspruchung.

Streng korrekte Führung der Innenteile durch Spindelgang. Spindelgang in der Messingführung jetzt aus dem Vollen geschnitten.

		Stück RM
Nr. 1	**komplett (wie Abbildung) mit loser Tischklammer**	**35.—**
„ 2	**ohne Tischklammer (nur zum Aufschrauben auf den Tisch)**	**32.50**

Nr.	**Ersatzteile**	Stück RM
71	**Griff komplett mit beiden Bügeln**	**12.50**
71a	**Holzheft**	**0.40**
72	**Verbindungsstück**	**1.50**
73	**Bügelschraube**	**0.25**
74	**Querbolzen mit Kappenschraube**	**1.—**
75	**Komplette Innenausstattung**	**10.15**
76	**Messing-Nuß mit Führungsstab**	**3.—**
77	**Messing-Kolben**	**3.65**
78	**Spindel**	**2.—**
79	**Krätzer**	**1.25**
80	**Gummiring**	**1.15**
81	**Komplette Tischklammer**	**2.50**
79a	**Ersatz-Krätzer mit engl. Gewinde zur The Don Maschine**	**1.50**

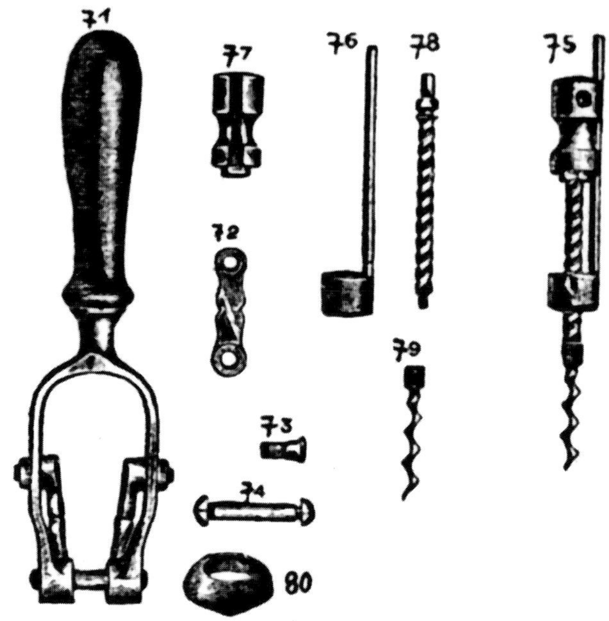

Die komplette Innenausstattung läßt sich auch in das englische Don-Modell einbauen.

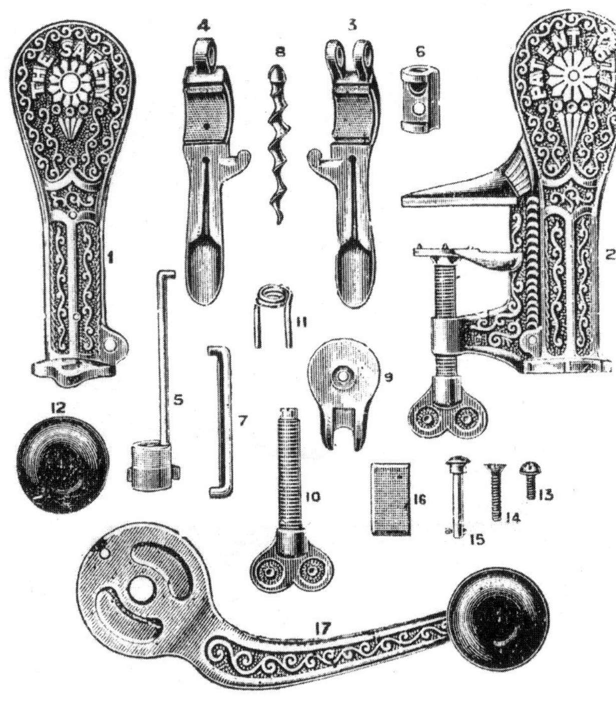

"Safety" Cork Drawer Parts.

No.		
1.	Oil Side	3/6
2.	Clamp Side	4/-
3.	Left Bottle Clamp (double side)	2/-
4.	Right ditto (single side) ...	2/-
5.	Nut with Guide Rod ...	1/8
6.	Plunger	5d.
7.	Link	5d.
8.	Corkscrew Worm	10d.
9.	Clamp Plate	8d.
10.	Clamp Screw	6d.
11.	Spring	2d.
12.	Knob	2d.
13.	Bottom Screw	1d.
14.	Top Screw	1d.
15.	Cotter Pin and Bolt ...	4d.
16.	Rubber	3d.
17.	Handle and Knob... ...	4/-

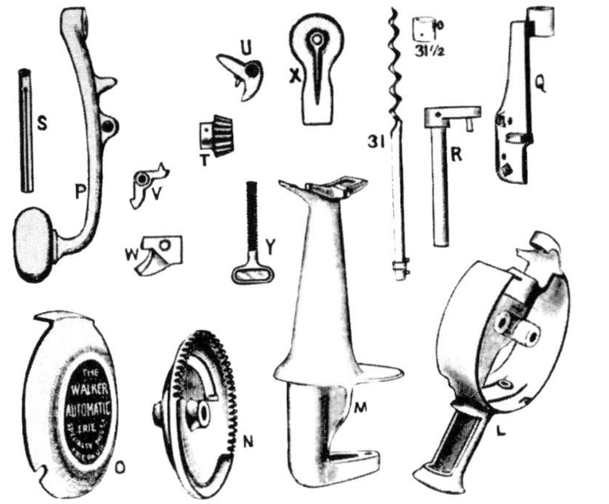

Extra Parts for No. 27.

WALKER'S

Automatic Cork Puller.

For convenience in ordering repair parts, this list is arranged with retail price of each.

	EACH		EACH
L—Body	$3 00	T—Small gear	$0 20
M—Stand	1 50	U—Upper dog	10
N—Large gear	50	V—Lower dog	10
O—Name plate	30	W—Catch	10
P—Lever	50	X—Washer	10
Q—Lifting sleeve	50	Y—Thumb screw	20
R—Crank	50	31—Screw	50
S—Steel sleeves	30	31½—Nut	50

N. B.—In the first machines made, a short screw was used 3⅞ inches long. If this screw is wanted, mention short screw, otherwise the long one as now used will be sent.

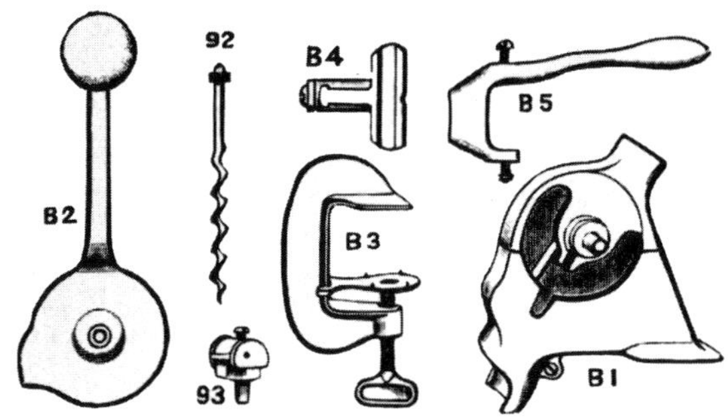

EXTRA PARTS FOR

WALKER'S

Bull Dog Puller.

For convenience in ordering repair parts this list is arranged with retail price of each.

B 1—Body	Price each,		$1	20
B 2—Lever	"	"		80
B 3—Clamp	"	"		50
B 4—Inside sleeve	"	"		70
B 5—Bottle clasp	"	"		50
92—Screw	"	"		50
93—Nut	"	"		50

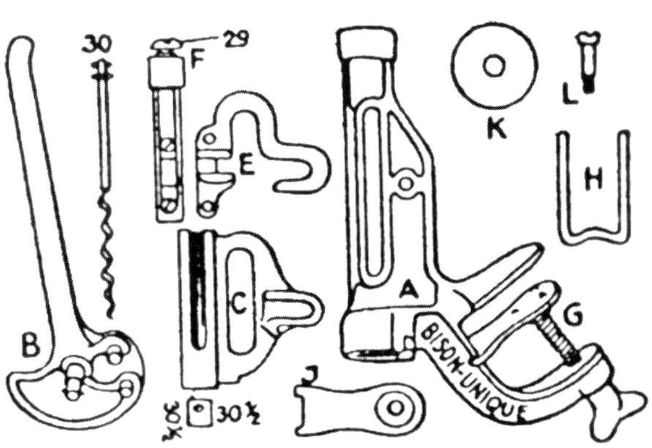

Ersatzteile

			vernickelt	lackiert
A	Hauptteil oder Körper	Stück	M. 13,50	M. 10,50
B	Kurbel	"	" 4,05	" 3,—
C	sog. C-Teil	"	" 3,—	" 2,55
E	Hakenteil oder E-Teil	"	" 2,55	" 2,10
F	Führung oder F-Teil	"	" 1,95	" 1,80
29	F-Teil-Schraube	"	" 0,45	
G	Tischschraube	"	" 0,75	
H	Flaschenhalter	"	" 0,45	
J	Tischplatte	"	" 0,45	
K	Holzknopf	"	" 0,30	
L	Knopfschraube	"	" 0,45	
30	Krätzer (oder Korkzieher)	"	" 1,10	
30 ½	Nuß	"	" 1,20	

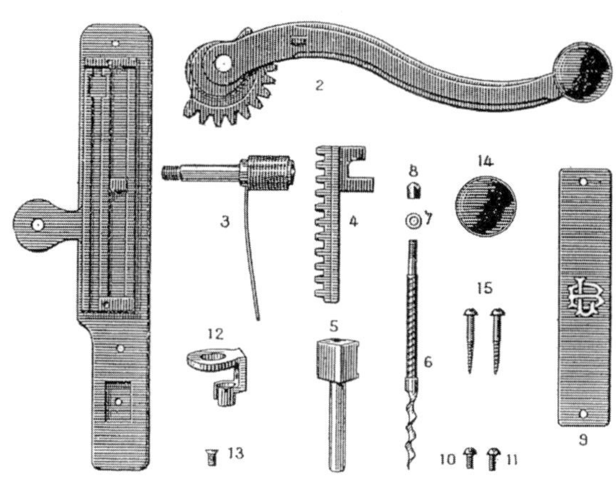

Pièces détachées de la Déboucheuse 331

Nº des pièces	DÉSIGNATION	PRIX
1	Bâti	15. »
2	Levier	12.50
3	Ressort de levier avec axe	3.50
4	Crémaillère	4.50
5	Écrou bronze	5. »
6	Mèche	6. »
7	Rondelle pour mèche	0.15
8	Écrou » »	0.25
9	Plaque	2.50
10	Vis de plaque (basse)	0.25
11	» » » (haute)	0.25
12	Embouchoir	2. »
13	Vis pour embouchoir	0.25
14	Poignée bois	0.75
15	Vis de fixation	0.30

Les mèches de rechange sont livrées avec rondelle et écrou. Prendre soin lorsque l'on remplace la mèche de s'assurer que l'extrémité supérieure seule sert de pivot.

Appendix 2
BAR CORKSCREW ACCESSORIES

CIRCULAR No. 35.

N[illegible]28

"RAPID" CORK PULLER

[PATENTED APRIL 21, 1891.]

DESIGNED FOR USE IN HOTELS, RESTAURANTS, DRUG STORES, CLUBS, BARS, ETC.

ILLUSTRATIONS ONE-THIRD FULL SIZE.

THE "RAPID" IS THE BEST AND MOST COMPLETE CORK PULLER MADE.

IN POSITION READY FOR USE.

POSITION AFTER CORK IS REMOVED.

DIRECTIONS FOR USE.

Screw the Puller to a Table or Bar, that is firm enough so it will not spring.

Hold Bottle by the bottom with mouth firmly up into mouth of Push-off, then pull Handle forward and down until it hangs straight with body of Puller; this cuts the wires and removes cork from bottle.

Then pull Handle back into "position ready for use," and Cork will drop from Screw.

KEEP PULLER WELL OILED, by dropping a little Oil in "Oil" hole just above Left-handed Screw which holds Push-off to Body, also by removing Cap marked "Rapid" on top of Body and dropping a little Oil inside of Body.

THE "RAPID" is Best for the following reasons:

Is Strong, Simple and Perfect in Construction.
Is smaller than other Pullers of the kind, requiring less room.
Cuts Wires and pulls Cork with one motion of the hand.
Never breaks Bottles, as strain is on the strongest part of bottle.
Is so made that any part can be replaced without returning entire Puller to the Factory.

....MADE BY....

BRADLEY & HUBBARD MFG. CO.,

MERIDEN, CONN.

BOSTON, 160 CONGRESS STREET. NE[illegible]YORK, 26 PARK PL[illegible]RCLAY STREET. CHICAGO, 131 WABASH AVENUE.

(OVER)

THE "SAVEALL" CORK-CATCHER.

(REGISTERED)

A simple Contrivance for fixing under counter to catch Corks.

Small size...	...	...	1/6 each
Medium size	...	...	2/6 ,,
Large ,,	...	...	5/- ,,
Nickel-plated Frame		...	1/- extra

No. **5003**

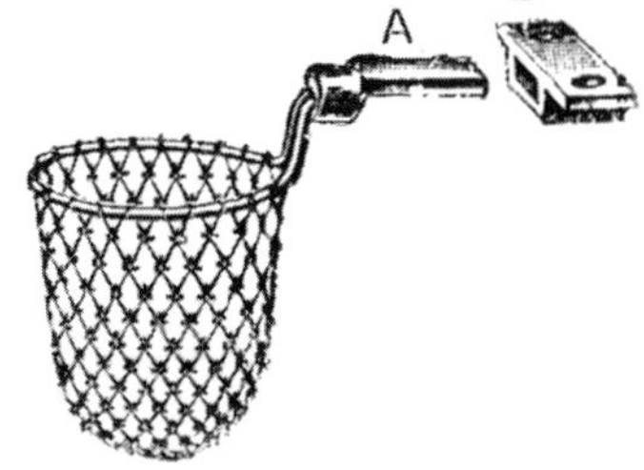

No. **5003**

The Eyelet marked B, No. 5003, is fixed to the underside of the counter to hold the Detachable Net Holder A.

THE NET CAN READILY BE REMOVED.

For Bottle Guards, see No. 5251, page 204.

Rotary Eclipse, showing Rubber Bottle Guard fixed.

No. **5251.**

Rubber Bottle Guard, for Cork Drawers.
Prevents Accidents.
Self Adjusting, 5/6 each.

No. **5252**

A Rubber Bottle Guard, with Metal Clip for fixing on Cork Drawer.
3/6 each.

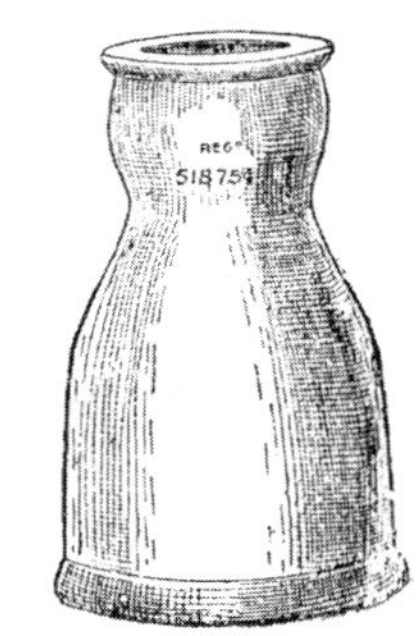

No. **5251.**

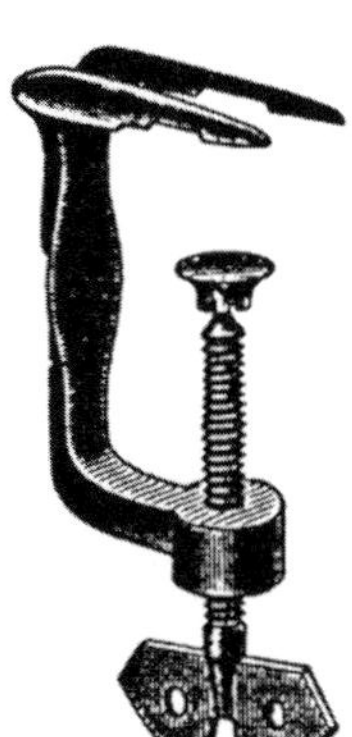

PER DOZEN.

Extra Clamps, Tinned, for Fastening Samson Cork Pullers to Table or Bar, ... $4.50

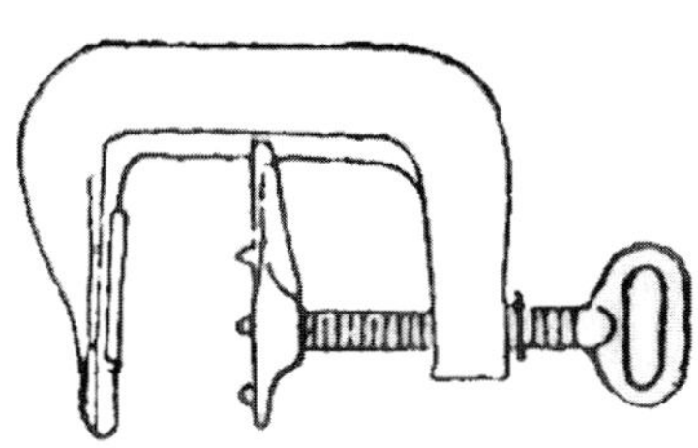

EXTRA PARTS FOR THE "QUICK AND EASY"

Clamp.. Price each .50

Daisy Cork Puller Parts

Screw Clamp.................... .50

Appendix 3

Manufacturers and Distributors

Arcade Manufacturing Co.

(INCORPORATED 1885.)

L. L. MUNN, *Pres.* A. BAUMGARTEN, *Vice Pres.* L. L. MUNN, JR., *Sec'y.*
E. H. MORGAN, *Treas. and Gen'l Mgr.* CHAS. MORGAN, *Supt.*

Authorized Capital, = = $125,000.
Paid in Capital, = = = $120,000.

Fine Light Gray Iron Castings Made to Order.

HAVE ALSO LATELY ADDED TO OUR PLANT A

Thoroughly Equipped Nickel Plating Outfit

AND ARE PREPARED TO DO JOB WORK IN THIS LINE.

FREEPORT, ILL., U. S. A.

These are some of the manufacturers and distributors associated with the production and distribution of bar corkscrews. The distributors have been included if their name is found marked on bar corkscrews. Very little historical documentation has been found, thus much of the company histories and dates of operation is very sketchy. It is hoped that the inclusion of even the smallest amount of information will be of some assistance to researchers in the future.

d' Acier Poli operated their business from approximately 1824 to 1946 in Vieux Moulin, France. From approximately 1914 – 1927 it was owned by Eugénie Sitbon, who was the inventor and manufacturer of LE PELICAN.

F. F. Adams Co. operated their business from approximately 1847 to an unknown date, in Erie, Pennsylvania, USA. Owned by Francis Adams, their name is found on the SAMSON corkscrew.

ALEXANDERWERK started their business in Essen, Germany around 1885 and are still in business. They were possibly only a distributor of bar corkscrews.

American Wringer Co. operated their business from approximately 1898 to 1954 in New York City, New York, USA. The "AWC" trademark is not found on any bar corkscrews. In one advertisement they claim that they were the only manufacturer of the SAMSON; it is not known which version this was.

Arcade Manufacturing Co. operated their business from approximately 1885 to 1945 in Freeport, Illinois, USA. Owned by Albert Baumgarten, Edgar & Charles Morgan and L. L. Munn, Arcade's "AC" trademark is not found on their corkscrews. Arcade located their foundry in Freeport due to the very fine sand found on the riverbank. The sand was said to be perfect for casting very delicate and intricate cast iron toys. In one newspaper account, they claimed to have shipped over 1,000,000 toy coffee grinders to France.

Barraud & Lerenard operated their business from approximately 1921 to 1942 in Paris, France. Owned by Paul Lerenard, the B&L trademark is found on most corkscrews they made

B. Olaneta Juaristi, S. A. have operated their business from approximately 1905 to the present in Eibar, Spain. The "BOJ" mark is found on all of their corkscrews.

Box & Coy operated their business for an unknown time period before and after 1890 in Dublin, Ireland. Owned by John and Thomas Joseph Haslam, Box & Coy described themselves as "Wholesale Saddlers, Ironmongers and Manufacturers"; the Haslams patented a few bar corkscrews.

Bradley & Hubbard Mfg. Co. operated their business for an unknown period of time in Meriden, Connecticut, USA. Owned by Walter Hubbard, their name was found on an operating and parts list brochure for the US RAPID.

Camion Frères operated their business from approximately 1900 to 1979 in Vivier, Ardennes, France. Owned by Georges and Charles Camion, the "CF" trademark is found on L'AUTOMATIQUE.

Franco Cicogna & Co. operated their business for an unknown time period, before and after 1975 in Milano, Italy. This is possibly an Italian manufacturer, as their name was found on a 1975 Italian patent document.

Drehteile und Korkenzieher operated their business from approximately 1958 to 1992 in Steinbacht- Hallenberg, East Germany. Owned by Kasper Kirchner, Friedrich Holland-Cunz and Franz Hoffmann, the DREKO trademark is found on most of the corkscrews they manufactured.

W. G. Edmonds & Co. operated their business for an unknown time period in Dublin, Ireland. Their name was found on a DON bar corkscrew, so they were presumably an Irish distributor.

Enterprise Mfg. Co. operated their business from approximately 1866 to 1920 in Philadelphia, Pennsylvania, USA. Owned by Asbury, Smith & Seltzer, they produced many cast iron kitchen items including the ENTERPRISE corkscrew.

Erie Specialty Co. operated their business from approximately 1892 to 1917 in Erie, Pennsylvania, USA. Edwin Walker and E. T. Brindley owned the company; this "ESC" mark was found in their 1901 catalog, but is not found on bar corkscrews.

Erie Specialty Mfg. Co. operated their business from approximately 1889 to 1892 in Erie, Pennsylvania, USA. It was owned by Edwin Walker; there is some confusion as to the exact dates that Walker's company changed its names.

Eskilstuna Järnmanufaktur Aktiebolag operated their business from approximately 1868 to an unknown date, in Eskilstuna, Sweden. The "EJAB" mark is found on Swedish versions of the ACME and QUICK & EASY.

Farrow & Jackson Ltd. operated their business from approximately 1798 to 1921 in London, England. They were wine and spirit merchants, and manufacturers of storage bins. They distributed bar corkscrews.

James D. Frary (1832 - 1890) operated his business from 1888 to 1890 in Meriden, Connecticut. Frary contracted with Meriden Malleable Iron Co. for the production of the 5th AVENUE and SULLIVAN corkscrews. Frary was initially a partner in the Landers, Frary & Clark company which operated from 1865 - 1955 in Meriden.

Freeport Novelty Co. operated their business from approximately 1900 to 1901 in Freeport, Illinois, USA. Albert Baumgarten owned this company; when Baumgarten left Arcade he owned or was associated with two other Freeport manufacturers for a very short period of time. There is no clear indication of the dates, but a very few Baumgarten corkscrews marked Freeport Novelty exist.

Frings & Co. o. H. G. have operated their business from approximately 1906 to the present in Hurth, Germany. Owned by Gerhard Frings, a "F. u C." (Frings and Company) mark is found on the HEKTOR 1. Frings manufactured all of the HEKTORs, and the CYKLOP, AJAX and AJAX 2.

The Guarranty Manufacturing Co. operated their business for an unknown time period before and after 1892 in Chicago, Illinois, USA. Owned by Raymond Beardsley Gilchrist, the Guarranty company patented Gilchrist's COLUMBIA corkscrew in Germany and France.

Peter Gaskell operated his business from an unknown date until approximately 1920 in Dale End, Birmingham, England. The "hand & star" trademark was cast into the inside of all of his bar corkscrews; the trademark registration has not been found. Very little has been discovered about Peter Gaskell. He appears to have operated the company independently until about 1920, after Chambers purchased it in 1897.

G&C

Gaskell & Chambers Ltd. have operated their business from approximately 1897 to the present in Dale End, Birmingham England. Owned by Cornelius Chambers, Gaskell & Chambers used the "G&C" trademark until the "optic" mark was registered. This "optic" trademark was registered Sep. 20, 1920 (# 407,991) and was used exclusively after about 1925. The "optic" and the "G&C" trademark are found stamped or cast into most of their bar corkscrews. Gaskell & Chambers trace their roots back to 1797; corkscrew production ended in about 1963.

HGB

Helmut Gebel operated his business for an unknown time period, before and after 1936, in Berlin, Germany. Owned by Helmut Gebel, the "HGB" mark is found cast into the internal components of all of the corkscrews they manufactured. Gebel initially distributed Gilchrist's BISON No 5 and BISON No 6.

Gilchrist Mfg. Co. operated their business from an unknown period of time around 1890 in Chicago, Illinois, USA. Owned by Raymond Gilchrist, there is no record of other products being manufactured, other than his bar corkscrew.

Paul Hammerschmidt operated his business from approximately 1906 to 1980 in Remscheid, Germany. A simple "PHR" is found on their corkscrews.

JUMA operated their business for an unknown time period, before and after 1970 in Gijon, Spain. They manufactured an unmarked bar corkscrew.

W.R. Loftus Ltd. operated their business for an unknown period of time in London, England. They distributed bar equipment, including bar corkscrews.

Lovell Mfg. Co. Ltd. operated their business for an unknown period of time in Erie, Pennsylvania, USA. Their name is found on one version of the LEVER; it is assumed that they were a manufacturer.

Erste Mainzer Metallkapsel-Fabrik operated their business for an unknown period of time, before and after 1930 in Mainz, Germany. Owned by Franz Zahn, this company may have been the manufacturer of the HELIOS and the VIKTORIA.

Maison Ruben operated their business over an unknown period of time in Bruxelles, Belgium. It is not known if they were a distributor or a manufacturer of the TITAN and other bar corkscrews.

Manning, Bowman & Co. operated their business for an unknown period of time around 1899 in Meriden, Connecticut, USA. They manufactured corkscrews for A. Baumgarten.

Markt & Co. operated their business from approximately 1920 to 1951 in Paris, France. It is not known if Markt was the manufacturer or just the distributor of the ALP corkscrew, or what the initials A. L. P. represent. Their "Indian head" trademark is not found on the ALP.

E. Martenet operated their business from approximately 1928 to 1978 in France. Owned by Ernest Martenet, they were possibly only a distributor of the PERFECT bar corkscrew.

Parnall & Sons operated their business for an unknown period of time in Bristol, England. They distributed bar equipment, including bar corkscrews.

Sachs, Druden & Co. operated their business for an unknown time period around 1886 in Dayton, Ohio, USA. Their name is found on the September 07, 1886 Hurley; whether they were a manufacturer or a distributor is unknown.

Samuel Mason Ltd. operated his business from approximately 1865 to 1910 in Dale End, Birmingham, England. Owned by Samuel George Mason, the "sun" trademark was very lightly stamped into brass or cast into many cast iron corkscrews as part of the case decoration. The "sun" trademark registration has not been found. Chambers purchased Mason's company in 1910.

Meriden Malleable Iron Co. operated their business for an unknown period of time (around 1888) in Meriden, Connecticut, USA. They manufactured bar corkscrews for H. Williams and J.D. Frary. Meriden Malleable may have produced the unmarked SULLIVANs after Frary's death in 1890.

Merritt & Chambers operated their business from approximately 1890 to 1892 in Dale End, Birmingham, England. Owned as a partnership by Cornelius Chambers and John Merritt, presumably their bar corkscrews were manufactured by Mason, until approximately 1892. Another name, J. T. Haywood, appears in conjunction with Chambers name, in registration documentation.

Novelty Iron Works operated their business from approximately 1868 to 1885 in Freeport, Illinois USA. Owned by Charles and Edgar Hazen Morgan, this company became Arcade Manufacturing Co.

M. J. Ordi & Co. Ltd. operated their business for an unknown period of time in Dublin, Ireland. Their name was found on an A1 bar corkscrew; presumably they were an Irish distributor.

Perez-Quintanilla operated their family owned business from approximately 1920 to 1990 in Gijon, Spain. The "bottle with a lever" trademark is found on versions of the ALFREDO. This trademark or logo has an "A" beside the bottle; it is also found with "AYM" beside the bottle.

PIX

Albert Pick & Co. operated their hotel and restaurant distribution business for an unknown period of time before and after 1895 in Chicago, Illinois, USA. Pick may have used the "PIX" trademark as a number of the items he sold have the "PIX" mark on them, including his private label version of the CHAMPION.

Rogar International Corp. have operated their business from 1978 to the present, in Texas and later in Richmond, Virginia, USA. Rogar manufactured the VINTNER, ESTATE and the Centennial CHAMPION.

Scovill Mfg. Co. have operated their business from approximately 1802 to the present in Waterbury, Connecticut, USA. Owned by J. M. L. and W. H. Scovill, they manufactured non-ferrous metal products; their name was found on the brass ferrule of a US Rapid.

Stover Mfg. Co. operated their business from approximately 1900 to 1901 in Freeport, Illinois, USA, owned by Albert Baumgarten. There is no clear indication of the dates, but a very few Baumgarten corkscrews marked "Stover Mfg." exist.

F. R. Sucesores operated their business for an unknown period of time, before and after 1920 in Gijon, Spain. They manufactured the SISTEMA bar corkscrew, which is very similar to the ALFREDO.

E. Walker Tool Co. operated their business from approximately 1883 to 1892 in Erie, Pennsylvania, USA. It was owned by Edwin Walker.

Wintenberger operated his business from approximately 1930 to the present in France. Very little is known about Paul Wintenberger's company. The (G) trademark is found on the PRESTO that he patented, but it is not known if this is Wintenberger's trademark. If Wintenberger was only a distributor, this (G) could be the trademark of the company that manufactured the PRESTO.

V & T Co. operated their business for an unknown period of time before and after 1888 in Meadville, Pennsylvania, USA. This name was found on the July 10, 1888 BARRETT corkscrew and is presumed to be the manufacturer; it is not known if this was Barrett's company.

Unknown French mark (possibly a worm manufacturer) found on the shanks of the worms in L'AUTOMATIQUE bar corkscrews.

BCM **Unknown German initials** (possibly the mark of the foil cutter manufacturer) found beside the foil cutter on versions of the HEKTOR 1 and HEKTOR 2 bar corkscrews.

HMK **An unknown German initial**, the "HMK" mark is found on the FORTSCHRITT.

JHE **An unknown German initial**, the "JHE" mark is found on a HERO NO 5 type of corkscrew marked JHE.

RIMO **An unknown German initial**, the "RIMO" mark is found on a grape leaf version of the HEKTOR 2 bar corkscrew.

Unknown German mark (possibly the mark (K) is by the thumb screw manufacturer) found on many of the German thumbscrews.

Unknown German mark (possibly the mark of a tool and die maker) "PxP" is found on the internal components of all CYKLOPs inspected.

AP 3 **Unknown German mark** (possibly the mark of a tool and die maker) "AP3" is found on the internal components of all HEKTOR 3s inspected.

AP **Unknown German mark,** (possibly the mark of a tool and die maker) "AP" is found on the internal components of some HEKTOR 2s inspected.

Unknown Italian mark, the "fly" trademark was found on a version of the US RAPID.

Appendix 4

STEM-NUT THROATS

10 GOLD MEDALS — GASKELLS — HIGHEST AWARDS

Cork Drawers.

Repairs to every Pattern Cork Drawer.

New Parts Supplied.

The "Merritt."

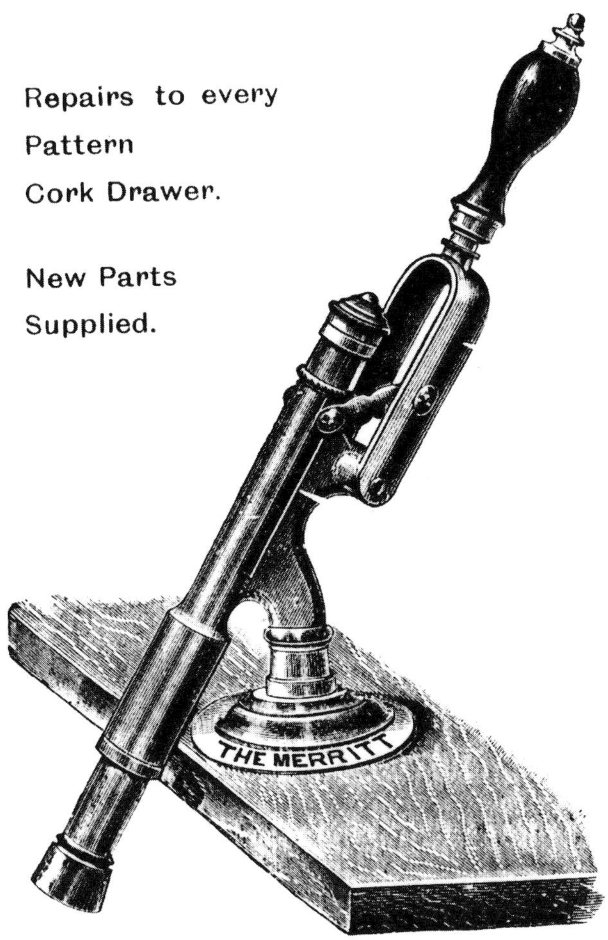

No. **5001**—On Stand.

To screw on Counter Top, as illustrated :—
Nickel-plated on Brass ... 35/- each
Polished Brass ... ... 33/- „

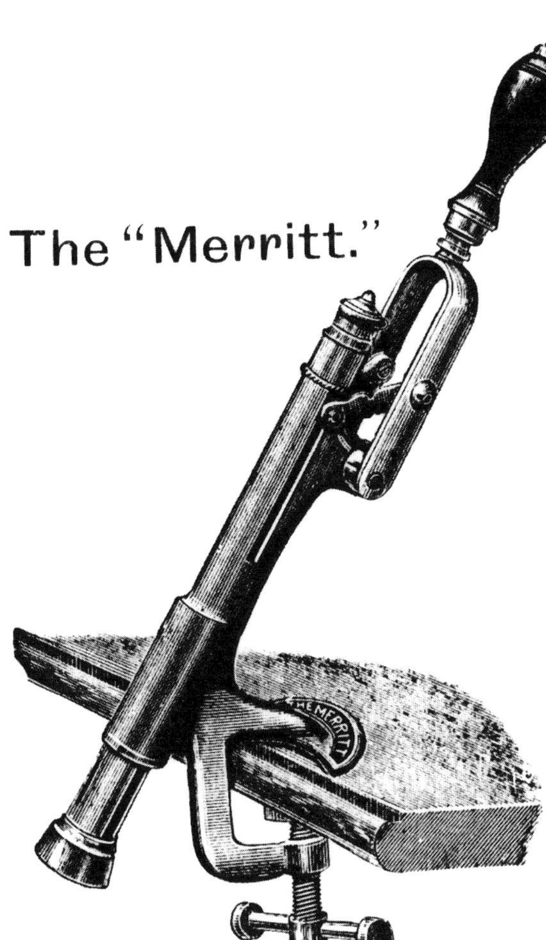

No. **5002**—To Clamp.

Nickel-plated on Brass ... 35/- each
Polished Brass ... ... 33/- „

These stem-nut throats were required because the channels for the stem-nut had to be machined inside the barrel. The stem-nut mechanism was inserted, and then the throat screwed on. These screw-in throats would have been relatively complex to manufacture, thus expensive. Chambers' DON patent in 1903 eliminated the requirement for these throats.

In 1889, J. and T. Haslam's patent included the idea of cutting holes in the top of the throat. The patent claimed: *The nozzle having an open* [sic] *on the upper side the operator is enabled to see that the bottle is held straight to the screw.* (It is difficult to see well enough through the hole or holes to see this, but one can definitely see if there were still a cork on the worm.) Curiously, there is no cutout in the throat on the only known example of this patent. It should be noted that in 1888, Chambers' patent drawings clearly show a slot cut into the throat of his MERRITT patent, but he did not claim it. We know that he actually used this, as a MERRITT marked "PAT. APL'D. FOR" has the cut out as shown in the patent drawing.

Another simple, but important, use for the hole pattern has been noted. The diameter and pitch of the screw threads are consistent with the cutout pattern. In other words, if the customer had somehow damaged the throat on his corkscrew, he could order the replacement part by specifying this pattern. It is assumed that this was also valuable from a factory inventory point of view.

The following types have been found.

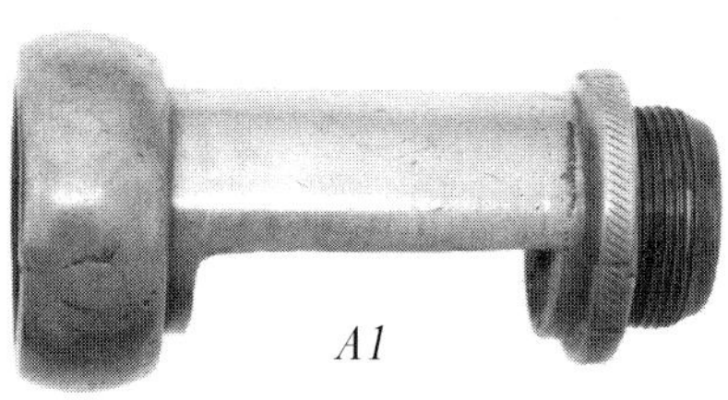
A1

A1 A throat without a hole, as found on what appears to be a very early SHAMROCK. As the SHAMROCK utilized the same style of operating lever and single link as the RAPID this was probably made prior to 1888.

A2 A massive open throat as found on the ECLIPSE.

A2

A3

A3 An open throat with integrated bottleneck rest as found on Mason's A1 and A739. Presumably this throat is earlier than the A4 throat.

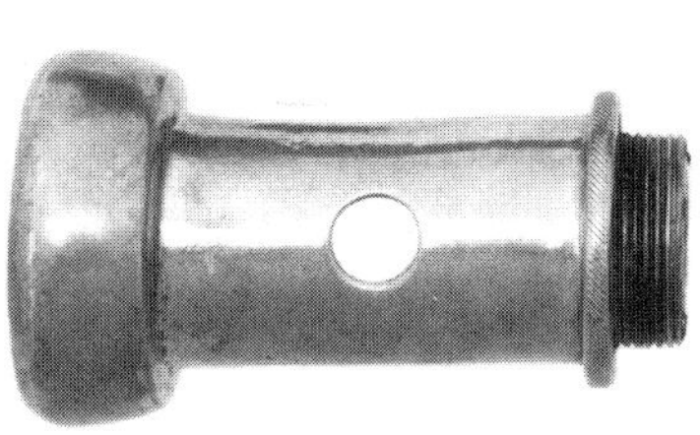
A4

A4 A one-hole pattern as found on the A1, A739, SUN and SLAM. The screw diameter and pitch are the same as A3, but the threaded portion is longer.

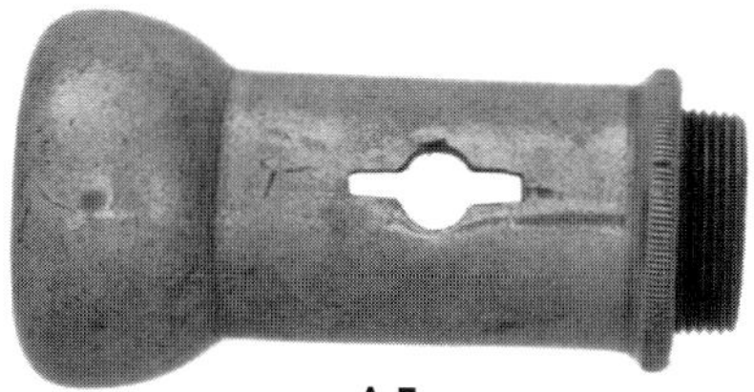

A5

A5 A one-hole and slot pattern as found on the RAPID style of bar corkscrew.

A6 A three-hole pattern as found on the ACME and the SHAMROCK. This pattern can vary widely; depending on how closely together the holes had been drilled, this pattern may be found varying from three separate, spaced-out holes to a single lumpy hole. More typical examples are seen on the ACMEs in the *IDENTIFICATION* section.

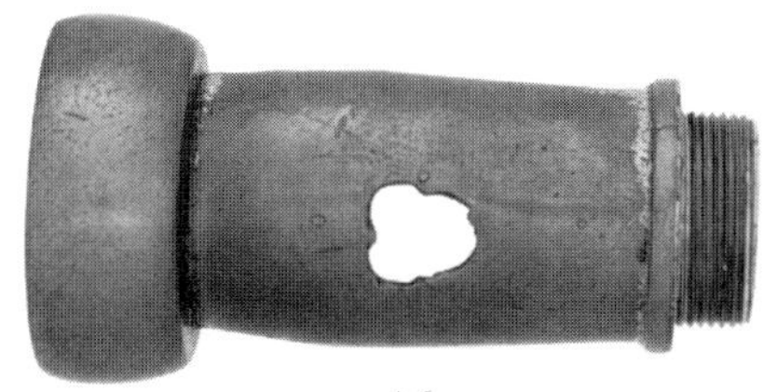

A6

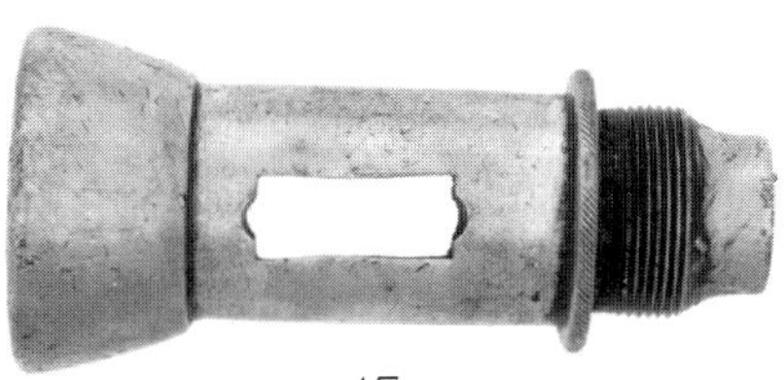

A7

A7 A two-hole and slot pattern as found on the MERRITT and SWIFT. This pattern can vary depending on how far into the holes the slot was cut.

A8 A two-hole pattern as found on the DON. This single-piece casting replaced the screw-in throat.

A8

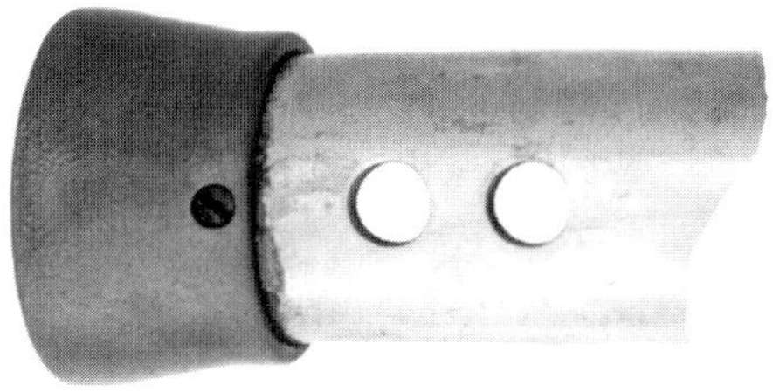

A9

A9 A two-hole pattern as found on the NEW DON. This illustration also shows the NEW DON's attached bottle lip. (It must have been cheaper to add this lip to the casting than to cast it all as one piece.)

Appendix 5
THUMBSCREWS

SOMETHING NEW!

First Introduced Sept. 5th, 1890.

Columbia Patent Automatic Cork Puller.

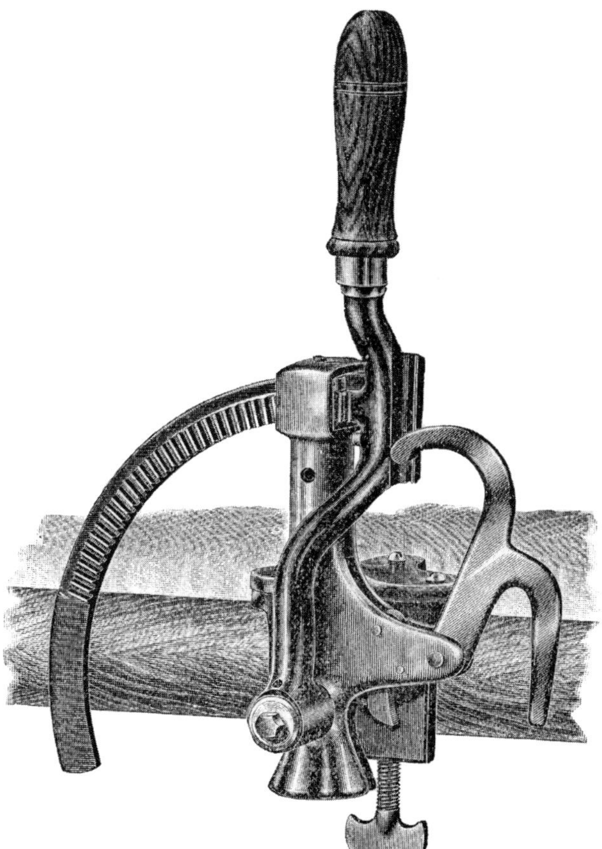

THIS AUTOMATIC CORK PULLER is the most RAPID AND PERFECT MACHINE on the market, and with ordinary care will last for YEARS WITHOUT GETTING OUT OF ORDER. It has been put to the severest test in all the largest hotels and saloons in Chicago, and other large cities, giving entire satisfaction.

The corkscrews are all made by hand OF THE FINEST QUALITY OF STEEL, and spring tempered so as to avoid breaking.

No hotel or saloon can afford to be without one, as the saving in time soon pays for it. One motion of the lever breaks the WIRE, pulls the cork and drops it on the floor without any danger of BREAKING THE BOTTLE which comes in contact with a soft RUBBER CUSHION.

I am prepared to furnish the machine in three different styles of finish, i. e.: ANTIQUE COPPER BRONZE, NICKEL PLATE OR JAPANNED. They are HIGHLY FINISHED so as to make an attractive ornament to a first-class bar.

I wish to call attention to the fact that this CORK PULLER can be attached either to the counter, back bar or wall, by means of an adjustable clamp or bracket. All necessary fixtures, clamp, screws, oil can, etc., accompany each machine, also full directions for setting up and using.

Price, $6.00 each. Clamps, 50 cents each.

All orders and communications will receive prompt attention.

ADOLPH KEITEL,

Sole Agent for Southern States,

51 Tchoupitoulas Street, NEW ORLEANS, LA.

When combined with trademarks, dated advertising and patent drawings, the findings (anything screwed, bolted or riveted on to the frame) can be of assistance in both dating and identifying the foundry where a corkscrew was produced.

All clamp-mounted corkscrews have a clamp plate, threaded rod and thumb piece. Each foundry would have made its own casting model for the thumb piece and clamp plate. In some cases these are found on other clamp mount items they manufactured, such as cherry pitters and lemon presses.

The foundry used the pattern until a cheaper-to-produce design was found, or some outside force caused a production change. So, once a shape has been correctly associated with a foundry, the shape of the clamp mount components should reveal one or more of the following: which country it was manufactured in, the manufacturer and, in some cases, the approximate date of production. Who manufactured many of the bar corkscrews is still a mystery.

Italy

A10 Found exclusively on Italian corkscrews after about 1950, this thumbscrew utilized a threaded rod, through which a cross pin was inserted. In a few rare cases this style of thumbscrew has been found on corkscrews from other countries; these include the very early MERRITTs circa 1890, the German VAMPIR circa 1950, and a massive clamp mount BL.

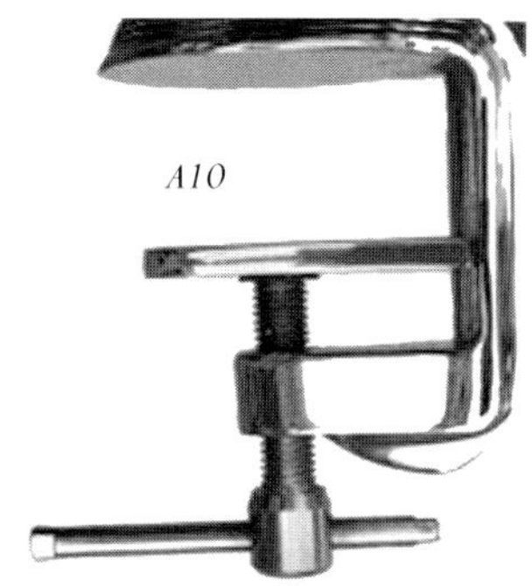

A10

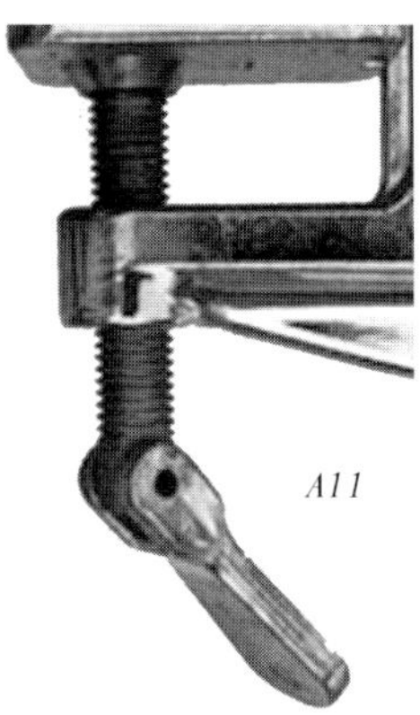

A11

Switzerland

A11 Found exclusively on the Swiss RAPID corkscrews, this thumbscrew used a hinged toggle, pinned to the bottom of the shaft.

East Germany

A12 Found exclusively on the East German DREKO corkscrews, this thumbscrew used a sliding bar pinned into the cap of the threaded shaft.

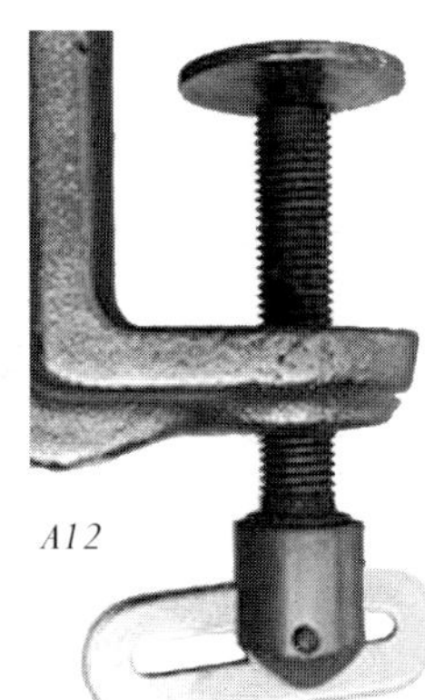

A12

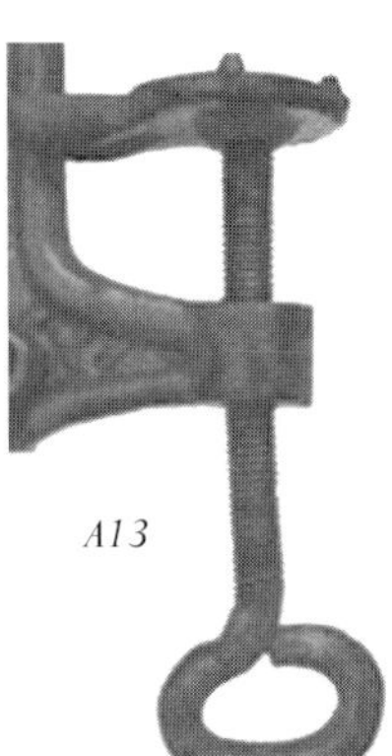

A13

Germany

A13 From a very crude copy of the ARCADE, presumably manufactured sometime between 1890 - 1910 in America for the European market, this thumb piece pre-dates the German loop thumbscrew by more than 10 years.

A14

A14 Found on a cast iron, grapevine decorated PHR, this very ornate, freestanding clamp plate and unrefined thumb piece would indicate a very early version of the German loop thumb piece; later versions of the PHR utilize the standard (K) thumb piece.

A15 Found exclusively on German manufactured corkscrews circa 1925 to the present, this thumbscrew used a rod threaded to approximately half of its length, with the unthreaded portion bent into a loop and slightly flattened. This very common thumbscrew was marked with a (K) from about 1925 to sometime after WWII. The (K) mark is not found on the recent versions of German corkscrews.

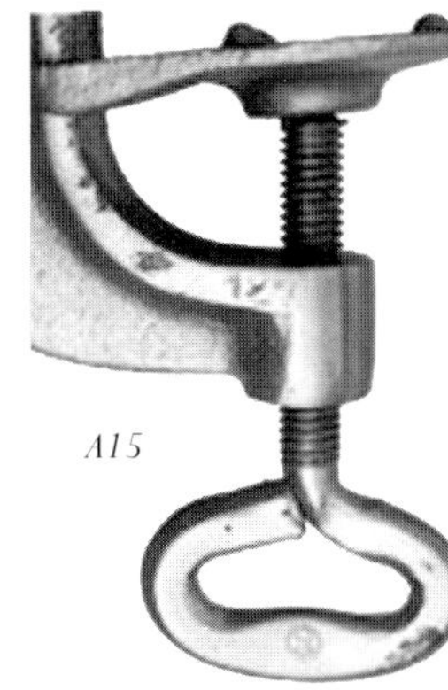

A15

The HERO N05 was copied in Germany, so there are a number of German thumbscrews that resemble Gilchrist's, until one looks more closely. Different manufacturers will have made these slightly different shapes.

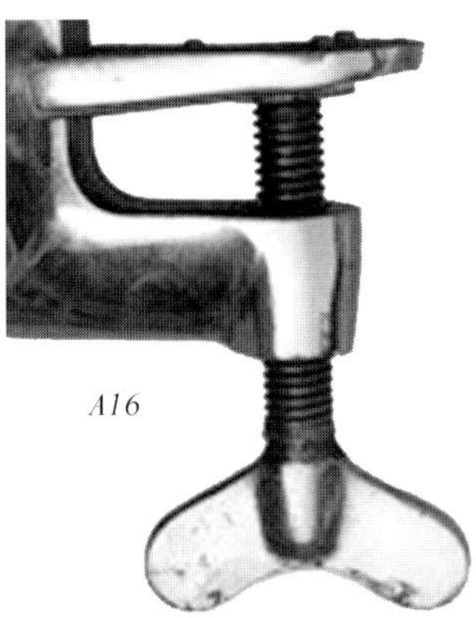

A16

A16 A Gilchrist look-alike thumb piece, found on the HELIOS.

A17 A Gilchrist look-alike thumb piece, found on the JHE.

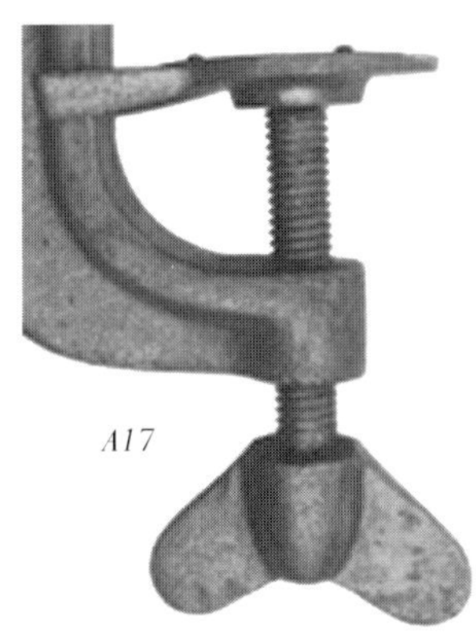

A17

America

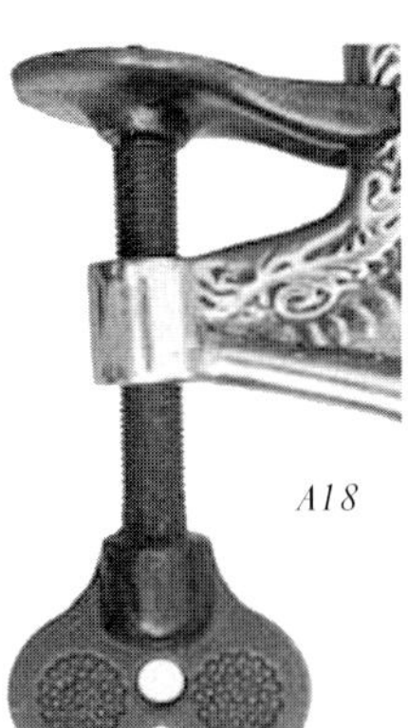

A18

A18 Manufactured by Arcade, circa 1893 - 1896, this thumb piece was found on the first versions of the ARCADE. When the ARCADE design moved to England, Gaskell eliminated the hole in the thumb piece and it became his standard thumb piece for all of his smaller bar corkscrews.

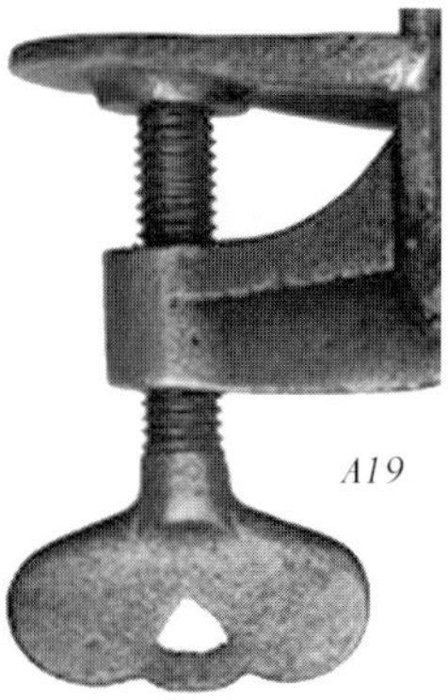

A19

A19 Manufactured by Arcade, circa 1896, this thumb piece with one or more holes was found on the earliest "pat pending" version of the CHAMPION.

A20 Manufactured by Arcade, circa 1896, this thumb piece was found on the BEAUMONT and later on the LITTLE GIANT. This is the only example of a freestanding clamp plate that the author has found on an Arcade corkscrew. This thumb piece is approaching the final Arcade shape.

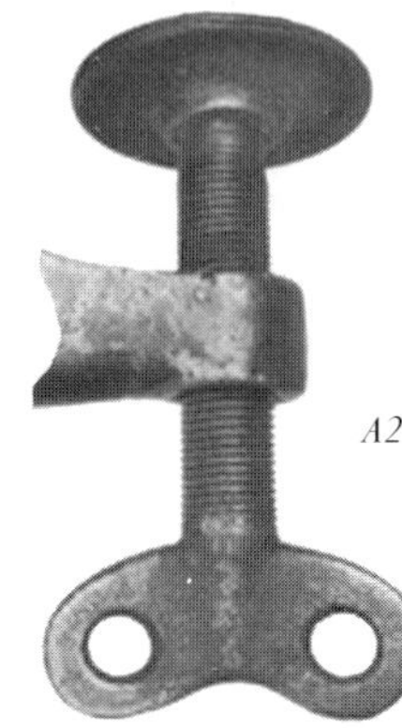

A20

A21

A21 Manufactured by Arcade, circa 1897 until the end of their corkscrew production, this was their final thumb piece shape used on all of the corkscrews distributed under the Arcade name.

A22 Manufactured by Arcade, circa 1915 - 1920, this thumb piece was used exclusively for the private label pieces manufactured by Arcade for Albert Pick.

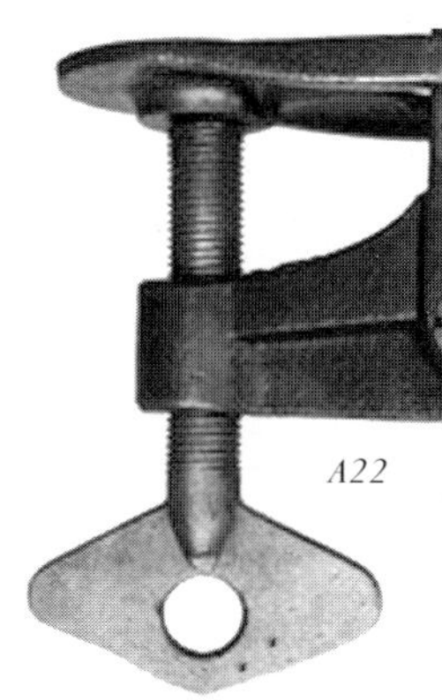

A22

A23

A23 Manufactured by Arcade, circa 1894 to the end of production, this thumb piece was used exclusively for the private label pieces manufactured by Arcade for Raymond Gilchrist.

A24 Manufactured by Enterprise Manufacturing Co., circa 1886 - 1910, this thumb piece was found on the ENTERPRISE 113 and on Enterprise cherry-pitting machines.

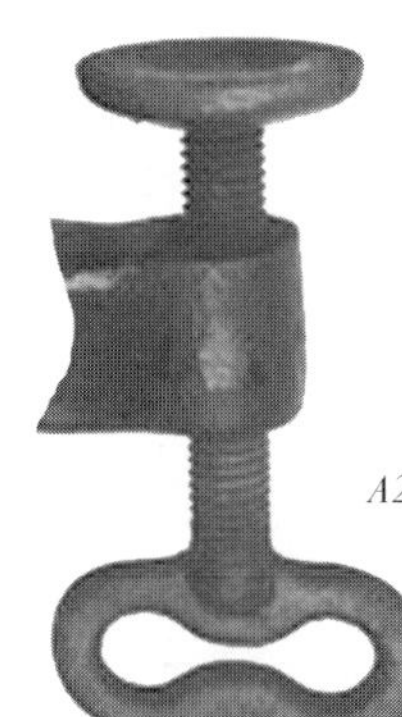

A24

A25 Manufactured by Meriden Malleable Iron Co., circa 1888 - 1890, this thumb screw is found on the 5th AVENUE.

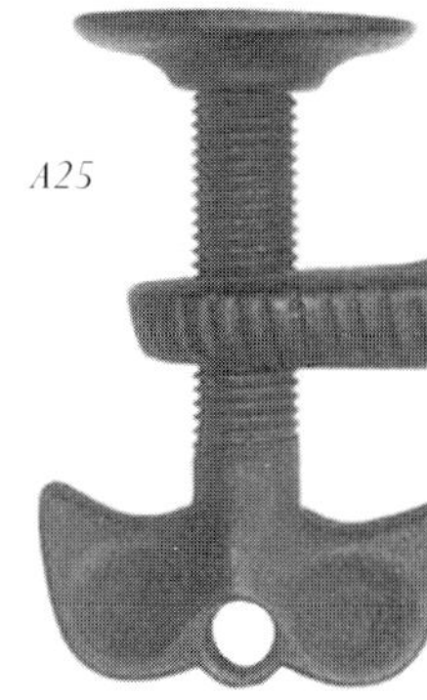

A25

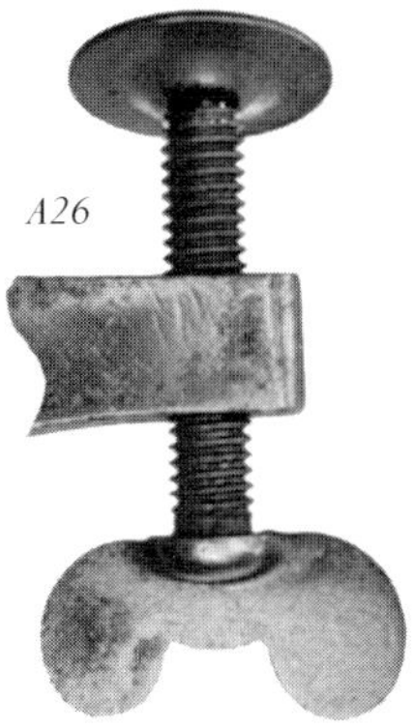

A26

A26 Manufactured by Meriden Malleable Iron Co., circa 1897, this thumb piece was found on the INFANTA. It is made up of a standard round head screw with the thumb piece soldered into the screw slot.

A27

A27 Manufactured by Meriden Malleable Iron Co., circa 1891 - 1910? this thumb piece was found on the American RAPID and lemon presses made by the Meriden Malleable Iron Co. This oval thumb piece is quite similar to the Manning & Bowman thumb piece.

A28

A28 Manufactured by Bradley & Hubbard circa 1910 to the end of production, this thumb piece was found on the later American RAPIDs, and exclusively on the bottle clamp version.

A29

A29 Manufactured by Manning & Bowman, circa 1900, this early version of their thumb piece was found on the PAT. APLD. FOR version of Baumgarten's SHOMEE.

A30

A30 Manufactured by Manning, Bowman & Co., circa 1901 to the end of production, this random stippled pattern, which is different on each side of the thumb piece, was found on the patented version of Baumgarten's SHOMEE. On six different examples of this corkscrew, manufactured by Manning & Bowman, each thumb piece was made with a different pattern.

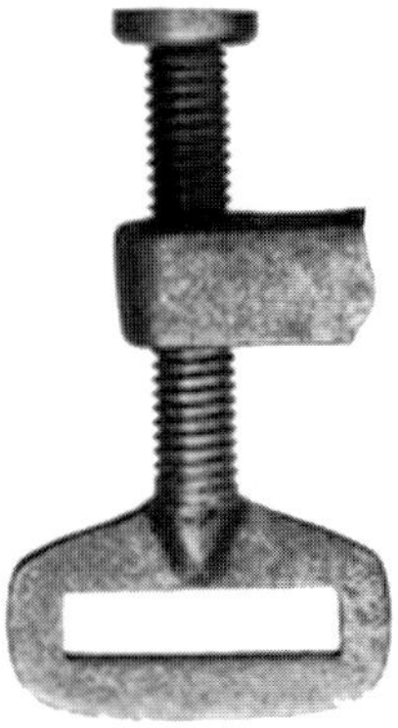

A31

A31 Manufactured by E. Walker, circa 1888, this thumb piece with its rectangular pierced opening and free standing clamp plate was found on the 1888 Walker patented corkscrew.

A32 Manufactured by E. Walker, circa 1893, the pierced opening of the thumb piece has changed from rectangular to oval, and was found on the WALKER AUTOMATIC.

A32

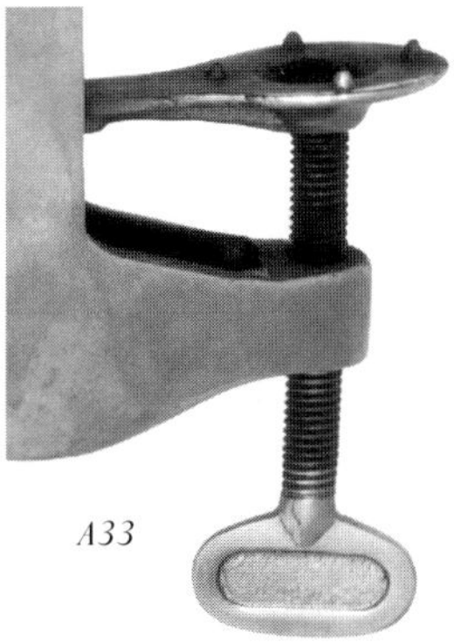

A33

A33 Manufactured by E. Walker, circa 1895 - 1917, the thumb piece has changed from an oval pierced opening to a closed oval. This thumb piece was found on all Walker manufactured corkscrews after approximately 1895.

Britain

A34

A34 With its three-hole thumb piece and three-point clamp plate, this was manufactured by S. Mason, circa 1889. The three-point clamp plate is shown in Vaughan's 1886 patent application for the Mason manufactured ACME. These large clamps were used on the larger corkscrews and are found only on the earliest small bar corkscrews, such as the A1.

A35

A35 This was manufactured by S. Mason, circa 1889 - 1910, with its three-hole thumb piece and what became Mason's standard large round clamp plate on the large bar corkscrews.

A36 Manufactured by S. Mason, circa 1900 - 1910, with its two-hole scalloped thumb piece and small round clamp plate, this became Mason's standard clamp on his smaller bar cork-screws.

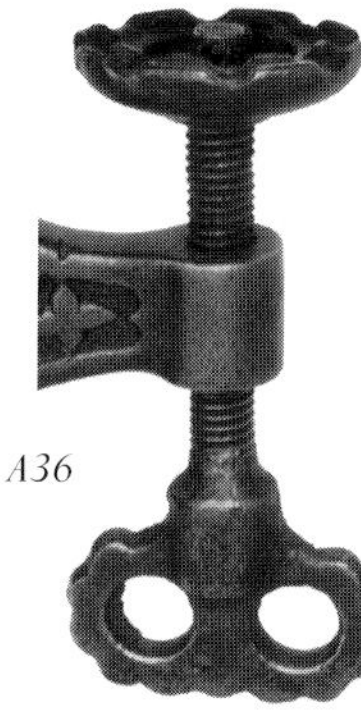

A36

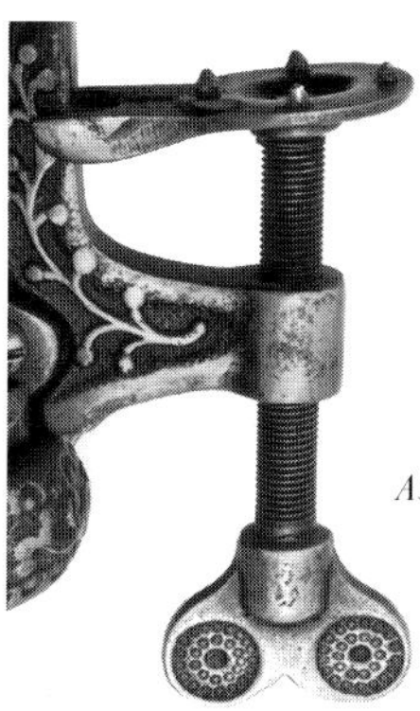

A37

A37 Manufactured by P. Gaskell, circa 1895 to the end of production, this thumb piece and "U" shaped clamp plate became Gaskell's standard clamp on his smaller bar corkscrews. This design (minus the little round hole in the thumb piece) originated with Arcade and moved to Gaskell, through Gilchrist, as part of the ARCADE design.

A38 Manufactured by P. Gaskell, circa 1910 to the end of production, this thumb piece and four-point clamp plate became Gaskell's standard clamp on his larger bar corkscrews. This closed version of Mason's three-hole thumb piece was probably produced after Chambers purchased Mason's company.

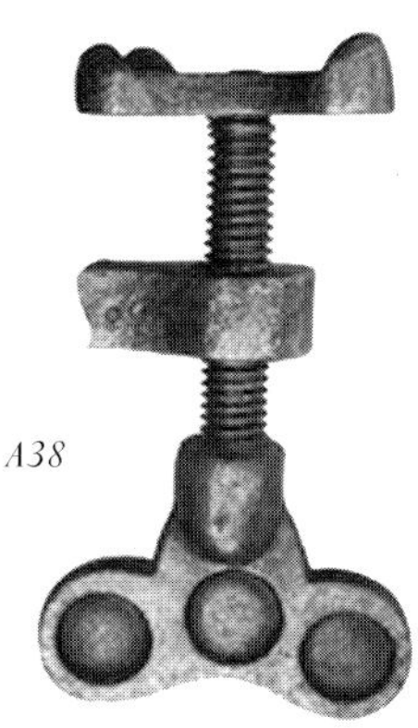

A38

Bibliography

Berntson, Buster & Ekman, Per. *Scandinavian Corkscrews.* Täby, Sweden, 1994.

Bidault, Gérard. *Fabriques les Françaises de Tire-bouchons 1820-1970.* France, 2000.

Brown, Henry T. *Five Hundred and Seven Mechanical Movements.* Mendham, New Jersey, U.S.A. 1995. ISBN 1 8793 3563 8.

Bull, Donald A. *The Ultimate Corkscrew Book.* Atglen, Pennsylvania, U.S.A. 1999. ISBN 0 7643 0701 0

Heckmann, Mannfred. *Korkenzieher.* Berlin, Germany, 1979.

O'Leary, Fred. *Corkscrews (1000 patented ways to open a bottle).* Atglen, Pennsylvania, U.S.A. 1996. ISBN 0 7643 0018 0.

Olive, Guy. *Tire-Bouchons Français Brevets 1828 – 1974.* France, 1995.

Peters, Ferd. *German Corkscrew Patents and German Corkscrew Registrations 2nd Ed.* Heel, Netherlands, 1997.

Peters, Ferd. *Mechanical Corkscrews.* Heel, Netherlands, 1999. ISBN 9 0805 0581 1.

Tresise, Charles E. *Tavern Treasures.* Poole, Dorset, England, 1983. ISBN 0 7137 1192 2.

Wallis, Fletcher. *British Corkscrew Patents from 1795.* Brighton, England, 1997. ISBN 1 8988 2505 X.

Index

Notes:

Notes: